British Cinema History

British Cinema History

Edited by
James Curran and Vincent Porter

Weidenfeld and Nicolson London

First published in 1983

George Weidenfeld & Nicolson Ltd.
91 Clapham High Street, London SW4

ISBN 0 297 78186 3 cased

ISBN 0 297 78223 1 paperback

Filmset by Deltatype, Ellesmere Port
Printed in Great Britain by
Butler & Tanner Ltd., Frome and London

Contents

Introduction

The academic study of the cinema is still in its infancy in Britain. And, as the opening chapter in this book argues, what serious film history there is sometimes suffers from a rather narrow and restricted focus. This book is not intended to be a definitive history of the British cinema, even if such a history were possible to produce. Rather it attempts to illuminate certain key developments and movements in the history of the British cinema through nineteen essays, some of which are surveys and others of which are case studies. The selection has been determined by what seemed to us to be important or interesting; necessarily, it has also been determined by what is possible in an area where there is only a limited amount of research activity.

The arrangement of the book is as follows: Part One provides two linked overall perspectives of film history. Part Two traces the evolution of the British film industry and the parallel development of government film policy. Part Three examines different aspects of the organization and practice of film-making through a series of case studies. Part Four considers the ideological and cultural significance of a number of important movements and genres since the 1920s.

Part one begins with Raymond Williams's critique of conventional film history, which separates the history of film from other aspects of life, such as economics or politics, on the one hand, or from literature and drama on the other. The reasons for this traditionally narrow formulation of film history are not hard to divine. Early film enthusiasts felt the necessity to prove both that a study of films was intellectually viable in its own right and that the intensive emotional charge to be obtained from such film-viewing was not simply a minor branch of some broader overarching academic discipline. Conversely, academics working in disciplines such as English literature, history or sociology have generally ignored the cinema for reasons of snobbery, tradition, or lack of an appropriate academic methodology with which to deal with the film-going experience. All too often film-going has been dismissed as simply a way in which the masses 'wasted' their leisure time and has therefore not been considered worthy of serious study.

It is to this last area – the nature of the film-viewing experiences of large audiences – that Philip Corrigan addresses his contribution to this volume. It never ceases to surprise us that the area of film activity where most people have been involved – that of watching films – is the one area of British film history where there is least data. Even recent developments in historical methods (such as, for example, the practices of oral history) seem to have ignored the exploration of how films have influenced the working lives and beliefs of ordinary men and women, both at a conscious and at a subconscious level. Philip Corrigan's chapter represents a pioneering enquiry into a field where there is a woeful lack of empirical analysis.

Part Two examines the rise and fall of the British film industry from its origins in the 1890s, through its expansive phase as a major entertainment industry during the thirties and forties, to its decline during the post-war period. It begins with a chapter in which Michael Chanan traces the evolution of the British cinema from its humble beginnings as a cottage industry at the end of the nineteenth century to its full internationalization by the 1920s, when British film producers lobbied effectively for government protection against American domination. Simon Hartog takes up the story from 1927, arguing that government legislation not only saved the British cinema from probable extinction but also played a significant part in forming its character. The third chapter, by Margaret Dickinson, examines the marginalization of the British cinema since the 1940s, culminating in the current moves to dismantle the state support system for the British film industry.

The collapse of the 'film industry' – a term which lumps together cinema exhibition and film production – is usually mourned by cinema enthusiasts as an irreparable loss, even though films have assumed an important role in television. Most people now watch films, of course, on television rather than in the cinema. Television has also become one of the major producers of British films, for both foreign and domestic consumption. Indeed, the introduction of a fourth television channel has already proved to be a positive stimulus both to mainstream and independent film-making in Britain. However, the role of television in the production and exhibition of filmed material is a large subject that lies outside the compass of this book and warrants a separate study in its own right.

Part Three takes a closer look at the structures and practice of film-making, beginning with Stuart Hood's account of John Grierson and the documentary film movement. He traces the strange and contradictory alliances between the imperialist state, Grierson (whose political position was an inch to the left of whichever political party was in office) and his considerably more radical employees. For all the apparent radicalism of the movement, however, many documentary films were in fact rather condescending in the way in which they represented the working class on the screen. To be sure, they occasionally evoked spontaneous applause from audiences used to seeing themselves portrayed as idiots or buffoons in comedies, but most documentaries were about industrial or economic processes in which workers played a subordinate and allegedly contented role.

This approach contrasts markedly with that of the workers' film movement of the thirties, surveyed by Trevor Ryan. The aim of this movement was to build up an autonomous, proletarian film culture in direct opposition to that of Hollywood and the dominant film industry. Despite its limited financial resources and circumscribed distribution outlets, the workers' film movement was a significant part of the left-wing political and cultural milieu of the 1930s.

While the British Labour movement was struggling against the cultural and ideological hegemony of Hollywood at home, the British government was struggling against it in its overseas colonies. Rosaleen Smyth looks at the direct involvement of the British government in financing films designed to portray the British way of life and intended for colonial consumption in Africa. Its weapons, however, were extremely limited and it concentrated on education and instruction rather than on entertainment, with, Smyth suggests, only limited success.

If the movements charted by Trevor Ryan and Rosaleen Smyth were comparative failures, the operation of British propaganda and censorship during the Second World War was extremely successful, as Nicholas Pronay and Jeremy Croft demonstrate. In the period of total war, film played a significant role both in unifying the nation and in selling the British point of view to people in foreign countries, particularly the United States. This was accomplished more by covert pressure than by formal censorship, exerted by a complete web of control about which most people at the time knew little. Yet, as Pronay and Croft argue through an extremely careful rereading of the evidence surrounding the production and the release of *The Life and Death of Colonel Blimp*, this film was a piece of deeply laid Ministry of Information propaganda, designed to influence American attitudes to involvement in the war, in a way of which even Churchill himself was probably not aware.

One of the great illusions encouraged by the success of British films during the Second World War was that the British film industry, led by the Rank Organization, could successfully compete in the world market after the war had ended. Robert Murphy's essay looks at the reasons why Rank failed to penetrate successfully the largest market of all: the United States. Conflicts between a capitalist film industry and a reforming Labour government, between film production and exhibition, and between management and creative film makers, to say nothing of Rank's personal shortcomings as a film entrepreneur, all contributed, according to Murphy, to the failure of the Rank Organization to contend with the big American companies.

In his contribution, Vincent Porter takes up the question of the role played by the producer in film production through an analysis of the parts played by two very different film producers whose careers dominate the post-war history of British film production: Sir Michael Balcon and Sir James Carreras. He points to the ways in which they shaped British films by their choice of subject and of key creative personnel, and by the degree of freedom they allowed their picked employees in film-making. Yet both producers operated within the constraints of the market place. Whereas Balcon sought refuge from these constraints within the Rank Organization, Carreras positively celebrated their 'vulgarity'. Despite their differences, however, the studios which they led suffered similar economic histories in a shrinking world market and both came ultimately to offer similar, although by no means identical, mixtures of exoticism and escapism to the American market.

Janet Woollacott argues that it is necessary to examine not only the constraints of the market system, and the specific conditions of production, but also the ideological climate in which films are made. She takes as an illustrative example the ways in which the character of James Bond has been modified, and his relationship to his girl-friends has been altered, in the long-running series of Bond films.

Simon Blanchard and Sylvia Harvey take up some of these themes in their survey of the structure and organization of post-war independent cinema in Britain. They chart the struggles of independent film-makers to find a structure for film-financing which does not leave them either dependent on the ideologically limiting patronage of the television organizations or on the vagaries of state support. They conclude with an examination of the role of independent film-makers within the cinema industry, and of their relationship to the public, that echoes – in the altered context of post-war Britain – some of the central concerns of the workers' film movement of the 1930s.

Part Four, concerned with the cultural and ideological significance of selected film genres, begins with Jeffrey Richards's survey of the imperialist films of the thirties. He distinguishes between Korda's nostalgic evocations of a timeless empire and Balcon's more candid celebrations of imperial dominion as a glorious adventure story. Both genres, he argues, served to project the empire in an idealized form that fostered pride in Britain's imperial destiny.

Tony Aldgate in his contribution questions the conventional view that British audiences stayed away from British films during the thirties and that the British Board of Film Censors prevented any dissident points of view from being expressed in certified films. He points to evidence indicating that British films were more popular than American films in the middle of the decade and to the possibilities that existed for film-makers to outwit the restrictions of the British Board of Film Censors. However, Aldgate concludes that the conservatism and traditionalism of much of the British cinema contributed significantly to the stability and cohesiveness of British society during the thirties.

Sue Aspinall addresses her contribution to the problems of gender, and in particular to the role of women in society and the way in which they were portrayed in films between 1943 and 1953. This was a period in which the emancipation of the war years, opening up the possibilities of a relatively independent working and sexual life, gave way to a renewed emphasis on the subordinate and domestic role of women during peacetime. The British cinema, Aspinall argues, played a part in containing women's emancipation by reaffirming traditional gender norms.

Ian Green also attributes a conformist, conservative influence to the Ealing Studio fantasies. He argues that, although they ruptured political and social conventions in the context of comedy, their effect was to encourage the integration of audiences into the social and political structure.

John Hill writes about a film genre that consciously rejected the class-bound 'theatricality' of the Ealing Studio comedies – the socially realist films of the late fifties and early sixties. He argues that they were not as significant a 'breakthrough' as has often been suggested, not least because they represented women and female sexuality in a form that 'work[ed] against and ultimately undercut their claims to be "progressive" '.

The last chapter examines the longest-running British comedy series, the 'Carry On' films, which are the cultural legatees of the neglected British comedies of the thirties discussed by Aldgate. Marion Jordan examines their comic picture-postcard world, revealing the different ways in which they reflect and comment upon the repressions, fears and humours of a masculine working-class culture that is fast disappearing.

The book concludes with an appendix, summarizing in statistical form historic changes in the British cinema, and a selective bibliography of the fast-growing literature on aspects of British film.

This symposium of essays has benefited from help and advice from many sources. In particular, we should like to thank Philip Corrigan, Gillian Hartnoll, Simon Hartog, Sue Honeyford, Keith McClelland, Tony Smith and Janet Woollacott for their very helpful suggestions during the initial planning and commissioning of this book. We should also like to thank the students taking part in the different courses which we teach for encouraging us to edit this book in the first place.

Part I
Historical Perspectives

I

British Film History: New Perspectives

Raymond Williams

What is the history of film? In considering this question, we are likely
to pass lightly over 'history' and put a defining emphasis on 'film'.
'Film' is the noun that brings us to our subject. Its history, or any
other intellectual process relevant to it, seems to follow naturally from
its already defined properties.

This has certainly been the procedure in most histories of film, or
cinema. The properties of the subject are taken as known, and their
components are then traced as precedents of these properties. In the
simplest versions, film and cinema are treated as unitary subjects,
which are then made to disclose their historical stages of development:
the early technology and its institutions; the silent film; the sound
film; films for television. In what appear more complex versions,
tendencies or schools or (very commonly) national 'traditions' are
identified within the more general phases: a form of history which can
then be developed into a form of criticism – the identification of key
directors, actors, techniques, described and then evaluated as leading
factors in the general historical development. Collected writing on
these bearings is now vast. Some, perhaps much, of it is obviously
useful.

Yet there are hard questions underlying the assumptions within
which such writing is undertaken. The hardest question is in the
biggest assumption, if we stop·and really consider it. This is the
assumption that there is a significant unitary subject, film, with
reasonably evident common properties. In fact the only unifying
element, of a definite kind, is a particular material process or
repertory of processes. Yet this, evidently, is not all that is indicated
by a proposed history of film. There is a useful current distinction
between 'film' and 'cinema', in which 'cinema' is used to describe the
institutions of the production, distribution and reception of films,

while 'film' is used to describe the material processes and the uses made of them by those who compose or watch them. This is a valuable kind of distinction, in its necessary discrimination within the loose unitary subject. But what can then happen is that 'cinema' and 'film' become, in their turn, unitary subjects, with known properties to be traced in the elements from which they are eventually assembled. There is 'social and historical' narrative and analysis, and there is also, but elsewhere, 'critical' narrative and analysis or, at more basic levels, 'formal' analysis. Some, perhaps much, of these different kinds of writing is again obviously useful.

History, however, is something else, both in practice and in any adequate writing. Particular areas of attention and emphasis have of course to be distinguished, not only in historical accounts but also in practical living. Yet in any full assessment of history it is necessary to be aware that these temporary and provisional indications of attention and emphasis – of 'subjects' – can never be mistaken for independent and isolated processes and products. For they are at best provisional intellectual identifications of significant areas of a common life. At worst, and frequently, they draw hard lines around certain areas, cutting off the practical relations with other 'areas' (which are indeed then seen only as 'areas' – 'the economy', 'the family', 'literature') which are in fact necessary if we are to understand not only the 'outward' relations – how 'the economy' affected 'the cinema' – but also the 'internal' relations and compositions, the supposed fixed properties of 'cinema' or 'film', which can often only be clarified if the specific processes are seen in the context of much more general processes. Lines have indeed to be drawn, to make any account possible, but it is always necessary to see ourselves as drawing them, and willing to redraw them, rather than to suppose that the marks on this one of many maps are hard features, of similar content and isolation, on the ground.

There are many ways in which this general proposition can be illustrated. I was myself very struck, reading histories of cinema, to see how indifferent most of them were to the preceding history of theatre. Indeed this was more than a hard line around the separated subject of film. It was often a defiant rejection of the idea that 'theatre', or 'literature', or any other of those marked areas, could have anything significant to do with the practice of film. Or should we then say Film, for what often followed was an account of how 'theatre' or 'literature' had diluted or destroyed the pure essence of 'Film', which was then not a name for a body of actual practice and works but an idealized projection of supposedly pure and inherent properties?

This is in fact the false form of what could, on different bearings, be an important argument: that certain cultural (or other) influences limited or misdirected actual practice and development in this specific material process or group of processes. But to write a critical history of 'film' which is actually going to exclude, on such grounds, those films which were 'really only theatrical or literary bastards' is a procedure so astonishing that it could only ever be undertaken in the same spirit of misplaced confidence that is shown in similar histories of Literature (excluding not only all 'non-imaginative' writing, but also most actual novels and poems which fall below the proper standard of 'literature') or of Theatre (restricting drama to one of its places of performance – the theatre – and to work of certain types, while excluding other places of performance and rejecting all other types as 'popular entertainment'). What we really find, in each case, is a categorical argument, based on what, if it were not categorical, could be openly offered as a justified opinion, which manages to reduce the actual diversity of its real subject and to offer its highly selective version as the whole real history of its now necessarily hard-line area. We can argue against such reductive procedures, but the best cure, usually, is to look up from these categorical histories and see the astonishing actual diversity within the practice itself. It is true that this can lead the historian to adopt the mode of an indiscriminate miscellany, in which the endless is finitely preferred. But in all real history, while the necessary starting-point and control lie in the recognition of diversity, the essential next steps are provisional analyses and groupings which are intended to clarify, rather than merely register, the diversity itself.

It is a disadvantage of the most common historical mode that the usual forms of such analyses and groupings are chronological periods, or types assigned to such periods. This method produces a kind of prehistory, devoted to early technological developments and uses of film, followed in order by the silent film, the early sound film, the modern film and so on. A linear view is set out in a linear way. But it is my own understanding of the history of film/cinema that while there are very significant periods of development, in which certain emphases and uses are possible or dominant, there are also, from the beginning (a notion that in itself must be examined), diverse actual elements and possibilities which often, and perhaps always, run

through such fixed periods. If I then separate these out, to try to
clarify them, it will be difficult not to suggest, or to be understood as
suggesting, that these are steps in some development of fixed
properties or known categories. What I shall in fact be suggesting is
that the history looks very different according to the bearings that are
chosen to run it on. It may then be through putting the bearings side
by side that we can begin to distinguish an actual, rather than an ideal
or categorical history.

The four bearings I shall use are: (a) the actual technology and its
uses; (b) film and popular culture; (c) film and established culture; (d)
film and modernist culture. These do not form a linear progression
but a set of lateral and eventually interactive relations. What I shall
write under each heading will, equally, not be a summary, nor an
attempt at a definitive account, but an exploratory one. I shall finally
try to indicate some of the diverse practical ways in which the bearings
come together, in an actual and active rather than a narrated history.

It can reasonably be argued that the only true common property of
film is its technology. But what we usually separate out as 'film' is a
variable and, in fact, changing selection from a wider body of systems.

It may nevertheless still be possible to talk of a technology of film.
This has to depend on a firm distinction between 'technical invention'
and 'technology', which are usually employed interchangeably. A
technical invention is a specific device, developed from practical
experience or scientific knowledge and their interaction. Such devices
have been carefully recorded in what is seen as the prehistory of film.
Yet we have only to stop and look at these, as the narrative rolls them
before us, to realize that the selection refers to what are at least two,
and perhaps more, technologies. Thus there are a number of
inventions and devices which belong primarily to the development of
still *photography*: the daguerreotype; the sodium thiosulphate negative (for which the term 'photography' was invented); wet collodion;
the gelatin dry plate; the nitro-cellulose roll (by which time the term
'film' was established for straightforward descriptive purposes); reflex
and roll-film cameras. All these and further developments were
eventually brought together, by exclusion, selection and improvement, into a systematic technology of general photography, embodied
in major industrial and commercial enterprises. Equally, however,
there are a number of inventions and devices which belong primarily
to the development of the display of *moving images*: the technique of

the *camera obscura* refined and extended to the magic lantern; the phantasmagoria, the thaumatrope, the praxinoscope, the zoetrope; the developments from still photography in sequences of cameras and revolving plates; the kinetograph and the kinetoscope, using new celluloid strip film; the *cinematographe* and the vitascope. It can be said that these were selected, improved and developed into a systematic technology of 'film' or 'cinema', embodied in what soon became, in this field, major industrial and commercial enterprises likewise.

Yet the point is not just the obvious one that there were two major lines of development: towards the recorded and reproducible image and towards the moving image. It is that there is a problem of what we then say when we find the two lines of scattered technical development combined in the 1890s in the invention of 'cinema'. It is ironic that the often preferred term, 'film', comes from the group of photographic developments, with which it still shares certain physical properties. And it is interesting that the popular term, 'movie', comes essentially from the properties of the other group, the work on moving images. But can we then not say that the film camera and the associated projection systems mark a qualitative new stage, in which moving images can be recorded and reproduced?

We have of course to say something like that. For this is the point at which the diverse technical inventions were assembled and developed into a systematic technology which eventually attracted enough further investment to become an independent industry. Yet in the rush to that conclusion we can easily fall into a simple technological determinism. The inventions come along and 'make' a new industry and a new art. Simple historical retrospect shows everything leading to what we now have. But this is where the difficulties, and many of the interesting problems, start. For in fact we do not have, in that simple unitary way, a 'new art', or even, in any unitary way, a 'new industry'. Diverse and in some cases alternative possibilities, in both art and industry, are there in the material history from the beginning, and even after the qualitatively new phase of the 1890s. To put it at its simplest, a fundamental argument about the nature of film and its uses, which is still at the centre of many of our most serious discussions, is already inscribed in the diverse technical and technological history. Some say that film is a major medium because it can record and reproduce life and its movements, in a physical world, so clearly and permanently. Others say that film is a major art because, with it, an artist can compose with moving images. At their extremes these positions are often argued in typically absolutist ways: 'true film' or 'authentic cinema' is one or other of these seemingly opposed things.

Thus no account of the technical inventions, or even of the systematic technologies, can function as a prehistory to some unitary version of the history of cinema, whether presented either from any of these, or from any similar, positions. Already in the earliest years the basic elements of the technology were being used for the radically different purposes which were inherent in what was never a series but always a scatter of inventions. Lumière recorded events on film and projected them; Méliès used a different property of film to project tricks and illusion. Edison, meanwhile, wanted moving pictures to accompany his phonograph – the ironic opposite of the eventual development of silent into synchronised sound film. Nor are these simply early uncertainties. The whole subsequent practice of film shows both the intense development of the alternative emphases of record and illusion, in these simple senses, and the diverse development of many forms, taking these emphases into more complex uses or attempting simple and complex syntheses beyond them. Very little of this history is explicable or predictable from the technical history or the systematic technologies. Rather, these provided certain new possibilities, at times themselves entailing further technical developments, within the general presures and limits of a wider social and cultural history.

Film – the 'motion picture' – has been used, throughout its period of availability, for strict record of a scientific or historical kind, and this remains a major use. But the early and most of the subsequent development of cinema has been firmly within the area usually defined as 'popular culture'. Most of the early shows were held in tents and booths, or in music-halls – while films made for purposes of factual record were screened in scientific institutions. Already by 1914 cinema had become the most widely distributed cultural form that there had ever been, and the scale of this distribution had been vastly increased by 1945.

Yet there was no simple transition from the technical prehistory to the new universal art form. Film took its place, and then made its own new place, in an already dense, complex and changing popular culture. In Britain this has been especially clear.

The 'popular culture' of a predominantly urban and industrial society comprises a radically different set of phenomena from preindustrial popular, or 'folk', culture. The latter is relatively traditional in form and content, and its contrast is with 'court' or 'aristocratic' – or 'polite' ('liberal', 'learned') – culture. Modern popular culture however is not only a response to predominantly urban and industrial living. It is also in its central processes, (1) largely urban-based, (2) an application of new industrial processes to a broad range of old and new cultural processes and forms, and thus (3) predominantly mobile and innovative, but with very complex relations to older and still persistent conditions and forms. Film arrived at the end of a century of such developments.

Two related areas can be briefly characterized. By the time of the first film-shows the newspaper press had been transformed, with popular Sunday, and then new daily papers, building up circulations of more than a million copies each. At the same time there had been an intense and novel development of both popular and 'society' drama.

The popular newspaper should not be primarily related to the need for information in a new kind of society, though it marginally served this purpose at different times in history. We misunderstand the press if we attempt to trace a simple line from the early newsletters to modern 'quality' newspapers. The most widely distributed news-papers, from the early nineteenth century onwards, were firstly those of a radical character, opposing the political establishment, and secondly, when these had been largely defeated by repressive legislation and by the rising costs of capitalization in new methods of production and distribution, newspapers of commercial 'entertain-ment' (their main topics being crime, scandal, sport, pastimes and spectacle). The minor element of pure 'news' continued in the cinema through the equally minor medium of the newsreel, following much the same principles of selection and presentation but of course with major visual advantages.

The other elements of the popular press were congruent with much of the popular drama, and the development of cinema, in one of its main tendencies, has to be seen in relation to both press and drama. Yet we can usefully emphasize the congruence and even the continuity of certain theatrical forms which permit more direct comparisons.

These forms are often crudely summarized as 'melodrama', but the real history is more varied. Melodrama began in the established, 'legitimate' theatre, in about 1800. It was a form of play with music and with a large element of mime. If we try to generalize 'mime', or silent 'gestural' acting, from the conditions and achievements of the silent film, we overlook this whole previous history. In many early melodramas certain characters were represented as, for some reason, dumb, so that mime could be employed by the actors who took these roles. A whole rich tradition of predominantly visual acting, stemming from travelling popular entertainers with a very long history behind them, was thus taken into theatre and was again to be heavily drawn on and developed in silent film. As melodrama became popular, from the 1820s, its plots increasingly resembled events reported in the popular press: sensational crimes and seductions – though in melodrama these were eventually concluded by providential rescues and escapes – at times presented in a radical perspective. From the 1860s there existed in effect two broad kinds of melodrama: this well-remembered type, but also the earlier and always numerically more common 'costume epic', peopled by pirates, bandits, soldiers, sailors and 'historical' figures of all kinds. Each type was to contribute massively to cinema: at first by direct adaptation (*Pearl White*, *Jane Shore*, *Ben Hur*); later by the cinematic adaptation of similar plots, themes and shows, and (as in Britain before 1914) by the addition of such new but congruent techniques as the close-up and the chase.

But there was more than melodrama in each of these kinds. In the established theatre, by the time of the first film shows, there was a century's tradition of extraordinary spectacle: the vast development of elaborate costuming, by period or for display; the great elaboration of 'sets' – the new (nineteenth-century) theatrical device of fully furnished places of action and rooms; the highly ingenious staging of mechanical and lighting effects, from fires and volcanic eruptions to shipwrecks, railway crashes and even naval battles. Film was to develop many even more ingenious technical resources, but mainly it was to show much the same things with even more 'spectacular realism' and conscious display. It is very difficult, when considering this line of development – as when considering the derivation of film from the two kinds of melodrama – to see any real qualitative change, though there were obviously more resources and possibilities once film had been mastered, and there were the usual changes of style over the passage of time, so that a contemporary film 'melodrama', essentially similar in form and plot to its nineteenth-century predecessors, may not seek to be 'melodramatic' in that older style. To these continuities, with their local variations, we have to add those elements which lay outside the 'legitimate' theatre: the acrobats, conjurors, tumblers and dancers, who carried on both old and new tricks in film; the performers of farces and sketches in the music-halls; the skilled horse-riders, prominent in the circus from the eighteenth century onwards and now finding new openings – in one special case, the 'Western', in a major way – in film.

Thus majority cinema, in both the silent and the sound periods, can be reasonably seen as the flowering of a whole body of drama, theatre and entertainment, which in its essential interests and methods preceded film but was then at once enhanced and made much more widely available by it. Indeed, the qualitative change can be seen less in what was done – there are really very few films, by proportion, for which there is not a nineteenth-century precedent in drama or entertainment – than in what then happened, in the genuinely new factors of multiple and recurrent reproducibility and distribution.

Film was to become the central art form of the twentieth century, but it took a long time – longer in some nations and in some classes than in others – for this centrality to be recognized in relation to already established culture. From its marginal beginnings, within both the content and the institutions of popular culture, it made its way to a qualitatively different position: not only or even primarily because of its individual qualities as art, but mainly because of the radical change in the means of artistic production employed.

In the early decades most cinema industries tried to move towards respectability within the terms of the established culture. The earliest settled sites of distribution were modelled on theatres, and often went on being called theatres. The process of the luxurious refurbishing of theatre interiors, which had been such a feature of theatre building and adaptation from the 1860s, was extensively continued in the period of the 'picture palaces', with a further continuity of characteristically aristocratic or exotic names. Most of the films shown in them were derived from various forms of the popular culture, especially the commercial popular culture. But there were also many attempts to draw on the more prestigious theatre (both in the enlistment of stage actors and in the adaptation of plays), on musical comedy and light opera, on novels in the established literary tradition and on other literary forms such as biography. As late as 1940 the quality of film was often evidenced from these borrowings and adaptations – a thin blue line above the assumed typical 'vulgarity' of the cinematic popular culture. Yet what went into film from these sources formed, of course, a real contribution to the medium. Dismissal of such work as merely 'theatrical' or 'literary' can only emanate from an arbitrary idealization of film. In one cultural area after another, film, as it became (before television) the dominant form, was in effect a common carrier of many different kinds of art, and cinemas were the central institutions of this wide range of drama and entertainment.

Yet alongside these adaptive and incorporating processes something more fundamental was happening – something consequent on the nature of the new means of distribution. The prestige of the established cultures was very closely linked with the predominance of the old metropolitan centres. London and Paris, Berlin and New York were the places where high art, especially in drama, music and painting, was produced or exhibited. This situation corresponded with a phase of political and cultural centralization and with the general dominance of orthodox metropolitan criteria. What happened beyond the metropolis – in what, during this whole phase, from the eighteenth century onwards, could be defined as 'the provinces' – submitted itself, for the most part, to these allegedly superior and fashionable centres. In fact however in some of the relevant arts, and especially in drama, this became an inherently false situation, particularly in Britain. During the period from 1870, when European drama was moving into a new great period, it was not from the fashionable metropolitan centres and the dominant national cultures that creativity was flowing. It was from what were regarded in most countries of Western Europe as marginal or distant cultures: Scandinavia, Russia, Ireland. In Britain the established theatre was locked into social fashion rather than into anything which could be even momentarily mistaken for high art. Indeed, the persistence of this enclosed and self-reflecting 'West End' is at least a contributory reason for some of the failures of British cinema, if only because its exceptionally class-marked enclosure raised, in its shadow, what was often a reductive and self-impoverishing 'provincial' and popular culture.

One major factor shifted the old kind of metropolitan dominance, and eventually, and ironically, produced a quite new form of dominance. The central material characteristic of film was that its productions and performances could be fixed, and could then be distributed in standard multiple forms. Thus, quite apart from its new technical capacity to enhance and extend older forms, there could be a simultaneous high investment of both talent and resources in any single production, and, when such a production was achieved, very widespread and indefinite reproduction. Obviously this matching of potentialities made sense in financial terms also. Thus the dominant centres of production became, first, less dependent on the established metropolitan centres, and, in all later phases, in effect dominant of them. In the theatre the old kinds of prestige persisted, in remarkably reproductive ways, but whereas they had previously dominated all relevant activity elsewhere, they were now in a less important position, with major new institutions and forms surpassing them – nationally, and, even more crucially, internationally – in the eyes of newly enlarged, regular audiences.

The results have been complex. In relation to the established culture – a very different matter from traditional culture – film and cinema have been in general quite remarkably liberating. Yet, quite apart from the effects of new kinds of centralized dominance, which must be separately examined, there has remained a certain parasitism on established forms and styles, often most noticeable when the 'industry' has taken itself most seriously and produced 'serious' films. It is clear that in much mainstream cinema there have been nothing like the cultural breaks that might have been predicted from the new possibilities of the technology and from its new and potentially new social relations. There has been some evidence, from time to time, that this situation may be changing, but the continued prestige of 'theatre', as opposed to 'film', is remarkable after a half-century in which it is quite clear that film has produced much more important new work. Moreover, deference towards the forms and styles of the established culture seems continually to re-establish itself within cinema, for predominantly social rather than artistic reasons.

Yet the history of film looks different again when we relate it to modernist culture, itself the conscious antagonist of established culture in every field. Such a relation however is necessarily complex.

It has always seemed to me significant, since I first noticed the dates, that the years in which the motion-picture camera and projector were being effectively developed – the 1880s and 1890s – were also the years in which there was a decisive break, within avant-garde drama, towards new kinds of mobile and dynamic composition. To read Strindberg's *Lady Julie* (1888), but even more his *The Road to Damascus* (1898) and the later *Dream Play* and *Ghost Sonata*, is to find a stage dramatist writing what are in effect screenplays, embodying shifts of location, sequences of images, fragmentations, transformations and dissolves which were only just technically possible (if that) in the most experimental kinds of stage production, but which would eventually become even commonplace in film. There is hardly any evidence of direct influence either way. The experiments were going on in widely separated and non-communicating sectors. The correspondence, or even congruence, is at a different level, where not only experiences of mobility, dislocation and alienation, but also an intense curiosity about movement and about newly possible dynamic forms, were parts of a deeper and more general cultural movement. The same underlying movement can be seen, for example, in the paintings of Munch; it went on into expressionism and in fact quite directly into early German cinema. The profound perceptual shifts embodied in a whole succession of movements in the visual arts, from impressionism to cubism, belong to the same general cultural transformation.

The hostility of this kind of modernist culture to the characteristically fixed and enclosed forms of the established culture was intense. What are much harder to analyse are its then very complicated relations to the forms of popular culture, and beyond these to the altering social relations within which both tendencies – at first sight so far apart – were trying to develop.

There is a quite clear line of development from the subjective expressionism of Strindberg and Munch, with its uses of dynamic distortions and dream imagery, to a whole body of expressionist and surrealist film. But there is also a very different yet related line, also within general modernism, in two tendencies which came to define the most influential modernist film-making: on the one hand, shifts of location, point of view and perspective in narrative, including non-linear time sequences (all of which had been developing in modernist fiction, and continued to develop interactively in both fiction and film); on the other hand, the more specifically filmic use of composed and associated (linked or contrasted) images, whether in the original theory of montage $(A + B = C)$ or more generally. In the kinds of film developing (with other differences) through Griffith and Eisenstein, these new processes of dispersed narrative and edited imagery led not only to a modernist cinema but also to a repertory of film techniques which were eventually incorporated into mainline cinema in its still basic adaptations to the established non-modernist culture. They were then commonly perceived as the specific properties of 'film'.

Yet there was also a more diverse progeny in the general anti-bourgeois character of modernism. In the formal senses already referred to, modernism broke up the fixed frames and images of established bourgeois art. But its commitment to the dynamic was never solely, and not always even primarily, formal. Its rejection of the forms of bourgeois theatre and representational painting was often combined, in ways that break up the conventional formal categories, with an interest in popular forms, in two senses: (1) popular movements in history, whether explicit revolution (as in early Soviet cinema) or a more general extension of the actions of history to the characteristic and technically possible 'crowds' of the 'epic' film; (2) the non-representational and non-realistic elements of popular culture, which had by now become available in silent film comedy and melodrama. The outcome of this complex of conflicting influences has been, as might be expected, very complicated indeed. The 'art film' of one kind of modernism (composed images, or dispersed narrative with composed images) has to be set beside forms which appear, at first sight, to be wholly in contrast with it: the revolutionary epic, which used the mobility and scale of developed cinema and also composed non-representational images within these; but also what came to be called the 'documentary', in which the specifically 'theatrical', the 'staged' event, was so thoroughly rejected that a new, apparently unmediated, relation between 'the camera' and 'reality' was proposed and created. The old dual potentiality of film – (1), that the camera could create illusions and that the film itself could be worked on to create new visual effects; (2) that the motion-picture camera made possible the most accurate and thorough representation and record of real life – has thus been recognized and used, selected from, combined and recombined, in extraordinary and unprecedented ways which ought not to be reduced to apparently separate and distinct 'periods' and 'genres'. What is necessary, by contrast, is to distinguish those genuinely modernist elements (over the range from expressionism and surrealism through dispersed and extended narrative and symbolic montage to the documentary and *cinéma-vérité*), which have been used for conscious social and artistic purposes in a diverse and continuing series of films, from the more common 'technical' or 'professional' adaptations of this or that method or device which were uncritically incorporated into an apparently neutral technology of 'film'.

It is clear that when we look at the history of film on these different bearings – the material processes; the relations with popular culture; the relations with established culture; the relations with modernism – we find something very much more complex, but also more interesting, than the ordinary categories of film history or film criticism can contain. Moreover there is every reason to resist the temptation of arriving at some synthesis of which these elements are components. All are real in the sense that they describe actual work in actual places at actual times. But no present place or time can be permitted to absorb or order them, because what they are, in practice, has been and remains contradictory in the full sense: diversely alternative and often irreconcilable practices, within the diversity and opposition of actual and foreseen social and cultural relations.

This sense of diversity and contradiction must be firmly sustained against the forms of any unitary 'aesthetics of film' or unitary developmental history – and, as urgently, against the industrial and commercial structures which, with their command of means and resources of production, impose more practical forms of (marginally varied) unification.

What needs emphasis in this context, where the question of the industrial and commercial structures is concerned, is the effect of the decisive material factor in film – its indefinite and multiple reproducibility. Within capitalist and state-capitalist economies, it came to seem natural that this led, by a familiar financial logic, to an extreme concentration and relative monopoly of production: massive production costs made affordable by a controlled system of mass distribution. Yet the material factor itself could, within different general relations, lead as easily to more diverse centres of production, beyond the old metropolitan fixed points, and to a radically extended and more diverse distribution of this wider range. Thus there is no technological determinism running from 'film' to 'Hollywood', or to anywhere else. And whatever may be said about the past, there are now new opportunities for diversity in the increasing distribution of films through television, though they can only be exploited if the television institutions are themselves consciously reformed to make independent production and extended diversity more possible. This remains a more hopeful line of development than what has hitherto been settled for: the fusion of commercial popular culture and established culture in a massively organized capitalist cinema, which in turn adapts to control television and video-cassettes and discs. The alternative, at the fringe, is of a festival and art-house cinema, as a conscious minority culture.

It is how this fusion relates to the bearings already examined that needs emphasis. Popular culture should not be romanticised, either that which existed before the coming of film, or after. Neither 'melodrama' nor 'mime', music-hall song nor icon, is a simple fixed element. Most of the ways in which these forms were put together were absorbed, without effort, into what became an established popular culture of commercial consumption. That they did not have to go this way, and that the 'popular audience' is not predisposed to what is eventually made of it, is better evidenced from film than from any other area of the culture. At the same time the radical elements in modernism, widely apparent in many areas of minority culture, have been expressed more generally – and with less specific ties to social minorities – in film than in any other medium. Yet the tendencies to monopoly, to incorporation and to agency or outpost production in terms of the dominant centre have been so strong that only relatively brief periods of fully independent production, and then more often than not in 'national' terms, have escaped them. At the same time, as in the related case of twentieth-century theatre, it has been almost wholly in these comparatively independent centres that work of real value has been done. What has been lost, in the whole process, is not so much the consciously modernist work, which can find a not uncongenial place at the margins, but the fully autonomous development of native popular cultures, which keep showing their strength whenever there is even a half-chance, but which have been denied any mature expression and growth by the pressures and prestige of a skilfully homogenized and falsely universal cinema: popular *cinema* rather than popular films.

Yet it is important to realize that the old economy of the cinema is beginning to break up – under the pressure not only of general economic, but also of mainly new technical, developments – and that some new kinds of opening are becoming apparent, in which the history, already in any full sense of the term so diverse, can be reinterpreted by being changed.

2

Film Entertainment as Ideology and Pleasure: A Preliminary Approach to a History of Audiences[1]

Philip Corrigan

'The task I'm trying to achieve is above all to make you see.'

D. W. Griffith[2]

The preceding chapter connects with a number of moves, both in the study of film[3] and, more generally, especially in the study of literary forms, where an explicit challenge from 'history' (and 'institutions') has been made to 'theory'.[4] The points made by Raymond Williams are valid both for the sources[5] of film drama and for the continuities of 'theatrical' architecture, decor, and related conventions in cinemas.[6] But these do not prevent a persistent evaluation which sets 'live drama' above and against 'film'[7] or which separates the forms quite unhelpfully: 'Dramatic theatre (now mediated by television) and the classic realist novel are still the dominant popular modes. The cinema, *too*, is still dominated by narrative illusionism. . . .'[8]

There is, of course, another approach to the history of film and cinema – from the point of view of the audiences. This is still almost completely undeveloped, even unconsidered. Before the advent of mass television the estimated annual admissions to various popular paid entertainments in England, Scotland and Wales were as in Table 1.[9] Cinema attendance was more extensive in these countries (with important differences within them) than in any other country.

Table 1

(Millions of admissions)	1950	1951	1952
Cinemas	1611	1498	1458
Theatres and music-halls	84	82	83
Football matches	84	77	81

England, Scotland and Wales averaged twenty-eight admissions per head in 1950, compared with twenty-three in the United States, and there was no other country with an average of more than twenty.[10]

This least studied feature of the relations of cultural production – the audience – is, where mentioned, characteristically reduced to two unequal parts: a mass of consumers and a minority of critics. From a variety of starting-points this is now being challenged.[11] Even that most mystified, because seemingly most private, of cultural activities – that of reading – is currently being rethought.[12] That is to say, in the phrase of the late Roland Barthes, 'A text's unity lies not in its origin but in its destination . . . the birth of the reader must be at the cost of the death of the Author.'[13]

By locating the study of film and television within the framework of cultural studies, I hope to avoid some of the limitations of the dominant approaches to audiences. I would stress, finally, that, apart from the severe space limitations to cover a period of almost one hundred years, the undeveloped nature of the field of study means that I shall be offering what Bill Nichols calls an 'exploratory foray',[14] informed (after Barthes' suggestion)[15] by imagination.

The arrival of large-scale audiences – characteristically called masses[16] – coincides with many other changes in social relations and cultural forms. Recent investigations have shown the danger of seeing the earlier moments of the different cultural forms as simply primitive, inadequate attempts to achieve the final (and fixed) forms within which we are represented today. Technological determinism in particular has the additional effect of reducing the audience to so many *consumers*: empty vessels into which the 'messages' are poured and which have their 'effects'.

In the case of film, investigation of early cinema,[17] the 'coming' of sound[18] or colour,[19] histories of particular studios,[20] or of the arrival of the B movie,[21] all show that technological determinism and its associated images of the audience are totally inadequate. What they reveal is that there are multiple determinations at work in any history of a cultural form.

There is a further qualification to set against the conventional ways of categorizing audiences as solely a problem for the social sciences and their second cousins twice removed – the survey analyses of markets. We need to encompass the views of audiences and assumptions about them inscribed in (1) official reports and legal regulations; (2) statements of producers, distributors and critics;[22] and (3) the expressed opinions and actions of the audiences themselves. The meeting-point of all three is no less than the sign around which there have recently been so many battles; it happens to be how the audience is placed in the production of meaning. That this had to be 'taught', and that it is not a fully controlled (controllable) practice, is at last being recognized. We forget that media *mediate*. The same point can be made in relation to all the 'great failures' – those attempts to repeat a success by using a supposed formula, believing in the 'power' of a performer or director.[23]

From a very early moment Hollywood dominated (as it still does) the product shown in cinemas in Great Britain. As early as 1925, 95 per cent of the films shown in Britain were Hollywood products and Hollywood earned well over a third of its total foreign earnings from screenings here.[24] Between 1929 and 1935 there were never more than 190 British 'long' films registered for 'renter's quota' in a total of all films registered that never fell below 600.[25] Manvell states that Hollywood in 1939 produced 65 per cent of the films shown throughout the world; and Hollywood itself, was, of course, dominated by the 'Big Five'.[26] It was not until the late 1930s that the 22 'British' studios (using 65 sound stages) produced over 200 films. We can contrast the 40 or so films (over 72 minutes long) produced in the 9 'British' studios (using 30 sound stages) in 1945–6.[27] In the period between 1945 and 1979 there has never been a year when 100 'British' films of that length were registered with the Board/Department of Trade, while in the same period the number of feature films submitted to the British Board of Film Censors was never less than 324.[28]

So much for 'product'. Films have to be seen *in certain places*. Such places, in their early multi-media context and their later single medium development, have to be central to any provisional understanding of what 'going to the pictures' means or could mean for large audiences. The 'wonderful' rise of the picture palace needs to be related to good social histories of the period.[29] The key periods are from the 1890s until about 1918, from the 1920s until the early 1950s, and the current period (defined by mass television – on which, of course, many movies are shown). From the start, as Manvell points out, sound (originally music only) was central. By 1919 a library of appropriate musical extracts had been built up, although the first piece of music specifically composed for filmic accompaniment dates from 1908.[30]

Moving pictures arrived in London, Manchester and many other places in 1896, emerging from the earlier forms (the zoetrope and kinetoscope) which, like others (the bioscope) were part of a wider set of popular forms,[31] such as the circus, fairground, and mobile music-hall. That development, however, was not the only one possible. Theatres, along with music-halls, showed films and, in some cases, were fully converted into cinemas. As late as 1979, 'out of 318 existing theatre buildings still identifiable in Britain, 43 were in use as cinemas.'[32] The period of itinerant or multiform film-screenings starts to end after 1904 or so. Atwell finds earlier instances outside London, but dates the Bioscope, Victoria, from 1905, and the Daily Bioscope, Bishopsgate, from 1906.[33] But as important is Chanan's setting of such changes within the context of wider changes in production and distribution: the systematization and the stabilization for the conditions of 'realizing' surplus – instead of the product being sold, what could be sold was the right to exhibit, 'ownership' remaining with the production company.[34]

The 'moment of cinema' was clearly established by 1914; 500 cinemas in London by 1912, 111 and 22 in Manchester and Liverpool respectively by 1913, 24 in Portsmouth by 1914 and four in Rochdale.[35] The overall audience may have been some 350 million a year, for a population of about 40 million[36] with the 4000 to 5000 cinemas already being organized in circuits, some 109 of which already accounted for between 15 and 20 per cent of all cinemas.[37] By 1914 going to the picture palaces had become a normal activity.[38]

In 1921 there were about 4000 cinemas – most of them still of the open-hall, 300–600 seat-plan form. Since the 1934 figure is about 4300, there had clearly been a complex reconstruction of sites, a view confirmed by one estimate of 3000 cinemas open in 1926.[39] One immediately noticeable difference is that by 1934, 28.3 per cent of all cinemas contained over 1000 seats (that is, 47.6 per cent of all seats). The first 4000-seat cinemas date from 1925, in Glasgow, and from 1928, in Croydon.[40] Second, by 1930 the circuits had become firmly established: Gaumont-British (which took over the Provincial Cinematograph Theatres, controlled Shepherds Bush studios and had connections with Fox) owned 299 cinemas by 1929; the Associated British Picture Corporation (controlling Elstree, with connections with First National and Pathé) owned 73 cinemas in 1929, 225 by 1943. Bernstein's Granada and Deutsch's Odeon circuits were also significant. By 1943, when there were 4750 cinemas, Manvell estimated that there were 2000 key or first-run cinemas, of which over 1000 were controlled by the 'Big Three': the Odeon with 315, Gaumont-British with 304 and Associated British Cinemas with 442. By 1941 J. Arthur Rank had brought Gaumont-British and the Odeon circuits together, and controlled about 600 cinemas, together with about 50 per cent of the reduced studio space.[41] In 1951 there were still about 4600 cinemas, but although only a quarter of all cinemas had over 1000 seats, these accounted for 57 per cent of all seats and 65 per cent of receipts. For circuits with more than 50 cinemas the figures are also striking: they accounted for 25 per cent of all cinemas, 38 per cent of all seats and 48 per cent of receipts. The circuits were far more dominant in the South than in the North of England, Wales or Scotland.[42] Between 1952 and 1962 the two major circuits – Rank and ABC/EMI – increased their total of seats from 33 to 41 per cent. In London in 1961, Ivor Montagu also states, Rank took 44 per cent and ABC 28 per cent of newly registered English-dialogue films.[43] Of course, these were the years of the locust: between 1951 and 1979 the number of cinemas was reduced from 4581 to 1564 – a rate of annihilation which slowed and perhaps stalled in the 1970s. Seating capacity during the same period was reduced from 4.2 million to 721,000.[44]

Concurrently with these general changes, changes in programming have also taken place: for example, from short and cheap screenings, through the stabilization of the two-feature performance (with newsreels, organ music and advertisements), with two programmes a week, through (although unevenly) the single feature (with a 'short') kept for a whole week, to the multi-screen 'complex' which can offer up to four feature films in any one week. The closures have been dramatic. Today, for many people in many areas of the country, seeing films in cinemas necessitates a special day-trip. In 1977 Greater London had 130,000 cinema seats out of the total of 764,000 in England, Scotland and Wales, took 22 million of the 103 million admissions, and receipts of £24 million out of a total of £85 million.[45]

Cultural products do not only entail production and circulation to particular sites. Both products and sites are regulated by the state and other agencies. The pattern of legitimation and regulation in film and cinema is similar to that obtaining for other media, particularly in that various 'technical' regulations have social outcomes forming part of a general standardization of product and systematization of production and distribution – that is, the shift from small-scale competitive capitalism to monopoly capitalism. In turn, this raises the cost of entry into production and, an emphasis normally totally ignored, what is a standard example of a given cultural product (that is, what is a proper film, or a proper cinema) is defined by the oligopolic exemplars. Chanan helpfully shows the parallels between the 1898 'Suitability Act' (for music-halls and variety theatres) and the 1909 Cinematograph Act,[46] which led to many more purpose-built cinemas. Successive regulations – together with the relevant parts of other legislation, such as the Sunday Entertainments Act, (1932) and the Children and Young Persons Act, (1933; 1937 for Scotland) and various Manuals of Safety Requirements – need to be traced through the cultural form of cinema in the way that this has been done, for example, for newspapers and literacy.[47] Two other Acts are important, in relation to what has been shown in regulated cinemas: The Cinematograph Films Act of 1927 (which established the 'quota' of British films)[48] and the Cinematograph Films Act of 1957 (which established the 'Eady Levy').[49]

Censorship has long been wrongly construed as being concerned with morality. Again, and equally fortunately, this view is now being challenged from two directions: by a study of the censorship of groups of people who tried to make and show political films to working-class audiences,[50] and by a reconstruction of the history of the British Board of Film Censors.[51] The board dates from 1912 and its membership was appointed by trade organizations, although the choice of the president, and later of the secretary, were 'approved' by the Home Secretary. Apart from 'moral panics' about the film form and working-class audiences, the need for some form of self-regulation followed from powers granted to local authorities by the court decisions broadening the scope of the 1909 Act.[52] The principal individuals associated with the board were all *political*. Furthermore there was only one secretary – Brooke Wilkinson – from 1913 to 1948. The forty-three basic rules of the board were established by T. P. O'Connor (president, 1916–29).[53] Thirty-three of these were concerned with morality in its usual narrow sense, but the other ten were political. One rule – in force until after 1945 – banned all 'subjects . . . which dealt with relations between capital and labour. . . .'[54] This was a specific case of a rule clearly obtained to prevent film-makers from dealing with controversial subjects. As Lord Tyrrell, President in 1936 said, 'Cinema needs continued repression of controversy to stave off disaster.'[55]

Above, I have sketched the outlines of a materialist history of 'availability' – product, sites and their regulation. Finally we can turn to the audience, or to what we know of audiences. Rounded up to the nearest million, cinema admissions and television licence-holders are compared in Table 2. The key years are 1954–8, when some 500 million disappear from the annual attendances at cinemas. But the same years also saw other changes in the gender, age and class composition of audiences.

Table 2

	Cinema admissions (millions)[56]	TV licences (millions)[57]
1914	364	–
1934	903	–
1940	1027	–
1944	1575	–
1946	1635	–
1947	not available	0.015
1950	1396	0.343
1953	1285	2.142
1955	1182	4.651
1958	755	not available
1965	327	13.516
1971	176	15.300
1973	134	17.100
1976	104	17.700
1979	111	

Although I have compared these two sets of figures, I am not implying any simple correlation. In particular, we have to note, first, that films are shown on television. Buscombe described how, in 1970, 'in the London area . . . with just one set you could watch something like fifteen hours of feature films during the week.'[58] Second, Manvell calculated that anyone who went to the cinema twice a week in 1943 would have seen two hundred or so feature films and spent six hours a week (three hundred hours a year, 'plus perhaps a hundred hours queuing') at the pictures. These figures remind us how little time regular cinema attendance occupied.[59] BBC figures suggest about twenty hours a week for the average viewing of persons over five in the late 1970s, with above-average viewing for the under-fourteens and over-fifties, and below average figures for those aged fifteen to nineteen.[60]

The cinema as a setting for films had effects of its own, as many comments from the 1930s onwards show.[61] Even Montagu, writing with a clear sense of the film as a capitalist commodity, agrees that the 'name picture *palace* [his italics] is far from inapt'. Moreover, rather 'than individual films, the cinema sold a habit . . . : To "go to the local", meant, in the language, not only a visit to the pub but, equally, a visit to the cinema.'[62] As Manvell noted in 1944, 'there is more in cinema-going than seeing films. There is going out at night, the sense of relaxation combined with the sense of fun and excitement. . . . It is to be expected that success of this sort will breed a habit and habit a fashion.'[63]

As well as the setting, we have evidence that the symbolic structure and specific conventions of film have other consequences.[64] Despite the specific position he advances,[65] J. P. Mayer's two books – particularly the second – still form the basis of any qualitative study of audiences. In each book Mayer draws upon material collected from readers of *Picturegoer*.[66] The resulting material represents a rare collection of the contradictory discourses concerning films which were in play during the 1940s. It confirms what has been said about the habit of 'going to the pictures', as well as being relevant to other debates – for example, about whether or not English films were liked. Of course they are 'creatures' of their times in relation not only to the high tide of Hollywood but also to the experience of the Second World War.[67] But they are starting-points.

There is a range of practices and materials which we cannot afford to ignore: the range of promotional devices. Dyer's work on stars, and more generally on entertainment, is important here, but it requires a wider study, along with the whole apparatus of memorabilia[68] and fan-mail.[69] It is of some interest to study how people learn about films and what influences their decision to go and see a particular film.[70] In 1937, of the 100,000 or more people attending Granada theatres who were surveyed, 41.5 per cent listened to BBC radio programmes on films; in 1947 the figure was 69 per cent.[71] In a *Kinematograph Weekly* survey (12 October 1945) 14 per cent of a sample admitted that newspaper critics influenced their choice of films to view, but 76 per cent said they read the critics for information. Of the 660 regular cinemagoers interviewed in a 1963 London survey, 31 per cent were *alerted* to a film by word of mouth, no other medium of information reaching above 15 per cent.[72] Although it is no longer correct to argue – as Sidney Bernstein did in 1937,[73] when he stressed the specific importance of local advertising – 32 per cent of the Londoners interviewed in 1963 knew that a film was being shown from an advertisement in the local paper, and 29 per cent from posters outside the cinema.[74]

The moment of cinema is in fact a brief one. Significantly in 1950 the Hulton survey included cinema attendance together with greyhound racing and football pools, among 'Some New Habits', in contrast with 'The Reading Public' or 'It makes a Change' (holidays).[75] Within two years, the statisticians were attributing 'three-quarters of the decline in admissions' to the cinema 'to the competition of television'.[76] Although the British Federation of Film Makers planned a detailed national survey for 1958 and again for 1961, it was not until 1963 that one was carried out, and it was restricted to Greater London, obtaining a thousand interviews of people aged between sixteen and forty-five. Of the six hundred and sixty regular cinema-goers, it was a formal event ('a bit of an occasion') for 41 per cent. The general conclusion of the 1963 survey reflected the changes already rapidly taking place and made recommendations, many of which have been put into effect, to alter the 'image' of the cinema more towards 'a special night out'. The *habit* had died.

So much for some general indications of the audience. It was never, of course, homogeneous. To begin with, national and regional differences must be taken into account. Until recently Scotland and Northern England were the areas of highest cinema attendance, with South Wales also ranking as a high attending area: as late as 1960 the average number of cinema visits per person per year was 27 in Scotland and 20 in London.[77] London has always been a special case: by 1934 half the cinemas there had more than 1500 seats (compared with 28 per cent in Scotland; nowhere else had more than 20 per cent). Also, London had 52 cinemas with over 2001 seats (Lancashire, 25; Scotland, 21).[78] In 1951 London led the field with both circuit and long-run cinemas, and in the change to one programme a week scheduling (57.4 per cent of its cinemas, the eastern region being runner-up, with 26 per cent. By contrast, 38.2 per cent of the cinemas in Scotland were showing three programmes a week).[79] However, the general profile of the London audience was not to differ markedly from the national profile in 1963[80] nor in 1966.[81]

The West End audience was very distinctive. It is worth noting that in 1963, of 660 regular London cinema-goers, 10 per cent had never been to the West End, and of those who had been, 44 per cent had not been there that year.[82] The best guide to the distinctiveness of the West End audience is the 1970 survey by Pearl and Dean.[83] Of those who had visited cinemas in the previous four weeks, 30 per cent in the West End (25 per cent in the GLC area, 21 per cent in London), compared with 14 per cent of the national audience, were classified as in the social categories 'AB'. By contrast, only 5 per cent of the West End audience (9 per cent in the GLC area, 7 per cent in London), compared with 18 per cent of the national audience, were classified as 'DE'.

Age is also relevant in determining who are regular cinema-goers – as is clear from the recent Cinema Advertising Association survey (1980), which gives statistics of how many members of each relevant age group had seen such films as *Grease* or *Star Wars*.[84] Even if one sets aside films addressed primarily for the young – which imply a recognition by producers that the market is not homogeneous – the cinema's audience has, for perhaps twenty-five years, been essentially made up of people aged between the mid-teens and the mid-twenties. In 1976 this group, who made up some 18 per cent of the UK population, represented 56 per cent of the cinema audience. 85.2 per cent of people in this age group were cinema-goers.[85] Until 1959 the twenty-five to thirty-four years age group also visited the cinema with more than average frequency;[86] in 1943, 57 per cent of regular cinema-goers were eighteen to forty, although they made up 42 per cent of the population.[87] Equally long–standing has been the under-representation of those aged over forty-five, and particularly of those aged over sixty, in the cinema audience. According to the 1946 Social Survey, 61 per cent of those aged over sixty never went to the cinema.[88]

The proportions of the sexes represented in cinema audiences have also been significant. Here too there has been change over the years. Women were dominant in the mass cinema audience of the 1940s: 34 per cent of the women civilian population interviewed in 1943 went to the cinema at least once a week, compared to 28 per cent of male civilians, paid working women going much more frequently than those engaged in unpaid domestic labour.[89] During the mid- to late 1950s, however, the former dominance of women in the cinema audience changed to that of men.[90] Apart from the writers quoted in Mayer's books, we have some indication of gender-based 'likes' and 'dislikes' from the Bernstein surveys and from the 1980 Cinema Advertising Association study.[91]

And so, finally, we come to the subject of class. Lindsay Anderson told Peter Harcourt in 1977:

The class division of the British Cinema echoes the class division of British society: on the one hand we have our 'popular' films, which the 'ignorant' people with their 'degraded' taste enjoy – i.e. the *Carry On . . .* pictures; on the other hand, you have the reputable bourgeois art-works, which the intellectual critics can applaud because they give them a comforting feeling of having good taste, but which have absolutely no relevance to this country.[92]

Alas for such an analysis, 'Them' have triumphed over 'Us': the great DE masses have dwindled to the significant AB others. Thirty-three per cent of those who went to the cinema at least once a week in 1943 had had only an elementary schooling (as against 31 per cent with secondary or further education, and 14 per cent with university education). For the same year, 42 per cent of those who attended with this regularity were employed in heavy or light manufacturing and among them munitions workers were the main attenders.[93] To quote one pithy summary from the 1946 survey '. . . the lowest economic and education groups show the greatest rigidity in their cinema-going. . . .'[94] In 1949, 43.4 per cent of regular cinema-goers were from groups DE,[95] a figure which is almost identical to the later figures given by the Screen Advertising Association surveys: 43 per cent of attenders in 1960; 121.5 million DEs from a total of 168.6 million in 1961.[95] But, in 1963 and for London alone, we find that in a survey of 660 regular cinema-goers, 18 per cent were DE and 16 per cent AB; and in the national survey of 1965–6, of all those of the 15,685 sampled who went to the cinema at least once a month, there were 15 per cent DE and 16 per cent AB.[97] The JICNAR survey for 1976 presents contradictory figures in this context: of an average cinema audience, they estimated that 26 per cent were DE and 13 per cent AB, but of the total population who were cinema-goers, they estimate that 31.8 per cent were DE and 60.3 per cent AB.[98] Pearl and Dean's survey show the particularity of the West End audience: of those who had visited a cinema in the previous four weeks, 30 per cent were AB and only 5 per cent DE.[99] Finally, the Cinema Advertising Association, in its sampling of a hundred places, asked people about the number of visits to the cinema which they had made during the period December 1979 to January 1980, and arrived at these figures: for DEs, 0.28; for ABs 0.46.[100]

Class preferences have been far less coherently investigated, but information on this point can be found in Mayer's two books and in the Cinema Advertising Association survey.

Richard Dyer concludes his immensely valuable book, *Stars*, thus:

> First of all, there is the question of the audience. Throughout this book – as throughout most film studies – the audience has been conspicuous by its absence. In talking of manipulation (pp. 12f.), consumption (pp. 39f.), ideological work (pp. 22f.), subversion (pp. 59f), identification (pp. 19f.), reading (pp. 72f.), placing (pp. 137f.), and elsewhere, a concept of the audience is clearly critical, and yet in every case have had to gesture toward this gap in our knowledge and then proceed as if it were *merely* a gap. But how one conceptualizes the audience – and the very empirical adequacy of one's conceptualizations – is fundamental in every assumption one can make about how stars, and films, work.

He goes on to indicate other major areas of ignorance, but concludes, 'Yet these are as nothing compared to our ignorance, theoretical and empirical, of how films work, for, on, with audiences. . . .'[101]

Part 2
The Development of the British Cinema Industry

3
The Emergence of an Industry
Michael Chanan

Between 1896 – the year when, in Britain, the cinematograph made its public commercial bow – and the passing of the Cinematograph Films Act in 1927 – the year after the General Strike – a great many things changed in these islands, and in the world whose image the cinematograph traded in. The very shape of British capitalism changed.

The British economy never properly recovered from the First World War. Its leading heavy industries failed to regain their previous levels of productivity. Although in the nineteenth century Britain, by building on the early advantages acquired in the course of the Industrial Revolution, had become the dominant imperial power in the world economy, by the turn of the century it had already fallen behind rival capitalist economies, such as Germany and the United States, in technological development of the forces of production. The destruction of people and resources caused by the first world war intensified the contradiction that this already implied between the monetary and financial superstructure of the imperial system and the conditions necessary for the internal development of the productive forces. The country's internal credit system was subordinated to the international credit system that enabled British finance capital to appropriate much of its imperialist super profits. This subordination was maintained, until 1931, through the gold standard, which kept the pound at an overvalued exchange rate against gold, the world money form. This resulted in an arbitrary restriction of credit and high interest rates, thus accentuating the already existing tendency towards depression. There was not yet any structural crisis in the economic system, but finance capital, by maintaining an outdated budgetary policy and high interest rates, impeded and obstructed capital accumulation.

It was in this context that the accumulation of capital in the film industry began. During its first few years, the industry suffered no particular disadvantage from this situation because, as Peter Bachlin observed,[1] at this stage it was a branch of the economy without any tradition, and its mode of production was artisanal, hardly yet industrial. Consequently there was room for it to grow before conditions in the economic environment would be felt as constraining.

Indeed, the problems which the dominance of finance capital created for internal economic development impeded neither the early expansion of the cinema nor, in general, the prosperity of the economic sector it was born into, the sector controlled by what can be called entertainment capital. This was because cinema-goers were initially recruited from the strata of the urban population with the lowest incomes; in the latter part of the nineteenth century these strata had won for themselves a reduction of working hours, without a fall in real income, and consequently an increase in leisure hours and at least a minimal amount of money to spend on them. This basic condition operated right up to the second world war and even until the beginning of the 1950s, leaving its mark on the marketing policies which the industry pursued. In 1919, for example, the trade weekly *Kine Weekly* carried the comment that 'Though there is a good deal of unemployment in Blackburn owing to the slackness in the cotton trade, the kinemas are doing well. Their success is likely to continue as long as the unemployment benefit goes on. The latter has been a boon to the kinemas, for without it there would have been little money in circulation.'[2] And almost twenty years later, Orwell, writing in *The Road to Wigan Pier* of the dreadful life of the single unemployed man, who was forced to spend his days loafing around in public libraries or in any other place where he could keep warm, observed that 'In Wigan a favourite refuge was the pictures, which are fantastically cheap there. You can always get a seat for fourpence, and at the matinee at some houses you can even get a seat for twopence. Even people on the verge of starvation will readily pay twopence to get out of the ghastly cold of a winter afternoon.'[3]

Entertainment capital corresponded mainly to interests which had emerged in the 1880s, following an Act of Parliament passed in 1878, which was concerned with theatre safety regulations. This piece of legislation was known as the 'Suitability Act', because it required certificates of suitability for music-halls and variety theatres. The effect of the 'Suitability Act' was that some two hundred halls across the country were forced to put up shutters because their managements could not afford to make the alterations which it stipulated, although some of them managed to struggle on until, with the growth of the cinema, they acquired a new lease of life. But many went out of business because the economic depression which began in the mid-1870s restricted the availability of investment funds needed for rebuilding. As a result, big business, with readier access to such funds, bought them out and moved in, forming syndicates and chains. As the recession abated in the late 1880s and 1890s, these new business interests began to put up bigger and plushier halls, and the middle-men of the industry – for this is what it had now become – the agents through whom the artists were booked, began to flourish. Music-hall programmes for this period show that while there were different types of hall for different classes of audience, the entertainment they presented was becoming more and more uniform. It was largely because syndicates and chains had created a uniformity of music-hall entertainment that moving pictures penetrated the music-hall with such speed, became diffused by and through it, and took much of their early aesthetic from it.

In the early years of the twentieth century, entertainment capital, widely absorbed by the 1930s into what Adorno called the 'culture industry', passed from the wings to a commanding position upstage, ready for its sweep down to the footlights after the Second World War. In the course of this process cinema, which was born into the interstices of the entertainment world – in the fairground and among popular itinerant entertainers, as well as in the halls – grew up to usurp the music-hall and acquire the position of market leader of the culture industry, before giving up its place to its own usurper, television.

In Britain, however, finance capital in the City was slow off the mark in exploiting this market, because its interests lay in a different direction. In particular it was slower than the City's cousin Wall Street. The spread of cinema had been no less rapid in Britain than anywhere else, and Britain had quickly become the largest film market outside the United States; nevertheless, largely because of the City's apathy, the British film production industry rapidly lost ground, in its own market, to its North American counterpart. In the long term the British film industry came to recognize that it could only sustain its position by accepting symbiotic allegiance to the American leaders in the field – that is to say, through a mutual agreement to share the exploitation of the British market – since neither party was properly able to do without the other. But it was an agreement in which the British played the junior partners and acceded to American domination. The Cinematograph Act of 1927 is a dividing line because, before it, the methods used by the Americans in the exploitation of cinema in Britain were pretty much the same as those they were using and have always used in underdeveloped countries, like those of Latin America.[4] It was only after the 1927 Act, and with the coming of sound, that Hollywood, as it had now become, learned to adopt more subtle methods of penetration in the case of other metropolitan countries, such as Britain.

The cinema, Bachlin wrote, is a branch of the economy without any tradition:

it has developed sometimes in an autonomous way and sometimes by assuming forms of organization from other sectors. In a very short time, this industry has been through almost all forms of capitalism, which were born before cinema itself, from personal enterprise to trustification. The very considerable risks it entails and the arrangements made to remove or reduce them give to its production, distribution and exploitation a very peculiar character.[5]

This peculiarity first showed itself in the trade which rapidly grew up between the pioneer producers and the individual showmen who mounted the new form of entertainment. The small entrepreneurial inventors, on the one hand, their fine imaginations schooled in Victorian empiricism and common sense, and on the other the motley crowd of magic lanternists, fairground showmen, itinerant theatre people and music-hall magicians, all began by treating film as if it were cloth – a commodity to be bought and sold at a uniform price of so much per foot. Thus there also appeared, very rapidly, a second-hand market in which – since film, like cloth, wears out – prices were calculated according to the age of the copy. At first, different kinds of film were all treated in the same way, even though a keen sense of genre developed very quickly in the producers' publicity. Within a few years, however, it was new films of any genre that gathered themselves a premium, as travelling exhibitors sought to gain the advantage over competitors by always being able to guarantee an audience something they had not seen before – by learning, in other words, to trade on novelty and fashion.

Initially, the price of all new films was fixed by the dominant primary production cost, which was that of raw film stock. Practically nowhere, at first, in the primitive conditions which prevailed during the infancy of film production, was there any of the developed business sense that insists on the making of proper accounts – the kind of rationalizing intelligence which Max Weber (in *The Protestant Ethic and the Spirit of Capitalism*) located at the origins of modern capitalism and which, in the United States, the banks began to impose on the film business as a condition of financing it. This undeveloped business sense could be found at both ends of the industry and several individuals noted its effects. The pioneer distributor, A. C. Bromhead, an ex-army colonel, described the problems of collecting accounts from fairground showmen: 'A representative meeting a showman who was behind with his accounts was immediately invited to 'come and collect it yourself . . . on the roundabouts . . . in tuppences'.[6] At the other end of the business, the first time the pioneer producer Cecil Hepworth recalled paying his actors was not until 1905.[7] These are hardly the characteristics of proper capitalist operation, and in fact the vast majority of people involved in film in the first few years could hardly be called capitalists. Some, like Bromhead and Hepworth, were *petit bourgeois* aiming to become capitalists, but in this respect the Americans were further advanced. It is not surprising to find Hepworth acknowledging this. He mentions how an American visitor to his studio in 1912 advised him of the distinction between the producer and the director. The terms were still unfamiliar in Britain at the time, he remarks.

The names recorded by history are mostly those of the budding capitalists (Hepworth, Bromhead, Urban and others), but the social origins of the anonymous majority were mostly proletarian. Few of them managed to start a business that lasted for longer than their own generation. On the other hand, the initial absence of fully blown capitalist relations, which has misled many would-be historians of cinema, is only one face of the early film. Film is a hybrid, and the language of the early film business itself shows another face. The making of films was not in the beginning, called 'production', but 'manufacture', and the first film studios were called factories (much as the first factories, in the early years of the industrial revolution, had often been called mills). Moreover, the rule of the world of industrial capitalism which, after all, brought film into being, showed itself in the course of the first couple of years of the industry's existence in the fall in price that exhibitors found themselves paying for their copies, as the supply of ready-coated raw film on which films were made and printed began to increase.

Also early to manifest itself was the international character of the film industry, already anticipated by the manner in which the French company of the *Lumière frères* launched itself into operation in a series of countries in quick succession from the end of 1895 to the beginning of 1897. This aspect became clear in what was later to be called the distribution market. It did so as a consequence of the singularly rapid expansion which engulfed this new sub-branch of the entertainment business, by which the market was both extended geographically and intensified locally. The consequence of this unsatisfied demand was that no single country was able to produce enough films for its own home-market. Individual producers consequently found themselves, at the outset, able to gain from developing an export trade, as long as they could produce a sufficient number of copies. At the same time, there were dealers setting themselves up to sell exhibitors films they had imported. One of these was A. C. Bromhead. Also, from the outset, there were companies which operated in foreign territories, although for a long time most of them did so only through licensing arrangements. The earliest examples of foreign companies operating in Britain include the French Pathé and Gaumont companies; Gaumont's British operations were built up by Bromhead, who had started as their import agent. Such international cross-links grew and multiplied over the years at a steady rhythm, ending with markets across the world being carved up among the biggest competitors. From the start, these included the Americans, but until the first world war they were not in the dominant position. Nevertheless, viewed from the international perspective, the film industry, together with the gramophone record industry, offers a remarkable parallel, in the cultural sphere, with the conditions which Lenin observed in 1917 in the electrical industry, and whose paradigmatic character for the mode of production of late capitalism he detected in *Imperialism: The Highest Stage of Capitalism*.

The similarity between the cinema and the gramophone record industry is a reminder of the force with which film exploded into history, for the mechanical reproduction of sound had remained little more than, on the one hand, a rich man's toy and, on the other, a fairground sideshow for a quarter of a century before it reached the industrial stage. But cinematography was more than a means of mechanical reproduction. In creating so suddenly a huge and hungry following, the primary characteristic of the film, in its early days, was the sense, and the fact, of unsatisfied demand. The *sense* of unsatisfied demand lay in the baffling fact that, like the primary, basic material needs of human existence – for food, clothing, a dwelling and warmth – the demand for the cinema seemed to anticipate the particular means of satisfying it. This is an undeniable fact of social history. And while the idealist explanations of this phenomenon, by film critics like Bazin, made unsupportable claims for it, the immediate demand which film created arose from the most intimate characteristics of the invention, which inevitably made it a new means of aesthetic expression.

The early conditions of the film industry reveal still another aspect in the absence, as yet, of any formal division of labour in the actual processes of mounting and shooting – 'manufacturing' as it was originally called – a film, since the machinery was originally simple enough for almost anyone to operate. Similarly, there was no established compartmentalization of the industry into the various sectors which later came to characterize its structure: namely, production, distribution and exhibition. Thus, many of the firms which established positions of leadership in the first few years were those with a primary interest in the production of equipment rather than in films – in what is nowadays colloquially called 'hardware', as opposed to 'software'. But, like subsequent hardware producers, such as those of the radio industry in the 1920s in the United States, they undertook software production in order to capture a sector of the hardware market. Hardware and software are linked commodities, inseperable twins, but it is generally the creation of a software market that creates the demand for the hardware. This means that software manufacture must sometimes be undertaken at the beginning, according to the criteria of what, in the language of marketing, has come to be known as the loss leader. In other words, the firms we are speaking of did not make equipment in order to sell films; they made films in order to sell equipment: their own. Because competition was in fact extraordinarily intense, the result was a lack of standardization. For example, makers of projectors, in order to gain an advantage over competitors, would typically incorporate an idiosyncratic feature in the design of their equipment, such as an odd type of perforation. This would correspond to the same manufacturer's camera, in order to ensure that purchasers of the one would also have to buy the other –

and get their films from the same source. For what was happening was happening was that these small workshop manufacturers were selling their apparatuses to showmen of various kinds, including those who made their own films to supplement the supply they bought in the film exchanges. These were often itinerants, working the fairground, music-hall or local and town hall circuits, who would offer in their programmes a locally shot scenic view, or topical film on a local municipal event, to attract the audience as they travelled around – a practice much susceptible, because of the crudeness of the early state of the art, to cheating, misrepresentation and what is nowadays called 'hyping' – constant features of commercial cinema ever since. A handful of these itinerants became major producers, but few survived the First World War.

In 1899, however, Eastman Kodak, in the United States, introduced a new method of film stock manufacture: a method of continuous casting on revolving drums which produced an unending sheet of celluloid, coated it with photographic emulsion, split it into thin strips and perforated them, running non-stop for twenty-four hours a day. It was a semi-automatic type of manufacture which so enormously raised the productivity of labour power, greatly improving the organic composition of capital, that it quickly led to the establishment of the industry's first monopoly. The small equipment firms were steadily disadvantaged as a result, the ones with the quirkiest standards first. Others survived by adapting their equipment to the standards imposed by the monopolists, at the same time running down their film production side, including production of their own film stock.

One of the main exponents of the original pre-monopolist manufacturing-based operation in early British cinema was R. W. Paul, by trade a precision instrument engineer with his own small workshop. It was British companies like Paul's which were among the first to find, over the years, that international competition and the international nature of the industry put them at a disadvantage – although Paul had entered the business as the inventor of a projector mechanism, after copying Edison's Kinetoscope, the original what-the-butler-saw machine, when he discovered that it was not covered by a British patent. He originally undertook to make films in order to provide a personal supply for his own exhibiting activities. The fate of Paul's operations, however, provides perhaps the first hint of what were to be structural weaknesses in the future British film industry. The author of some fine, imaginative and delightful examples of very early British film, Paul was forced to withdraw from production after only a few years, although his company survived to become part of Cambridge Scientific Instruments in the 1920s.

Another early film producer, and a more imaginative film-maker than most, the Brighton-based Williamson, began as a portrait photographer with experience of magic-lantern lecturing. He too gave up making films to concentrate on the manufacture of equipment. This kind of specialization fulfilled a positive function: it placed the aesthetic development of the medium, which at that time depended largely on the elaboration of basic technical facilities (such as camera panning heads and viewfinder systems), in the hands of manu-facturers with personal knowledge of these needs. There is nothing, of course, in the history and laws of capitalist development that makes this unusual. It is also perfectly usual to find such craftsmen-entrepreneurs being eclipsed sooner rather than later. Williamson's company did not, as Paul's did, survive.

At the manufacturing end of the film business, the peculiarities of film still lay dormant. They would not appear until the development of a division of labour in the film crew and the emergence of a new kind of cultural craft-worker. Meanwhile there was also the chaos, at the manufacturing end, created by the state of patents legislation. It was not until the Patents Act of 1907 that, because of growing confusion in technological competition in a whole range of branches of production, the Patents Office stipulated that the novelty of an invention must be investigated by the Office itself before a patent could be granted. Many of the enormous number of early film patents would plainly not have been granted if this provision had been in operation earlier. Its effects in promoting the rationalization of the industry were immediate, as the ensuing history of patent litigation over Urban's Kinemacolor process shows.[8] The importance of the relation of patents to the industrial structure is well known from the history of the cinema in the United States.

Bachlin drew attention particularly to the fact that the film is not an ordinary kind of commodity. In the first place, it is not used up in a single act of consumption, but remains available for repeated exploitation until the copy is physically worn out. Even so, worn-out copies can always be replaced by new prints. Indeed, in the case of a particularly successful early film, Cecil Hepworth's *Rescued by Rover*, the film was actually remade, twice, because so many copies were needed that the negative itself also wore out twice!

This capacity for multiple consumption is not a unique property of film, but something which in some measure it shares with certain other aesthetic objects: those works of art from which exchange value can be raised by means of an admission charge to view them. This is like the admission charge for the performing arts, which in turn is like the gate money paid at football matches, with which in other respects too, the mode of exploitation of film bears singularly close similarities. For the spread of film is also a consequence of its characteristically collective mode of consumption, the aspect under which its social impact is felt within the community.

It was because of the durability of film, both materially and aesthetically, that a brisk second-hand trade developed so quickly. This was initiated by enterprising showmen, who saw the benefits in exchanging, renting out and even selling their mounting stocks. In Britain, there was the example of J. D. Walker and E. G. Turner, whose company was called Walturdaw, and who were already, like Paul, involved in the exploitation of the Edison Kinetoscope when they bought their first film projector, the first to be made by the English manufacturer, Wrench. Walturdaw concentrated their operations among the entertainment bureaux: the booking agencies for music-hall and other circuits. In turning from selling to renting operations, they and other incipient distributors realized that the film need not pass physically into the hands of the consumer for its exchange value to be realized, nor need it pass into the ownership of the exhibitor, since the exhibitor can rent it instead.

Bachlin describes the significance of this discovery of the properties of rental:

The distributor took the risk of purchasing films on his own account, while the exhibitor did no more than rent them; and the distributor's intervention improved economic conditions for the exhibitor by allowing more frequent programme changes. This created a growth in the market for the producer: films could reach the consumer in greater number and more rapidly; moreover, the new system constituted a kind of sales guarantee for their films. In general, the distributor bought copies of one or several films from one or several producers and rented them to many exhibitors; by doing this it was possible to obtain for them a greater sum than their cost price [at the same time that the exhibitor now had to pay less]. The old system of selling the individual copy, which means ceding a piece of property, was replaced by the *temporary concession of the right to exhibit*.[9]

'It is undeniable,' Bachlin continues, 'that the birth of the branch of distribution accelerated the development of the film industry: the reduction in the price of films, their diffusion and greater distribution led to an increase in the number of cinemas.'

It was in order to deal with a variety of problems which this spread of cinemas created, including certain social problems, that Parliament passed its first Cinematograph Act in 1909, which like the 1878 'Suitability Act' for the theatre, dealt ostensibly with safety regulations in the buildings in which cinematograph exhibitions were taking place. Whether by anybody's design or not, the effects of the 1909 Act were like those of the earlier one. It was after this Act that exhibition capital began to become organized and to grow. In 1908 there were only three exhibition companies registered in Britain, with a total capital of £110,000 (although buildings where films were being shown numbered thousands). By the eve of the first world war there were 1,833 such companies, managing about four thousand cinemas and with a combined capital of just over £11 million.

At the same time, in the year this first Act of Parliament devoted to the cinema industry was passed, British production accounted for only about 15 per cent of programmes shown in British cinemas, 40 per cent being accounted for by French companies (under the leadership of Pathé), 30 per cent by American and 10 per cent by Italian. While the Italian proportion rose to about 17 per cent over the next few years, the American proportion rose even faster, and in the year of the outbreak of war the American share of the British market reached 60 per cent. (The estimate of *The Times* that British production by that date had fallen to only 2 per cent of its own home market is probably an exaggeration since the figures were difficult to assess, but it was nevertheless indicative of the situation.)

The intensifying conditions of the market during the pre-war years prompted the trade to organize itself more efficiently. The first of the trade organizations, the Kinematograph Manufacturers' Association (KMA), was formed in the summer of 1906, only a few months before the creation of the industry's first trade union, the National Association of Cinematograph Operators (NACO). As Rachael Low has observed, it is not perhaps surprising that the manufacturers were the first to come together in this way, since they were the fewest in number among the various employers in the industry.[10] Then, in 1910, the Incorporated Association of Film Renters was formed – in secret. It acquired weight from the membership of important renters, like William Jury, whose interests were widely spread, and spent its first secretive months aiming for an agreement with the KMA, which was trying, not for the first time, to limit the circulation of films, to fix prices and thus control the market. Agreement was reached and implemented a year later. Provisions were made to undertake boycotts of companies which infringed its code of practice, and to check illegal copying and the sale of films before release dates, for both practices were sufficiently widespread to constitute a nuisance. The rest of the trade responded, not for the first time, with vociferous accusations of interference and monopoly. This was not, however, the source from which the threat of monopoly was subsequently to come. For, meanwhile, the renters found themselves divided by an agreement whose implementation menaced their small and second-hand members, as well as the mass of industrial exhibitors, and the organization was unable to sustain its offensive.

It would have been natural to expect a massive injection of capital into the film business at the end of the First World War. For the imposition of an entertainments tax during the war had shown how inelastic the demand for cinema had become. Indeed, in 1920 Lord Burnham said at a Cinematograph Exhibitors' dinner that 'the high financiers of the world are flocking into the cinema industry. Formerly it was difficult, I believe, to raise even a small capital for a cinema enterprise. Today, if you ask for a million you get half a million oversubscribed.'[11] But this was capital that went principally into exhibition costs. When Cecil Hepworth tried to launch a production company not long after Burnham spoke these words, the capital he proposed was £250,000, the flotation was badly undersubscribed, and by 1924 he was bankrupt.

There is a clear relation between what happened in the exhibition field and what happened in production. Production in Britain was driven into a corner by the same factor that attracted British finance capital to the exhibitors: the profits were to be made from showing American films, which, as a result of the enforced curtailment of production in Europe during the war, were now a long way in the lead on British screens.

Growth figures quoted above for the years 1908–14 show that in the course of those years the exhibition-business emerged from its itinerant beginnings. But the phase it now entered was one of under capitalized, pre-monopolistic competition in which accumulation of capital was still largely primitive and disorganized. In Britain, local exhibitors began to attract small amounts of capital from local businesses; in some cases, successful local businessmen, usually shopkeepers, invested private profits in setting up cinemas. Sometimes, of course, there was money from local renters. But in 1908 it was already evident to the seasoned observer that developments were taking place much faster in the United States. There, according to the British trade journal the *Bioscope*, 'the numerous capitalists and syndicates have been quietly watching the business for a good long time, and now, having gleaned satisfactory proof of the profits, they are putting heart and soul into it as only the American speculator knows how. . . . When they can't buy or lease theatres they buy sites and erect picture houses.'[12]

Also, it was in the United States, much sooner than in Britain, that the process of vertical integration of production, distribution and exhibition in the industry began. The only example of this in Britain before the war was embodied in Provincial Cinematograph Theatres, the largest of the pre-war circuits, which had the backing of a financier, Sir William Bass, and incorporated a subsidiary, the original London Films Company, with studios at Twickenham. The company survived the war only with difficulty and by renting out its studios to other producers, as other studio-owners were also forced to do. But, after the war, even the largest circuits in Britain were not big enough to resist the marketing methods introduced by the American distributors. The Americans began establishing their own distribution offices in Britain even before the First World War. Vitagraph (subsequently Warner Brothers) registered a British company in 1912; Fox moved in in 1916, and in 1919 a distribution company set up in 1915 by the old hand, J. D. Walker, of Walturdaw, was taken over to become the Famous Lasky Film Service (subsequently Paramount).

American distributors realized that they enjoyed the advantage of having the largest home market of any film industry of the time. In the words of the Moyne Report of 1936, the size of their home market meant that the American producer was 'able to recover the whole or a high proportion of the costs of making the film by exhibiting it in his own market. The receipts in this country and elsewhere represent, therefore, apart from the cost of the positive prints and of distribution, additional profits.'[13] This situation enabled the Americans to offer their films, when necessary, at a cheaper rate in foreign markets, and hence in the British Market, than their competitors, the home producers in the markets concerned. Thus, as the 1952 PEP Report comments, the purely commercial advantage of booking American films had a powerful effect in 'prejudicing British exhibitors against British films'.[14] To ensure the necessary outlets for the increasing production of their studios – some might call it overproduction – the American companies employed other means of selling which were typical of the chain-store mentality. Two particular distributive malpractices were involved, known as 'block-booking' and 'blind booking'. The former consisted in the distributor foisting upon the exhibitor films he did not want, as part of a package including those he did want. In the latter case, the booking included films which were as yet unseen – or, in some cases, even unmade – but which the parent studio in the United States had already contracted for production. These measures were adopted because the film, like all aesthetic products, is an especially risky commodity for investment. It has always been the practice of the film industry to find methods of reducing the risk, either by fair means or foul.

These pre-1927 methods were particularly foul. Since they resulted in the advance booking of screen time for months and months ahead, they had a disastrous effect on home production in the market under attack. Adrian Brunel reported in his autobiography[15] the effects of these practices on his company, Minerva Films, which he had formed shortly after the war with the collaboration of Leslie Howard, A. A. Milne and others. They embarked on the production of short comedy burlesques in a dry, satirical vein characteristic of the genteel intelligentsia in Britain. Their first films were well received at the trade shows, but the most advantageous distribution agreement they were able to obtain gave them an advance of 25 per cent against bookings no earlier than eighteen months ahead. With no immediate return against expended capital, the company was simply unable to survive. Commenting on this point, Hepworth wrote in his autobiography that many film-makers at the time preferred in such circumstances not to take the risk of producing more ambitious films, but continued instead to turn out the same kind of short pieces as before. This only exacerbated the problem by flooding the market with the kind of film which was less and less in demand. Once again, quite a number of producers went out of business. As a result, the decline of the British film industry reached crisis proportions in 1924. November of that year has gone down in British film history as 'Black

November': every British studio was dark; not a single foot of film was exposed. Ironically at the same time, the trade was promoting a special British Cinema Week to show off its wares. This crisis can easily be correlated with the state of control in distribution. In the same year, 84 per cent of all films distributed in Britain were handled by only fourteen companies; 44 per cent of these films came from the United States, and this figure gave every impression of growing steadily. Several companies handled no British films at all. The three largest, all American-owned, handled 33 per cent of the total. One American magnate was reported to have said early in 1923 that the big American sales organizations would finally oust the British renters and that British producers would eventually be forced to distribute films through American firms – if, he might well have added, any British producers were still left.

In these conditions, the exhibition business had reached a stage where the renter understood clearly enough that if, as Rachael Low puts it, 'in order to give publicity and good presentation for a special film, he gave his own pre-release run, he could skim the profits and, by puffing the picture, could even put up its eventual price'. 'It was suspected before long', she continues, 'that this treatment was employed to build up unremarkable films, the renter's expenses on the pre-release run being made up later by inflated prices for the ordinary runs'.[16] In this way publicity costs came to be absorbed into distribution costs, to the advantage of the distributors and the disadvantage of both the exhibitors and the audience – a further strengthening of the already strong position of the distributors, in whose hands the real power in the film industry came to be concentrated. Low points out that this situation aroused much resentment, especially among showmen with large cinemas in parts of London other than the West End, who had been accustomed to securing genuine first runs before. But there was one important difference between the British distributors and their American competitors. The position of the former, who so largely relied on American products, was not securely enough founded in production and therefore lacked the necessary pull towards the vertical integration which existed in the United States, where it was promoted by the banks in order to take advantage of the United States as the largest national market in the world.

In this context, it is important to note that the growth of the cinema in Britain has been linked to the development of London's West End, with its strong concentration of commercial and office life. In this district, the entertainment (and in particular, the cinema) industries, taking advantage of the improvement in the capital's public transport system, have built on the position already held by the London theatre. This same transport system promoted the dispersal of studios in a ring around the London suburbs, where, during the course of the First World War, the country's leading producers all took up residence, eclipsing a number of important early producers in the provinces.

As the West End rose to prominence, American distributors, setting up offices in London, acquired cinemas for first runs in key West End sites. Famous Lasky was especially aggressive: in 1926 it acquired a number of such sites in provincial cities. But the Americans played the game of denying that they wanted to compete directly with British cinema-owners. In 1924 the heads of First National, Jury-Metro-Goldwyn and Famous Lasky had

each made categorical statements in public denying that the organizations which they represented had any intention of buying or building cinemas in this country. Each of the firms mentioned derives its income from the ordinary exhibitors, and is naturally alive to the importance of maintaining the best of relations with them. To allow an impression to get about that they were contemplating direct competition would be the worst of policies, for amongst other results there is every possibility that the next counter-move would be the formation of a co-operative renter-exhibitor concern which might easily grow into a powerful rival.[17]

The truth is that the Americans did not need to own cinemas in Britain in any number in order to maintain and extend their control over distribution in this country: it would serve their purposes to own only a few. In the case of underdeveloped countries, this approach had the advantage that, since the cinema-owners were drawn from the bourgeoisie, they had to spend money not only on American films but also on American equipment. With the coming of sound, just after the 1927 Cinematograph Act, the company most intimately concerned with forcing the pace of conversion, that of William Fox, succeeded in applying the same principle to Britain, when it contrived to invest in Gaumont-British the sum of £80 million, drawn from British banks – an action which confirmed the subordination to American interests of British finance capital in the field of culture and communications.

During the 1920s renters considered 20 to 25 per cent of box office receipts to be a fair rate of profit, with the cost of the film to the exhibitor varying according to its age, as it had previously done in the second-hand market before the introduction of the rental system. Booking prices being asked in Britain in 1925 by the American company Associated-First National for five classes of films and for various runs were said at the time to descend from £300 for the first run of a full-length film to £3 for the oldest and shortest film. But film hire was charged at a flat rate, not on a percentage of the receipts, and so the system worked doubly to the distributors' advantage: it was the exhibitor who had to bear the cost of a flop. If, therefore, anyone alleges that British finance capital was invested in cinema exhibition rather than in production because production was insufficiently promising, then it must also be explained why the production business was so uninviting, and how it deteriorated further as a result of the way in which the exhibition sector was manipulated by the big, and growing, American distributors. This also applies to the way in which British finance capital responded to the challenge of the Americans. By 1927, however, a definite trend towards the rationalization of the exhibition sector had begun. Authorized public capital stood at the same level as in 1914, a little over £11 million, but the number of registered public companies sharing this capital had been reduced to fifty-three.

The cornerstone in the domination of the British market by the big American distributors was simply that the additional profit they drew from overseas operations gave the American film industry the surplus profits with which to attract increasing investment funds. This was feasible because as Thomas Guback has pointed out –

a motion picture is a commodity one can duplicate indefinitely without substantially adding to the cost of the first unit produced. . . . The economic and technical nature of a film compels the . . . distributor, to try to achieve the widest possible circulation for it. Extra prints represent little further investment, and it is in their interest to make many, distribute them widely, and attempt to recoup their total costs as quickly as possible. Although additional effort is involved in selling the product overseas, a print sent abroad does not deprive the domestic market of anything. In these terms, a given film tends to be an infinitely exportable commodity; prints exported do not affect domestic supplies nor the revenue resulting from domestic exhibition.

As an American, he adds, 'We can have our film and foreigners can have it too'.[18] Yet Guback himself has misinterpreted his own insight. He maintains that not until the American market began to contract after the Second World War did the major American distributors begin to regard their additional income from foreign exploitation as something to be protected by every available means. He fails to see that, because finance capital follows not simply profit but surplus profits, such as those which are guaranteed by technological rents in successful new branches of production, the foreign market, the principal source of surplus profits, has always been regarded as essential. As an American producer told a class of Harvard business students in 1927, discussing the question of 'how we are trying to lessen sales resistance in those countries that want to build up their own industries':

We are trying to do that by internationalizing this art, by drawing on old countries for the best talent that they possess in the way of artists, directors and technicians, and bringing these people over to our country by drawing on their literary talents, taking their choicest stories and producing them in our own way, and sending them back into the countries where they are famous. In doing that, however, we must always keep in mind the revenue end of it. Out of every dollar received, about 75c still comes out of America and only 25c out of all the foreign countries combined. Therefore you must have in mind a picture that will first bring in that very necessary 75 per cent and that secondly will please the other 25 per cent you want to please. If you please the 25 per cent of foreigners to the detriment of your home market, you can see what happens. Of course, the profit is in that last 25 per cent.[19]

Surplus profit, that is, but whether the speaker meant profit, or surplus profit, his last sentence gives the game away.

It is hardly surprising that, as a result of this situation, the British cinema, such as it was, lost its self-confidence. It was unable to sell in the American market, and in other foreign markets was forced to compete against the Americans on unfavourable terms. As the British Consul-General in Havana blandly put it in 1923 in a report on market conditions for films in Cuba, 'British prices are said to be too high.'[20] With their own films being kept off their own screens, British film-makers quite simply developed an inferiority complex. This was a typical effect of neo-imperialism in the cultural sphere: cultural imperialism. What Britain in its long history had had a hand in inflicting on its own empire, it now in turn, began to suffer in the field of cinema and was subsequently to suffer throughout the whole culture industry. British financiers, discouraged from investing in production, offered their excuses. The cultural prejudice which they already nurtured against the cinema and the inimical orientation (towards the exploitation of imperialist super-profits) of the financial system, allowed them to suspect the Americans of over-investment. So they hung back in the City, waiting for a crash in the American industry. The general trade recession no doubt encouraged them in this expectation. A crash did come – one that was not expected in that it affected everyone, but it was the Americans who had to bear the brunt of it. Audiences in Britain did not fall as much as in the United States.

It should not be overlooked that between 'Black November' in 1924 and the Cinematograph Act of 1927, a small caucus, one might say, began to form within the British film industry, which saw something of the likely future pattern of development and how to gain advantage from it. For it was during these years that the foundations of the two British cinema monopolies of the 1930s, ABPC (Associated British Picture Corporation) and Gaumont-British, were laid, both of them being planned as fully vertically integrated concerns. John Maxwell, the founder of the former, originally a solicitor who acquired interests in cinema exhibition through foreclosures, gathered investment funds and, in 1926, erected studios, with a separate laboratory designed by an American technician, on the outskirts of London at Elstree. Gaumont-British was built up by a firm of merchant bankers with notably wide-ranging interests, the Ostrer brothers, who bought the company's proprietory rights when Leon Gaumont withdrew his business interests from Britain at the beginning of the 1920s in the face of American competition in both Britain and France. The most exceptional of the brothers, Isidore, stands as an intelligent representative of certain forward-looking elements within British capitalism in the interwar years. He was a friend of the economist Maynard Keynes, the man who in the 1930s was to provide capitalism with the reformist state economic policy which it needed to overcome its torpor (although it was not adopted until later). Isidore imbibed Keynesian ideas and even wrote a book attacking the gold standard on which the established capitalist hierarchy depended.[21] Apart from his work in films, Isidore Ostrer set up the Bush Radio Company, and bought Baird Television (the company founded by the inventor of television, John Logie Baird) and the commercial radio station, Radio Luxembourg. Last but not least, there were also Ostrer interests in the press, in the shape of the *Sunday Citizen*. This was the portfolio of someone who saw the emerging shape of the culture industry in his own way – just as clearly as Adorno and Horkeimer who *called* it the culture industry.

There is an ironic footnote to be added. Paul Rotha has recorded[22] how, at the demise of the Empire Marketing Board Film Unit in the mid-1930s, the Ostrers offered to buy the Unit and its film library. They were interested, Rotha said, not in any genuine educational purpose, but in developing the educational market as a customer for the manufacture of 'sub-standard' (16mm) projectors. A short while earlier, in 1931, at a moment when Gaumont-British was in a weakened position, Isidore is said to have offered the Ostrers' controlling interest in the company to MacDonald's Labour government, presumably thinking that they might be tempted to purchase it because of the rhetoric of concern that had grown up for the role of 'the film in national life' (the title of an official report published a year later). But the government turned the offer down, unprepared to step on the toes of the film industry and of the powerful interests which ultimately lay behind it.

4
State Protection of a Beleaguered Industry
Simon Hartog

Direct and specific intervention by the state in the British film business began with the Cinematograph Films Act (1927). Since then each new decade has had its own new Films Act, and the state's involvement in films has been crucial to the development of the business, and particularly of British film production. Prior to the 1927 Act a variety of laws and policies dealing with such matters as safety, taxation, copyright and censorship had affected film production, distribution and exhibition in Britain, but these measures sprang from the general responsibilities of central and local governments to raise revenue and to protect the public. The first Cinematograph Films Act was a new and controversial type of intervention, designed to foster and protect Britain's film production industry in the face of the almost total domination of Britain's domestic market by American film companies. The 1927 Act and its successors saved British production from probable extinction and also played a major part in forming its character.

Although there had been occasional, isolated calls for action by the government to support and protect British film-making during and after the First World War, they had made little impact on either the public or politicians. In November 1924 there was a crisis. All British film production stopped, and the studios went dark. British production had never been particularly healthy, and, during the war, while attendances grew, production virtually ceased. American films filled British screens. After the war British production tried to re-establish itself, and the 1924 crisis signalled the failure of this attempt. Lacking both finance and imagination, British film producers were unable to compete with the endless torrent of 'bigger and better' films made in Hollywood.

The campaign for government action gathered force early in 1925.

The major film trade associations, the Cinematograph Exhibitors' Association (CEA) and the Kinematograph Renters' Society (KRS), were not part of the campaign, and there was, as yet, no association of British producers. The small and relatively unknown British Association of Film Directors (BAFD) was the only film group calling for government intervention. The demands of a handful of mainly unemployed British film directors, acting alone, would not have made much impact, but they brought the plight of British films to the attention of more influential interests. The *Morning Post* publicized and supported the directors' campaign. The Federation of British Industries (FBI), an important association of industrialists and a forerunner of the Confederation of British Industries, became interested in the films crisis and convened a gathering of patriotic, imperial, military and educational bodies to broaden and co-ordinate pressure on the government for action, as yet undefined, to save British production. There were calls for a Royal Commission or some other form of official enquiry. The House of Lords debated the films question. The government's initial response was not encouraging: the civil servants were investigating the situation, and no major enquiry was needed.

The films issue smouldered on until the summer without any clear indication of the government's intentions. In June, a bizarre incident inflamed patriotic sentiment. The British subsidiary of the American company, Universal, tricked a group of British soldiers into providing a guard of honour for a print of *The Hunchback of Notre Dame* on its voyage from Southampton to London. The men were told that the camera crew filming them was making a recruitment film. The national press gave the story sensational coverage, and questions were asked in the House of Commons. On the day the Secretary for War assured MPs that the film shot by the American company had been confiscated, Stanley Baldwin, the Conservative Prime Minister, included a mention of the film industry in his speech against an Opposition censure motion on unemployment:

I think the time has come when the position of that industry in this country should be examined with a view to seeing whether it be not possible, as it is desirable, on national grounds, to see that the larger proportion of the films exhibited in this country are British, having regard . . . to the enormous power which the film is developing for propaganda purposes, and the danger to which we in this country and our Empire subject ourselves if we allow that method of propaganda to be entirely in the hands of foreign countries.[1]

The Prime Minister's statement was brief, vague and, perhaps, impromptu, but it was the first clear indication of the government's concern. Early in July it was announced that responsibility for dealing with the films issue had been given to the Board of Trade and to its President, Sir Philip Cunliffe-Lister. In spite of the far-reaching consequences of this decision, no serious consideration was given to any other option. No alternative was publicly proposed or discussed. Even the opponents of official intervention regarded the Board of Trade as the obvious choice.

After the First World War, the Board's traditional responsibility for foreign trade had been expanded to include domestic industrial and commercial policy. The films crisis was seen in Westminster and Whitehall, and by the Federation of British Industries, as a very visible symptom of the nation's economic problems, at home and abroad. American and Continental competition was eroding Britain's foreign trade and the pre-eminence of Britain's manufactured goods within the Empire was under threat. The Americans and Germans had proved, it was argued, that trade follows the film, so British films were needed to show British goods to both foreign and domestic buyers. Faced with the decline of Britain's traditional industries and exports, the prospect of a new industry to make films for the healthy and expanding domestic exhibition market was also alluring.

The choice of the man to deal with the matter was, however, as important as the choice of the department, particularly since the Board of Trade was traditionally in favour of free trade and opposed to intervention. The Board's President, Sir Philip Cunliffe-Lister, a Tory stalwart of the post-war generation, a protégé of Baldwin and a great believer in propaganda, was a pragmatic protectionist and a cautious interventionist. Soon after his new responsibility was announced, he received official deputations from the FBI and the CEA. The problem was thorny and the trade was divided. The exhibitors and the American distributors were bitterly opposed to any type of legal interference in the film business. On the other hand, the majority of the very small number of British producers and of the equally small number of British distributors wanted the state to intervene and protect British films. In the wider political arena, the alliance of patriots, producers and the FBI was asking for the government to restrict free trade and to limit commercial contracts. Cunliffe-Lister approached the minefield extremely carefully. He told the major interest groups to try to reach a voluntary agreement among themselves on the protection of British film production.

The FBI had taken the initiative and made the early running. First, it published a memorandum that outlined the options open to the government, without expressing any preference. Then, in order to overcome the real difficulty caused by the lack of an organization to speak for British film producers, the FBI set up its own film producers' group, and, finally, it published a draft Bill based on the quota principle. The most obvious technique for protection was the tariff. A duty had in fact been imposed on film imports during the war, but it was a low, flat-rate duty on footage, which did little to inhibit imports. An *ad valorem* tariff, which based the duty on the commercial value of the exploitation of the film in Britain, was thought by most to be impractical.

The most successful existing technique for protecting national film production was the German *Kontingent* legislation. This limited the number of films that could be imported annually and required renters operating in Germany to distribute a percentage of German films. The British producers adopted the German model but made two major changes. First and most important, no limit was placed on the number of films that the distributors could import and, secondly, the British producers proposed that the quota of British films must apply to both distributors and exhibitors. Both changes were intended to lessen the opposition of American distributors and British exhibitors to quota legislation.

British producers, distributors and exhibitors set up a joint trade committee in an attempt to work out a voluntary agreement to protect national production. The CEA put forward a plan to curb the restrictive trading practices of the large American renters. 'Block-booking' required an exhibitor who wanted to book the most commercially promising films from a renter to hire a large number of other films as well. 'Blind booking' forced exhibitors to take films sight unseen, and often even before the films were made. It was these practices, according to the exhibitors, which were the real cause of the failure of British films to obtain an adequate number of bookings in the domestic market.

The joint trade committee did work out a voluntary plan which established a quota for British films and banned the renters' restrictive trading practices, but a referendum of exhibitors rejected the plan at the end of 1925. The Board of Trade was annoyed, but the trade was, nonetheless, given another chance to agree on a voluntary solution.

With the quota system, which in essence gave British films a guaranteed home market and forced the major American distributors to finance the production of a number of British films, vetoed by the exhibitors, the joint trade committee tried to negotiate 'reciprocity' with the American renters. Though it was plain that the American companies opposed any kind of restriction, they had, up to this point, taken little part in the trade's discussion. The idea of 'reciprocity' was that the Americans must use some of their enormous profits, gained by their free access to the British market, to finance British films. The joint trade committee met the London heads of the American companies. The Motion Picture Producers' and Distributors' Association (MPPDA) of America, better known as the Hays Office, sent over a representative to attend the meetings. Although the British were told that the decision on participation in a reciprocity scheme was the responsibility of the head offices in the United States, they drew up a detailed plan, but, as a result of opposition by a number of producers on the joint trade committe, who felt that the scheme gave too much control over British production to the major American companies, the 'reciprocity' option was rejected.

The trade informed the President of the Board of Trade that there was no agreement on a voluntary solution to the British films problem. Cunliffe-Lister, prompted by the FBI, then put the films question on the agenda of the 1926 Imperial Conference. The British government and the producers wanted an Imperial quota, so that the guaranteed market for British films could be larger than the national market. The 1926 Imperial Conference, however, was more concerned with increasing the dominions' autonomy and with decreasing Westminster's central control. The British proposal for an Imperial films quota received almost no support from the dominions, but the conference did approve a vague statement on the films question which gave the British government the justification it needed for introducing legislation.

The government's Bill was published early in 1927. Apart from the creation of an advisory committee, the Bill embodied little more than a fusion of the FBI's quota proposals and the CEA's plan for banning the renters' restrictive booking practices. The quota was to start at a low level and rise slowly over the years. Penalties for renters and exhibitors who violated the law were fixed. The Labour Party and some radical Liberals opposed the legislation. Though, in their opposition, there was an element of concern about Tory ministers telling the poor what they must watch at the pictures, the Labour leadership attacked the Bill on the grounds that it violated the principles of free trade and freedom of contract. With a large Parliamentary majority, the Government had no difficulty in winning the debate on the second reading. In committee, Labour adopted obstructive and delaying tactics, but, apart from making the Bill's committee phase one of the longest on record, the only apparently substantial concession that they obtained from the government was the imposition of a time limit, eventually ten years, on the duration of the Act.

The key questions for the producers were the level of quota and the legal definition of a British film. Giving in somewhat to the pressure from exhibitors and renters to keep the quota percentages low, the President of the Board of Trade fixed the first year of the renters' quota at 7½ per cent and of the exhibitors' quota at 5 per cent. Both were set to rise gradually to a maximum of 20 per cent in 1936. Not all types of film were automatically eligible as quota films. Newsreels and advertising, educational, scientific, industrial and scenic films did not qualify unless they had 'special exhibition value', a judgement to be made by the Board of Trade after consulting its trade-dominated advisory committee. If the film was to be registered as British, the author of the scenario had to be a British subject, the studio scenes had to be filmed in a studio in the British Empire, and at least 70 per cent of the labour cost of the film had to be paid to British subjects or residents in the Empire. The most hotly debated requirement for British nationality was that the film had to be made by a British company. Patriots and most producers thought this to be inadequate protection. The quota system, as they saw it, was intended to make the major American companies pay for their predominant position in the British market, and to do so by financing the production of British films. The producers' worry was that an American company could, under the government's definition, simply set up a British company to make British films, and, thus, totally undermine the value of quota protection for British producers. The government, however, was unable to devise a stronger definition. The American companies, in any case, found another way in which to undermine the quota legislation.

As soon as the government's Bill was published, a film production boom began. New production companies, with respectable board members, went to the Stock Exchange, which was itself booming, for capital to finance films. The failure rate of these new companies was high, and the Stock Exchange was never again tempted to provide the capital for production. One factor, apart from foolish speculation, which played a significant role in the failure of the 'bubble' film companies was the coming of 'the talkies'. Sound had been totally ignored during the debates on the Cinematograph Films Act of 1927, though the impact of sound films on attendances and profits in America had been widely reported, particularly in the film trade press. Few British producers thought talking pictures were anything more than a passing fad. Even those who wanted to make sound films did not have sound-proofed studios and the recording equipment needed to make the films. The problem of raising the finance to buy sound equipment was compounded, for both producers and exhibitors, by the confusion surrounding the patents on the new sound systems. There were two important American systems and hundreds of others. The British production boom evaporated while the British trade waited to see the outcome of the complex jigsaw of sound. Though patent suits were to continue throughout the 1930s, within a few years British cinemas were wired for sound with American sound systems, and British film production, protected by the quota, rose each year until, in the early 1930s, Britain became the most important centre of European film production and began to believe that it could beat Hollywood at its own game.

The 1927 Films Act had an objective that is not mentioned in its text: the creation of one or more British film combines. During the 1920s the United States had seen its private film producing, renting or exhibiting companies transformed into public companies combining production, distribution and exhibition. Wall Street's role in the transformation was crucial. The major American companies, however, were not the only film combines to have emerged. In Germany there was the UFA firm, a vertically integrated company linked closely to national high finance and industry. In Britain there was no giant to lead the way. There was only one small national circuit, controlled by Lord Beaverbrook. Most exhibitors owned only one cinema or a handful of cinemas. Apart from the American renting companies, there were only three or four small commercially successful British renters, and their success was due, almost entirely, to the American films they distributed. The inefficiency and fragmentation of production, hovering as it was on the edge of oblivion, was even more marked. The implicit pact that had been made between the government and the FBI was that if the government enacted the quota the FBI would encourage a re-organization of the film business by creating a British film giant, and, marching almost in parallel with the legislative process, the first British film combine took shape.

The Gaumont-British Picture Corporation was built by merging existing companies, studios, renters and cinemas, and the leading figures in all branches of the film trade joined, with their companies. The operation was master-minded by an ambitious and eccentric City man, Isidore Ostrer. Having established the nucleus of his vertically integrated combine, Ostrer set out on a cinema-buying spree. When he acquired control of the Beaverbrook circuit, Gaumont-British was a national film giant. Almost as soon as it reached its full size, the nationality of the giant was in constant doubt. Ostrer, it appears, needed capital to finance the acquisition of sound equipment for Gaumont-British's films, and for its three hundred cinemas, at a time when the Stock Exchange was extremely wary of new issues by film companies. So he sold a majority share, but not control, of Gaumont-British to William Fox, the American film mogul. Fox, who thought he had bought control, threatened a lawsuit. He then lost control of *his* company to Wall Street interests, and suits were threatened. Ostrer held on, but the Fox company's claims haunted Gaumont-British throughout the 1930s. At one point, early in the decade, Ostrer offered to give his controlling interest in the combine to the Board of Trade, but his offer was refused.

The department's officials advised rejection primarily on the grounds that it might be a manoeuvre by Ostrer to defeat or discredit John Maxwell and his Associated British Picture Corporation. Maxwell, a Scottish solicitor who came into the trade through exhibition and distribution, was threatening Gaumont-British's pre-eminence. In the wake of the Quota Act, Maxwell at first concentrated on production.[2] He made a number of expensive, impressive silent films aimed at the international market. The coming of sound shattered Maxwell's dream of creating the British Hollywood in Elstree, and he then began buying cinemas with the aim of making his ABC chain the largest in the country. ABPC's production activities now took second place.

Since the passage of the quota legislation, British producers and those who financed production found themselves on the horns of a dilemma. The 'talkies' and the common language made it worse, and it persists even today: whether to make modest films for the protected national market or to make expensive films for the international – or, more precisely, the American – market? The outcome of Maxwell's attempt, the Great Depression, and the transformation from silent to talking pictures, all combined to convince British producers and their financial backers that production for the home market was the safest course. Then in about 1933, with its exhibition base stabilized, its studios re-equipped and its corporate and financial structure re-organized, Gaumont-British set in motion an ambitious programme of production clearly intended to be prestigious at home and successful in the United States. The major American film companies had still not recovered from the financial collapse of 1929, and there seemed to be room for British films in the world's richest market. Gaumont-British's cautiously optimistic long-term plan was pushed into the background by the quite unexpected world-wide success of a British film, directed by a Hungarian and financed by United Artists, *The Private Life of Henry VIII*. Alexander Korda, the film's director, turned himself into an instant myth. With the financial backing of United Artists and the Prudential insurance company, he became a producer, and his London Films company began the production of a series of extravagant internationally produced films. The pot of gold across the Atlantic seemed within reach. Gaumont-British's assault on the American market also went into high gear. The wildest claims of the advocates of the quota system looked like becoming realities.

The commercial and industrial approach of the Board of Trade to its film legislation meant that cultural questions and aesthetic judgements were scrupulously ignored. Two separate, but not entirely distinct, pressure groups grew up in the wake of the 1927 Act, both of which reached crucial stages at the time the production boom was beginning, and both raised questions which the 1927 Act had avoided. The documentary movement, led by John Grierson, wanted public finance for its productions, and educationalists wanted official action to aid the non-commercial and intellectual aspects of the cinema. The documentary movement, which grew up almost by accident within the Empire Marketing Board, was facing the closure of the Board, endangering its own future. The educational lobby produced a report, *The Film in National Life*, the product of research and discussion over a number of years. The report's main demand was for the creation of a national film institute under a royal charter. The trade did not like the ideas and ambitions of what it called 'the uplift brigade' and moved quickly to veto the report's most concrete proposals for the institute's activities. Without a royal charter and restricted by the trade, the British Film Institute was established in 1933. It was financed by the Lord President's office from a fund, created by Parliament, which collected profits from cinemas open on Sunday. At about the same time, the documentary movement was reprieved when the Empire Marketing Board's film unit was transferred to the Post Office.

The creation and development of a national film production industry by the use of legal protection rather than public funds had been the prime objective of the 1927 Act, and the annual improvement in Britain's film production statistics seemed to provide objective proof of its success. In fact, the figures also demonstrated its prime failure. About half of the British films produced each year were made to be registered, but not to be shown. The major American companies continued to exploit all their films in their most valuable foreign market. In order to fulfil their distribution quota, they financed British films which were cheap, awful, and just long enough to qualify as feature films under the 1927 Act. The films, which were usually financed at a rate per foot, became known as 'quota films' or 'quota quickies'. By complying only with the letter of the law, the American renters funded the production of hundreds of British films which discredited both British film production and the quota legislation.

After the failure of its advisory committee to reach anything like a unanimous view on the legislation required to replace the 1927 Act when it expired, the Board of Trade appointed a departmental committee under Lord Moyne to make recommendations. The Moyne committee published its report in November 1936 after almost a year of submissions and discussions. Its members included the chairman of the films advisory committee, Sir Arnold Wilson and A. C. Cameron, the guiding spirit behind *The Film In National Life*. It was the first and only films enquiry set up by the Board of Trade in which trade interests were not represented.

Protection was no longer controversial, and it was no surprise when the committee recommended the continuation of the renters' and the exhibitors' quotas, though few in the trade thought that the committee's suggestion of an eventual 50 per cent quota was either desirable or practical. The documentary movement won its case for a separate quota for short films with both the committee and the government, but the two most radical recommendations of the committee, the creation of a Films Commission to administer the films legislation and of a quality test for British films, did not please either the Board of Trade or the dominant trade interests. The producers objected to the quality test on the grounds that it would be impossible to find the finance to make films if it was not certain that they would qualify as British quota films until they had been completed, and the Board of Trade agreed. To eradicate the 'quota quickie', the government adopted a minimum cost requirement for registration. If the film's budget was adequate, it was argued, the quality problem would solve itself, and a judgement based on cost was objective and verifiable. The committee's proposal for a Films Commission was vague. The film trade press interpreted it as state control of the film industry, while its few supporters justified the commission by citing the example of the BBC. Officials in the Board of Trade opposed the Films Commission on the grounds that they did not want the films legislation to be administered by such a body, and the commission was excluded from the government's Bill.

The political context of the legislative stage was quite different from that of the 1927 Act. Protection was no longer an issue, and the Bill was considered to be non-partisan. The departmental interests of the Board of Trade were a new factor. The producers had spokesmen among the MPs. The influence of the film trade unions, led by the newly formed Association of Cinematograph Technicians (ACT), was much more noticeable and direct. The Americans, who had played virtually no part in the politics preceding the 1927 Act, were this time well prepared and organized: public pressure came through the KRS in its evidence to the Moyne Commission; private pressure came from the London representative of the Hays Office and from the State Department, Joseph Kennedy, the new American Ambassador and a former film mogul, met the President of the Board of Trade on a number of occasions to put the American case. The United States was in the process of negotiating a bilateral trade agreement with the United Kingdom, and threats were made that these negotiations would end unless the government gave way on the films legislation.

While the process of preparing new legislation, from the Moyne Report to the 1938 Act, moved slowly along, the production bubble exploded. Gaumont-British stopped production as a consequence of massive losses from its assault on the American market. Korda's extravagant production programme was not a financial success.

The British Film Trade in 1936*

Renter	American affiliation	British production affiliation	Exhibition affiliation
(A) AMERICAN RENTERS			
Metro-Goldwyn Mayer	Loew's Inc. (MGM)	Various quota producers	London pre-release hall
Radio Pictures	R.K.O. Radio	Various quota producers	—
Warner & First National	Warner & F.N.	Own subsidiary with studio in Teddington	—
Fox Film Co.	20th Cent. Fox	Fox British, Wembley & New World Pict. Denham	—
Paramount Film Serv.	Paramount Inc.	British & Dominion, Boreham Wood studios and quota producers	14 super halls and tie-up with Union Circ. (250 halls)
Columbia	Columbia Pict. Corp.	Paul Soskin Prod. & others	—
(B) ANGLO-AMERICAN RENTERS			
United Artists	U.A. Corp.	London Film Prod., British & Dominion Films Ltd., Criterion Film, Brit. Cine Alliance, Bergner-Czinner Prod., Trafalgar F. Pr., V. Saville Pr., E. Pommer Pr., Garrett-Klement Pr., Atlantic Films, Pall Mall Pr., Denham, Worton Hall & Pinewood Studios	Participation in Odeon (about 150 halls) & County Circ. (about 50 halls)
General Film Distr.	Universal	Pinewood Studios, British & Dominion Films Ltd., H. Wilcox Prod., Capitol Prod., City Films, Universal-Wainwright, Brit. National Films, Cecil Films, Grafton Films, etc.	New circuit in process of formation

* Source: F. D. Klingender and Stuart Legg: *The Money Behind the Screen*

Renter	American affiliation	British production affiliation	Exhibition affiliation
(C) MAJOR BRITISH RENTERS			
Gaumont-Brit. Distr.	(20th C.-Fox).*	Gaumont-British Pict. Corp., Shepherds Bush, Gainsborough P. Corp. Islington	Gaumont-Brit. Circuit, over 300 halls
Wardour F. & Pathe Pic.	Various occasional contracts	B.I.P., Elstree and Welwyn and other indep. units	A.B.C. Circuit, about 290 halls
(D) OTHER BRITISH RENTERS			
Ass. Brit. Film Distr.	Grand Nat. Films Inc.	Ass. Talking Pict., Ealing studio., and indep. prods.	None
Twickenham F. Distr. (incl. P.D.C.).	Various	Twickenham F. Stud., New Ideal P., Hammersmith, J. H. Prod., Boreham Wood	None
British Lion Film Corp.	Republic Corp. of America	Beaconsfield Stud., also Hammer Prod.	None
Equity Brit. Films	Various	Various quota prods.	None
Butchers F. Serv.	Various	Various indep. prods. in ass. with Butchers	None
Ass. Produc. & Distrib. Co.	Various	Sound City Studios, U.K. Films & indep. prods.	None
Ace Films (shorts)	Educat. Film Corp. of America	Ace Films	None
Reunion Films	Mainly Continental films	Various indep. prods.	None

23 other renters distributed from one to six films (Brit. and/or foreign) in 1936. Total no. of Renters' Licences issued 1935/6: 65; total no. of producers of long films in 1935/6: 76.

* Note. Gaumont-British are the only English company having their own distribution organization in the USA.

Companies failed, financial scandals filled the national press and the Board of Trade opened an enquiry into the affairs of Gaumont-British. New studios were empty and half the production labour force was unemployed. The only apparent bright spots on the horizon were the establishment of a distribution and production finance company (led by Lord Portal, including J. Arthur Rank and brimming with capital and financial respectability) and the growth of Oscar Deutsch's Odeon circuit.

Money Behind the Screen, a courageous and original report on the structure and finances of the British film industry, written by F. D. Klingender and Stuart Legg, was published early in 1937. Its revelations played some part in persuading the City to withdraw from film production financing. Its detail remains unsurpassed. The first table in *Money Behind the Screen* provides a panoramic view of the British film trade in the autumn of 1936 (see pp. 70–71).

In the new economic situation, the government's draft legislation was largely irrelevant. There was little unity within the British film trade. Each of the trade organizations was split within itself, mainly between large and small companies, and there were very few proposals which were unanimously supported by the FBI, the KRS and the CEA. The key decisions about the shape of the new legislation were, thus, left to Board of Trade officials, who did not like the more radical proposals for change put forward by the Moyne committee and gave the major American companies a most sympathetic hearing.

In Parliament, the Conservative party whips were not brought in for the film legislation, so there was a possibility of defeating the government proposals in committee. Labour, together with some Liberals and some Tories, tried to put the Films Commission back into the Bill, but, by relying on the government's 'payroll vote', the President of the Board of Trade just managed to defeat this. By way of a concession, the government introduced an amendment to create a Cinematograph Films Council, with a majority of independent members to advise the Board of Trade. The major concession made to the Americans was to allow them to concentrate the money they had to spend on British production on fewer films by establishing double and triple quota values for films made for double and triple the average production cost.

In the short period between the enactment of the 1938 Cinematograph Act and the outbreak of war, the new legislation did nothing to resolve the production crisis, though the Americans and the exhibitors were satisfied with the new law. The opportunity for a radical change in the perspective of Britain's film legislation was lost in 1938. The innovations introduced by the post-War Labour government, the National Film Finance Corporation and the Eady Levy, were options outlined in the FBI's 1925 memorandum to the Board of Trade. The cultural objectives of the first Cinematograph Act, as described below by R. D. Fennelly of the Board of Trade in his evidence to the Moyne Committee, were never fundamentally challenged or changed:

By 1925 the depressed state of the British industry was causing general concern. Apart from the purely industrial aspect of the matter it was felt that from the point of view of British culture and ideals it was unwise to allow the United States to dominate the cinemas of this country. At that time nearly every film shown represented American ideas set in an American atmosphere, and the accessories were American houses, American materials, American manufactures, etc. Whatever the position today, cinematograph audiences then were made up of the most impressionable sections of the community, and it was felt to be of the utmost importance for our prestige, for our trade and, it was even asserted, for our morals, that they should see at least some proportion of British films.[3]

Judging the 1927 'Quota Act' on its own ground, the terse comment to be found in *Money Behind the Screen* needs no revision: 'The passing of the Quota Act, while virtually creating the British production industry as far as feature films are concerned, did not, however, put an end to the predominance of the major American producers in the English market.'[4]

5

The State and the Consolidation of Monopoly

Margaret Dickinson

Between the 1940s and the 1960s the role of the cinema in British society changed radically. From being a very influential mass medium and an important business in its own right it became a minority entertainment and a sideline of the leisure industry. The political debate surrounding the film industry consequently lost much of its former intensity. Yet the issues remained remarkably constant. Although decline and competition with television introduced new questions, many arguments which took place in the sixties and seventies were essentially re-runs of favourite themes from the forties. Three problems have consistently attracted attention: the dominant influence of America; the monopoly exercised by the major British interests; and the lack of a stable domestic production industry. From a political point of view the 1940s, the years of the Second World War and its immediate aftermath, are by far the most interesting. It was then that the commercial structure often called the 'duopoly' became entrenched. But the process was the centre of an intense struggle. The government was very much involved with the industry and considered various ideas which, if implemented, might have resulted in a very different outcome. By the early fifties, however, most of the options had been closed. Future relations between the government and the industry had been settled. Since then, the form of the institutional framework has changed very little although the way it functions has altered as the character of the business has evolved.

The Second World War, unlike the First, was a time of relative prosperity for the British film industry. The exhibition business experienced the greatest boom it had ever known, with weekly admissions rising to thirty million. The production sector was forced to contract, but what remained of it was healthy. British films enjoyed

unprecedented popularity and both the critics and the trade acknowledged a great improvement in quality. In the long term the industry
was most deeply affected by the changes the war brought about in
Anglo-American relations. Britain became a suitor first for American
help to defeat the enemy, and afterwards for American finance to pay
for economic recovery. Her increased political and financial dependence on America made it harder to tackle the particular problem of the
cinema's dependence on American films. The British market was a
vital source of revenue for Hollywood and the Motion Picture
Association of America was prepared to use its considerable political
muscle to retain that market. During the war it established a special
foreign affairs section, the Motion Picture Export Association, which
soon became known as 'the little State Department' because of the
power it exercised. The British government, however, had new
reasons to worry about the scale of film imports. The war effort at once
put a strain on currency reserves and in the long run wrecked the
balance of trade, so that both during the war and for some years
afterwards it was necessary to reduce non-essential imports. The
Treasury regarded films as luxury items and therefore singled them
out for cuts. Thus the reason that the government was drawn deeply
into the affairs of the industry after 1939 had more to do with relations
with the United States than with an increased official concern with
propaganda or morale. The government was preoccupied with trying
to reconcile the conflicting objectives of correcting the adverse
balance of trade and of avoiding a serious confrontation with
Hollywood which might have unfortunate political repercussions.

The kind of measures which might have permanently solved the
problem by reducing the United States' share of the market involved
radical changes in exhibitors' practices. British films occupied only
about 20 per cent of screen time and it was unrealistic to expect
producers to increase their output suddenly, especially in wartime.
But if fewer films were shown, the same number of British films could
occupy a larger share of screen time and so earn a larger proportion of
revenue. This was a plausible approach because the existing pattern of
exhibition was decidedly extravagant. Most cinemas showed at least
two different double-feature programmes every week and, as there
were three competing circuits, this meant that in most urban centres
the public was offered six different programmes in a week, involving a
total of twelve films. By enforcing weekly programme changes and
single-feature bills an annual requirement of about 600 films would

have been cut to 150. The cheaper second features would have been eliminated and the demand for first features halved. The British industry had produced about 200 first and second features in a good prewar year, and so, if resources were redeployed for first feature production, could be expected to turn out about 100. There were problems, such as how to ensure that only American films were excluded by the changes, but in 1940 officials at the Board of Trade began to research the posibilities. The idea was dropped, partly because of the opposition of exhibitors, who advised that such cuts would cause a damaging fall in attendances. It was considered again in 1945 but abandoned for similar reasons.

Direct import restrictions were considered only during the first weeks of war, when it was thought that many cinemas, in any case, might be permanently closed because of air raids. The American Ambassador responded sharply to this threat and insisted on being consulted in future about measures affecting the film trade. Discussions with the Americans resulted by the end of 1939 in a compromise whereby the major Hollywood companies entered into a voluntary agreement to repatriate no more than 17.5 million dollars, about a third of their revenue, the rest being blocked. From the British point of view the arrangement was unsatisfactory, both because the sum saved fell short of the Treasury target and because the blocked funds would one day have to be released. One feature of this agreement which did, however, correspond with a long-standing Treasury objective was that the blocked funds could be used to make British films or to buy rights in films already made. The Treasury was anxious to encourage American investment in British production, partly because such investments would tie up revenue which would otherwise leave the country and partly because it was thought that the Americans might make the British industry more efficient by introducing the practices which had made Hollywood so successful.

American remittances, 1939–40[1]

Year ending in October	£ million
1939	10 (estimate)
1940	4.8
1941	5.7
1942	8.5
1943	26.5
1944	15.6
1945	17.0

The agreement was renegotiated annually, with minor changes, until 1942, when America had entered the war. The blocked earnings were then released and all restrictions removed. Although the cost of American films continued to worry the Treasury and to attract adverse public comment, no further attempt was made to find a solution until 1947. The effect of the agreements on the remittances can be seen in the table on the previous page.

The government's intentions with respect to film production remained unclear until well into the second year of the war. While the supply of American films seemed to be threatened, consideration was given to increasing output. Yet at the same time facilities for production were gradually being eroded. By the end of 1940 plans for expansion ceased to be taken seriously, partly because competition for resources had increased and partly because, after the second Anglo-American agreement, it seemed neither necessary nor politically practicable to substitute any significant proportion of American films with British. The question which remained was whether the government should make arrangements to ensure that the production of entertainment films should continue at all.

Several factors influenced official thinking on the subject. One was the memory of the lasting effect that the previous war had had on the industry. Related to this was the consideration that the dollar shortage would continue after the war and that it would be desirable then to be in a position to step up the supply of British films. There was also an active film lobby in Parliament and the press, which ensured that the financial case was heard and also put forward cultural and patriotic arguments for the value of a national film production industry.

Such considerations led the government to a policy of maintaining what was described as a 'healthy nucleus'. In practice this turned out to mean an industry with the capacity to make about fifty films a year, less than half the pre-war output. What this nucleus should consist of remained the subject of bitter controversy. Which producers and which companies should remain? On what principle should resources be allocated – fair shares for all or the survivial of the fittest? In this atmosphere of increased competition the conflicts of interest within the industry took on a new significance.

The long-standing differences between producers and exhibitors, and employers and employees were complicated at this time by tensions arising from the recent growth of cinema circuits and of vertically integrated companies, like Associated British and

Gaumont-British, with interests in all sectors. Between 1938 and 1943 further changes became apparent which greatly aggravated this tension. J. Arthur Rank, the son of Joseph Rank, the flour miller, accomplished a series of transactions which made him the most powerful man in the industry, uniting in one group the Woolf distribution interests, the Odeon circuit, the Gaumont-British interests, the studios Korda had built at Denham and the studio Rank had built at Pinewood. The only comparable group was Associated British Pictures, which also had production and studio interests and owned the ABC cinema circuit. The emergence of the Rank empire therefore gave the industry the structure of 'duopoly' which has since characterized it. It also marked a new development in the relationship between the industry and finance capital, since Rank, unlike most of the earlier film magnates, started off with very considerable capital of his own, a sound business reputation and good personal contacts in the banking world.

Elements in the industry outside the two big combines felt extremely threatened by the progressive concentration of power. These were the producers and exhibitors usually described as 'independent', although 'would-be independent' might be a more accurate description. Exhibitors were, in practice, dependent on distributors and producers were dependent both on distributors and financiers. Their problems revolved round the fact that in the distribution sector the process of concentration was most complete. The big distributors were the subsidiaries of the major American companies and General Film Distributors, which was owned by Rank. The links which already existed between the American companies and the British circuits became, if anything, more rigid once there were effectively only two British companies to deal with. Each American company had an arrangement either with Rank or ABPC, so that competition was virtually eliminated. The financial ties between some of the big American companies and British companies were another facet of the relationship. Rank inherited the Gaumont-British connection with 20th Century Fox and on his own account acquired ties with Universal and United Artists. Warner's big share in ABPC had long been a subject of comment and after John Maxwell's death in 1941 there were fears that Warner might gain complete control over the company.

As a result of these developments, the issues of domestic monopoly and of American competition were inextricably linked. The combines were, on the one hand, closely associated with the Hollywood companies, but, on the other, as producers in their own right, and in the case of Rank, an important distributor, they were potential competitors. The battle between independents and the combines therefore also became an argument about tactics for facing American competition. Rank recommended a strategy, based on Hollywood methods, which would involve producing expensive pictures designed for export and negotiating a share of the American market by exploiting links with the major American companies, using control of the British market as a bargaining counter. During the war the personality who came to represent the opposing view was Michael Balcon, head of Ealing studios, who thought the first step should be to recapture a larger share of the British market. The character of the controversy was neatly stated in an article in *Documentary News Letter* in 1944:

> The trouble is of course that the issues keep on getting confused. Everyone is agreed that we need a truly national film industry, and need equally a share in the world's screen time. The methods of achieving this, however, are the source of the conflict. The danger of domination by United States interests is clear enough. But on the other hand you have big interests associated especially with the names of Rank and Korda, who claim that we must make films costing from a quarter to half a million and break into world markets on production values comparable to those of Hollywood. On the other hand there are the smaller independent groups at Ealing and Elstree, who would limit expenditure from fifty to a hundred thousand, in the expectation of gearing their economies to home cinemas, breaking into the world market on merit, as specifically British products but not depending – at any rate for some time – on receipts from overseas.[2]

The dispute had obvious implications for government policy. The course proposed by Balcon presupposed the introduction of new measures to control the internal affairs of the industry. For one of the obstacles preventing British films from capturing a larger share of the home market was the structure of distribution and exhibition itself, the fact that exhibition was effectively controlled by two companies, both of which had long-standing commitments to show American films. Rank's plan, on the other hand, required minimal intervention. The conflict between the combines and their critics therefore found expression very largely in a struggle to influence the government.

The problem of monopoly was formally raised by the Cinematograph Films Council in 1943, but before that Board of Trade officials had already been considering the implications of the growth of the Rank interests in another context. In 1940 the Films Council had recommended that the government should set up a films bank to ensure the continuation of British production. As a result, a series of consultations began, involving the Treasury and the Bank of England as well as the Board of Trade. By 1942 a consensus was reached that the industry's financial problems were in part caused by its own structure and practices and that it was more in need of independent supervision or control than of new sources of finance. Further discussions about a bank were therefore postponed, but the President of the Board of Trade, Sir Hugh Dalton, put to the Lord President's Committee a general proposal to set up an independent authority, referred to as a Films Commission. The proposal was accepted, subject to the submission of more detailed plans, but these plans were never presented. Instead, in the face of vociferous opposition from the major trade interests, the whole scheme was reconsidered. At that time support for such an authority did not necessarily imply concern about monopoly. On the contrary, one view was that the industry was in need of supervision because it was fragmented and disorganized, because there were too many transient production companies working with speculative capital and offering no security. In that context the appearance of Rank could be interpreted as a healthy development. This was the conclusion reached by the Board of Trade officials. In consequence they advised that because of the recent process of concentration, the reasons for wishing to impose controls on an unwilling industry had to some extent been superseded. Dalton subsequently withdrew his proposal with the explanation that 'Some of the strong arguments for setting up a Films Commission have lost much of their significance and urgency while the difficulties in the way are greater than supposed'.[3]

The Films Council, however, disagreed. Michael Balcon, who was at that time one of the two producers' representatives, was able to convince some of his colleagues that a dangerous monopoly was developing. The Council sounded a warning in its annual report of 1943. Dalton responded by obtaining personal undertakings from Rank and the acting head of ABPC that they would not acquire more cinemas without the prior consent of the President of the Board of Trade. The Films Council were not satisfied and Dalton asked them to advise on what other steps they thought should be taken. The Council then appointed a committee of four independent, or non-trade, members to study the problem. The committee, which was chaired by Albert Palache, a partner in a City firm, was responsible for the report *Tendencies to Monopoly in the Cinematograph Industry*,[4] which provided the basis for a vigorous campaign for state intervention during the term of office of the first post-war Labour government.

The authors of the report came up against the problem from which all subsequent reports on this subject have suffered: that much important information was either unobtainable or was made available in confidence on the understanding that it would not be published. The data was therefore rather sketchy. Although the report established that 56 per cent of studio space was owned by Rank and 70 per cent by the combines between them, and that a third of all cinema seats were controlled by the combines, it did not provide information about the proportion of the box-office receipts taken by the combines or the proportion of film rentals paid by their circuits. Nevertheless, it stated coherently the general case against the combines: that they did exercise monopolistic powers: 'It has been made clear to us that, save in quite exceptional cases, a booking by one of the three major circuits . . . is indispensable for successful exploitation of a British feature film in the United Kingdom;'[5] that the powers might be used to further American aims: 'the statement that ultimate control over the three major exhibition circuits reposes in as few as two hands may not adequately convey the gravity of the situation in which independent British producers have suddenly been placed. For it may further be the case that these two hands are, or may ultimately be, guided by American interests;'[6] and that the structure by its nature tended to discriminate against British independent producers: 'When the exhibition circuits themselves are also controlled by an interest which controls competing production, and which has long term arrangements in addition to distribute American feature films, the independent producer must assume that the best dates and locations will be reserved by the circuits for the associated producers and the American companies.'[7]

When making recommendations the authors restated the need both for a films bank and for some independent supervision, although, rather than reviving the idea of a Commission, they suggested that the Board of Trade should be given wider powers and that an independent tribunal should be set up to arbitrate in cases of trade disputes. They also proposed legislation to forbid specific restrictive practices and to prevent the expansion of the existing circuits. Most of the arguments and ideas in the report had been aired before, but the document was

important in that it publicized them and invested them with some
authority. The full Films Council, although unable to agree on the
detailed recommendations, unanimously accepted the 'broad conclusions', which could then be taken to be those of the government's
official advisory body. For some years the films debate focused on the
report and its recommendations.

Not surprisingly the Film Council's report was violently attacked
by the interests associated with the combines, interests which were
influential in all the main trade associations. The Cinematograph
Exhibitors' Association, the Kinematograph Renters Society and the
British Film Producers' Association each supported some particular
recommendations of value to their own members but rejected the
wider intentions. All three strongly opposed the idea of a tribunal.
The report, however, appealed to quite a broad spectrum of opinion,
both inside and outside the industry, partly because, by stressing
cultural aspects of the problem, it bypassed the highly controversial
question of how far the state should intervene in commercial matters.
The case was made forcefully in the introduction that

> Cinematograph film represents something more than a mere commodity to
> be bartered against others. Already the screen has great influence both
> politically and culturally over the minds of the people. Its potentialities are
> vast, as a vehicle for the expression of national life, ideals and tradition, as a
> dramatic and artistic medium, and as an instrument for propaganda.[8]

The campaign for intervention was nevertheless led by pressure
groups committed to state control in industry as well as to state
support for culture. The most active were the film trade unions, the
documentary movement and the Tribune Group of the Labour Party.
Between them they canvassed several ideas for more radical measures
than those suggested by the Palache committee. The Association of
Cinematograph Technicians had published a report in 1941 advocating partial nationalization.[9] This included the suggestion, later
elaborated elsewhere, that cinemas might be put under municipal
rather than national ownership. In the mid-forties the ACT threw its
weight behind the Palache recommendations, rather than pressing for
nationalization, but it also proposed some tougher measures for
dealing with American competition, including the use of import
restrictions. In a private memorandum requested by the President of
the Board of Trade in 1945,[10] John Grierson and Paul Rotha, pioneers
of the Documentary Movement, outlined a plan for a Government

Film Corporation, which would have powers not only to regulate the activities of private companies but also to engage in production, distribution and possibly exhibition. Two pamphlets produced in 1946 strongly promoted the view that the British combines served American interests. *Monopoly: the Future of British Films*[11] was published by the ACT; *Films, an Alternative to Rank*[12] was by Frederick Mullally, an assistant editor of *Tribune*. Both argued that the export drive would fail because the major Hollywood companies would never give the films of competitors a fair chance in the American market. Mullally considered that the Tribunal mentioned by Palache would not be sufficiently effective and proposed that a Films Commission, although one differently constituted from that discussed during the war, should take over the existing functions both of the Board of Trade and of the Films Council and acquire new ones such as those projected for the Tribunal. The effect would have been to create a national film authority in some respects similar to the Centre National de la Cinematographie, which had recently been put in charge of the cinema in France. The Film Industry Employees' Committee, an association of film unions which included the ACT and the more conservative NATKE, called for a body like the newly formed Arts Council to help finance films of artistic merit. Another set of proposals was influenced by the progress of the anti-trust suits in America, which eventually forced the big American concerns to divest themselves of their huge cinema circuits. They stressed ways of breaking up the combines, rather than of setting up new structures, but in some cases the two ideas were combined. A plan promoted by a group of Labour MPs involved the creation of a fourth cinema circuit.

The campaign failed to make much impression on policy. The Palache Report itself was completely out of tune with Board of Trade thinking. The civil servants' advice, that the industry needed large-scale commercial units, was in direct conflict with that given by the Films Council. The former apparently carried more weight since the conflict was resolved by changing some of the members of the Films Council, rather than by reviewing policy. Neither Michael Balcon nor the other producers' representative, a maker of short films, was reappointed when their term of office ended in the autumn of 1944. They were replaced by Rank and Korda. Meanwhile consultations with the trade on the various recommendations were allowed to drag on for nearly a year, so that no decision could be made before the end of the war.

The election of a Labour Government in 1945 did not result in a sudden change of course. The new President of the Board of Trade, Sir Stafford Cripps, at first showed some interest in the cause of the independents. It was he who commissioned the memorandum from Grierson and Rotha referred to above. But the Parliamentary timetable was packed with legislation already promised in the election manifesto and, by this time, the Films Council as well as the civil servants were advising caution. Cripps agreed to postpone any legislation until the Cinematograph Films Act was due to expire in 1948. As an interim measure he made another voluntary arrangement with the circuits, enabling the President of the Board of Trade to obtain release for a limited number of independent films previously rejected by the circuits. Aggrieved producers had to submit their films to a selection committee which would advise on whether, on the criterion of entertainment value alone, the films merited a general release. A committee was appointed, but it never met, since, apparently, no producers considered it worth-while risking the displeasure of the combines by presenting their films for assessment.

During the period of inaction several independent producers signed agreements either with Rank or with Korda, who had recently returned from America and acquired a studio and distribution company. Even Balcon's concern, Ealing Studios, signed a distribution agreement with Rank. Thus, by the time the new Films Act was being drafted in 1947, the anti-monopoly lobby was depleted of some of its most influential elements, leaving the employees' organizations relatively isolated. It was not surprising, therefore, that the Films Council advised against any reshaping of the exhibition business, nor that their conclusions[13] were accompanied by a note of dissent from one of the employee members, George Elvin, the General Secretary of the ACT. The advice of the majority was followed and no new anti-monopoly measures were devised, although the existing voluntary arrangements were made statutory. Instead of strengthening the non-trade voice in administration, the Act[14] altered the composition of the council in a way which had the opposite effect. Independent members were reduced from eleven to seven; representatives of producers and of employees were increased from two to four in each case and those of exhibitors were increased from four to five. Thus the employers, among whom there were several associates of the combines, held an absolute majority in the full council, while among the trade members, although production interests had been strengthened, the representatives of the distribution and exhibition sectors still had a marginal majority. The council never again caused embarrassment, as it had in 1943–4, by giving advice diametrically opposed to that both of the major financial interests and of the civil servants involved.

The 1948 Act otherwise made few changes in existing legislation. It abolished the renters' quota – not because this was considered in itself desirable but because the Americans had fought for the change during the GATT negotiations. As far as the exhibitors' quota was concerned, the regulations for fixing the percentages were made more flexible, as the Board of Trade was allowed to determine the figure after consulting the Films Council.

Before the new Act was passed the monopoly debate had been overshadowed by a new crisis arising more directly out of relations with the United States. The question of the American remittances had been left in abeyance while the post-war loan and general trading arrangements were being negotiated between the two countries. Matters were brought to a head, however, by the economic crisis of 1947. The loan was, by then, nearly exhausted, but by the terms of the loan agreement sterling had to be made convertible with the dollar by July. Marshall aid was only an idea. The government urgently needed to narrow the balance of payments deficit and to restrict more effectively expenditure on exports; by this time it was ready to take fairly aggressive measures which might shock the United States into appreciating the gravity of the British position. Sir Hugh Dalton, as Chancellor, announced in August the introduction of an *ad valorem* duty on all imported film, which would absorb 75 per cent of remittable revenue. The MPEA reacted immediately by calling on their members to stop all exports to Britain.

The British government was completely unprepared for a boycott. The civil servants who, during the war, had warned that government interference in the film trade might well provoke such a response, in 1947 advised that a boycott was unlikely. Because of the *laissez-faire* approach of the previous two years, the government lacked the administrative machinery to direct the industry. Faced with the fact of the boycott, the Board of Trade at last began to take steps to set up a film bank and in the meantime appealed to the big producers to use their resources to boost the output of British films. The BFPA, although critical of the duty, agreed and Rank announced plans that autumn for a much expanded programme of production.

In the short term, the main effect of the boycott was to frustrate the Treasury's intentions rather than to starve the cinemas of films. There were enough American films in the country to keep the cinemas supplied for at least six months, and since these went on circulating, rather than gradually being replaced by new ones on which duty would have had to be paid, very little saving was achieved. Negotiations between the government and the MPEA were hastily resumed and in March 1948 an agreement was reached which was similar to those concluded during the war. The government agreed to withdraw the duty and in return the MPEA agreed to repatriate only seventeen million dollars. Blocked earnings, as before, could be invested in British production, an arrangement which opened the way for the future penetration of American capital and which was severely criticized in some quarters for this reason.

The agreement caused an abrupt setback for British films. The market was flooded with the American films withheld during the boycott just at the time when the films Rank had begun in the autumn of 1947 were reaching completion. As a result there was a glut both of American films and British films, but whereas the former included the cream of a normal year's production, many of the latter suffered from having been rushed through in unusual circumstances and were decidedly second-rate. Not surprisingly, British films lost more money than usual that year. The losses, following on the period of uncertainty caused by the boycott, provoked a crisis of confidence. Small producers found it almost impossible to get loans; Korda's company, British Lion, was on the verge of bankruptcy by mid-1948; Rank, the most important single source of production finance, had sustained particularly heavy losses and in 1949 announced a plan for retrenchement which included a big cut in the production budget.

Opinions differed about how far the episode of the duty alone was to blame for the losses and how far bad management had contributed. It was also recognized that, whatever special reasons there might be for the failure of those particular films, production still suffered from a chronic problem of low profitability and that for some years costs had been rising faster than revenue. Many British films released before 1948 also lost money. Opinions differed again about the principal cause, rival theories being that producers were extravagant and incompetent; that the box office takings were insufficient, or that they were incorrectly distributed. Those who held the last view were further divided about who was taking an excess share and whether restrictive practices were involved. Some thought the exhibitors' share or the distributors' fees too high, while others regarded the Exchequer as the main culprit, complaining that, at about 40 per cent, the Entertainments Duty was unreasonably high.

The period of recession coincided with a new phase in government thinking about the industry. Two months after the imposition of the import duty Cripps was appointed Minister for Economic Affairs and Harold Wilson President of the Board of Trade, his first Cabinet post. Wilson was at once thrown into film industry affairs, as he had to take charge of the negotiations with the MPEA. In the course of this work he developed a keen interest in the problems of British production and began personally to pursue several schemes for putting the industry on a sounder footing. Up to a point he agreed with the case for intervention, accepting that there was a need to check monopolistic practices and to safeguard the production of British films with measures which might not meet with the approval of other sections of the industry. Unlike the left wing of his party, however, he thought this could be done without interfering fundamentally with the structure of ownership and control. He set out to develop techniques of co-operation and persuasion, hoping to persuade rather than compel, the industry to introduce reforms.

One obstacle he soon encountered was that even the production interests were not wholeheartedly committed to the cause of British films. This was nowhere more evident than in the context of quota percentages. Shortly after the Anglo-American agreement was signed Wilson used his powers under the 1948 Act to raise the quota to 45 per cent hoping, in this way, to mitigate some of the damage done by the resumption of American imports. As might have been expected, the move provoked an outcry from the MPEA and from exhibitors. More surprisingly, Rank and the BFPA, although initially in favour of a high quota, did not persist in defending it. Within two years they had joined the chorus of complaints, although, in deference to the exhibitors, the quota had already been dropped to 40 per cent. In 1950 it was lowered to 30 per cent, where it remained for the next thirty years.

Another drawback was the absence of a consensus within the industry about the nature of its problems. Faced constantly with conflicting advice, Wilson called for more information and more discussion. He set up a National Film Production Council, a committee of producers and production employees presided over by a representative of the Board of Trade, hoping that this would lead to greater co-operation between management and workers. The results were disappointing, mainly because the producers refused to supply information which they thought the unions might use against them. Wilson also initiated three new enquiries into different aspects of the industry. A working party was set up to look into ways of reducing production costs; a committee was appointed to advise on whether there was a need for a state studio; another committee was appointed to examine distribution and exhibition and advise on ways of increasing the revenue reaching producers.

The enquiries yielded some useful information but they failed to remedy the real problem of lack of access to essential data. The committees had no power to force companies to open their books and complained that they themselves had not been able to obtain all the information they required. Also their assignments were limited, whereas what was required was a permanent service of statistics. In all three cases the conclusions reached were rather negative. By the time the Film Studio Committee was collecting evidence, the slump had emptied the studios and, far from there being a shortage of space, stages were lying idle. The committee therefore concluded that there was no urgent need for the state to step in to provide facilities.[15] *The Report of the Working Party on Film Production Costs*[16] confirmed in general terms that there was some foundation for accusations of extravagance and mismanagement, but did not publish much detailed evidence and did not offer specific remedies. The enquiry into distribution and exhibition was a much more elaborate affair and the result, the Plant Report,[17] provided a good deal of new data and served as a useful source for a more comprehensive study carried out shortly afterwards by Political and Economic Planning.[18] The findings substantiated many of the comments made in the Palache Report but, considering the nature of the evidence, the conclusions are cautious. The committee recommended against either divorcement or nationalization in any form and instead made a series of detailed recommendations on steps the trade might take to eliminate restrictive practices. It did, however, make a case for independent supervision and suggested the establishment of a film authority with more complex functions than those of the proposed tribunal, but with rather less power than Mullally's suggested commission. The need for some such body was thus a persistent theme, recurring as an element in almost every programme of reform and in each case hotly disputed by the trade. The Plant proposal proved no more successful in winning acceptance than its predecessors; but it is interesting to note that the idea was revived in the seventies with the proposal for the British Film Authority.

The main practical achievement of the Wilson era was the introduction of two forms of financial aid for producers: a film bank and a type of subsidy. The film bank came first. Wilson was convinced during his first months of dealing with the industry that special arrangements should be made for the financing of independent production, but his ideas on the subject were quite different from those of the Palache Committee or the ACT. He did not intend the provision of money to be a step towards forming a state sector in competition with private enterprise. He hoped, rather, to use it to encourage private companies to develop in competition with the existing big two. The initial plan envisaged that some, at least, of the finance would come from private sources, and it was only when it proved impossible to interest existing financial institutions that Wilson decided to create a specialized finance corporation and provide a Treasury grant. Even then the scheme was designed specifically to avoid competing with private capital. There were no plans to provide the finance corporation with a distribution agency and at first it was only allowed to lend through existing private distributors, the theory being that the distributor would acquire a group of satellite independent producers and together they would form a viable commercial unit. Wilson thought that Korda's British Lion already had the makings of just such a group and could, with a little assistance, become an effective third force in the industry. He was, therefore, partly motivated by the aim of saving this particular company. The Act[19] setting up the National Film Finance Corporation was passed early in 1949, but before this, as an emergency measure, a state company had been formed which was then absorbed by the corporation. The NFFC was provided with a revolving fund of £5 million, increased to £6 million in 1950. But the company had already advanced £1 million to British Lion and a further £1 million was lent by the corporation the following year. Korda continued to lose money on a grand scale and in 1954 the decision was taken to call in the receivers. By then the corporation had committed about £3 million, almost all of which was lost.

Many of the former advocates of a film bank were disappointed by the character and behaviour of the corporation. Paul Rotha voiced the principal criticisms when he wrote, 'Seeking to encourage British production the Government has already spent a lot of money putting on the screen mainly what the distributor – the middle man – wants. It has bolstered up trembling concerns and given out a handful here and there to "keep things going". It has not touched the roots of the problem.'[20] The funds sunk in British Lion could not be retrieved, but one minor concession to the critics was that the restrictions preventing the corporation from lending directly to producers were lifted. The role which the NFFC came to play was, however, in keeping with the original brief to supplement, not compete with, private capital. For it specialized in providing high-risk capital. The usual pattern of film finance was that about 70 per cent of a film's budget would be covered by a loan raised on the distributor's guarantee. The distributor would provide the capital to repay the loan as soon as the film was completed and would have first call on the film's earnings until it had recovered the capital. The remaining 30 per cent, known as the 'end money', came from another source and was only repayable out of earnings in excess of the distributor's investment. Since it was often lost, producers had great difficulty in obtaining 'end money'. The NFFC became the main source, spreading its resources over a large number of films and leaving the more profitable business of 'front money' to the distributors.

The other form of aid was the Levy, known as the Eady Levy, after Sir Wilfred Eady, the Treasury official who helped to devise the scheme. By the end of 1949 it was apparent that further action was needed to end the slump. Film production still seemed so unprofitable that producers were finding it hard even to raise 'front money'. The solution favoured by the trade and endorsed by the Plant Report was a general reduction in Entertainment Duty. The BFPA, however, proposed that instead of a simple lowering of the duty part of the proceeds of the tax should be used to increase the earnings of British films. There were precedents for such an arrangement in that parafiscal aids had recently been introduced in France and Italy. Wilson decided to offer a compromise which would benefit both exhibitors and producers. A voluntary arrangement was worked out whereby, in return for a reduction in Entertainments Duty, exhibitors agreed to pay a levy on the price of each ticket, which was paid into a fund, to be distributed to producers of British films according to their box-office earnings.

The Levy was the last of the innovations made under the Labour

Government. Wilson had not given up the idea of taking some action to check restrictive practices, but was unable to work out a plan before he left the Board of Trade.[21] After the Labour government was thrown out of office in 1951 no further changes were contemplated. On the other hand, fears that the Conservatives might undo much of the work of their predecessors proved unfounded. Both the NFFC and the Levy were reluctantly accepted as being essential to the survival of a national film industry. The Levy was made statutory in 1957. The NFFC was slightly restricted by a new obligation that it should operate commercially. This was virtually impossible to comply with and only inhibited the corporation from playing a more adventurous role in the industry by backing unorthodox projects or relatively unknown film-makers. The possibility that the industry might become self-supporting receded when the decline in cinema admissions, which had begun in the late forties, began to accelerate during the fifties. The government responded to the industry's changed circumstances by reducing Entertainments Duty, and finally by abolishing it in 1960.

It was not altogether surprising that the Conservatives were content to leave film legislation as it was. The form of administration bequeathed by the Labour government was not fundamentally different from that which it had inherited. The trade had been left to regulate its own affairs, with minimal supervision by the Board of Trade. The main source of advice was the trade. The state had become more involved only in the provision of assistance to keep the production sector going. The forms of this assistance – the exhibitors' quota, the NFFC, the Levy – corresponded with the wishes of the trade. Although similar to aids to the film industry used in parts of Continental Europe, they were far less interventionist. They rewarded whatever the market rewarded and so could not encourage developments of a kind the trade was unlikely to foster.

The legislation remained virtually unchanged for the next thirty years allowing the industry to evolve according to the logic of market forces. The tendency to monopoly became very much more pronounced. The British combines diversified into other fields and became progressively less dependent on their film interests. ABPC was taken over by EMI in 1969. But the British cinema became progressively more dependent on them. The third force in the field of production and distribution gradually disintegrated. After British Lion went bankrupt in 1954 the distribution company was kept in being under NFFC management, but was sold in 1964 to a private group which later resold it at a profit. In 1972 it changed hands again and was subsequently dismembered. In the exhibition field the share of the market controlled by the two combines steadily increased: in 1944 they owned between them 22 per cent of all cinemas, in 1965, 29 per cent and in 1972, 32 per cent. By then they were taking 52 per cent of box-office revenue.[22]

The other dominant trend in the industry was the growth of American interests in distribution and production. Between 1950 and 1970 there was a spectacular increase in the amount of American capital invested in British production and in the proportion of British films distributed by American companies. In 1950 the major American firms distributed 68 per cent of all films distributed in Britain, but only 10 per cent of these were British films; in 1970 the figures were 75 per cent and 60 per cent respectively.[23] The flow of American capital into British production reached its height at the end of the 1960s, and in 1968 90 per cent of all production capital was American.[24]

Both developments were the subject of continuing criticism, as they had been in the forties, but the government showed less interest than ever. The one concession made to the constant complaints about restrictive practices was that the industry was referred to the Monopolies Commission in 1964. The commission found that there was a monopoly and that it operated against the public interest, but was unable to recommend that the government should use compulsion to bring about changes.[25] The influx of American capital met with less resistance, since it brought many benefits to precisely those groups who had been most critical of American influences – independent producers and the employees in film production. The NFFC, however, monitored the development and published some cautious warnings about the possible dangers.[26] More attention was paid to the problem when the American companies began to withdraw at the beginning of the seventies, precipitating a new production crisis. As British films seemed again in danger – this time, in danger of disappearing altogether – a new cycle of debate began.

The withdrawal of American capital, however, began too late to influence the character of the 1970 Cinematograph Films Act, which, like its predecessor of 1960, was an essentially conservative piece of legislation, extending, with minor modifications, the existing arrangements for a further ten years. One provision intended to give additional help to British producers was that the lending power of the NFFC was increased by a further £5 million, but, before the funds were advanced, a general election brought to office a Conservative government which declined to make full use of the clause. Eventually, in recognition of the NFFC's efforts to raise capital from a consortium of private interests, £1 million was provided from public funds. The NFFC therefore continued to function, but the scale of support which it could offer was so far reduced as to be hardly comparable with that provided by it in the early sixties.

A further factor which contributed to unsettle the industry throughout the seventies were doubts about the future effects of the revolution in audiovisual technology, which, if not in practice developing as fast as its prophets had suggested at the beginning of the decade, was nevertheless felt to be only just round the corner. The 1970 Act, however, offered no recognition of the possibility that, by the time it expired, its terms of reference might be outdated. It did not even take any steps to tackle the question which had long been preoccupying the industry, that of the regularization of its relations with conventional television.

The decline in film production began to affect employment opportunities well before there was an obvious reduction in the supply of British films. The sums spent on British labour costs fell from 1971 onwards, with a spectacular drop from £22,427,640 in 1971 to £12,642,468 in 1973.[27] A number of studio closures and, most importantly, the closure of MGM, one of Britain's three top studios, contributed to a sense of crisis. At this time the call for nationalization was revived within the ACTT and in 1973 they published a report, *Nationalizing the Film Industry*, which developed the arguments about the relationship between domestic monopoly and American dominance and also set out some specific guide-lines for how a state industry might be organized. Nationalization was temporarily adopted as union policy, but was subsequently dropped in favour of a less radical approach, which emphasized the need for increased state aid and some adjustment of relations with television.

The setback in terms of creative opportunities in the British industry was arguably more pronounced than the adverse effect on the earning power of the work force. For the remaining American investment tended to be concentrated into very expensive films, which were rarely particularly 'British' in character. A good deal of work consisted in servicing films which had been conceived and shot mostly in the United States. American producers, in so far as they were gambling on risky projects at all, were doing this in their own country. The best course for the aspiring British director or writer was, as it had been before the war, to cross the Atlantic. The weakness of the NFFC naturally aggravated the situation. At the time when American financiers had been most enthusiastic about the British industry, the NFFC had had the resources to give many film-makers a first chance, to contribute considerably to 'discovering new talent' for the American companies. But from 1972 to 1974 the NFFC was only able to assist a total of six long films altogether. The overall effect was that the opportunities, always scarce enough, for new directors or producers to enter feature production or for known ones to realize an unconventional project, seemed likely to vanish completely. One response was the formation in 1976 of the Association of Independent Producers. At that time this was not, strictly speaking, a new trade association, but rather a pressure group representing the interests of a rather miscellaneous body of producers, directors and senior technicians, many of whom had gained prominence in television but who were finding it difficult or impossible to develop their work in the feature film industry. The AIP made extensive use of cultural arguments, stressing the need to make films which looked and felt 'British', and campaigned vigorously for a policy of aid which would promote the production of relatively low-budget feature films.

By this time the industry's problems had received some official recognition. Harold Wilson, as Prime Minister, remembered his early dealings with the industry with affection and, just before he retired, appointed a Working Party to look into the needs of a 'viable and prosperous British Film Industry'.[28] In its report[29] the Working Party revived the recommendation, familiar from earlier enquiries, for the establishment of a single body responsible for the cinema, to be called (so they proposed) The British Film Authority. In the meantime an Interim Action Committee was set up to take over the Working Party's advisory role and to elaborate some of the proposals already made. The first of its reports dealt in detail with the constitution and functions of the suggested Film Authority.[30]

In 1979 the Labour government was planning to incorporate into the new Cinematograph Films Act, due in 1980, some of the proposals made by the Interim Action Committee, and was considering other measures to encourage small-scale and experimental production, when the general election intervened. The new Conservative government was also of the view that existing legislation was unsatisfactory, but for completely different reasons. The time available for revising the Bill was, however, very limited, and an Act was hurried through which postponed major decisions by prolonging for five years most of the provisions of the existing legislation, although with some significant modifications. The Act ended government financing for the NFFC, providing instead for contributions to be made from the Eady Levy. It also allowed for the suspension of the quota at any time during the life of the Act, an encouraging sign for exhibitors who had, during the preceding years, been forcefully putting the case for the abolition of the quota. The Secretary of State subsequently took advantage of this clause and announced in the summer of 1982 that the quota would be suspended from January 1983. The trend was thus set for a policy of dismantling, rather than reforming, a structure of state support which was clearly failing in its avowed objective of guaranteeing the continued production of British films.

Part 3
British Film-making:
Structures and Practice

6
John Grierson and The Documentary Film Movement
Stuart Hood

'It is worth recalling that the British documentary group began not so much in affection for film *per se* as in affection for national education. If I am to be counted as the founder and leader of the movement, its origins certainly lay in sociological rather than aesthetic ideas.'[1] These are the words of John Grierson (1898 – 1972), who was without doubt the founder of the British school of documentary film-making – a school which came into being in the late twenties, continued through the Second World War and died away in the fifties in the face of lack of government interest and of competition from television.

Naturally, when Grierson first became interested in film he did not know that he was about to found a movement or group; he was drawn to film and the cinema because he saw in it 'the only democratic institution that has ever appeared on a world-wide scale.'[2] His use of the word 'democratic' to describe a medium which has always been overwhelmingly in the hands of large-scale financial interests is curious. What he presumably meant was that, during the twenties, it was the most popular medium – a universal one, far outstripping its rivals: radio, which was still developing, and the press, which was not regularly read by the working-class, even in industrial countries like Britain or the United States, whereas a large proportion of the population of these countries (and of others less highly developed) went regularly to the cinema. Film was therefore an ideal tool for the task which Grierson had in mind, which was to explain to the citizens of modern societies how these societies work; this was a task which he felt to be of great importance, since, because 'under modern conditions, the citizen could not know everything about everything all the time, democratic citizenship was . . . impossible'.[3] The idea of using film to educate citizens in democracy and in an understanding of society came to Grierson when he was a post-graduate student in the United States in the early twenties. There he met Walter Lippmann, an American writer whose views on public opinion and on education made a lasting impression on Grierson. Lippmann, in Grierson's words, 'pointed to the growing complexity of the modern world, its spreading communications and the national and international horizon of every economic and social problem. He drew a sad portrait of John Citizen, tired after the day's work, being asked to express his free and rational judgement on matters he could not possibly be equipped to judge.'[4] It is a condescending view of John Citizen, but it inspired Grierson with the belief that film could explain the workings of society not in a fictional but a 'documentary' way and thus allow John Citizen (and his wife?) to make better judgements.

Grierson's background made him particularly receptive of Lippmann's ideas about society and education. He was the son of the headmaster in a small Scottish town and so grew up in an atmosphere of admiration for education as the key to advancement for both the individual and society, as a weapon which allowed people to 'get on' in life. It was a tradition which combined a certain radical independence of spirit – 'a man's a man for a' that' – with considerable respect for established authority in the shape of the local 'dominiec' (the headmaster) or the local minister of religion. Central to it was the concept of the dignity of labour, a concept which can be adapted to fit into the most reactionary of political philosophies (Fascism, for instance), but which was to become an important element in the work of the British documentary group. Respect for education, respect for authority and respect for those who carry out the labour without which society could not function were all elements from his early background which Grierson brought with him to his work as a producer of films.

The kind of film which he believed could best educate people for citizenship was the documentary. He first appears to have come across the genre when he was still in the United States and writing about film for various American publications. At this time he met Robert Flaherty, who was to collaborate with him later and who in 1921 had produced the celebrated documentary on Eskimo life, *Nanook of the North*, and had just completed *Moana*, which Grierson described as 'a poetic record of Polynesian tribal life' which had 'documentary value'.[5] 'Documentary' he was later to say was as a 'clumsy description';[6] the French had first used it in the sense of a travelogue but Grierson came to apply it to 'all films from natural material' and added 'where the camera shot on the spot . . . in fact was documentary.'[7] That he was able to embark on a career making or, more frequently, supervising the making of 'documentaries' was due not simply to his interest in film but to the fact that he found a patron who supplied the finance and collaborators who helped to make the films, because they broadly shared his views on the function of film and above all shared his enthusiasm for the medium.

His patron was Stephen Tallents, a civil servant who in 1928 had been appointed to run the Empire Marketing Board – a man of liberal views, whose later career was to be closely connected with both film and broadcasting. The task of the Empire Marketing Board was to promote the consumption of the products of the Empire as part of the attempt to make the Empire function as a self-sufficient economic system. The board launched campaigns which involved graphic artists whose work covered schoolroom walls with pleasing pictures of workers picking cotton, cutting copra and harvesting tea, and copywriters who invented such slogans as 'Be British. Buy Empire Bananas.' Tallents shared Grierson's conviction that film was ideally suited to an educational campaign aimed at a broad public and, after overcoming resistance from members of the Conservative government of the day as well as from civil servants suspicious of film, had Grierson appointed in 1928 head of the Empire Marketing Board Film Unit, with the brief 'to bring the Empire alive'.[8]

Grierson's acceptance of that brief and his later positive assessment 'without apology'[9] of the EMB raises the question of patronage and its effect on the work it commissions – a question which is still alive today. The problem is: given the cost of film-making, where are film-makers to turn for financial help and how much must they compromise if they accept it? Today there is talk of the need to exploit the contradictions in institutions – chiefly the broadcasting ones – in order to produce work which is radical or innovatory or both; this in many cases is what the members of the British documentary group tried to do when working for the EMB Film Unit or for its successors, the General Post Office Film Unit and the wartime Crown Film Unit, or indeed when working for industrial sponsors. In the EMB Film Unit they were fortunate in that, as Grierson says, the Board permitted 'a unique degree of freedom' within 'the necessary propaganda limits'.[10] These limits he accepted and defined as 'the degree of general sanction',[11] which corresponded to what today would be called the 'consensus', or, as Grierson puts it, 'the degree of sanction allowed by all the parties of Parliament'.[12] This, he recognized, 'imposes a clear limit on the creative artist',[13] for that general sanction 'does not easily allow of forthright discussions on such highly controversial problems as, say, America's record with the Negroes of the South, or Britain's record with the Indians in the East'.[14] The creative artist, he insisted, if he is 'a practical reformer',[15] will accept the situation as one of the disciplines he must learn.

The effect of patronage can be seen in such famous films produced by members of the British documentary group as Basil Wright's *Song of Ceylon* or *Housing Problems* by Anstey and Elton. *Song of Ceylon* enjoyed an immense success and won the top award at the Brussels International Film Festival of 1935. It is a beautiful and interesting film, with remarkable film and sound montage, to which Graham Greene was inclined to apply the epithet of 'perfection';[16] but it totally avoids the question of colonial labour and the economic exploitation of the colonies – which is not surprising, since it was produced by the GPO Film Unit in conjunction with the Ceylon Tea Propaganda Board. *Housing Problems*, a dramatic exposé of living conditions in South London, was made for the gas industry, which was concerned that the London County Council was beginning to instal electric heating in council flats. The fact that it made a social statement at all was due in part to the social concern of the film-makers, in part to the wish of the public relations man involved, 'as a merely personal bonus', to 'do something positive to lift us out of the mass of poverty in which so many are floundering, at least to the extent of making the facts better known'.[17] But the message of the film was the one required by the industry: gas is best. As Joris Ivens, the famous Dutch documentary film-maker, has said, 'If the British films had been sponsored directly by social organizations fighting the bad housing conditions instead of by a gas company, they would have closed in on such dramatic reality as rent strikes and protest movements'.[18] However, as Paul Rotha, another member of the group, comments, *Housing Problems* would not have been made at all if the gas industry had not sponsored it.[19]

Grierson's collaborators were overwhelmingly middle-class and mostly graduates of Oxford or Cambridge. Grierson himself made only one film, for his real gifts lay in dealing with organizations that would provide funds, in generating interest in film in general and in the production of his group in particular, in arguing about aesthetics and about how films should be edited and in recruiting talent. *Coal–face* is a good example of his ability to spot and use the gifts of others. The film is largely made up of shots from material left over from other productions, together with a little fresh shooting. But it was put together by Alberto Cavalcanti, a Brazilian film-maker who had made an intelligent film about Paris, *Rien que les heures*, and was particularly interested in the problems of sound montage. Grierson set him to work on the material, which was supplemented by a poem by a teacher at a minor public school, W. H. Auden, and a pupil at the Royal College of Music, Benjamin Britten. Both were to become famous in their own right, as did the film editor, William Coldstream who ended his career as Professor at the Slade School of Fine Art. This was a period during which many middle-class intellectuals were drawn to film and to the politics of the Left, and the group acquired a radical reputation, due in part to the importance which Grierson and his followers rightly attached to the example of contemporary Russian film-makers like Pudovkin and Eisenstein and to the study of their works. The EMB, Grierson explained in an article written in 1933, was 'the only organization outside Russia that understood and had imagination enough to practise the principles of long-range propaganda' and 'was not unconscious of the example of Russia'.[20] This consciousness of what was going on in Russian film-making was due to the fact that Grierson arranged screenings of films like Turin's documentary on the building of the Turkestan-Siberian railway, *Turksib*, Pudovkin's anti-colonial, anti-British *Storm over Asia* and Eisenstein's *Battleship Potemkin*. These screenings were occasions at which film-makers like Pudovkin were present, just as the Hungarian artist, photographer and film-maker, Laszlo Moholy-Nagy, or the German composer, Paul Hindemith, came to the informal discussions Grierson held on film-making.

Yet the interest of the group in Russian films was not necessarily primarily political. This is made clear by Paul Rotha, who was to become an important and genuinely radical member of the documentary movement. To him the interest 'was in the main an aesthetic interest. We were interested in montage and so on. . . . It wasn't until later that we developed the sociological and political inspiration.'[21] That was to come with the intensification of the great economic depression of the thirties and with the rise of Fascism in Europe. By that time, as Harry Watt, one member who did not come from either Oxford or Cambridge, remembers, 'we were left-wing to a man. Not many of us were Communists, but we were all socialists.'[22] He goes on to recall that during the days of the EMB a Special Branch man was infiltrated as a trainee editor, and that until the late thirties there were always people who wanted to shut down the GPO Film Unit, for which he worked. This bears out Anstey's view that the documentary film-makers with whom he worked were 'premature anti-Fascists'. Politically, Grierson himself was more cautious, in spite of his radical-sounding phrases, and as his biographer, Forsyth Hardy, recalls, defined his position as being 'an inch to the left of whichever party is in office'.[23] Certainly, in spite of his proclaimed interest 'in this question of putting the working class on the screen',[24] there is no evidence that he was critical of imperialism, for instance; indeed, he wrote, apparently without irony, that in the twenties 'our original command of peoples was becoming slowly a co-operative effort. . . . For the old flags of exploitation it substituted the new flags of common labour.'[25] This point of view allowed him to describe in curiously naive terms the role of Shell Oil, one of the earliest and richest companies to sponsor industrial documentaries; he saw Shell as 'the greatest of sponsors', because the company saw the full implication of film sponsorship, 'in terms of social welfare and the preaching and teaching of social welfare'.[26] The example he gives of Shell's interest in welfare is instructive. Shell had found that in the Persian Gulf it took two men to lift a bag of cement, 'therefore they [Shell] were in the nutrition business'[27] – and the business, one might add, of seeing that each man could carry his own bag and thus increase productivity and Shell's profits. Such thoughts do not seem to have troubled Grierson, whose approach was purely pragmatic, as is demonstrated by the account by Basil Wright of how Grierson gave him 'some very rusty cans of mostly very, very old instructional films about cocoa on the Gold Coast [Ghana] and told me "OK. Sell the British public the idea that cocoa comes from one of our great colonies." '[28]

Besides casting light on Grierson's attitude to colonialism, Wright's reminiscences illustrate in an interesting way the working methods of the documentary group in the early days. They were all beginners who had no fixed ideas about the allocating of roles in film-making and no detailed professional codes of procedure about shooting and editing. 'We were thrown in at the deep end and,' says Harry Watt, 'at the lowest job you were projectionist, you were film-joiner, you were electrician, but of course you were talking and studying, and film was everywhere and you would work all god's hours and all week and you slept sometimes on the cutting room floor.'[29] This pooling of talents and resources sometimes makes it difficult today to discover who made a particular film, for they were joint efforts. For instance, *Industrial Britain* is made up of footage shot during film tests by Flaherty, who had been invited over to instruct the group on photography, supplemented by material shot by Basil Wright and Grierson himself. 'It represents,' says Grierson, 'the kind of thing we could do at that time because we all sort of fitted into each other. We could all cut together or shoot together or whatever.'[30] Some of their work, as Wright demonstrates, was carried out with 'found' material – a practice which is reflected in the way the same shots appear in more than one film, or material shot for one purpose was used for another or abandoned by one film-maker and taken over by someone else. Stuart Legg, who is remembered for his documentary *BBC – The Voice of Britain*, shot some material on the plum harvest in the Vale of Evesham. 'The rushes made Grierson sick and the theatre reverberated with his curses. Finally I managed to get rid of it onto somebody else . . . who was working at the EMB . . . and finished it.'[31] What comes across from all the evidence – and the anecdotes – is that Grierson was a dominating presence not only in the units for which he was directly responsible – the EMB Film Unit and the GPO Film Unit – but in the documentary movement as a whole, to which he dedicated his immense energy and his passion for film. Also, in spite of his acceptance of the principle of respect for 'the degree of general sanction' and his skill in refusing to be labelled politically, he quite clearly stood between the film-makers and their patrons and protected the members of the documentary group from excessive interference.

Grierson himself made only one film, *Drifters*, which shows the work of fishermen as they follow the herring shoals down the east coast of Britain from the Orkneys to Lowestoft and Yarmouth. With his usual flair for publicity, which was another of his contributions to the documentary movement, he screened *Drifters* in 1928 at the London Film Society – a club at which banned films could be shown – along with Eisenstein's *Battleship Potemkin*, which the censor considered too dangerous politically to be publicly released. *Drifters*, although some members criticized it as being technically weak, was 'an immense revelation to everybody . . . a revelation of Grierson's theories that life at home is just as interesting as life in fiction, if only you could be made to see it so'.[32] These theories of Grierson were concerned with what he called 'documentary proper' – as distinct from either film journalism or purely didactic films. They were based on three main principles. One was the belief that 'the cinema's capacity for getting around, for observing and selecting from life itself, can be exploited in a new and vital art form. . . . Documentary would photograph the living scene and the living story.'[33] The second was that 'the original (or native) actor and the original (or native) scene are better guides to a screen interpretation of the modern world . . . than the studio mind can conjure up or the studio mechanician recreate.'[34] This view is coloured by Grierson's well founded dislike of the dramatic conventions and accents of the West End stage of the day and of the restricted, middle-class view of life presented there. The third was the belief that 'the materials and the stories thus taken from the raw can be finer (more real in the philosophic sense) than the acted article'.[35]

Grierson had studied philosophy at Glasgow University and taught it briefly at Durham, but it is difficult to see what he means by 'more real in the philosophic sense' although one interpretation could be – using *The Oxford English Dictionary*'s definition of 'real' – 'having an existence in fact and not merely in appearance'. But that raises more questions about the 'fact' of documentary than it answers. What is certain is that Grierson believed that the making of documentary film entailed the passage from 'the plain (or fancy) descriptions of natural material to arrangements, re-arrangements, and creative shapings of it'.[36] So material is to be manipulated – a view which fits in with his frank admission that he was always a propagandist. Aesthetics came second to propaganda, but would 'come in good time to inhabit the statement which is honest and lucid and deeply felt and which fulfils the best ends of citizenship'.[37] This sense of social responsibility, he felt, 'makes our realist documentary a troubled and difficult art. . . . It has given itself the job of making poetry where no poet has gone before.'[38] It is the lack of social and civic element that leads him to oppose the 'film symphony' – a genre common at the time, examples being Cavalcanti's *Rien que les heures* or Ruttman's *Berlin, Symphony of a Great City*, which is a portrait in which aesthetic values, the choice of interesting and visually exciting shots, dominate and in which there is no explicit social content. In Grierson's mind this was 'the most dangerous of all film models to follow'.[39] He cites his own *Drifters* – Grierson was not falsely modest – as an example of the true method of making documentaries, because the aesthetic had a social-aim in mind: to celebrate 'the high bravery of upstanding labour'.[40] (He was also given to a turgid style of rhetoric.)

Grierson's interest in 'upstanding labour' was shared by other members of the documentary group, such as Edgar Anstey. In *Housing Problems* which he codirected, working men and women spoke directly to camera about their lives and living conditions for the first time in the history of cinema. Many years later Anstey spoke of his romantic belief (in those days) that 'the working man can only be a heroic figure'.[41] This attitude reflects the interest in and idealization of the working class, common among middle-class intellectuals in the thirties. They shared an urge to discover the hidden people of British society: the miners, train-drivers, industrial workers, housewives, whose existence was so remote from their own and whose culture was so different. This interest led George Orwell to explore working-class life and write *The Road to Wigan Pier*, venturing among the workers as if they were a strange tribe. Similarly Tom Harrison, who founded Mass Observation, a movement which aimed to apply the tools of anthropology to British society, returned from work in the Far East to study what he called 'the cannibals of Britain'. Grierson himself talked of the need 'to travel dangerously into the jungles of Middlesbrough and the Clyde'.[42]

In photography there were Humphrey Spender's studies of working-class life in the North West. In film there was *Spare Time*, a film based on his work for Mass Observation by Humphrey Jennings, one of the most talented of documentary film-makers, but one whose work and talents did not appeal to Grierson, who found him too much of an aesthetic. Jennings was indeed unlike most of the other members of the group in that he was a poet and painter, involved in the Surrealist movement. But he was also a man with a strong sense of tradition, essentially conservative and not interested in group or team work. *Spare Time* was considered to be 'a patronizing, sometimes sneering attitude towards the efforts of the lower-income groups to entertain themselves'.[43] But films like *Coalface* and *Industrial Britain*, which were highly regarded, were also open to criticism in that they avoided a number of crucial questions about wages and conditions, while making what are in their own way rather condescending comments on the dignity of labour. In *Coalface*, while there are references to industrial accidents and industrial mortality, there is none to the fact that the miners had been starved back to work after the General

Strike, an event still vividly alive in people's memories, nor is there
any comment on a shot showing men coaling a liner manually. In
Industrial Britain the stress is on workers as craftsmen, with little
suggestion that industrial labour is predominantly collective and no
reference to working-class organizations or unions. On the other
hand, it has to be said that the images of workers in such films had an
extraordinary effect. It is difficult to convey to people to whom shots
of workers are the routine images of television documentaries the
impact of such pictures on audiences in the thirties; as Grierson
records, their appearance on the screen caused spontaneous applause
from spectators used to the representation of workers in British
feature films, in which, as Ralph Bond, a Communist member of the
movement, has explained, 'when workers did appear . . . they were
always the comedy relief, the buffoons, the idiots or the servants'.[44]

Yet the pictures offered of the working class by the Grierson school
did not go as far as some members would have wished. Thus Rotha
complained that although Grierson's films were very good technically,
'the people in them were mostly the men behind the machines; you
knew nothing about them'.[45] The hero of *Night Mail* 'is the train, not
the people on the train' – the post-office workers, the railwaymen.

There were, however, other film-makers active at the time who
were closer to the working-class and more committed politically than
the bulk of Grierson's followers.[46] They were the members of bodies
like the Workers' Film and Photo League (founded in 1934) or of
Kino Productions and Kino Films (the reference to Vertov, the
Russian film-maker, with his film *Kinoglas* – cinema eye – and
Kinopravda – cinema truth – is obvious). Both were Communist
Party front organizations at a time when the party had adopted the
Popular Front tactic. They produced left-wing films and distributed
others (usually Russian); made newsreels of the hunger marches and
of May Day parades in the belief that 'the time has come for workers to
produce films showing their own lives, their own problems, their own
organized efforts to solve these problems'[47]; and held summer schools
on films and film-making at which Paul Rotha, Arthur Elton and
Ralph Bond, all members of the documentary movement, lectured.
Their productions included *Bread*, a semi-fictional documentary
about life on the dole, which ended with footage of the 1934 hunger
march. *Revolt of the Fishermen*, aesthetically strongly influenced by
Grierson's *Drifters*, dealt with a strike by the same fishermen whose
dignified labour Grierson had celebrated while at the same time

avoiding the question of pay and exploitation. *Construction*, shot partly in secret by workers, told the story of a strike on a building site. *The Merry Month of May* was a 'satirical document' on the coronation of George VI. During the Spanish Civil War Kino teams shot film in Madrid and Barcelona. The work of such organizations does not approach in volume the four hundred or so films which Grierson's followers had produced by 1938; but it is a challenge to the claim implicit in Grierson's statements, and in those of his followers, that no one else was seriously engaged in making documentaries in the thirties.

In 1938 Grierson left for Canada, where he was to set up the National Film Board of Canada, which aimed to diminish sectionalism and to give Canada 'a sense of its relationships at home and overseas'.[48] It was the kind of quasi-independent governmental agency in which he seems to have been happiest. It produced some good film-makers and attracted to itself talents like those of Norman MacLaren, who, as a student at the Glasgow School of Art, had made an anti-war film *Hell Unlimited*, had experimented in abstract colour film-making, and had shot the footage that went to make *The Defence of Madrid*. He left behind in Britain a group of film-makers who, after the outbreak of the Second World War, were to make a considerable contribution to wartime propaganda. It is an apparent paradox that a movement which was seen as and thought of itself as being radical and socially critical was so easily swung behind the wartime concept of 'one nation'; but in this its members were simply following the political tide of the time, which few – especially after Russia entered the war – were able to resist. The figures of workers which had featured in pre-war documentaries were now recruited for propaganda ends; thus, in Harry Watt's *Squadron 992*, which contains a reconstruction of the German raid on the Forth Bridge in September 1939, two miners coursing a hare with a whippet provide a simile for the fighter that shoots down one of the raiding bombers. Jennings' *Diary for Timothy*, perhaps the most accomplished of the wartime documentaries, uses shots that might have come from *Coal Face* or *Industrial Britain* and has four protagonists (apart from the baby Timothy round whom the film is built and to whom it is addressed): a miner, a train-driver – both stock figures from pre-war documentaries – a farmer and a fighter pilot, all class differences being reconciled in the struggle to preserve the British way of life and the traditions by which Jennings set such store.

As in prewar films, so in the wartime productions there is often great attention to the work process; firefighting is described in Jennings' *Fires were Started* as a job slightly more dangerous than others but with its own routines. Harry Watt's *Target for Tonight* describes a day in the life of a bomber squadron – including a raid on Germany – in a way that stresses the routine nature of their job. Grierson's theories about 'the original (or native) actor and the original (or native) scene' were also perpetuated. *Fires Were Started* was acted by 'real' firemen; the part of the middle-class copywriter who joins an East End fire crew was taken by the writer, William Sansom. In *Target for Tonight* all the parts, from the head of Bomber Command to the aircraftsmen, were played by RAF personnel. *Western Approaches*, set for the most part in a lifeboat adrift after a torpedo attack on a convoy, was cast entirely from merchant seamen. The question remains whether *Western Approaches* – with a story invented by its director, Pat Jackson – is made any truer, 'more real in the philosophic sense', by the use of 'real' people – any truer, say, than the feature film, *In Which we Serve*, directed by Noel Coward and David Lean, which is based on a true incident but acted by professionals, and which – unlike the documentary features, such as *Western Approaches* – admits that there is such a thing as fear in war and that people actually get killed in quite large numbers.

Many of the Grierson group worked during the war for the Crown Film Unit, which was set up by the Ministry of Information. Like workers in other media, they were not encouraged to raise questions about what sort of society should emerge in Britain after the war – a subject which Churchill thought would merely distract from the war effort. In 1940 some members of the documentary group had begun to publish *Documentary News Letter* to 'express the documentary idea';[49] they included Rotha and Basil Wright. They saw their wartime task as being 'to fortify national morale with an articulation of democratic citizenship as a constructive force that can mould the future'.[50] They recalled that 'our present European war against Fascism began in Spain' (an assumption not at all shared by Churchill and the conservative forces in British society) and detected 'a nervousness in some quarters to face the implications of a fully matured anti-Fascist policy'. 'Films of democracy on the social offensive' were missing.[51] Curiously enough, one of the films which does take up the social future of Britain is Jennings' *Diary for Timothy*, in which the commentary by the novelist, E. M. Forster, explicitly asks what sort of future the baby Timothy can expect and puts into the mouth of the miner a statement of confidence in the capabilities of the working class. Presumably Jennings was able to raise such questions because his film was put together in the spring of 1945, when the war in Europe was almost won.

The documentary movement founded by Grierson did not flourish in the post-war years. The Labour Government was not interested in or willing to use a relatively expensive medium like film. The cohesion of wartime which had concealed differing class interests gave way to what Humphrey Jennings, for instance, felt to be an unhappy mood. He recorded his reactions to post-war Britain in his *Dim Little Island*, which makes nostalgic use of some of his own wartime material to establish his point. It is a dim little film.

In 1952 the Crown Film Unit was dissolved. Rotha had an unhappy interlude in BBC Television, which was beginning to absorb the talents of documentary film-makers and to dispense immense patronage, the price being acceptance of the limitations of a consensual view of society and of film's function in it. It is a method of working which continues to this day, for even the observational film-making of people like Roger Graef and Charles Stewart does not break through the constraints. The challenge to the Grierson tradition comes from film-makers like the members of the Berwick Street Collective or of Cinema Action – who are more radical, aesthetically or politically, or both.

One of the dangers of hindsight is that it is liable to produce judgements that appear to diminish the work of a man like Grierson. The coolness induced by historical distance can minimize the difficulties and constraints under which he worked in the thirties, the years which saw his most important achievements. These were accomplished by a brilliant exploitation of the contradictions in British society during a period that combined the complacency of politicians like MacDonald and Chamberlain, on the one hand, with, on the other, widespread political activity, which brought about the radicalization of sections of the middle class and intelligentsia (from which the bulk of Grierson's followers were drawn) in the face of economic depression, mass unemployment and – above all – the rise of Fascism in Italy, Germany and Spain. That activity produced support for the hunger marches and for the Spanish Republic, including enlistment in some cases in the British Battalion of the International

Brigade, and membership of the Left Book Club. In this political climate, thanks to Grierson's astuteness, energy and enthusiasm, the documentary film movement was able to survive the paranoid investigations of the Conservative administration and to find both a voice and a strong echo in those audiences that saw their films, either in cinemas or at meetings held in support of the Spanish Republic or for peace meetings often organized within the framework of the Popular Front movement, with whose political vagueness the social documentaries of Grierson's followers fitted comfortably. Grierson, like Sir John Reith, was a man whose formation and background of Scottish Presbyterianism fitted him well for his task of educating and 'improving' the ordinary citizen through his chosen medium – film. Like Reith, he was authoritarian. Like Reith, he basically accepted the society in which he functioned. Like Reith, he founded a tradition which fittingly finds its last refuge in the BBC documentary, which accepts social and institutional restraints and which still believes in the unquestioned truth of documentary.[52]

7

'The New Road To Progress': the Use and Production of Films by the Labour Movement, 1929–39

Trevor Ryan

Between 1929 and 1939 a number of organizations within the labour movement became involved in the production, distribution and exhibition of films, largely for political purposes. There had been earlier attempts to use film in this way by the Labour Party and the British Section of the Workers' International Relief, but little had been achieved.[1] By 1929 however there was clear evidence of a growing interest within some sections of the labour movement in the political utility of the medium. The first labour film group, the Federation of Workers' Film Societies (FWFS), was launched in London in October 1929 to show 'Russian and other working class films' and 'arouse working class interest in films of special importance'.[2] The Federation viewed its activities in specifically political terms, as Alfred Williams, recalling his work as a member of the Manchester and Salford Workers' Film Society, explained: 'if we could get these Russian films . . . in to trade union branches, and get trade union members talking about them, it would be a means of political education. Now that was my prime and only concern – using films as a means of political education.'[3] Its origins can be traced to decisions taken in Moscow in 1928, instructing both political and industrial sections of the international communist movement to develop workers' clubs and societies for recreation, education and culture.[4] Under the guiding hand of members of the Communist Party the Federation was one of several attempts to broaden the basis of revolutionary trade union work, and also build up an authentic 'proletarian culture'. By showing Soviet films, the FWFS sought in addition to generate interest in and support for the Soviet Union, corresponding to decisions taken by the Communist Party in response to a rapidly deteriorating international situation.[5] But production was considered vital by the Council of the Federation, because 'every aspect of the social struggle ought to be presented in the setting most familiar to the mass of workers in this country'.[6] At the heart of the federation therefore was Atlas Films, registered as a company in December 1929 and founded to import, distribute and produce 35mm films.

For a year or so the Federation was quite successful, with workers' film societies, in most cases run by left-wing activists, established in ten or twelve towns and cities. But some societies depended on Atlas for financial support, and by the end of 1931 Atlas itself had accumulated losses of £500. Within a further four months Atlas, and the Federation, had collapsed. Other factors had of course played their part: continual harassment by the police and censorship restrictions prevented many societies from arranging regular exhibitions; and early in 1932 the supply of new Soviet films virtually ceased.[7]

The distribution network of Atlas took the form of workers' film societies as a direct consequence of the censorship system. As the group's films were on inflammable 35mm nitrate stock they were automatically subject to the censorship procedures which arose from the conditions stipulated in the Cinematograph Act of 1909. A few of the films which Atlas obtained had already been banned from public exhibition by both the British Board of Film Censors and the London County Council, which made it unlikely that other licensing authorities would grant permission for their public exhibition.[8] But because the Film Society had been allowed to show these films (notably, *Battleship Potemkin* and *Mother*) before private audiences, there was clearly a precedent for the exhibition of 'controversial' material. A workers' film society was consequently established in London in November 1929, quickly followed by others in Glasgow, Bradford, Liverpool, Edinburgh, Cardiff and elsewhere.[9]

Most films from the Atlas library therefore were exhibited in cinemas and halls before audiences restricted to members of these societies, each of which could usually only obtain permission to give eight or nine shows each year on a monthly basis.[10] This was rather a narrow platform upon which to build what Ralph Bond called 'the workers' film movement', exhibition being a function of film society activities rather than an aspect of the routine work of established labour organizations, such as trades councils or trade union branches.

Attempts were made to broaden the basis of the Federation by giving shows to trade union and other labour groups in London, in local halls which were not licensed for exhibition.[11] But these moves were unsuccessful, owing largely to the strategy of the Communist Party, to which the leaders of the Federation conformed.

As political work within social democratic trade unions was strictly forbidden, the communist cadres who formed the basis of many individual workers' film societies were probably unable to establish positions of influence within these 'reformist' trade unions, in order to generate formal organizational support for their societies. In some cases the severely hostile attitude of the Communist Party towards the leaderships of the social democratic sections of the labour movement antagonized many local trade union and Labour Party activists, who might otherwise have been interested in these film groups. Audiences for the FWFS shows therefore consisted largely of members of and sympathizers with the Communist Party and its auxiliary bodies, and most of these were workers, although this was not true of every society. The films made by Atlas certainly conform to this pattern. The events reported in the three issues of *Workers' Topical News* were concerned largely with the activities of communist groupings; and the techniques of presentation pre-supposed a knowledge of both communist leaders and the party's policies. Similarly, the agitational film *1931* was made by Bond to 'popularise filmically the Workers' Charter, the militant programmes of the revolutionary workers', launched by the National Minority Movement, the trade union organization of the Communist Party.[12]

The work of the FWFS was clearly of the cadre type, conforming to general Communist Party practice. But the Council of the Federation was also keen to publicize more widely the existence of a 'workers' cinema'. Atlas actively sought to secure exhibition of its material in public cinemas, and some films, such as *Turksib* and *The General Line*, were passed by the British Board of Film Censors for public exhibition and appear to have been shown quite widely.[13] Moreover, a small number of licensing authorities in England and Wales (twelve at the most) granted permission for two Soviet films banned by the BBFC to be shown publicly.[14]

Despite the collapse of the Federation, interest within the labour movement did not subside, and the release of *Soviet Russia: Past and Present* (by either Bond or Ivor Montagu) in July 1933 led to a resurgence of film exhibition. The film was on Kodak's newly available 16mm reversal stock, which was far more reliable than other

16mm stocks, and was not inflammable. Its use therefore was not subject to the conditions stipulated in the 1909 Act and, providing that exhibition was in unlicensed halls, it was free of the censorship restrictions which had hampered the FWFS. By November 1933 a 16mm production and distribution group, Kino, had been formed; and this arranged exhibitions of *Battleship Potemkin* in co-operative halls and trade union clubs.

During its first year Kino survived on meagre resources. Since Kino possessed a single 300-watt projector with only five Soviet films and as many made by its own production unit, its distribution/ exhibition work was confined largely to the London area. As few labour organizations had the equipment or the expertise to handle films and projectors, Kino appears to have been extremely reluctant to send its *only* projector and the *only* prints from its library to unknown people in distant parts of the country.[15] Profits on individual shows were so small that fifty or sixty shows were needed to provide a surplus sufficient for Kino to acquire another film for its collection.[16] There were of course other problems, not least of which was the attention which Kino was attracting from local watch committees, the police and the state.[17] But although it was unable to obtain more than single prints for its library until late 1936, the scope of Kino's activities expanded rapidly. By the end of 1935 two more projectors had been acquired, together with a further eleven Soviet films and several British productions. Distribution channels began to open up in 1934–5, and by mid-1937 Kino had effectively become a national organization, with an extensive distribution/exhibition service based on a web of regional agents and a large number of local contacts in branches of the Labour Party, the Communist Party, trade unions and Left Book Club groups.

Kino continued the work initiated by Atlas Films and the Federation of Workers' Film Societies. Until the end of 1936 it was concerned mainly with the exhibition of Soviet films, and much of its energy was devoted to convincing labour organizations of the political value of using films in their routine activities. Kino was not however tied to exhibition through film societies. Films from its library were screened at film shows convened simply for entertainment; at social and cultural gatherings, exhibitions and bazaars; at educational classes and summer schools; at meetings to raise funds or promote specific campaigns, and at political meetings and conferences. Many exhibitions were held at meetings largely with the object of attracting people, and in some cases these films had no immediate relevance to the subject of the meetings in question.[18] Consequently, Kino's material was shown in a variety of non-theatrical venues: mechanics' institutes, co-operative halls, trades clubs, town halls, and other places, such as the Whitechapel Gallery and Transport House. These were supplemented, in 1939, by Kino's own mobile daylight cinema van, with which the group toured seaside towns and holiday camps, giving several shows a day before moving along the coast.[19]

Atlas and Kino were the two most important labour film agencies between the two world wars. There were several others, of which the most notable were the Workers' Film and Photo League and the Progressive Film Institute. Formed in November 1934 and surviving for approximately four years, the Workers' Film and Photo League was the most productive of all labour film agencies in this period, making at least twenty-four 16mm silent films. Originally the group was Kino's production unit, but political and personal differences led to their separation. The League set itself the task of promoting and co-ordinating a 'left cinema' within the labour movement.[20] However, in practice, it tended to duplicate the activities of Kino. But where Kino retained a coherent political perspective, the League appears to have developed a two-sided character. Its leading members were divided between vaguely left-wing cine enthusiasts and politically motivated film-makers, and the League became increasingly dominated by people who were interested in making films rather than in producing material for political work.[21] Politically fragmented, the group began to lose its cohesion and sense of purpose and produced only one film after January 1938. By the end of that year the League had collapsed, with its more politically committed members joining Kino's production group, the British Film Unit.[22]

The League was 'a small and staffless society' in 1935, with only two provincial groups affiliated, and almost all its members lived in London.[23] With few outlets beyond London, and extremely meagre resources, the League was saved from obscurity by a strategic alliance with the Left Book Club, whose groups provided for it a relatively large potential audience and a nationwide distribution network.[24] The dramatic rise in the Club's activities had a profound effect on the League's status and accessibility, and by 1938 it had thirty affiliated groups across the country, many of which were local labour organizations, such as Aberdeen Independent Labour Party, Urmston and District Labour Party (Manchester) and Nottingham Co-operative

Society Education Department. Despite this remarkable transformation however the League continued to function on the most meagre of funds. Its structure and policy focused primarily on production, leaving 'the field of distribution to Kino Films'.[25] But production and distribution/exhibition were inextricably linked. Because the League concentrated on providing films specifically for small gatherings for which there was usually no entrance charge, little income was derived from exhibition, with the result that the League could not afford to make copies of its films.[26] Since it possessed only cutting copies, the League's distribution/exhibition work was at the mercy of its customers. Some failed to return films promptly, or to pay hire charges, and films were frequently returned in a damaged state. Consequently, in December 1937 the League resolved to confine its hire service to affiliated bodies and members. Limited co-operation with Kino enabled it to circulate some of its productions among more widely distributed audiences, and its affiliates were constantly ordering League material for their meetings. But the League's political incoherence, organizational disarray and extremely small funds ensured that exhibition was limited and production work haphazard, lacking a clear political focus.

Of far greater importance than the Workers' Film and Photo League was the Progressive Film Institute. Kino and the PFI were registered as companies in March 1935, the former to distribute 16mm films, the latter to distribute 35mm films which could not otherwise secure a distributor in Britain.[27] In practice, the PFI was concerned mainly with the importation and distribution of Soviet films until the Spanish Civil War broke out. Ivor Montagu, was able to negotiate an unprecedented agreement with the Soviet import/export agency, Soyuzintorgkino, in February 1935, by which Soviet material would be supplied free of charge, and the PFI was granted 35mm distribution rights in Britain for all Soviet films, if it wished to take them. Similar rights were given to Kino for 16mm distribution.[28] Thereafter the PFI worked closely with Kino, allowing the latter to make 16mm prints of almost all its imported material and producing a sizeable number of films for Kino to distribute.

The Progressive Film Institute attempted to encourage independent exhibitors to take its foreign material. With at least one-third, and possibly almost a half, of the 4,300 cinemas in Britain independent of the cinema circuits, there was clearly some scope for penetrating the commercial cinema.[29] Some cinema-owners were sympathetic.[30] A small number of specialist cinemas often took PFI material; and Sidney Bernstein apparently opened his 26-cinema circuit to the group.[31] But the majority of cinemas which used PFI material were controlled by sections of the labour movement: co-operative society cinemas, miners' institute cinemas, and others, such as the Popular Picture Palace owned by Miles Platting Independent Labour Party (Manchester).

The PFI attempted to penetrate the commercial cinema in two other related ways: by persuading cinema circuits, or independent cinemas, to take its news-film material for inclusion in their newsreel programmes; and by selling footage to newsreel companies. The Bernstein circuit for example took *Prisoners Prove Intervention in Spain* and *Madrid Today*,[32] and *Pathé News* took various items on the bombing of British shipping in Spanish waters for inclusion in five issues of its newsreel.

While considerable importance was attached to this work, the PFI's principal function was the distribution of 35mm films for non-theatrical exhibition. As with Kino, the origins of the PFI can be traced to the activities of the international communist movement. There was a need to distribute *Free Thaelmann*, a film commissioned by the World Committee for the Relief of Victims of German Fascism, an immensely influential campaign organization established by Willi Muenzenberg, the propaganda chief of the West European Bureau of the Comintern.[33] The PFI was formed specifically to distribute the film in Britain,[34] and the subsequent work of the group was of a fundamentally political nature, corresponding broadly to the activities of the Communist Party. This work was concerned largely with the provision of film material for exhibition at large prestige meetings in town halls, or in other large public auditoria such as Kingsway Hall in central London. The Institute's larger gauge material was far more suitable than Kino's films for these meetings, rendering larger images with greater definition. Moreover, its films could be shown in cinemas: the Communist Party in East London frequently arranged political meetings at the People's Palace in Mile End Road, and meetings of the Friends of the Soviet Union in the Cambridge Theatre, Seven Dials, were regularly accompanied by similar shows. Other organizations used the PFI library, such as the National Joint Committee for Spanish Relief and the International Peace Campaign, but the Communist Party and its orbital groups were probably the

PFI's most frequent customers.

The other key aspect of the Progressive Film Institute's activities was its production work. Two trips to Spain in 1936 and 1938 resulted in twelve films (either news film or documentary reportage) in support of the Republican cause.[35] The Civil War had become a central focus of the Communist Party's political work to generate a popular front, and it was in this context that these films were used. Moreover, the PFI gave considerable assistance to the National Joint Film Committee for Spanish Relief, helping to raise funds for relief work through the organization of shows of its own productions. Other PFI productions, such as *Peace and Plenty*, *Britain Expects* and *Communist Party 15th Congress*, were intended to contribute directly to the Communist Party's recruitment and propaganda.

The activities of Kino illustrate more clearly than those of any other agency the full range and nature of labour film work. The mainspring of the group's work was the Communist Party, from which it drew political and strategic guidance. The party organized the political life of its members as individuals and provided Kino's chief organizational contacts with other sections of the labour movement. However, the party leadership attached low priority to the use of the medium of film in its national political work, in view of the meagre resources at its disposal.[36] Consequently, it did not generally co-ordinate film publicity or propaganda with its national campaigns, and appears to have left the initiative regarding film work with Kino, the PFI and local Communist Party branches.[37]

Although Kino was not under formal Communist Party control, its work was consistent with that of an organization which identified with the party. It produced films which reported events or focused on issues of particular relevance to party propaganda, and made several films either at the request of the party, or to publicize explicitly the party's activities and policies. Production was always a subsidiary activity however: Kino's principal functions were the distribution and exhibition of films. From the beginning there was an emphasis on the showing of Soviet material. This was in part a response to a genuine demand for such films. But it was also part of the communist movement's concern to publicize the achievements and culture of the Soviet Union as an essential preliminary to building up sympathy and support for the USSR. From 1933 the party's work focused largely on the promotion of an anti-Fascist, anti-war platform, and by the end of

1935 this had taken the form of a 'united front' embracing all 'progressive' organizations and individuals opposed to Fascist aggression and to the policies of the National Government in Britain. Much of the party's work therefore was conducted through local branches of Spanish Relief groups, the International Peace Campaign, the League of Nations Union, the Left Book Club and several other organizations. Under these circumstances Kino occupied a strategically important position, as the principal non-theatrical distributor of films covering the wars in Spain and China and anti-Fascist activities in Britain. Kino worked in close conjunction with the International Peace Campaign,[38] the Left Book Club,[39] and the National Joint Committee for Spanish Relief, producing three short films for the latter in 1938 after the committee had sponsored a Kino expedition to Catalonia in December 1937.[40] But Kino did not simply provide a service for the party, or for these organizations: as the party's 'people's front' strategy began to assume priority over all other political work Kino appears to have adopted a more active political role, organizing its own shows to contribute to party campaigns, providing its own speakers from within the Kino group for shows before meetings convened by other groups, and using its material specifically for recruitment to the party.[41] Finally, Kino, like the Progressive Film Institute, made a small but important contribution to inner-party life. Even though a more open stance was permitted by the party from 1935 onwards, its members saw the organization as a refuge, and their immersion in the party naturally extended to their social lives. In London at least Kino quickly became part of the social and cultural foreground of inner-party life shared by the Unity Theatre, the Forum Cinema, the *Left Review*, the Nanking Restaurant, Marx House, Shoreditch Town Hall and many other cafés, pubs, bookshops and halls.[42]

Kino attempted to use film for broadly educational purposes and acquired a number of films of an educational or instructional character produced by William Hunter's Dartington Film Unit and by Cambridge Film Productions, run by James Harris. It also organized classes, lectures and schools to provide education for workers in film appreciation and theoretical analysis, and gave practical lessons in camera use and editing technique.[43] Politically opposed to the commercial cinema, Kino sought to cultivate the critical taste of labour and working-class audiences through its own shows, publicity and reviews in its own regular bulletin, and through demonstrations and protests against either the exhibition of reactionary films or the censorship of 'progressive' material.[44]

Kino however did not reject the film as a medium of entertainment. Imbued with a 'workerist' ethic, the group sought to provide film entertainment as part of an assertion of an authentic workers' culture, and even tried to broaden the social basis of Kino's support by organizing 'socials', dances, trips and rambles. But in the field of entertainment priority was given to a long-term project to cultivate among the group's audiences a critical attitude towards the commercial cinema, not merely as a form of resistance to what Kino believed to be 'manipulation' and 'dope', but to mobilize public opinion and thereby bring pressure to bear on the industry, which it was hoped, would eventually be forced to make more acceptable films and, more immediately, create a space within itself for a different conception of film – one designed to further 'culture, education and enlightenment'.[45] Kino even considered the production of a 35mm 'super-film' by public subscription, along the lines of Jean Renoir's *La Marseillaise*.[46]

These projects, ambitious and long-term, were integral to Kino's non-theatrical activities. Films were used as a means of generating class consciousness, contributing to the long process of building a more unified, politically knowledgeable and resolute labour movement. Kino's work was an additional channel for political activism and a means of publicizing the leading role of the Communist Party in the struggle of the working class against capitalism. But Kino was never a mere extension of the party's publicity and propaganda work, and it was precisely because of its independence that it achieved such widespread support within the labour movement.

We can provide a clear indication of the scope of labour film work in various ways. Between 1927 and 1939 labour organizations produced 112 films; at least a further three were produced but never released, and an additional six may have been produced. For the entire decade of the 1930s film output averaged almost one film every month. These figures moreover represent the lower limit of production: there are more about which there is very little information.[47] Furthermore, they do not include the publicity/propaganda films of the commercial sector of the co-operative movement, which advertised co-operative trade, promoted specific co-operative products and expounded the principles of co-operation.[48] Table 1 provides details of the principal

Table 1
Labour Film Production, 1929–39

Atlas	6
Kino Films	17
Workers Film and Photo League	24 (4)
Progressive Film Institute	18
Socialist Film Council	3
London Co-operative Society	9
Royal Arsenal Co-operative Society	5
Workers' Film Association	5
People's Newsreel	2
British Film Unit	2 (2)
Others	21
Total	112 (6)

Note: Figures in parentheses refer to additional films which may have been made by these groups. A further three films were made but not released. The last entry refers to groups such as Glasgow Kino, the Scottish People's Film Association and Manchester Film and Photo League.

film production agencies of the labour movement.

The great majority of these films were made on 16mm stock, and roughly two-thirds were silent. All were shot by the organizations listed, with the exception of about ten, which were made by commercial companies, the main one being the Realist Film Unit. These exceptions, commissioned by the wealthy co-operative movement, were by far the most expensive: *Voice of the People*, for example, cost £1000 to produce (pre-war values), and *People with a Purpose* £1200.[49] Of the majority, only four films had comparable funding: *Spanish ABC*, *Behind the Spanish Lines* and *Peace and Plenty*, produced by the Progressive Film Institute, and *Blow, Bugles, Blow!*, produced by the Socialist Film Council. Several productions cost between £100 and £400, but most probably cost less than £40 each, accounting in part for the preponderance of silent films: a twenty-minute 16mm sound film would have cost over £100.

Details of distributions are provided in Table 2. It should be noted that the total for British films does not include all British films distributed by these groups – only those made by or for organizations of the labour movement. While no full comparison should be made with commercial distributors, it is interesting to note that the growth of Kino's library compares favourably with them. Rowson revealed in

Table 2
Labour Film Distribution, 1924–39

	GB	USSR	Spain	USA	Germany	Czecho-slovakia	China	France	Others	Total by group
Atlas Films	6 (1)	24	–	1	1	–	–	1	–	34 (1)
Zino Films	66 (2)	56	11	13	5	1	2	3	1	158 (2)
WFPL	28 (4)	–	–	3	–	–	–	–	–	31 (4)
PFI	14	46	13	7	2	–	2	2	–	86
International Sound Films	3	3	4	2	1	5	1	–	2	21
Workers Film Ass.	19	1	–	2	–	–	–	–	4	26
Others	15	7	–	–	–	–	–	–	–	22
Total by Country	112 (6)	92	22	20	7	5	5	5	5	273 (6)

Note: These figures represent the minimum totals of films distributed by each group. Some distributors handled the same films. Figures in parentheses refer to additional films which may have been distributed by each group. 'Other' film distributors were not strictly distributors but individuals or groups which occasionally issued films.

his survey of the cinema industry in 1934 that a yearly intake of 30-plus and 26-or-less were respectively large and small trading figures for distributors.[50] Kino's average yearly intake between December 1933 and September 1939 was 27 films. However, the contents of the group's library probably never exceeded 70 or 80 films in 1938, the busiest point in its history. Much of its collection was simply out of date or worn out by constant use; there were difficulties in obtaining replacement prints of Soviet material, and British films were often cut up and used as stock footage in other productions. By February 1939 Kino's entire collection amounted to only 62 films.[51]

As for the number and frequency of shows, the evidence is patchy and its reliability uncertain. Kino undoubtedly provided films for the greater proportion of all labour film exhibitions. Individual films were continually in demand. *Storm over Asia* was apparently shown on over 120 occasions within 12 months, and *Mother* approximately 75 times during the same period.[52] *Defence of Madrid* was reportedly shown on over 400 occasions within six months of release.[53] Individual shows attracting audiences of over 500 were common, and several of Kino's films were apparently shown before audiences of 1000 or more.[54] The size of the total audience for Kino's films in any one year is difficult to determine, as is the total number of exhibitions. But from the information available it is possible to provide tentative estimates. Between March 1935 and February 1936 the maximum number of people who attended shows given by Kino was 30,000. The total number of shows given by Kino was between 500 and 600, and the total for the exhibition of Kino's films by other groups was between 470 and 600. As it is unlikely that Kino achieved an *average* audience of more than 50 for its own shows, the upper limit for the total audience for all shows of Kino's films in that year was approximately 100,000.[55] Evidence for other years is scant, but in 1938 Kino apparently provided films for 1372 shows.[56] The group claimed that the total audience reached was 330,000 but this is probably too high, and a total of 200,000 is suggested as an extremely tentative estimate. Whatever size this audience may have been, and whatever the total number of shows in any one year, advertisements in the *Daily Worker* and other papers reveal that the use of films at meetings was widespread, regular and frequent – and, for many labour groups, a weekly routine.

It is necessary to suggest some of the elements which provided the context for labour film work. The most immediate and striking feature is the extent to which, as Joseph Reeves put it, 'The sound film is supreme today in the field of the people's amusements and recreations.'[57] Average weekly attendances apart,[58] the thorough assimilation of the commercial cinema within British social life in the 1930s is suggested by the siting of new cinemas in shopping precincts, and by many of the larger city-centre cinemas, which incorporated tea-rooms, restaurants, bars and ballrooms.[59] Cinema was conceptualized overwhelmingly in terms of entertainment, and recognition within labour film groups of the need to challenge this dominant view informed all their activities. But a note of urgency in the implementation of this task arose from a particular set of assumptions, widely shared within the cadre levels of the labour movement, concerning the cinema industry. Exception was taken both to the pervasive American influence on British audiences and to the disconcerting ease with which people were accepting the vicarious pleasures of the cinema and 'escaping' from the real world and its problems.[60] While the metaphor may have varied between 'drug', 'dope', 'opium' and 'soporific', the central idea that the cinema exercised a narcotizing influence received wide currency, and was reinforced by a commonly held belief that the media in general, and the cinema in particular, were 'homogenizing' thought and creating a 'mass psychology'.[61] Many observers on the left and centre of the movement however believed that the complacent conformity of the masses was not simply an 'effect' of the cinema but a direct result of manipulation. The cinema was not merely a source of profit but 'an instrument of class rule'.[62]

These arguments were of course familiar themes in the discussions of the press which punctuated labour politics throughout the inter-war period, and it was the combativeness of the communist movement in this context during the late 1920s which led to the initiation of the Federation of Workers' Film Societies in October 1929 and the publication of the *Daily Worker* from 1 January 1930. The paper was obviously of far greater value to the Communist Party, but a number of elements in the political conjuncture of the 1930s made film particularly attractive as a weapon in the class struggle. One was the need to counter the political and ideological content of the commercial cinema and to expose its alleged manipulatory function. Soviet films were considered to be excellent material in this respect because, in presenting the working classes on the screen and analysing their problems, they were considered the direct antithesis of Hollywood films. Moreover, originating within the 'first workers' state', they appeared to demonstrate the full range of possibilities of a socialist cinema, and the form it should take in Britain.[63]

The appeal of Soviet cinema also derived from an aesthetic of realism, which was a central motif in the work of labour film production. The cadre levels of the labour movement, while subscribing to the common view of the suggestibility of the masses, believed in the ultimate rationality of the individual.[64] A particular attraction of film for these film groups was its supposed capacity for reproducing 'reality'. The presentation of the 'real' on screen was a conscious aim, in direct opposition to the 'artificiality' of the commercial cinema. 'Workers' newsreels' were consequently a major aspect of labour film production, and exhibited as a counter to the 'bourgeois newsreels'.[65] Furthermore, these groups were influenced not only by the 'realism' of the Soviet cinema, but by the growing stature of the indigenous documentary movement. The documentary style was informed by a democratic impulse and a diagnostic technique with which these groups, in the absence of any sustained attempt within left-wing circles in Britain to formulate a theory about the relationship between politics and aesthetics, could readily identify.[66] Key components of this 'emergent form of social consciousness' were an ideology of facts, and the belief that film-makers possessed a social mandate to act as a voice in the defence of the

people.[67] Where the main personalities of the documentary movement eschewed any direct political involvement however, these
labour film groups were of course heavily committed. Nevertheless,
the documentary rationale tapped, and was underpinned by, the
deeply rooted rationalist tradition within the leadership of the labour
movement. A striking feature of labour film output is the extent to
which these films were confined largely to the immediately observable
and upheld the importance of visual accessibility. The prominence of
Griersonian ideas within film aesthetics in Britain ensured that labour
film production was confined largely to the construction of a
'documentary' social truth. Consequently, only a small number of
films were produced which used agitational techniques.

The development of film production, distribution and exhibition
within the labour movement took place largely within a communist
context. Originating in the needs of the Comintern, this activity was
clearly influenced by events in the Soviet Union.[68] But the Communist Party leadership was preoccupied with a utilitarian, political
approach and, despite a growing awareness within the party hierarchy
of the need to broaden its activity, its sustained neglect of cultural and
other forms of work prompted much criticism from within the
rank-and-file membership.[69] The various left-wing film groups were
independent of the party and, while receptive to its strategy, were
unrestricted by its narrow theory of politics. They occupied a
crucially important place in labour politics in the later 1930s, when
notions of class struggle lost much credibility and, paradoxically, the
Communist Party enjoyed an unprecedented national influence.
While the significance of the foundation work of the Federation of
Workers' Film Societies should not be overlooked, especially the
long-term project of creating a 'workers' cinema', it was in this period,
from late 1936 to early 1939, that labour film work enjoyed its most
important phase. Of the many organizations which thrived in these
years, comprising a general left-wing cultural thrust, Kino and the
Progressive Film Institute were two of the most important. Their
status and accessibility within the labour movement were impressive.
They were the principal oppositional sources of visual news of events
in Spain; the main sources of material of Soviet origin, and of films of a
left-wing nature from other countries. Their films were used by the
broad spectrum of organizations which subscribed to anti-Fascist or
anti-National Government perspectives, and enabled audiences of

plumbers and politicians alike to *visualize* what was happening in Abyssinia, Spain, China, France and Czechoslovakia. The significance of their work hinged largely on the emergence of a political and cultural alignment within the country which transcended class boundaries and the organizational fragmentation of the labour movement. The unifying force of anti-fascism appears to have been nourished and given greater clarity by the material in the libraries of Kino and the Progressive Film Institute. But their work was not confined to the passive provision of a service of which trade union branches or humanitarian relief agencies could take advantage. Both were deeply involved in cadre work, organizing shows, producing material for anti-Fascist agitation and propaganda, and providing speakers for shows mounted by other groups. In the absence of a more sophisticated theory of ideology, and under the pervasive influence of a distinctly 'documentary' aesthetic of realism, the films produced by them were tied largely to the immediately observable in directly political situations. Other factors played their part in shaping this work, but perhaps one feature which has so far received little attention is the extent to which these groups strove to present their films, and discuss the medium and its uses, in terms of direct opposition to the commercial cinema. This 'opposition' raises the question of the independence of these groups from prevailing cinema aesthetics, which involves a discussion of filmic representation and audience consumption. Such issues are beyond the scope of the present chapter. The term is therefore used in a limited sense, but left-wing film activity during these years was never simply subordinate to political work: this opposition had distinctly social priorities. These priorities were of course informed by particular political and ideological perspectives. But opposition to what was virtually a commercial monopoly of the medium also took place in a social context. Whether for entertainment, fund-raising or agitation, the non-commercial film shows organized by Kino and PFI, or for which they provided material, were, along with meetings of Left Book Club groups, part of, and helped to constitute, a *social* as well as a political milieu.

Movies and Mandarins: the Official Film and British Colonial Africa

Rosaleen Smyth

From the second half of the 1920s the Colonial Office began to explore the implications, for the colonies, and for the colonial power, of film and radio. The impact of the cinema was felt first; its potential as a propaganda medium was believed to be enormous. The question was: how to harness this propaganda power in the imperial interest? In the African colonies the concern of the Colonial Office was how the cinema affected British economic and political interests, and how Britain might use the cinema to promote what it determined to be the economic, social and moral welfare of the colonial peoples.

Britain felt that both her economic and political interests in Africa were threatened by the stranglehold which the American film had gained on the commercial cinema circuit in the 1920s. Not only was it believed that 'trade follows the film'[1], but also that the unsavoury image of the white race being projected in the Hollywood movie was a political threat, as it endangered the prestige of the white race. 'The success of our government of subject races,' warned a former colonial governor, Sir Hesketh Bell, in 1930, 'depends almost entirely on the degree of respect we can inspire.'[2] In India and the Far East the damage had already been done, but in his opinion, there was still time to avert the danger 'in our tropical African Empire'. Attempts to break the American stranglehold failed, however, mainly because many colonies had prior contractual obligations with South Africa, from where they obtained their commercial films.[3] The Colonial Office was forced to limit itself to the negative sanction of censorship and urged colonial governments to beware of showing any films which might discredit the armed forces[4] or 'rouse undesirable racial feeling'.[5]

As most Africans were illiterate both the cinema and the radio were thought to offer bright possibilities as a medium of instruction for adults. In 1927 Hanns Vischer, Secretary to the Advisory Committee on Education in the Colonies (ACEC), recommended to the Colonial Office conference that films be used to help spread general knowledge about 'health and economic development'.[6] In 1929 Julian Huxley went to East Africa for the ACEC to test African reactions to instructional films; he concluded that for the education of adults 'they will in the present state of tropical Africa be much the most powerful weapon of propaganda which we have at our command'.[7] Local experiments were already being made in instructional films by two government health officials, Dr A. Paterson in Kenya and William Sellers in Nigeria; Sellers obtained some assistance for his work from the Colonial Development Fund. The Colonial Office and the Commission on Educational and Cultural Films, which produced the highly influential report *The Film In National Life* (1932), both considered that the time was now ripe for a full-scale experiment, but financial backing could not be found.[8]

The financial solution was ultimately provided by the Carnegie Corporation of New York. In 1932 the Carnegie Corporation had financed an enquiry into the effect of industrialization on African society, carried out on Northern Rhodesia's Copperbelt by a team led by J. Merle Davis, of the Department of Social and Industrial Research of the International Missionary Council. Merle Davis urged that the cinema should be used to help illiterate Africans adjust to the coming of Western technological society, with its alien social and economic standards.[9] A follow-up to this Copperbelt exercise was the Bantu Educational Kinema Experiment (BEKE), sponsored by the International Missionary Council. The largest backer was the Carnegie Corporation, with contributions also coming from the Colonial Development Fund, the governments of Kenya, Uganda and Tanganyika and two multi-national mining companies with Copperbelt interests. The BEKE was under the general direction of Merle Davis; its technical director was Major Notcutt, who had experimented in making home movies with African actors in East Africa; G. C. Latham, a former Director of Native Education in Northern Rhodesia, was its education director, and the Colonial Office was represented on the advisory council.

The BEKE was conducted in East and Central Africa between 1935 and 1937; it was completely self-sufficient as the films were made and processed locally, and Africans were trained in all aspects of the work. The 16mm silent films had commentaries recorded by means of sound-on-disc. In two years the BEKE managed to produce thirty-five films, which included nineteen on agriculture and six on health. A singular feature was that the people who made the films showed them. They were taken by Latham on lorry tours throughout East and Central Africa, to test audience reactions. In five months, he travelled nine thousand miles and gave ninety screenings to more than eighty thousand people, most of whom had never seen a film before. He concluded that 'the moving picture is understood by quite unsophisticated Natives to a degree which astonishes people who have experienced their comparative inability to recognize still pictures'.[10]

The experiment was not an unqualified success. The sponsors and directors had high hopes that after two years the BEKE would be placed on a permanent footing. Latham had an ambitious plan for a central organization in London, with local production units in the colonies. The East African governments however were firmly against the institutionalization of the BEKE, both for financial reasons and because they were highly critical of the technical quality of the films, especially the imperfect synchronization of the sound-on-disc technique. Latham argued that, given the limited finance available and the fact that the instructional film was still at an experimental stage, one could not be too much of a technical purist; all that mattered as far as the African audience was concerned was that the film be 'intelligible'.[11] Northern Rhodesia was the only colony keen to see a continuation of the BEKE. It was more cinema-conscious than most other parts of black Africa because, as a result of the mine cinemas on the comparatively urbanized Copperbelt, it had probably the largest concentration of African cinema-goers outside South Africa.[12] Government officials saw the provision of 'suitable' films as a 'burning problem'.[13]

Part of the explanation for the foundering of the BEKE lies in the financial policy of the Colonial Office. Until the Second World War it was the policy of the British government that colonies should pay their own way. One would not expect that colonial governments would have much money to spend on experimental instructional films when many more fundamental areas, such as agriculture, health and school education, were starved of funds during the inter-war years. The meagre results of this financial policy in terms of development can be seen from the spate of reports critical of Britain's colonial administration which appeared on the eve of the war. The consensus was that much more money would have to be spent by the British government on colonial development: hence the Colonial Development and Welfare Act of 1940.

One positive result of the criticism of the British government's colonial stewardship was that the Colonial Marketing Board managed to find £4,175 to pay the Strand Film Company to produce a twenty-minute propaganda film, *Men of Africa* (d. Alexander Shaw, 1939).[14] The film used material from East Africa to show how British rule had brought 'peace' where life had been once full of 'fear and uncertainty'. The narrator describes how 'the enterprise of European officials and settlers and Indian traders had opened up the country. But there is still a long battle to be fought with ignorance, poverty and disease . . . ;' however, 'much can be achieved by money and the initiative of the white man. . . .'[15] The beneficent influence of the white man in Africa was also the theme of several British commercial films made during this period: films like *Palaver* (1926), *Sanders of the River* (d. Zoltan Korda, 1935), and *Rhodes of Africa* (d. Berthold Vietel, 1936).[16] The case of *Men of Africa* demonstrates that it was easier to find money for films in defence of the Empire, to counter criticism of British neglect of the colonies, than it was to find money for films as an aid in imperial development.

This argument is reinforced by the fact that when money was found for a colonial film unit it was for defence rather than educational purposes. The Second World War proved a great stimulus to film-making, as films were pressed into service for war propaganda and explanation. The Ministry of Information (MOI) set up the Colonial Film Unit (CFU) in 1939 to make and distribute war propaganda films designed to encourage the colonial war effort, chiefly in Africa. In addition, the MOI made available some mobile cinema vans to take this film propaganda into rural Africa. The CFU came under the MOI's Films Division, which had grown out of the Crown Film Unit of the GPO. Sellers was seconded from Nigeria to be the CFU's producer, while the veteran film-maker, George Pearson, was appointed director.

Sellers and Pearson developed a specialized type of film-making which they considered suitable for 'primitive people'; the films should be slow in pace, avoid trick photography, leave nothing to be inferred and pay special attention to continuity – the basic assumption being that the perception of film is an acquired skill rather than a natural talent.[17]

By 1944 the total number of films carrying the CFU label was 115, though not all were actually produced by the CFU. At first these 16mm films were shown with a spoken commentary, but later magnetic striping was introduced, which enabled commentaries to be recorded in local languages. By far the greatest number of films shown in the colonies were war propaganda films and newsreels. The war propaganda films can be subdivided into different categories: information, exhortation, good will and 'the projection-of-England'.[18] A series of information films, with titles like *This is an Anti-Aircraft Gun* and *This is a Barrage Balloon* (both d. George Pearson, 1941), sought to explain the mechanics of modern warfare in as simple a style as possible. *Food from Oil Nuts* (d. Pearson, 1944) exhorted Africans to produce more ground nuts to promote the production of margarine, while *We Want Rubber* (1943) urged them to help overcome the critical shortage of this commodity after the fall of Malaya. The image of a beleagured Britain enduring, with stoicism and good humour, the hardships and sacrifices of war was projected in *A British Family in Peace and War* (d. Pearson, 1944). *Comforts from Uganda* (d. Pearson, 1942) and *Katsina Tank* (1943) are examples of good will films made to show British appreciation of the colonial war effort, while others, such as *An African in London* (d. Pearson, 1941), *An African in England* (1945 or 1946), *Nurse Ademola* (d. Pearson, 1943), *West African Editors* (1944) and *Pilot-Officer Peter Thomas, RAF* (about a Nigerian who was the first African to qualify for a commission in the RAF; d. Pearson, 1943) showed Africans visiting England or working or studying there. As for the newsreels, *British News* was prepared by the British Council, from a compilation of items from five British newsreels, while from 1943 the CFU prepared a special newsreel, *British Empire at War* (1943–5) which ran to twenty-five editions.

The Colonial Office, which played an advisory role in the activities of the CFU, did not like this narrow concentration on war propaganda and lobbied successfully to have the CFU's work extended to include the making of instructional films. In 1942, as the CFU widened its scope, funds and staff were increased, although the Treasury insisted that the main activity of the CFU should continue to be the production of war propaganda films. The Colonial Office was looking forward to the coming of peace, when it expected that the CFU would concentrate on the production of instructional films. In anticipation of a drive for mass education, to be launched after the war, with funds to be provided under the Colonial Development and Welfare Act, the ACEC produced the report *Mass Education in*

African Society (1944), which recognized the film 'as the most popular and powerful of all visual aids' in mass education. The report further urged that documentary films be used to extend the horizons of rural villagers and help them to adjust to 'changing political, economic and social conditions', and that news films could help develop a 'national' outlook.[19]

The CFU firmly believed in the necessity for local background: films should be made in Africa with African actors, but because of wartime staff shortages it had to compromise on this principle for most of the war, with the result that its early instructional films were made in England.[20] It was not until 1945 that the first CFU unit went to Africa. As a stop-gap measure, a Raw Stock Scheme was introduced in 1941, under which some officials in the colonies were provided with film cameras and 16mm raw stock, so that they could send back African footage to Britain for processing, editing and titling. In order to provide a general channel of communication for all these film-making activities the CFU began the publication at the end of 1942 of a quarterly magazine, *Colonial Cinema*.

The films that were being made in Africa with African actors during the war were those made by the Directorate of Education and Welfare, East Africa Command. In 1944 the Directorate's Mobile Home News Unit began filming scenes of village life in Uganda, Tanganyika and Kenya for showing to soldiers on active service in Burma and the Middle East. They branched out and made several two-reel comedies using an African acting troupe from Bagamoyo in Tanganyika. East Africa Command found their efforts greatly appreciated, as the audiences rapidly accustomed themselves to cinema techniques.[21]

In an effort to find out what impact its films were having the CFU employed the questionnaire method, but found the results extremely contradictory.[22] In estimating the impact of the CFU films during the war, we have to rely, in the absence of systematic research, on a random collection of European reports of observed reactions. Captain Dickson, of East Africa Command's Mobile Propaganda Unit, which toured Rhodesia and Nyasaland in 1943–44, was quite scathing on the subject of war propaganda films from the CFU and MOI. He found them unimaginatively put together and too rapid in sequence. The European photography angles were unintelligible to Africans, who had never seen a gun or a shell, and Africans were bored by endless scenes of Cabinet Ministers visiting munitions factories. What they did enjoy were shots of actual combat.[23] The Crown Film Unit's *London Can Take It* (d. Harry Watt and Humphrey Jennings, 1940) was widely shown in East Africa with near-disastrous results; scenes of London in flame and ruin during the Battle of Britain caused 'virtual panic' in some areas, as the people thought 'the Germans are winning the War'.[24] Very popular in East and Central Africa was *Killing the Killer*, a CFU film made by Kodak about a fight to the death between a mongoose and a cobra, to which a commentary had been added which equated Churchill with the mongoose and Hitler with the cobra. Entertainment films were included in cinema programmes to make the programmes more appealing, and particularly popular were Westerns and Charlie Chaplin. One incontrovertible conclusion is that while the message did not always hit its target, the audience responded with great enthusiasm to the new medium which the exigencies of war had brought into the heart of rural Africa.

The Colonial Office is reported to have been somewhat dubious about the Chaplin films because of its concern about the prestige of the white race,[25] and so the CFU carefully edited some of his comedies to remove scenes which showed clergymen or policemen behaving in an undignified fashion.[26] Censorship in the colonies was carried out by censorship boards whose purpose, *Mass Education in African Society* pointed out, was to prevent 'the display of material which is blasphemous, or is likely to cause inter-racial feeling, or to encourage crime or juvenile delinquency or to undermine morality'[27]. In colonies such as Kenya and Northern Rhodesia, with a relatively large white population, segregated viewing and discriminatory censorship, censorship boards demonstrated a particular concern for the 'black peril' – assiduously censoring films which showed white women behaving seductively, for fear, it would seem, of arousing the black male.[28]

In the campaign to project a favourable image of Britain as a colonial power, the Colonial Office, dissatisfied with the documentary approach of *Men of Africa*, decided to commission a full-length feature film *Men of Two Worlds* (1946), which went into production in 1943. This Two Cities film, described by its director, Thorold Dickinson, as 'an intimate dramatic study of the two races working side by side',[29] is the story of the return of a celebrated African pianist to Tanganyika to teach in his home area. An outbreak of sleeping sickness occurs and the district officer orders the resiting of the village; the witch-doctor leads the local resistance and a battle of wills follows between the witch-doctor and the teacher, but the real hero is the district officer, who exhorts the teacher to stand fast. Some educated Africans found this simplistic theme 'offensive', with its 'conventional conflict between the familiar caricature of traditional Africa and the new era – claiming to be progressive – ushered in by a colonial power'.[30]

After the war, when the Central Office of Information (COI) replaced the MOI, the CFU became a department of the COI, under the administrative control of the Controller of the Films Division. The COI had no policy-making power; it was simply an agency whose function was to supply technical advice and facilities to ministerial departments. Production policy rested with the Colonial Office. During the war the CFU had been financed by imperial funds, but after the war, as its main function was now the production of instructional films, it was thought more appropriate for the unit to be financed under the Colonial Development and Welfare Act (1945) – with the exception of 'projection-of-England' films. An allocation of £250,000 was made in 1947, which financed the CFU until it was disbanded in 1955.[31]

The main objective of the post-war CFU was the promotion of film production in the colonies, whose governments, it was hoped, would ultimately assume full financial and administrative responsibility for the work in their territories. In working towards this local take-over emphasis was placed on decentralization and Africanization. As George Pearson told the British Film Institute Conference on 'The Film in Colonial Development' in 1948, the aim of the CFU was to produce 'films *for* Africans, *with* Africans, *by* Africans'.[32]

There were thus regional differences in the implementation of this policy in Africa, and the CFU did not operate in Central Africa where the Central African Film Unit was established in 1948 to serve Northern Rhodesia, Southern Rhodesia and Nyasaland. Between 1945 and 1950 the CFU had twelve production units in eight countries in East and West Africa. The units were to make films on subjects suggested by local governments, to train local people and to stimulate local film production. Some of the films of this period were *Towards True Democracy* (1947), *Village Development* (d. Lionel Snazelle, 1948), *Better Homes* (1948) and *Mixed Farming* (d. Snazelle, 1948), *Animal Manure* (d. Rollo Gamble, 1950). The training of local film technicians in West Africa was by means of a film school held in Accra in 1948. Africans trained here joined the Gold Coast Unit set up in 1949 and the Federal Film Unit established in Nigeria in 1950. In East Africa a different policy was followed. Africans were attached to the CFU units, but the European film-makers tended to be so occupied with film production that training was neglected.[33] East African government officials found the system of dual control by the COI and the Colonial Office by which the CFU was administered thoroughly unsatisfactory and insisted that if the CFU were to operate effectively in East Africa the Colonial Office should assume sole control of it. This change was effected in 1950. Dissatisfaction had arisen because of the administrative inefficiency of the dual control system and because the COI personnel were thought to be too remote from colonial problems[34] – a criticism with which John Grierson at the COI concurred.[35]

Another change in policy that occurred in 1950 was the decision of the CFU to cease its own film production. All the CFU units were withdrawn from Africa and the CFU then concentrated on providing technical and advisory services for the local colonial film units which were now established in some colonies; it continued to publish *Colonial Cinema* and to implement the Raw Stock Scheme, which provided newsreels and magazine films for colonies like Somaliland, Sierra Leone and the Gambia, which were too small to have their own film units. Begun as a matter of wartime expediency, the Raw Stock Scheme came to be regarded as one of the most successful aspects of the CFU's work; as C. Y. Carstairs, the Director of the Colonial Office information department, told a conference on the documentary film in 1952, 'So great is the relative importance of local content, as compared with technique, that such films are still generally regarded as the biggest "draw" and constitute the sugar that coats the pill of better drains, maternity centres and all the rest.'[36] (This conclusion would seem to justify Latham's defence of the BEKE.)

Some evidence of the effect of instructional films on rural African audiences is available for the post-war period. In Nigeria a cinema officer interested in the possibilities of the cinema in mass education tested the impact of a number of films, including two made by the CFU in West Africa soon after the war: *Weaving in Togoland* (d. P. Sargeant, 1946) and *Good Business* (which dealt with cocoa marketing co-operatives in Nigeria, d. Snazelle, 1947). He found that neither film was entirely successful in getting across its central theme of co-operative effort. He had high praise, however, for a film made by the Northern Rhodesian Information Office, *On Patrol* (d. Louis Nell, released under the CFU label in 1945), about the tracking down of a bicycle thief, which featured an exciting bicycle chase as its finale.[37] In Northern Rhodesia, by contrast, *Machi Gaba* (the village that crept ahead), one of Sellers's pre-war Nigerian films exhibited under the CFU label, proved ineffectual because the Northern Rhodesian African found the 'Mohammedan dress amusing and instead of being taught that clean village life makes for healthier living, he is left with the idea that Nigerians are funny people'.[38]

Films were an expensive means of mass education, and both the Treasury and the CFU were anxious to find out how effective they were, particularly in rural areas. In 1952 an experiment financed by the Colonial Development and Welfare Fund was conducted in rural Nigeria, the team being led by two Europeans – a former CFU film-maker and an anthropologist. Africans participated as commentators and projectionists. The principal finding was that films with a familiar background had a greater impact on the audiences, who quickly adapted to the cinema and remembered a significant amount of what they saw; but neither understanding nor familiarity was sufficient to get them to alter their behaviour. 'The response in action to the films,' wrote the anthropologist, P. Morton Williams, 'is disappointing.'[39] He concluded that films could only alter behaviour if they worked upon 'the established interests of the people', a conclusion that had already been reached by American theorists in mass communications.[40]

When the CFU was disbanded in 1955, with 280 short films to its credit, many of its agency services were taken over by a newly formed commercial organization located in London: the Overseas Film and Television Centre, run by some ex-members of the CFU. Sellers remained at the Colonial Office as Adviser on Overseas Film Production. In 1958 he told a conference in Brussels on the cinema in Africa south of the Sahara that films were more likely to be effective if they were made 'entirely by Africans'. Although the CFU films had been 'technically' and 'pictorially' of high quality, many had aroused 'little emotional interest in the minds of illiterate rural audiences', which he attributed to the fact that European film-makers did not have sufficient understanding of the customs and culture of the people for whom they had made the films.[41]

Several of the films used in the Nigerian experiment were made by the recently formed Gold Coast and Nigerian film units – evidence that the CFU's policy of encouraging local production had achieved some success, particularly in West Africa. (Outside Africa units were established in Malaya and the West Indies.) There was some degree of Africanization in these units in that Africans were employed as film technicians, but the units continued to be run by Europeans; it was not until 1965, for example, that a production of the Federal Film Unit was handled entirely by Nigerians.[42] Kenya had a film unit attached to its information office during the war and when the CFU withdrew its units from East Africa this was re-established. It did make some instructional films for Africans, but with the onset of the Mau Mau emergency in 1952 its main concern came to be propaganda films.[43] Some instructional films were made by government officials in Tanganyika and Uganda and in 1960 Colonial Development and Welfare funds were provided to set up a full-scale unit in Tanganyika.

In 1951 Tanganyika started an interesting experiment in the production of locally made entertainment films in Swahili, produced by a South African firm and sponsored by the governor, Sir Edward Twining. The experiment lasted two-and-a-half years.[44] The Colonial Office had frequently expressed an interest in the idea of government-sponsored feature films for Africans, partly because of its concern about the influence of Hollywood and partly because it was felt that Africans would appreciate films based on their own experiences. *Mass Education in African Society* had endorsed the idea. The BEKE had produced a few entertainment films, as had East Africa Command, the CAFU and the Gold Coast Film Unit. Entertainment was a strong ingredient in many instructional films, since it was believed that the propaganda would be more effective if the audiences were emotionally involved. But despite this interest and Sir Edward Twining's hopes, lack of finance prevented a government-sponsored entertainment film industry from developing in Africa. Film production was a costly business, so that, if money was available, priority was given to instructional films, newsreels and political propaganda films; and so Hollywood continued to dominate the commercial cinema circuits.

In 1948 the Central African Council, an inter-territorial body which linked the two Rhodesias and Nyasaland together before federation, had set up the Central African Film Unit with the primary aim of producing films to assist in African development. Until 1956 it was partly financed from Colonial Development and Welfare funds, the rest of the support coming from the territorial governments. The idea of the CAFU had been enthusiastically promoted by Harry Franklin, Director of the Northern Rhodesian Information Department, who had a special interest in the use of radio and films in mass education.[45] The CAFU had considerable success with its instructional films, many of which were in story form; government officials testified to the 'direct and startling' results that their showing often produced.[46] But when the Federation of Rhodesia and Nyasaland was established in 1953 the CAFU became a part of the Federal Department of Information and the making of development films was pushed into the background as the federal CAFU concentrated on making propaganda films and newsreels to win the Federation a respectable image overseas, to try and overcome African hostility and to encourage trade, immigration and tourism.

Another strand of British colonial film policy was concerned to project Britain to the colonies. As they moved towards post-war independence the aim of propaganda was now to ensure that the colonies stayed within the Commonwealth; they had to be persuaded that 'the western democratic way of life has more to offer than communism'.[47] In this campaign the weekly newsreel *British News* was considered invaluable and items were selected for 'their informational, prestige and trade promotional value';[48] items from colonial film units were also featured in order to strengthen the 'family' ties of the Commonwealth. A classic film of the 'English-way-of-life' genre was *Mr English at Home* (d. Gordon Hales, 1940), which showed, for African emulation, a day in the life of a carpenter and his family. Others which the Colonial Office joined the Foreign Office and the Commonwealth Relations Office in sponsoring were *An English Farm* (1954), *The Schoolmaster* (1954), *The Engineer* (1954) and *An English Village* (1957). The linchpin in this empire-strengthening propaganda exercise was the royalty film; a number were commissioned specially by the Colonial Office and the local colonial film units co-operated in the lavish coverage of the numerous royal tours.

After the war, as criticism of the Empire grew to a crescendo, the British government propagandists again employed the film in defence of their imperial stewardship. The chief effort was put into the £30,000 dramatized documentary, *Daybreak in Udi* (d. Terry Bishop, 1948), which was produced by the Crown Film Unit to demonstrate the progress being made in community development work[49] in the Udi division of Nigeria. It had the by now familiar scenario of the witch-doctor resisting progress, this time the building of a maternity centre initiated by progressive Africans, although the real hero is the fatherly colonial civil servant. The reviewer in *Corona* commented that 'without Mr Chadwick, one feels, nothing would have happened and the communal effort would fall off as soon as he left'.[50] *Daybreak in Udi* got maximum international publicity, as it was awarded the 1948 Academy Award for a documentary film and a British award for documentary film in 1949. The colonial film units themselves supplied much material for this Empire publicity campaign, which was used on BBC television and in commercial newsreels in Britain and from there was passed on to American and European commercial newsreel and television networks. The Colonial Office also encouraged film companies to make documentaries about the colonies and African features appeared in J. Arthur Rank's *This Modern Age* series – a more propagandistic adventure in screen journalism than the American original, *The March of Time*.[51]

In weighing the successes and failure of British colonial film policy it can be said that its practical application demonstrated that films could be used with some success in the education of illiterate peoples, but that it took an unconscionably long time to find out what were the most effective techniques because of the lack of continuity in policy. The BEKE and its methods were abandoned after two years, although the directors had probably hit upon the ideal formula of having the film-makers actually showing the films in order to get a rapid response. It took the CFU eleven years to mount an experiment in the impact of instructional films at a time when, in any case, it had ceased producing its own films. Furthermore, the Nigerian experiment in emphasizing variables like audience predisposition, self-selection, and selective perception which were culturally governed, seems to have had a sobering effect on the great expectations about the possibilities of film in colonial development.

The role of films in promoting development was further limited by the problem of distribution. Even in the most fortunate areas, villagers could not expect a visit from a cinema van more than two or three times in a year; according to a UNESCO survey reported in 1961, the average for the whole continent was once a year.[52] In an attempt to overcome the distribution problem the Colonial Office began to place more emphasis on the building of static cinemas in the villages, but this strategy seems to have had little overall effect. In post-war colonial policy broadcasting emerged as the more favoured channel for promoting colonial development. This can be seen from the relative size of allocations under the Colonial Development and Welfare Vote: for example, £250,000 for the CFU, £143,000 for the CAFU, but an initial £1,000,000 for the development of broadcasting, with an additional £250,000 voted in 1952.[53] The radio could reach more people than the film.

British and other colonial instructional films have come under some fire for their paternalism;[54] as in the feature films, there is often a European district officer, agricultural demonstrator or other authoritarian figure in the background, channelling African initiative. Some paternalism is inevitable in any didactic film – but never more so than in a colonial instructional film, reflecting as it does the political and social structure of colonial society. The only real solution to the dilemma of paternalism was for the Africans to make the films themselves. The CFU's Africanization policy was a step in this direction, but it was slow in implementation as no local film units had been completely Africanized by the time of independence. The CAFU was a different case. It did not pursue a policy of Africanization, and while it made some, in many ways admirable, instructional films, during the lifetime of the Federation of Rhodesia and Nyasaland it made crude propaganda films of the type of *Men of Africa* in support of the white-settler-controlled government.

In considering the contribution to political education made by colonial film policy it could perhaps be said that films did contribute (together with broadcasting, communications and migrant labour) in a small way to the breaking down of rural isolation, giving African peoples a sense of belonging to a wider territorial unit – but one has to be very tentative here, remembering the infrequency of cinema van shows in many areas. British colonial film policy may have made some contribution to the successful promotion of the idea of the Commonwealth, but there were, of course, other weapons in this discreet ideological arsenal, like the BBC and the British Council, as well as all kinds of other more tangible neo-colonial strings.

The 'Apologia for Empire' films cannot be said to have been a great success, as not only did the target audience, the Empire's critics in Europe, Britain and America, refuse to be disarmed, but the films antagonized educated Africans, who strongly objected to the heavy propaganda content of these and other British films about the Empire. In post-war Africa, when nationalist movements were agitating for independence, such films seem to have made some contribution to the anti-imperial mood. When the Crown Film Unit arrived in Nigeria for the filming of *Daybreak in Udi* in 1948, it was denounced by the nationalist press as 'yet another film unit come out to our country to depict us as naked savages and unfit to rule ourselves'.[55] The Colonial Office might tailor its film policy to suit different audiences but, unlike the policy, the audiences could not be kept in watertight compartments.

British Film Censorship and Propaganda Policy during the Second World War

Nicholas Pronay and Jeremy Croft

. . . film propaganda will be most effective when it is least recognizable as such. Only in a few rare prestige films, reassurance films and documentaries should the government's participation be announced. The influence brought to bear by the Ministry on the producers of feature films, and encouragement given to foreign distributors, must be kept secret. This is particularly true of any films which it is hoped to distribute in America and other neutral countries. . . .

Ministry of Information, *Programme for Film Propaganda* (1939)[1]

Contrary to some comfortable assumptions generally held, and which are implied here by placing film censorship in the context of the wartime history of the mass media in Britain, the cinema had in fact been under extensive political censorship long before the Second World War. No legislation to this effect had ever been passed by parliament – although the establishment of a State Censorship Board had been discussed in the Commons and rejected only because the existing extra-legal arrangements were felt to be working more effectively – nevertheless, the Home Office supervised and enforced a close system of censorship upon films exhibited in the public cinemas of Britain: a system which had been developing step by step since 1912.[2] It was run by the British Board of Film Censors. The BBFC was financed by the fees paid by those aspiring to obtain the 'Certificate' of the Board, thus in effect by the film trade itself, which obviated the need for public funds to be expended upon censorship; but its president was appointed by the Home Secretary. Theoretically, the Board's certificate only served the purpose of advising local authorities, which actually possessed the power to permit or ban the exhibition of a film in the cinemas of their district, as to the suitability of the film concerned. In practice, after a few, although much publicized, assertions of independence by some local authorities during the 1920s, the Home Office had succeeded in inducing all of them to require the possession of a BBFC Certificate as a precondition of exhibition. At the same time, the Cinematograph Exhibitors Association – that is, the 'film distributors' – made it a condition of membership that only BBFC certificated films should be handled. By 1931, therefore, the position was quite simple. There was no obligation on any film-*maker* to submit his production to censorship. He was free to *make* films about anything he wished and in any way he chose. But, if he desired to have his films shown to the great public in the cinemas, and to make a living from them, he first had to obtain the approval of the British Board of Film Censors.

The BBFC did not judge films on their merits as films, only on their 'suitability' to be exhibited to the public at large. The BBFC made no bones whatever about the fact that they regarded the political suitability of film as a major consideration. The list of the grounds on which a film would be refused a Certificate of Exhibition, and which by the 1930s ran to over ninety items, was organized in nine standard categories: (1) Religious; (2) Political; (3) Military; (4) Administration of Justice; (5) Social; (6) Questions of Sex; (7) Crime; (8) Cruelty; (9) Sound.[3]

Although it was chiefly the judgements on the 'social' grounds (that is, grounds of decorum), or on 'questions of sex', which tended to become famous – being often irresistibly quotable – the BBFC's main task was to control the power of the cinema to affect the political outlook of uneducated people, especially those who went to the cinema regularly in the 1930s: the urban working class. The Presidents of the Board appointed by the Home Secretary were not sociologists, educationalists or clergymen (as was the case with the genuinely 'morality' oriented Hays' Office of Hollywood) but men like Edward Shortt, PC (1929–35), Chief Secretary for Ireland in the Sinn Fein period and subsequently Home Secretary, and Lord Tyrell (1935–47), who rose from head of the Political Intelligence Department to Permanent Under-Secretary of State at the Foreign Office.[4] The actual film examiners in 1939 were Colonel J. C. Hannah, Lieutenant-Colonel A. Fleetwood-Wilson, Major R. H. W. Baker and Mrs N. Crouzet.[5] Colonel Hannah, the chief examiner and later vice-president, came to the BBFC in 1922 upon retiring from the Army as Deputy Chief of Intelligence in Ireland since 1918. The administrative head of the BBFC was J. Brooke-Wilkinson, who had been in charge of Film Propaganda to Neutral Nations during the First World War.

Until the late 1920s the BBFC confined its control of what the general public should be allowed to see in the cinemas to the examination of finished films, upon which it pronounced a general verdict, or in which it required certain 'cuts' to be made. From about 1932 the BBFC moved from post-censorship to pre-censorship; it 'encouraged' producers to submit to the BBFC first the outline scripts which they were considering for production for general 'advice', followed by submission of the full script, drawn up in the light of that advice, for detailed comment and amendments, prior to the commencement of actual production. By the mid-1930s this system, although it involved a truly amazing departure from the principles of free expression in a parliamentary democracy, came to be quietly and generally accepted by the film world in Britain; it was much cheaper to have your script amended or rejected than having to reshoot or, worse, having your investment denied exhibition altogether. Since much the same applied to the financial prospects of any foreign film for which distribution in Britain was sought, the habit of submitting scripts which appeared likely to raise problems, when they were considered in the light of BBFC's lists of 'objections', had also come largely to be acquired by the major Hollywood studios.

There was no need, therefore, to create a film censorship machinery when war came. Nor was it necessary to face agonised debates over the limits to which control of this medium was necessary, even in wartime, or to expect a running battle with film-makers accustomed to freedom, as was the case with the press and journalists. Film producers were entirely accustomed to working under conditions of practically total censorship and the war made little difference. Thus, when in October 1939 the pre-war planning arrangements were reviewed and finalized it was decided that 'films to which exception might be taken on the ground that they contained harmful propaganda' should be left to be suppressed under the existing censorship powers of the BBFC.[6] All that was necessary was, firstly, to close the loopholes which had deliberately been left open before the war for films which would only be shown to an intellectual minority behind the closed doors of cinema societies and the like, and, secondly, to introduce some new categories relating to the military security needs of wartime.

The most important loophole concerned the newsreels. After some hesitation it was decided at the end of the First World War that newsreels were not to be subjected to the scrutiny of the BBFC. To do so would have raised questions of press freedom and it would have required a huge machinery actually to be able to censor newsreels working to tight twice-weekly deadlines. Not that the newsreels in the 1930s actually enjoyed much of the principal freedom of the press – namely, to make life tough for the government. It was made painfully clear to their makers, as soon as the arrival of sound enabled them to make articulate political statements, that they were only free from formal censorship so long as they did not disregard such wishes of the Home Office, the Foreign Office or even the Conservative Central Office (under the National Government) as were conveyed to them, usually through the mouth of the Commissioner of the Metropolitan Police. Since legally they were obliged to obtain police permits to film in any public place, without which any newsreel company would have been instantly out of business, and since Lord Trenchard, as Commissioner, demonstrated in 1932 that he was quite willing to use his powers when Paramount News defied the order against filming the hunger march, the newreels had operated at best in a condition of guided freedom in peacetime.[7]

This was, however, more than wartime needs could allow, although initially it had been the intention that editorial control should be left with the newsreels, while the BBFC, reinforced with security censors supplied by the three armed services and with more staff, should check the footage proposed to be used in the newsreels for any *pictures* which might reveal secret military hardware or imperil security in other ways. It was thought that the BBFC could discharge this additional function because the bulk of the actual, military, footage in which such items were most likely to appear would in fact be supplied by the War Office itself, reviving the First World War system of 'official War Office cinematographers'. Within six months of the outbreak of war this system was recognized as unworkable. The War Office could not supply either the quantity or the quality of footage required, while the BBFC and its personnel could not supply the necessary balance between the needs of withholding from the enemy pictures of secret equipment and yet showing the British people and the world plenty of encouraging footage about how well prepared and powerful our forces were. It also came to be realized that insufficient thought had been given to the fact that war makes both the visual and

the audible presentation of 'news' especially important. The control
of what is being said and *how* it is being said is of vital importance in
the heightened, anxious, highly emotional atmosphere of wartime:
newsreel 'commentaries' could not be left uncontrolled, even if their
factual content had already been vetted through the normal operations of censorship. For newsreels do not communicate either by
pictures or by words in isolation from each other. Early attempts to try
and locate the control of words in the Films Division and of pictures in
the BBFC, or later in the Photographic Section of the Press and
Censorship Bureau, proved therefore unworkable also.[8]

The eventual solution, arrived at just in time for the Blitz but not
completely refined until 1941, was to give up the attempt to
distinguish between 'security censorship' and 'propaganda' and vest
the control of newsreels, as an integrated medium of communications,
in the Press and Censorship Division itself. A liaison officer (Captain
Donald Anderson) was appointed to maintain prior contact between
the newsreels and the Films Division: 'To convey our Do's and
Dont's to the newsreel companies', as Jack Beddington of the Films
Division put it.[9] The modus operandi of control/censorship in respect
of the newsreels for the rest of the war was summed up, although
minor modifications were still to be made later, in Director's Order S
13 issued in July 1941: (1) 'one or more censors' to go to the offices of
each company and there to view 'all pictorial material proposed to be
included in the newsreel'; (2) 'commentaries proposed to be given
with the newsreel must be submitted in writing, but if pressure of
time does not permit that, they should be dictated over the telephone
to a typist in the Censor's Office'; (3) 'between ten and eleven in the
morning on each Monday and Thursday the completed newsreels are
to be brought to Malet Street and there submitted to final Scrutiny
Viewing'. Further alterations might still be ordered. The order also
spelled it out specifically: 'The translation as far as practicable of the
Minister of Information's wishes in regard to propaganda into terms
of moving pictures and commentaries is to be regarded as a proper
part of the censor's duties.'[10]

The degree of sophistication with which the task of 'translating'
propaganda policy into the medium of news film was carried out may
be judged from the instructions which were given by the chief censor
to Commander Christopher Powell, of Photographic and Film
Censorship, at the height of the Blitz on 13 September 1940. Each
panning shot 'must start from an undamaged building and must

conclude on an undamaged building and it must not linger over damaged buildings'.[11] Christopher Powell had recently joined the department and such instructions were part of his training; as the war progressed, the censors came to know about the medium of film, the newsreel producers learned to work with them closely and such instructions became unnecessary. Newsreel men knew as well as the censors, or better, how to 'translate' propaganda policy into a usually effective, sometimes moving, occasionally powerful and, as far as possible, unobvious form for instilling the desired impressions into the minds of the viewers.

Far less important, in practical terms, was the second loophole, which was also to be closed in September 1939: the right to film entirely freely, as distinct from the right to exhibit the results. The Control of Photography Regulation, which was issued soon after the outbreak of war, made it an offence to take photographs of certain specified objects without a permit issued by the MOI. As Admiral G. P. Thompson, the Chief Censor, put it, 'The list covered practically everything which had war interest.'[12] A permit to film, the so-called 'red permit', was issued on the understanding that the resulting photograph (still or moving) would be submitted to censorship, and a record of the permit kept. As far as the film industry proper was concerned, there was not in fact much 'restriction of liberty' involved, for, as we have seen, film-makers had to have police permits for filming in any public place long before the war. Similarly closed was the minor loophole which permitted uncensored films to be shown to non-theatrical audiences such as cinema societies: all films had to be submitted to censorship.

The constitutional loophole which, more in theory than in practice, had allowed local authorities to ignore the refusal of the Board to 'grant a Certificate' to a film and to permit it to be exhibited under a local licence, in the name of the principle of municipal freedom, was effectively closed by making distributors liable for the exhibition of any film without a Certificate of Clearance. The attempt by some local authorities to salvage a measure of their legal status by asking if they could at least be represented on the Board was refused.[13]

Finally, a more significant extension of the theoretical basis of censorship was brought about by the necessity of subjecting to the BBFC all films destined to be exported – that is to be exhibited to people other than the British public. In practice, thereafter, a triple control was operated over the export of films: the BBFC viewed the film for security considerations and sealed the can containing it; the MoI Films Division certified that the film was or was not fit to be sent abroad; and the Board of Trade had to grant an export licence to the celluloid, which was classified as a strategic war material.

The machinery for censorship, and the extent of its powers to control feature films, both home-produced and imported thus changed little in wartime from what they had been before the war. The only criteria added to the list of those which decided what could not be shown – the considerations of military security – came in fact to contribute only an additional nine to the ninety-eight rules already in operation before the war. After some initial misunderstandings producers were eventually told either to avoid altogether, or to make sure that they thoroughly discussed with the authorities, any proposed scenarios concerning subjects which related to: (a) spies and counter-espionage, (b) delayed action bombs, (c) bomb disposal incidents, (d) parachute mines, (e) escape of serving personnel from enemy occupied territory, (f) treatment of prisoners of war, (g) use of gas, (h) parachutists, (i) commando raids (except as approved by censorship), (j) secret equipment'.[14]

More significant was the *relaxation* of some of the rules enforced before the war. The total ban on the use of 'relations between capital and labour' as the 'principal theme' of a film, or on the incidental portrayal of any manifestation of it in a film (such as a strike or the despair of unemployment) – the rule which more than anything else summed up the nature of film censorship between the wars – was significantly relaxed. Walter Greenwood's famous novel *Love on the Dole*, for example, was twice submitted to the BBFC, by two different companies, in 1936. It was rejected both times with the final comment, 'Even if the book is well reviewed and the stage play had a successful run, I think this subject as it stands would be undesirable as a film'.[15] In 1940 it was allowed, and in a form much stronger than the authors of the original scenarios had dared to suggest in 1936. The rule which banned 'the presentation of British officers and forces in disgraceful, reprehensible or equivocal light' was relaxed to allow a much more realistic treatment of the Army. *Waterloo Road*, in which going absent without leave to deal with marital problems was sympathetically treated, or *Next of Kin*, in which the guilty party was a drunken and indiscreet RAF officer, and many other films, would have been impossible to show publicly in peacetime. More fundamentally, the need, now, to mobilize people's minds, to politicize ordinary people, rather than dull them into passivity, caused the ban on the challenging treatment of matters of current foreign policy to be lifted. Thus the banning of any film which could lead to doubting the wisdom of the foreign policy of the government, whether towards Nazi Germany or any other country, the encouragement to leave all such matters to Mr Baldwin or Mr Chamberlain, and consequently any ban on portraying the internal affairs of a foreign country in any way which might make people feel involved, gave way to powerful arguments and powerful propaganda about the nature of Nazi government. *Pastor Hall*, a scenario for a film about the brutal persecution of a clergyman with a strong Christian conscience (in fact, a fictionalized story of Pastor Niemoller) was rejected in 1939 on the grounds that 'Its exhibition at the present time would be in-expedient'.[16] The same scenario was approved once war broke out and released in May 1940, less than a year after its first rejection. The powerful genre of 'docu-drama' – impersonations of actual persons and re-enactments of actual events, with or without a fictional element, perhaps the most politically stirring form of film or television – had been totally banned before the war under the rule, 'No representations of living persons', a rule which could not be circumvented by transparently fictitious names either. This too was now relaxed. Colonel Hannah announced in October 1939, 'During wartime our rule against the representation of living persons does not extend to enemy aliens.'[17]

The spate of films, which impersonated the Nazi leadership, warmly encouraged by the MoI Films Division, also released a genie from the bottle, as the experienced censors of the BBFC knew very well. The American film *Mission to Moscow* soon presented the inevitable dilemma: should Marshal Stalin's views of our statesmen of the 1930s be allowed to be expressed thus in an American film about the pre-war activities of their own envoy to the USSR?[18] It was allowed. *Mission to Moscow*, containing as it did a discussion of a semi-current political issue – namely, who *were* the 'guilty men' – provides a perfect illustration of just the sort of 'burning question of the day' which Lord Tyrell, in 1937, had been so proud to keep out of the 'public cinemas of this country' – and with which the relaxation of censorship in wartime allowed film-makers, for the first time, to enrich, or inflame, the fare of the cinema-going public. All this was in addition to the extension of the limits on realism as far as the portrayal of violence, brutality or 'salty' language was concerned which was permitted in response to the effect of war on public taste. Taken altogether, there can be little doubt that censorship during the Second World War had a far less inhibiting effect upon film-makers – especially those with aspirations to use the medium for purposes more ambitious than those of straight entertainment – than had been the case in peacetime.

It would, however, be misleading to leave it at that. Censorship before the war was indeed far-reaching, comprehensive and systematic and it imposed strict limitations upon what film-makers could show or tell the public through the potentially inspiring, inflammatory and powerful medium of the cinema. But it was essentially a negative control – and with well-defined 'Don'ts'. As long as film-makers avoided all the subjects proscribed by the ninety-eight rules and Colonel Hannah could use his strongest term of approval – 'harmless' – they were free to make films about whatever they wished. The cinema before 1939 had been censored, limited, neutered, but it was not directed, at least as far as feature films were concerned. It was here that a significant change for the worse *was* brought about by the war. Although, constitutionally, the Films Division had no formal powers to do more than commission, sponsor or produce its own 'information' films, to co-ordinate the information film work of other government departments and to supervise the censorship of all films, it nevertheless came also to exercise an almost complete direction over commercial film production.

From the early part of 1940 the Board of Trade agreed to consult the Films Division before allocating film stock, a strategic material, to film companies. It was clearly understood – indeed, stated in the course of the negotiations formalizing the arrangement – that it was unconstitutional to use the powers for the allocation of war materials for such purposes. Nevertheless, it was decided to take a robust view of the matter, especially after Hugh Dalton, fresh from the experience of being a partner in controlling Special Operations, including Political Warfare ('ungentlemanly warfare', as Churchill called it), took over the Board of Trade in February 1942. In deciding on an application for film stock, the Board of Trade required the submission of the proposed scenario and then acted upon the recommendations of the Films Division relating to it.[19] Production companies soon learned that the only way to obtain film stock was to submit their ideas to the Films Division in the first place, and also to engage a script consultant, or even a script writer, appointed by the Films Division.

Studio personnel, directors and actors were all in short supply owing to conscription – most of them were assigned to man the Crown Film Unit or the Army/Air Force/Navy Film Units, or to work in troop entertainment, release from the forces being in the gift of the Films Division. The Films Division also decided, as far as it wished to do in each case, who the director of a film would be and even the casting. Finally, the powers of the Board of Trade also extended to film stock required for the re-release of pre-war, previously approved films, as well as to the general importation of films for which it required the production of general import licences, owing to the problems of shipping space faced by an island at war. Although these powers were to be used with extreme care, because of the need to remain on good terms with Hollywood, they were known to be there. On at least one occasion they were actually used to cancel the exhibition licence of *Tobacco Road* (by the distributor who held the rights) after both the Films Division and the producer, Twentieth Century Fox, had agreed that it would be 'contrary to public interest' if the public were to be reminded of it again.[20]

The control by the MOI Films Division of the content, style and message of films was exercised in the British manner, more often over dinner tables than across desks, and it took some time to be perfected. Moreover, it was operated by people who not only had definite ideas about the need to control in depth the way the cinema mediated reality for the people in political terms, but also an intellectual belief in the need to raise the people's cultural and intellectual level. The policy of making resources available only for films impregnated with propaganda messages went hand in hand with one of favouring film-makers of quality and of encouraging studios to make films with culture rather than entertainment written all over them – above all, films which had a 'progressive cast' – 'culture' and 'progressiveness' being interchangeable terms in the minds of the intellectual elite. No doubt, as Thorold Dickinson wrote, under the 'benevolent despotism'[21] of the temporary civil servants of the Ministry of Information's Films Division, which included a glittering array of intellectuals, 'the quality of British entertainment film improved markedly'.[22] This should not, however, blind us to the fact that cultural censorship and direction are censorship and direction all the same. Cultural censorship was a net addition to the political, moral and social censorship existing before the war, and it needs to be weighed against the degree of relaxation which was allowed in these other areas.

Since 'the translation as far as practicable of the Minister of Information's wishes in regard to propaganda into terms of moving pictures' became, after 1942, the operating principle and practice for everybody in the films business, debate and conflict over censorship moved from the level of producers versus the censors of pre-war days to that of the Films Division versus other government agencies, or the MOI versus other ministries or the Prime Minister himself. 'Censorship', in the sense of the popular understanding of the word as meaning 'official or political interference' undertaken to suppress films – a mode of thinking based on assumptions about the conditions of film-making in Britain which, as we have seen, were very far from the actual reality either before or during the war – arose only as the result of disagreement between the more sophisticated propaganda experts of the MOI and (in this field) the less sophisticated officials or politicians outside it. The largest number of films actually suppressed – that is, after production had started, or a script had been completed and resources had been commited to the film – were in fact those included in the MOI's own internal film production programme. Between April 1942 and December 1944 a total of ninety-six 'official' MOI films were abandoned after financial authority to proceed had been granted. Many of these were, of course, abandoned because events overtook them, but thirteen were withdrawn because some government department demanded this. *The Battle of Steel*, a major semi-documentary project to be made by Ealing Studios for the MOI, was dropped under pressure from the Mines Department, who thought that by stressing the dangers of mining the film might discourage recruits to the industry. The policy committee of the MOI itself emasculated a Films Division 'information short' which explained the reasons for the operation of postal censorship, by ordering the cutting of the section which referred to the monitoring of telephone conversations.[23] Official interference, or censorship, of this kind was more common than political censorship deriving from differences of opinion or propaganda policy between the MOI and the government. But there were two notable examples of the latter. Pat Jackson, at the ministry's own Crown Film Unit, had spent six months on preparing a script for an official film about the Beveridge Report, which was planned by the ministry as part of a broad-ranging propaganda campaign on the projection of the aims of social reform when peacetime returned. The Home Secretary, Sir John Anderson, wrote to Bracken complaining about the general tenor of some MOI propaganda material relating to social policy: '. . . on various post-war topics extreme views seem to be catching the public imagination'; and it was thought to be high time that the balance should be redressed by gaining a hearing for more moderate and realistic views.[24] The result was that a 'blanket' was put over the Beveridge Report: the ministry's speakers were ordered not to allude to the Report and the projected film was dropped. Whether or not work on it was stopped because Pat Jackson's script itself was, as he believed, 'an exceedingly radical document indeed' or as part of a general abandonment of any MOI propaganda on the subject, is not clear. There is no doubt, however, that the MOI thought that it would be good propaganda policy to mount a campaign about post-war social reconstruction and that it was abandoned as a result of the views of others.

The case of *The Life and Death of Colonel Blimp* (1943) illustrates most clearly and fully the conflicts which could arise, by the middle years of the war, between the expert and sophisticated propaganda policies of the MOI, and the policies of the amateur propagandists outside it. It is also an illustration of Baldwin's dictum that 'propaganda work is very like anti-submarine work. It is work which is necessary, it is work as to which you cannot disclose to your adversaries how you are doing it and it is work that can be and must be judged by results.'[25] Secrecy and deception were, and are, at times, essential for its success. This was especially true of propaganda addressed to our great liberal-democratic ally, who had been badly stung when she discovered after 1918 how skilfully and effectively British propaganda had contributed to the pro-Entente alignment of the American people in the First World War. The effect of this hypersensitivity towards the possibility of any repetition of the exploits of Wellington House in the First World War led not only to legislation to try and block the infiltration of British propaganda agencies but was manifest in the fact that a major congressional investigation into pro-British propaganda through Hollywood was started in 1940 and only brought to a premature end with the Japanese attack on Pearl Harbor.[26] In the basic MOI document on film policy cited at the start of this chapter the central principle laid down in respect of propaganda towards the United States in feature films was that it should be 'least recognizable as such' and that it 'must be kept secret'. It was these two principles which charted the apparently strange course of *The Life and Death of Colonel Blimp*.

The producers and directors of the film, Michael Powell and Emeric Pressburger, had particular experience, throughout the war, of working in feature films which contained propaganda addressed at the United States: from *49th Parallel* (1941) (the first feature propaganda film sponsored – if secretly – by the MOI) to *A Matter of Life and Death* (1946) (the last MOI feature propaganda film of the war), made to the brief, 'Well, the war's nearly over, boys, but it's just starting from our point of view. We think you should make a film about Anglo-American relations, because they are deteriorating.'[27] In 1942, when, as the consequence of the 'Hitler first' decision, it was planned that American ground and air forces were to come to Britain, and to British-commanded theatres of war, to fight alongside the British, American attitudes towards their British ally in the field became a matter of top priority for the MOI and British propaganda policy. In this, of course, film propaganda had to play its part, leading to the production of both 'official' MOI films such as *Welcome to Britain* (1943) and 'unofficial' (that is, 'secret'), feature film propaganda. Whether the actual idea of what form that feature film propaganda should take came from Powell and Pressburger (as was the case with *49th Parallel*) or the other way round (as was the case with *A Matter of Life and Death*) we do not know. The film proposed was to show to the Americans, whose soldiers were to come over in large numbers, that the British Army had shed its ineffective, upper-class, 'Blimp' officer attitudes, that it had become essentially a 'democratic' citizen army and that it had also acquired the necessary mental attitudes to become an efficient, tough fighting force, capable of matching the professionalism of the Germans.

The film was designed, in other words, to tackle the existing stereotypes of the stuffy, undemocratic 'red-coats' image of the British Army which existed in North American perceptions, and to show that, while there had been some grounds for believing in the existence of these stereotypes in the past, a new generation had changed all this in substance, even if, externally, some of the traditional forms continued. The new British Army, the new British officer, was different from the old retired types which Americans might still meet in the army clubs and officers' messes – or continued to see on their cinema screens, embodied in such ex-British officers (now Hollywood actors) as C. Aubrey Smith. To put this over to the

American soldiers who were now coming to Britain was, politically and in propaganda terms, a very important task indeed, but it was not an easy one. In the first place, the new image represented neither 'the whole truth' nor the manifest truth. Senior officers (such as Montgomery) in the British Army were still talking in an impeccably aristocratic, officer-class language, however professional, or indeed 'democratic', their attitudes in the field might have become. In the second place, any British film trying to sell this idea, however subtly and elliptically, which could in any way appear to be officially inspired or even approved, was bound to be identified as propaganda, and thus be ignored at best, or backfire at worst, in the vigorous and still relatively free world of the American media.

Camouflage was, therefore, essential. If the War Office had provided the usual 'facilities' for the production; if the MOI had released Laurence Olivier, the one British superstar recognized in America, from his well publicized job in the Fleet Air Arm, so that he could act in this film; and, indeed, if it was produced by the Rank Organization (British Films), which was recognized by Americans as being as fully integrated into the wartime scheme as MGM was in their own country, the cloven hoof would obviously have protruded and negated the purpose of the exercise. The first puzzling feature of the much described production history of this film thus becomes clearer – namely, how could a film which was so widely known to have been 'strongly opposed' by the MOI, even to the extent of their refusing Laurence Olivier's release, and to which the War Office had refused service facilities, nevertheless receive film stock allocation? Nor did this seemingly disowned film receive an allocation of mere standard film stock: a newly formed production company, The Archers[28], with no apparent capital worth speaking of, for this, its very first production, pipped all the major British studios to the post and secured an allocation of that rarest and most rationed commodity of all, Technicolor film stock. Moreover, it secured enough to exceed by 60 per cent the limitation on length recently clamped on all productions, even MOI official films and newsreels, because of the shortage of stock which resulted from the shipping crisis in the Atlantic.

The War Office rejected the argument that had been put to it at some earlier stage, namely that it was:

intended as a tribute to the toughness and keenness of the new Army in Britain and shows how far they have progressed from the Blimpery of the pre-war Army. From this point of view he [the producer, Powell] urges that it would be valuable propaganda for the USA and the dominions in showing that we are conscious of any faults which we may possess, while telling the rest of the world that the rest of the faults are being eliminated.[29]

The War Office had already asked the Ministry of Information to suppress the film on the grounds that 'It would give the Blimp perception of the Army officer a new lease of life at a time when it is already dying from inanition'. The War Office had manifestly read the scenario, because the Secretary of State's letter referred to the opening of the film (the famous Turkish bath scene), commenting that 'Whatever it may do elsewhere the film has made a character built up by twenty years of brilliant cartooning into a figure of fun, and there is the inescapable suggestion that such a man is a type or at any rate an example of those who have risen to high command in the Army in the period preceding the war'.[30] The Secretary of State also objected that the Germans were depicted as 'very intense realists in war. The thug element in the make up of the German soldier is ignored and indeed the suggestion is that if we were exactly like the Germans we should be better soldiers.'[31] Although the War Office had made its views clear to the MOI, the Secretary of State was writing to the Prime Minister because 'the Ministry of Information knows of no way in which it can be stopped'.[32] Churchill – acting intuitively, and more in his former capacity as a subaltern in the 4th Hussars and as a brigadier on the Western Front in 1917 than as the Prime Minister in 1942 – instantly fired off one of his famous memos to Brendan Bracken at the MOI: 'Pray propose to me the measures necessary to stop this foolish production before it gets any further. I am not prepared to allow propaganda detrimental to the morale of the Army. . . .'[33]

Here was a classic case of different viewpoints on the aims and priorities of propaganda. For *Britain*, in which David Low's Blimp cartoons had appeared for many years – and were still appearing – there was very little point indeed in making such a film. Indeed, unless handled with extreme skill and care, such a subject could easily backfire as propaganda – in *Britain*. On the other hand, while it was perfectly possible to restrict an official MOI film to 'overseas distribution only' and even specify the particular countries, if this were done in the case of an apparently 'independent' feature film it would give the game away. As a matter of fact, the MOI made an official film with precisely the purpose of demonstrating to the Americans that British officers were no longer selected from the

'Blimp' class (*Personnel Selection in the British Army – Officers*),[34] which *was* so restricted.

An unusual and lengthy correspondence ensued after Churchill's intervention, in the course of which Bracken reiterated that the MOI had no powers to stop a feature film from being made. When the Prime Minister offered an extension of the MOI's 'powers' he modestly refrained from accepting the gift, and under further pressure – contradicting himself, in fact – he offered to submit the film, when 'it had reached the "rough cut stage" ', to a team of War Office and MOI experts, promising that, should they condemn it, the film *would* 'be withdrawn'.[35] This joint group of experts, representatives of the two viewpoints, in fact saw the film and agreed that 'it was unlikely to attract much attention or to have any undesirable consequences on the discipline of the Army'.[36] As always, when faced with the weight of professional opinion, even in military matters, Churchill grudgingly gave way. He was, however, not only at heart still in the 4th Hussars, he was also an avid cinema-goer, and in his own way fancied himself as an expert on the propaganda value of feature film, opining, for example, that *Lady Hamilton* was worth four divisions. When he came to see the première of *The Life and Death of Colonel Blimp* in London the old brigadier in him was cut to the quick – or so it appears. He ordered Bracken to try by all means to stop or delay the export of the film – taking Bracken's word for it that the MOI possessed no powers to stop the export of any film. Less than five weeks after the première of the film in London, when it went on release, Beaverbrook's *Evening Standard* (the home of the Blimp cartoons) printed what it assured its readers was the 'inside story' of the *banning* of this film for export, stated that Churchill saw the film at the Odeon at Leicester Square, did not like it and 'talked to his colleagues in the Cabinet and Whitehall officials' and that then they decided to ban the film for export, *not* because of the 'picture of the British officer drawn in the film and of his extreme conservatism', but because 'a young Army officer wins a victory over Home Guard Colonel Blimp by fighting a battle some hours before the appointed zero hour. This, says Whitehall, would advertise abroad that we countenance the ethos of the Japs at Pearl Harbour! Thus are great decisions made.'[37] A month later Bracken wrote to the Prime Minister, asking him to lift 'our illegal ban . . . it is now enjoying an extensive run in the suburbs and in all sorts of places, there are notices – "See the Banned Film" '. Three weeks later, on 25 August 1943, the film was permitted to be exported. The lifting of the ban happily coincided with the conclusion of the meeting at Quebec of Churchill, Roosevelt and the Combined Chiefs of Staff, at which, among other things, it was decided to launch the first allied invasion of the mainland of Europe in Italy, and under British overall command. By this time, of course, American correspondents in London had reported on the *unsuccessful* attempt by Churchill to ban this film from being exported to America, thereby creating not only far more advance publicity and interest in it than it would have been possible to achieve by any other means, and establishing conclusively the credentials of the film as being anything but official British propaganda, but also providing a wonderful demonstration for Americans that Britain was indeed a genuine democracy, in which not even an apparently all-powerful Prime Minister such as Churchill had the power to suppress a privately made film.

It seemed a famous victory: Powell and Pressburger had defied the Ministry of Information, the War Office, the War Cabinet and Churchill himself, who could not stop the film in the end, despite all the blustering, and who had all been made to look fools. Those who win such victories normally have to pay a price. Whitehall has a notoriously long memory, and Churchill, despite his cuddly appearance and 'in victory; magnanimity' rhetoric, was a bad enemy in politics. Those who thwarted him, particularly in public, such as Lord Reith, discovered this to their cost. But this is not what happened to Powell and Pressburger. While Whitehall and the Prime Minister were still 'attempting to suppress' Colonel Blimp a scenario for their next film was approved, the stock allocation was granted – and, yes, Laurence Olivier was released to be the star.[38] Two more films followed in quick succession while the MOI still held sway and Churchill remained Prime Minister.[39] And then it was they who were invited to make the last of the propaganda films, sponsored by the MOI, and receiving the surest token of 'most favoured production': Technicolor stock. Again, this was a film for American oriented propaganda: *A Matter of Life and Death*. If it was, then, not a famous victory after all, was the whole curious process of 'the attempted suppression of the film' a fabricated story, a camouflage exercise, conducted by Bracken, in line with some similarly devious exploits of Wellington House during the First World War?

There can be no question that if the MOI and Bracken had wanted to prevent that film being made they could have done so many times over. In Powell and Pressburger's own 'famous victory' version this is admitted: 'They (unnamed MOI officials) said: "We don't think you should make this film. You can't have Laurence Olivier". "You are going to stop us making it?" "Oh no, we are not going to stop you. After all this is a democracy, but we advise you not to make it. . . ." '[40] MOI officials talking to two film-makers who had already made, secretly made, propaganda feature films for them, were hardly likely to talk like this – unless it was for public consumption. Brendan Bracken was not in the habit of writing extended memoranda to Churchill, in whose living room he habitually slept – least of all memoranda full of large rhetorical statements which he knew to be entirely untrue: 'The Ministry of Information has no power to suppress the film. We have been unsuccessful in discouraging it by the only means open to us: that is by withholding government facilities for its production.'[41] Equally untrue was his statement to the War Office that 'there was no existing defence regulation under which the film could be suppressed',[42] even if we take the charitable view that he was referring to a film already made, as distinct from his powers simply to prevent it being shot on celluloid, let alone in Technicolor. On this point Churchill's memory was correct: the Defence Regulations quite specifically stated that anything, whether newspaper, book or film, which endangered morale or discipline *could* be suppressed.[43] Indeed, the BBFC's own rules, which had been in operation for more than twenty years already ('British officers . . . shown in disgraceful, reprehensible or equivocal light . . .') would have sufficed, and, before 1939, Colonel Hannah would undoubtedly have suppressed *The Life and Death of Colonel Blimp* without a second thought. And how did the whole file containing this unparalleled record of the government being unable to have its way over a minor matter, which could have been achieved simply by those MOI officials saying 'Yes' to Powell's question, 'You are going to stop us?', a '*Secret*' file belonging to the Prime Minister's office, come to be in the hands of B. C. Sendall, Bracken's private secretary, while he and Bracken were in the United States, just at the time when the ban had been lifted on the film and the American media were buzzing with the 'banned' story about it?[44]

For a man whose dominant character trait his biographers defined as 'incurable secretiveness'[45] and who is known to have had a capacity for 'deviousness', the game that these very curious facts suggest that he was playing would not seem to have been out of character.[46] It was certainly a dangerous game to play with Churchill, but Brendan Bracken was the one man who could safely risk it: as is well known, he had a strange psychological bond with Churchill, a quasi-filial relationship, formed in the early 1930s, which continued until his own death. He also had an impish sense of humour, and detested the Colonel Blimps of this world for political as much as for personal and social reasons of his own. Did the Blimps of the War Office innocently play the part expected of them in order to provide the ideal cover for this film? Since Bracken chose to destroy all his personal papers before he died this is one of the many mysteries of his career and relationship with Churchill which will probably remain unsolved. But a clue to it may be found in yet another curious episode. Bracken's only personal confidante in the latter years of the war was Lord Beaverbrook: another man who, temperamentally and socially, loathed the Colonel Blimps (indeed, it was in Beaverbrook's newspapers that the Blimp cartoon character appeared) and who also shared with Bracken a mischievous sense of humour. As we have seen, it was in Beaverbrook's *Evening Standard* that the 'inside story' of the laughable and ineffectual attempt to suppress the film appeared on 28 June 1943. And while Churchill, the War Office and Whitehall were still apparently fuming and were ineffectively trying to prevent the export of the film in July, Beaverbrook suddenly proposed, apparently out of the blue that Bracken should be made Britain's ambassador in Washington, on the grounds that he would make a much better job of this appointment than Lord Halifax. This 'mischievous' and 'inexplicable' recommendation,[47] coming as it did from the man who was Britain's first Minister of Information in 1918, and in defending whose work Baldwin described propaganda as being 'like anti-submarine work' – the man who told the Royal Commission on the Press in 1947, 'I run my papers for the purpose of political propaganda, and no other,' and who, if anyone, knew what his friend Brendan was actually up to, came to nought however. Bracken stayed at the MOI; Powell and Pressburger continued to make films.

Propaganda, as Baldwin also said in 1918, 'can be and must be judged by results.' *The Life and Death of Colonel Blimp* (which broke box-office records in the London cinemas of Rank's Odeon circuit, while Eisenhower's huge officers' headquarters' staff were settling in there, and was also successful in the United States), and the marvellous propaganda coup of having a film showing in London at the height of the war, with posters proclaiming 'See the Banned Film' stuck up outside the cinemas – these were indeed tangible results. The story of this film is an excellent illustration of the working of the sophisticated, intelligent and highly professional system for integrating the powerful medium of film into the wartime scheme for controlling perceptions of reality. It was one in which 'film censorship'[48] of the heavy-handed, extensive, pre-war variety, played almost no role.

Rank's Attempt on the American Market, 1944–9

Robert Murphy

The question whether to produce low-budget films which would recover their costs in the home market or to make prestige productions which would attract lucrative returns from an international market troubled the British film industry from its earliest days. The wish to emulate Hollywood, where lavish productions were virtually guaranteed distribution overseas, persistently tempted British producers into straying beyond the budgetary limits which would allow them a safe return from the British box-office.

In the 1930s the international success of Alexander Korda's *The Private Life of Henry VIII* (1933) led to a spate of big-budget film production which failed dismally to bring in the eagerly anticipated rewards. In 1937 Mark Ostrer, the Chairman of the Gaumont-British Picture Corporation, which had, like Korda, embarked on a series of costly epics in an attempt to break into the American market, complained to his shareholders that the disastrous failure of their films was 'not due to any lack of merit, but to the fact that we are not accorded playing time in the most important situations, these being almost exclusively controlled by American producing interests'.[1] It was a complaint echoed by every other British producer who failed to penetrate the seemingly open American market. As Thomas Guback points out, 'The structure of the industry was based upon the mass production of films exploited profitably in company-owned theatres and block-booked into independent houses. To introduce foreign films would have meant disrupting the production-distribution-exhibition chain and voluntarily giving away a portion of the box-office to foreign producers. In monopolizing the home market, American companies were following the dictates of economic self-interest.'[2]

Nonetheless, fascinating though they are, the quality of British films of the 1930s left something to be desired and their appeal to American audiences who were accustomed to Hollywood's production values must have been limited.

The war seemed to offer hopes of greater success, for, despite the requisitioning of studios and the call-up of personnel, those films which were produced displayed a competence and maturity hitherto lacking in British cinema. In America, pro-British feelings and a slow-down of Hollywood production opened a space for a more sympathetic reception of British film. Sidney Bernstein, as representative of the Ministry of Information, was able to induce the big American companies to accept eight British feature films a year for commercial distribution, one of which, *In Which We Serve*, proving successful enough to bring in gross box-office receipts of $1.8 million. It was amid these favourable circumstances that J. Arthur Rank began his concerted drive on the American market.

Alan Wood, in his witty, intelligent biography of Rank, gives the impression that Rank blundered into film production like some benevolent but rather stupid Renaissance despot: 'It was part of Rank's simplicity that he probably never realized the enormous advantages he derived from his ignorance. Subsequently, with his usual candour, he would remark that "the trouble really was that I didn't know anything about producing films, I only took it on because there was nobody else to do the job." '[3]

In fact, Rank had been involved in commercial film production since 1934, when he helped found British National Films with the jute heiress Lady Yule. In 1935 he provided most of the financial backing for the building of Pinewood Studios. Early in 1936, in collaboration with other leading industrialists, he established the General Cinema Finance Corporation, which, buying a controlling interest in C. M. Woolf's General Film Distributors and a 25 per cent share in the American Universal Company, rapidly became a major force in the industry.

During the next few years, as British film production attempted to recover from the bout of extravagance which had followed the success of *The Private Life of Henry VIII*, Rank, with his seemingly limitless financial resources, engaged in a protracted but successful mopping-up operation. In 1937 Gaumont-British closed down its distribution company and arranged for GFD to handle its films. In 1938 Korda, no longer able to keep the wolf from the door, lost control of Denham Studios to Rank. In 1939, pre-empting the emergence of any possible rival, Rank bought up the as yet unused Elstree-Amalgamated Studios. Finally, late in 1941 he acquired the modern and profitable Odeon chain of cinemas and the ramshackle Gaumont-British organization. Rank bought these cinema chains at exactly the right time, when exhibitors were still uncertain about the effects of the Blitz and cinema shares were at their lowest ebb. In fact, attendance rose to unprecedented heights and by 1946 10s G B shares, which Rank had bought for 6s 9d five years earlier, had risen to 28s 3d, while the 5s Odeon shares, which had stood at 7s 9d in December 1941, reached a phenomenal 50s 6d.[4]

Though it was the exhibition side of his empire which brought in the profits, with the renaissance of British film-making Rank was unlikely to forget his role as a major film producer. The old Gaumont-British/Gainsborough unit functioned virtually autonomously; Pinewood Studios had been requisitioned, but Rank still owned Denham Studios. His penchant for backing promising but rather off-beat independent productions – *Pygmalion* and *Major Barbara*, Powell and Pressburger's *The 49th Parallel* – led him into involvement in Filipo del Giudice's Two Cities Films. Giudice had been responsible for producing *In Which we Serve* (which Rank had refused to back) and its phenomenal success gave Rank a touching faith in the ability of established artists to make commercially successful films. Carried along by the critical and popular enthusiasm for British films, Rank not only lent Giudice financial support, but offered his backing to prestige director/producers such as Michael Powell and Emeric Pressburger, Frank Launder and Sidney Gilliatt and the Lean/ Neame/Havelock-Allan team, who wished to establish their own production companies.

In both Britain and the United States a shortage of films and bonanza box-office profits made independent production a much less precarious proposition than it had been in the past. In indulging in the sort of lavish prestige production which resulted, Rank was being neither naive nor foolhardy, but success depended on the films being distributed in a wider market. This he set about building.

Unlike any previous British producer, Rank, with assets in excess of $200 million, had an organization as large and as powerful as the American 'Big Five'. (MGM, for example, had assets of around $190 million.) Moreover, with control over two of the three major circuits which provided the chief outlet for Hollywood films in Britain, Rank had a powerful lever with which to force the Americans into granting him a share of their home market.

The Rank organization already had close financial ties with three American companies: 20th Century Fox, United Artists and Universal. Fox had been involved in Gaumont-British since 1929, when William Fox had been duped into buying what he thought was a controlling interest in the company. Relations between Fox and Gaumont-British were stormy throughout the 1930s and it was only after Rank's take-over that a satisfactory working relationship was established. By the agreement reached with the chairman of Fox, Spyros Skouras, early in 1944, Fox representatives were to sit on the Gaumont-British board, Rank was to provide Fox with production facilities in Britain, Fox was to distribute Rank's films in the United States and the two companies were to embark on two to four big budget pictures for international distribution.[5] Little came of the joint production plans and Fox distributed only a handful of British films in America, but relations remained cordial.

United Artists had a long history of involvement in the British film industry. After the massive success of *The Private Life of Henry VIII* (1933) they had welcomed Alexander Korda as a partner, and guaranteed the distribution of his films in America. Whether because of the indifferent quality of the films themselves, the resistance of American exhibitors or the inadequacy of United Artists' sales staff, box-office results were disappointing, and after 1938 Korda made only a handful of films for United Artists' release. By 1943 he was attempting to sell his shares in the company.[6] Rank seemed the obvious replacement, but United Artists was 'coming apart at the seams' and Rank found it easier to poach the two UA representatives sent to negotiate with him (Arthur Kelly, the vice-president, in charge of foreign sales, and Theodor Carr, the managing director of UA's British branch) than to reach agreement with UA's perpetually squabbling partners.[7] In March 1944 Rank announced the formation of a world-wide distribution organization, Eagle-Lion Films Ltd, which would be headed by Carr in England and Kelly in the United States.[8]

Establishing the English branch meant merely hiving off personnel and films from GFD, but establishing a completely new distribution network in the United States, particularly at a time when manpower and building materials were in short supply, was unrealistically ambitious and plans for building or buying thirty-one film exchanges were soon dropped. It would be some time before Kelly could build an organization capable of providing proper distribution services for Rank's films. UA, though piqued at losing two of its top men, was still prepared to help. In July 1944 Gradwell Sears came to London and negotiated a deal whereby UA would handle all Rank's top-budget pictures for the next two years. Kelly was to arrange for the distribution of the lesser films through a small company called English Films and to concentrate on building up his embryo Eagle-Lion organization.[9]

Unfortunately UA proved to be a particularly unsatisfactory partner. Riddled with internal problems, the company even managed to make a loss in 1944, the year that brought in massive profits to all the other big American companies.[10] Relations rapidly deteriorated, the Americans proving inflexible and dilatory in selling Rank's films to exhibitors. Powell and Pressburger's *Colonel Blimp* was drastically cut to fit the double-feature bill, and it was only under considerable pressure that UA agreed to handle *Henry V* at all, arrogantly insisting that Shakespeare was unsuitable for the American market and that the 'road-showing' strategy[11] recommended by Rank's agents was obsolete.

In June 1945 Rank himself came to America. Immediately after arriving, he spent two hours with Nate Blumberg, the president of Universal, and though he was careful to restore amicable relations with the UA executives, before leaving on 17 July he announced that, with the exception of those films specifically committed to UA (which included the $4 million *Caesar and Cleopatra*), all Rank's quality productions would henceforth be handled by Universal.[12]

Though Rank had played no active part in the running of Universal, he was, through the General Cinema Finance Corporation, the largest single shareholder. Universal, like UA, had no affiliated theatre circuits, but Rank did have the power to reorganize the company in such a way as to make the marketing of British films a more viable operation. Shortly after the deal was announced elaborate preparations began for the birth of a new production/distribution organization, United World Pictures, which was to be set up as a $10 million company, financed 50 per cent by Rank, 50 per cent by Universal. It was to be supplied annually with eight films from Rank and eight films from International Pictures Inc., a prestigious independent production company established in 1943 by William Goetz (the former head of production of 20th Century Fox and son-in-law of Louis B. Mayer) and Leo Spitz (the former president of

RKO). Universal was to acquire a 50 per cent holding in International. UWP, which was to commence operations on 1 January 1947, would have its own sales staff and function as an autonomous company, but would use Universal office space and transport facilities.[13]

The seven films produced in International's two-year existence had proved extremely successful, with average gross receipts of $3¼ million a film.[14] The idea behind the formation of UWP was to put the International and Rank films together as a package acceptable to exhibitors. It was a shrewd idea, realistic enough to recognize the real resistance to British films and the need to use American block-booking practices to crack open a difficult market. Unfortunately it reckoned without the crusading zeal of the Department of Justice, which, in its protracted fight to enforce anti-trust legislation on the American film industry, in June 1946 won a Federal court decision making block-booking illegal.[15] UWP, founded on that very principle, now became completely unviable. Ironically, Rank, offering real competition to the big American companies, would be condemned as a monopolist if he persisted with his strategy.

This was a considerable set-back. The American magazine *Variety* pessimistically forecasted that, 'floating entirely on their own, with the Department of Justice ready to pounce on any tie in or combination agreements, English pix, unless exceptional, can anticipate only minor grosses'.[16]

Rank, however, was not so easily defeated. UWP was abandoned, but the bonds between Universal and International were tightened. From the beginning of October 1946 Universal was to concentrate entirely on distribution and to form a new, wholly owned subsidiary, Universal-International Productions, which, with Spitz as chairman and Goetz as president, would deliver twenty-five pictures annually for distribution by the parent company. Twelve Rank films would also be handled, though now they would have to rely on their own merits for bookings.

The deal with Universal had made Kelly and Eagle-Lion virtually redundant, but Rank managed to use the still-born company to his advantage. In December 1945 E-L was bought out by Robert Young, the railway magnate, whose Pathé Industries group already owned the independent production/distribution company, Producers Releasing Corporation. Eagle-Lion was to absorb PRC production and distribution facilities and handle ten American films and ten British films.[17]

Rank now had a second-string distribution outlet, which, if it was unable to block-book his films along with the American product, could be relied upon to consider his interests and which already had a distribution network with twenty-two film exchanges.[18]

Rank was also expanding his interests in the rest of the world. In January 1945 he took over the 110-strong Odeon Cinema Chain in Canada; in November he acquired a 50 per cent holding in the Australian Greater Union Theatres Circuit; in March 1946 he bought himself into the 100-strong Kerridge Circuit in New Zealand, and early in 1947 he began building a large cinema in Cairo as a showcase for his films. He also beat 20th Century Fox to a deal with I. W. Schlesinger, the leading force in the South African film industry, and, by buying a 51 per cent interest in the Palace Amusement Company, won control of most of the important cinemas in the West Indies.[19]

At the beginning of 1947 Rank seemed to be at the peak of his power. As *Variety* saw it, 'J. Arthur Rank is rapidly winning the Anglo-American sweepstakes for foreign theatres, and the results to date have Yank film execs fretting and worried.'[20] UA was enjoying considerable success with the road-show distribution of *Henry V* – with only ten engagements played, the film had already made a net profit of $700,000 – and, with the help of a massive publicity campaign, *Caesar and Cleopatra* was raking in estimated gross receipts of $2,500,000 from its general release. Universal, distributing its first crop of British films, was finding *The Seventh Veil* encouragingly popular, and Eagle-Lion, beginning its operations with *Bedelia*, a medium-budget melodrama starring Margaret Lockwood, was doing better than might have been expected.

Of course, there were clouds upon the horizon. In May a disgruntled Nate Blumberg complained that the progress of British films was far from good and warned exhibitors 'that their welfare and the welfare of the American film industry depends a good deal on them giving British films a fair break here.'[21] The substance behind the threat lay in the critical situation of the British economy. A year earlier there had been some doubt about whether Congress would endorse a $3,750 million loan to Britain, and *Variety* had had to remind its political representatives that 'Britain, which provides by far the largest single share of the export market, would be virtually cut off from American films in the event the loan flops. Without the money, the English would have to tighten their belts still further and this would mean an end to all luxury imports, which includes films of course.'[22] The loan had been passed but had failed to solve Britain's chronic balance of payments crisis, and fear for their most lucrative overseas market made American film leaders amenable to compromise. *Variety* commented, '. . . most film moguls have figured it would be good business to help English pix in any way possible to find a market here since the income taken from the US by British films is inconsequential compared to what Hollywood product gets out of England. Any British retaliation for alleged injustices here could be very serious for American income from abroad.'[23] Seeking to convert these pious utterances into concrete cinema bookings, Rank returned to the United States in May 1947.

The poor economic climate in Britain had hardly affected the Rank Organization. Cinema attendance remained buoyant and British films continued to enjoy great popularity. Admissions rose from 990 million in 1939 to an all-time peak of 1,635 million in 1946, and, according to Rank's assessment of the relative popularity of British and American films in his Odeon cinemas, British pictures enjoyed an average weekly take of £694, compared to £583 for Hollywood pictures.[24]

Rank's power and prestige were such that the Americans were to make the mistake of regarding his interests as synonymous with those of the British government and of the British film industry as a whole. In an attempt to stave off discriminatory measures in Britain, each of the big five American companies agreed to provide Rank with $2-million-worth of play-dates on their affiliated circuits.[25] Universal and Eagle-Lion both reported a sudden upsurge in bookings, though there was still considerable resistance among the independent exhibitors in the provinces. *Variety* ('Stix Still Nix British Pix') reported on the continuing hostility to Rank's films in the small towns, where audiences remained obstinately insular:

> Situation was summed up neatly by one smalltown indie exhibitor, who told of the time he screened the March of Time's 'Challenge to Hollywood' which depicted British production units at work. Principal of the high school in his town, who's naturally recognized as one of the more intelligent citizens, walked out after the MOT short and told the manager. 'I don't know why you play such things. I wouldn't give you two cents for the best British picture made.'[26]

According to Rank, British films in Canada had managed to increase their share of the market from 4 per cent to 24 per cent, and it was hoped that, with a worth-while supply of films and the active co-operation of the big American companies, similar improvements could be affected in the United States.[27]

Unfortunately that co-operation was short-lived. For, far from being in Rank's pocket (as the American film moguls believed them to be), the Labour government regarded him with considerable hostility. Rank's allies and colleagues (Woodham Smith, John Davis, Lord Margesson, Lord Portal) were, like himself, staunch Tories, and Rank had made little effort to endear himself to the new administration. Filipo del Giudice, an Italian anti-Fascist, had cultivated the friendship of Sir Stafford Cripps and other leading socialists, but Giudice's extravagance in film production had finally proved too much even for Rank and he had been replaced as head of Two Cities earlier in the year.

On 30 June 1947 Hugh Dalton, the Chancellor of the Exchequer, announced the necessity for curbs on the import of semi-luxury goods, such as petrol, newsprint, tobacco and film. Hollywood clung to the hope that the concessions made to Rank would prevent the imposition of such measures against its films: 'New Finance bill which passed Parliament last week is only permissive in character and Rank's say should do much to slow its application. Armed as he is with assurances from US majors resulting from his American trip, Rank doesn't want the applecart upset now.'[28] Rank was later to complain bitterly about his upset applecart: 'All my work was thrown away. My 2 months in America went for nowt. All my sweat and perspiration in New Orleans with E. V. Richards [a Paramount executive] – right down the drain.'[29]

The tone of injured innocence glosses over a very complex situation, but Rank did, undoubtedly, find himself in an invidious position. The soft-sell approach engineered by his Chief American adviser (Jock Lawrence, who had worked as a publicity man for Sam Goldwyn) had been extremely successful. But, appearing as the American's friend laid him open to charges of selling out British interests. Left-wing writers, such as Ralph Bond and Frederick Mullally, virtually took it for granted that he was an agent of American imperialism, and though Rank could bring forward counter-arguments about the need to earn dollars and to show British films to the world, an insistence on supporting the Americans against the government might be construed as embarrassingly unpatriotic. The Cinema Exhibitors' Association, worried about the supply of films, and NATKE, most of whose members were drawn from cinema employees, were both vociferous in their condemnation of the government's precipitate action, but the boycott with which the Americans responded to Dalton's import duty seemed to offer Rank, as producer, the chance of breaking Hollywood's hegemony over the British market.

Rank vacillated for some months; as late as October he was insisting that 'the present time is unripe for any expansion of British film production', cutting back and warning his more extravagant producers that 'with the world situation upset . . . they must limit expenditure on pix to a range between $800,000 and $1 million'.[30]

But as hopes of an early settlement receded, and as the climate in America changed from one of mild sympathy towards Britain's economic plight to anger and indignation at the closure of a vital market, Rank reluctantly abandoned his conciliatory stance.

In August *Variety* had been able to report that exhibitors were 'leaning over backwards to avoid any resemblance of reprisals.' Once it became plain, however, that Rank could not or would not prevent the government going ahead with its 75 per cent import levy, box-office returns fell off rapidly. The situation was aggravated by events in Palestine, and the relatively few British films for which bookings were obtained became subject to the boycott of the Zionist Sons of Liberty. Their efforts proved suspiciously successful, and Alexander Korda bitterly accused the big American companies of colluding with the Zionists: 'The activity of a small group of fanatics is not what is keeping British product from American screens; the real "Sons of Liberty" are the Presidents of the American companies.'[31] Three of Korda's films released through 20th Century Fox (*Anna Karenina*, *An Ideal Husband* and *Mine Own Executioner*) brought in dismally meagre returns and Rank fared little better. Nate Blumberg, of Universal, reported that receipts from his British films dropped from $100,000 a week to less than $25,000.[32] After the grandiose hopes of a $12-million share of the American market, net remittances of less than $1½ million looked pathetically small. In December 1947 Rank announced an increased programme of thirty-six feature films – primarily designed for the British market, though still including a number of prestige pictures – and a major restructuring of his organization. The burden of film production had hitherto fallen on the GCFC (which controlled the Gaumont-British circuit as well as Rank's production interests); henceforth it was to be shared by the profitable Odeon Theatres side of the organization.

An attempt to wrest domination of the British screen from the Americans could attract support from the patriotic right and the anti-imperialist left, but hostility towards American films was not shared by the great mass of cinema-goers and the economic logic behind such an attempt was dubious. As the *Economist* pointed out, 'the circuits have been built on a foundation of free supply of American films', and, as became increasingly apparent, the profitability of the Rank Organization was built not on film production but on the Odeon and Gaumont-British cinema circuits.[33]

From the exhibitors' – and the cinema-goers' – viewpoint Hollywood films were a bargain: having already covered their costs in their home market, they could be distributed overseas at low rentals. There was no guarantee that the same level of cinema attendance could be maintained with a spartan diet of British films. The popularity of a small number of British films during the 1940s disguised the degree to which British cinemas were dependent on Hollywood. Of the 67 British films registered for Quota in 1945 only 28 were first features, and though by 1948 output had been increased to 170 'long films', only 63 of these were first features; the remainder were 'little more than featurettes on which very little money was spent and from which little entertainment was derived'.[34] Britain's 5000 cinemas, many of them changing their double-feature programmes twice a week, needed something more substantial than this.

Rank's attempt to involve the prosperous Odeon company in his production plans aroused considerable suspicion. United Artists, already disgruntled by the fact that their substantial (but non-voting) share in the company guaranteed their films no playing time in the Odeon cinemas, threatened legal action, but more important was the reaction of the English financial press. The consolidated balance sheet which Rank issued to counter claims that Odeon shareholders were being sold a pig in a poke hardly inspired confidence. The *Economist* called the merger 'One of the least meritorious financial schemes to be disclosed for some years' and concluded that 'All in all, a purchase at par of shares in a company which lost £1,667,070 on film production in 1945–6 (almost equal to the consolidated net profit of the Odeon group for 1946–7) and which has a deficiency of current assets approaching £1,000,000 according to its latest balance sheet does not represent an impressive bargain for Odeon shareholders.'[35]

Nevertheless, the deal went ahead. Rank actually produced only thirty-two feature films instead of the thirty-six originally announced, ostensibly because of shortage of studio space, more probably because of financial problems, but a serious attempt was made to make British films the mainstay of the two Rank circuits.

When the government reached agreement with the Americans and Hollywood films were again released onto the British market it looked for a moment that Rank's venture had been scuttled. In March 1948 *Variety* crowed that 'A year ago . . . the American industry greatly feared the competition of Rank. Now . . . the fear has been dissipated because Rank has proved he cannot compete with Hollywood's output in the US or elsewhere in the world.'[36] The celebrations were premature, though, for Rank refused to cancel bookings of British reissues to make way for the expected flood of Hollywood pictures, and American producers were soon complaining of 'arbitrary restrictions' on their films. Rank haughtily informed the American companies who normally released their films on his circuits that he would be unable to find space for more than twenty-five Hollywood pictures in 1948 and for more than seventy-five in 1949, and he then added insult to injury by offering them playing time as supports for his British films – poetic justice, as *Brief Encounter* had had to play second fiddle to *Song of Scheherezade* on its release in America.[37] The final shock was the revelation that now the Labour government seemed solidly behind Rank and prepared to ensure protection for his production programme by drastically raising the film quota from 17½ to 45 per cent from 1 October.

The Americans were outraged and threatened another boycott, but Eric Johnston, the president of the Motion Picture Export Association (MPEA), devised a more subtle policy. From the beginning of September no American film was to be double-billed with a British film: audiences were to be given a straight choice of programme.[38]

For a time it looked as if Rank had a chance of winning. Rather than playing his big films against the reissues and stand-bys on which the Americans had had to rely during the boycott period, he had hoarded them up for the big battle ahead. Now, with a programme of sixty new features, which included expensive (if disappointingly uncom-mercial) pictures like *The Blue Lagoon*, *The Passionate Friends*, *Eureka Stockade*, *Saraband for Dead Lovers* and *Scott of the Antarctic*, ten reissues, nine 'curtain raisers', half-a-dozen episodes of *This Modern Age* and several films from Universal and Eagle-Lion (whose contractual ties with Rank kept them from the Johnston dictum),

Rank seemed to have a reasonable chance of success.[39]

The Americans also faced the problem of finding suitable outlets for their films. With the Rank circuits virtually closed to them, they were forced into the indignity of cultivating the support of the small circuits and independent second-run cinemas. An attempt was made to put together a '4th Circuit', but the independents, rightly convinced that the feud with Rank would not last, were reluctant to commit themselves and preferred to exploit the unaccustomed solicitude of the big American companies for their own advantage. UA's Arthur Kelly, after several weeks of negotiations, was gloomily pessimistic. With the market glutted with surplus American films,

rentals on top-budget pictures have taken a tumble and because of the number of American pix the indies can lay their hands on, its practically impossible for the Yanks to get extended playing time. In addition, Kelly pointed out, J. Arthur Rank's Odeon and Gaumont-British chains control most of the London houses, from which the majority of British revenue accrues. Receipts will naturally fall off if bookings are confined to the indies in the provinces.[40]

Had the Rank films proved popular, the Americans would indeed have had something to worry about. As it was, there was a steep decline in quality and cinema-goers deserted the Odeons and Gaumonts in droves. Rank himself was eventually prepared to admit that

Unfortunately many of the films we produced were not of the quality to ensure reasonable returns. It can now be seen that our plans to meet an unexpected and critical situation were too ambitious, that we made demands on the creative talent in the industry that were beyond its resources, and that as a result, we spread our production capacity, in which I still have unshaken faith, too thinly over the films we made.[41]

Even before the end of the year defeat had become apparent. *Variety* was confident that this time 'the big British film bubble' really had burst, and as Rank Studios at Islington, Shepherds Bush and Denham were closed down Hollywood films began to appear again on Odeon and Gaumont screens. By February 1949 British film production was facing its worst crisis since 1936, and Rank's loss for the year came to a staggering £4,646,000.[42]

Rank's failure, then, was a much wider one than a failure to penetrate the American market. His challenge to Hollywood on its home ground had been conciliatory, co-operative and cordial; the bitter fighting and the big defeat occurred in Britain.

The attempt on the American market was by no means a complete failure. *Caesar and Cleopatra* had done much better in America than at home; *Great Expectations* looked set for a gross total of box-office receipts of over $2 million, until it was hit by the wave of hostility following the Dalton Duty. *Hamlet* emulated the success of *Henry V*, despite Rank's feud with Hollywood, and *The Red Shoes* overcame 'the double disadvantage of a long-hair subject and British antecedents' to become the only British film included in America's top one hundred all-time box-office record-holders.

Richard Griffiths, in a well informed series of articles on Rank's success and failure in America, argued that the future for British films lay in the expanding art-house circuit, citing the success of films like *I Know where I'm Going* at the 550-seater Sutton Theatre in New York.[43] Indeed, British films, particularly the quirky Ealing comedies, were to gain something of a cult status among middle-class Americans in the 1950's.[44]

Universal had set up a special unit to deal with the Rank films thought to have only minority appeal, booking them in to small theatres on a continuous-run policy. But though there was a healthy growth in this minority market, it represented only a tiny fraction of what could be earned from successful general release. For big-budget pictures of the type Rank was producing, art-house distribution was just not enough. The road-showing distribution method used with *Henry V*, *Hamlet* and *The Red Shoes* was rather different – an entirely appropriate intensive selling campaign concentrated on one area at a time – but its success depended on the film having the sort of exceptional qualities for which people would pay higher prices. After 1949 Rank produced few films which had such appeal.

Diplomacy, finance and marketing strategies were obviously of vital importance in determining the fate of Rank's attempt on the American market, but in the long run it was the quality and costs of the films which mattered. As *Variety* continually stressed, the United States welcomed with open arms outstanding British pictures, but if Rank was to offer a programme of films, as the big Hollywood companies did, in which a few outstanding pictures supported a number of mediocre ones, then he had to ensure that his outstanding pictures were at least as good as those of Hollywood, and his mediocre ones no more mediocre. This he signally failed to do. Britain did create excellent films, but in terms of production values their standards were generally lower than those made by Hollywood. Poor labour relations and poor production planning drove up costs, and an 'art for arts sake' ethos among British producers hardly helped. Maurice Cowan, *Variety*'s London correspondent, whose divided loyalties made him one of the most interesting commentators on British film production bitterly castigated

> those producers who plan a budget for a picture, almost double it halfway through production, and know that unless it is a world-beater the film must lose a fortune. But that doesn't worry them, they have collected press notices and prestige. . . . If they intend to keep up their scorn of Hollywood then let them at least earn their keep as Hollywood producers do. And if they are going to bleat about Art then let them stop spending $1½ or $2 million on a picture. They can't have it both ways![46]

Unfortunately Rank's producers did come near to having it both ways, moving over to Alexander Korda's London Films when curbs were put on their freedom. (Korda was to lose £3 million on film production in 1948–9.)

Blindly cutting back was little help, though, and substituting the unimaginative accountant for the irresponsible artist only made matters worse. The PEP report of 1952 makes the acute observation that the Rank Organization had become 'accustomed to, and adjusted to high cost production' and that even those films which started as modestly budgeted projects tended to end – in financial terms – in the 'prestige class'.[46] With the notable exception of Ted Black at Gainsborough and Michael Balcon at Ealing, the British film industry seemed incapable of turning out producers who could balance commercial acumen with creative flair. Without them the grandiose expansion envisaged by Rank was inevitably doomed to failure.

The Context of Creativity: Ealing Studios and Hammer Films

Vincent Porter

Since the end of the Second World War two areas of British film production have brought a sense of permanence and continuity to an industry which is more generally characterized by individual one-off productions. These have been the films produced at Ealing Studios between the end of the war and the mid-1950s and those (mostly as horror subjects) produced by Hammer Films from the 1950s until the late 1970s. By their very longevity these two areas of production appear, in their different ways, to represent something intrinsically and culturally British. In fact, however, the links between the films and British culture are substantially more attenuated than is immediately apparent, and their manifestation may be more readily understood by a closer examination of the creative contexts in which they were produced and in particular of the key roles played by the two producers primarily responsible: Sir Michael Balcon and Sir James Carreras. They also contribute some evidence to a more general debate about the relation between ideology in the mass media and the economic context of production.

The creative role played by a film producer has conventionally been ignored by film critics and theorists, who have tended to assign a more creative role to the film's director, or on occasion to the screen-writer. The producer has been seen as carrying out financial and administrative tasks and therefore as being of lesser cultural significance. But, in fact, the producer brings together under his or her unique control an assessment of public taste, the task of raising adequate production finance, the decision as to which individuals should be employed in the key creative roles in the film and on what terms, and the overall supervision and management of the production process. It is precisely through the way in which these four factors are interrelated that the producer imposes his or her creative mark upon the film. It is the producer who decides how the sources of production finance are to be related to a cultural assessment of the needs of the market-place; how that assessment is in turn to be related to the choice of creative personnel and to the degree of freedom allowed to them; and how in turn the money available for production finance can be administered to produce a film of suitable quality and length. Although the guiding hand of a producer may be difficult to perceive in an individual film, it is precisely in the longer term that the key role played by the producer becomes clear. For when a producer is successful in creating a stable and harmonious relationship between the financial needs of investment capital and a consistency of cultural output, it is because he or she has found a way of successfully resolving economics and ideology in a manner which may reflect a more general truth about the structural limitations imposed on British film culture from the outside and the constraints which can be imposed on individual creativity from within the production unit.

The Organization of Film Production

In many ways the organization of film production on a mass scale had been worked out by Thomas Ince between 1911 and 1916 at Kessel and Bauman's New York Motion Picture Company.[1] Ince adopted Frederick Winslow Taylor's principles of scientific management and adapted them to the needs of film production. The key to these principles lay in separating the craftsman from his control of the work process and in establishing a division of labour which separated mental labour from manual labour. In this way it became possible for management to control the production of films without having to be present during shooting. The key to the process was the development of the shooting script as the 'blueprint' for the film, which was then budgeted for and scheduled and then given to the director to 'shoot as written'. The daily rushes could be viewed by the producer as a form of 'quality control' of the manual labour involved in the production, and the shots thus approved were then edited together in the cutting room under his watchful eye.

This system, which was adopted by the big Hollywood companies in the twenties and thirties, was refined and adapted by Irving Thalberg at MGM to cater for its corporate needs for the mass production of high quality films which would be under his unique control'.[2] The work of the director was effectively relegated to the category of manual labour, while the key mental labourers were the script-writers and, to a lesser extent, the editors. The work of the mise-en-scène departments, the sets, the costumes, the make-up, the lighting, the photography, and later the sound recording, were streamlined and unified to give the studio's output a consistent appearance and technical quality which cinema-goers came to recognize and expect. The MGM look – brilliant high-key lighting, elegant sets, clean, smoothly draped gowns – set the pace for Hollywood and indeed, the world.

The problem with this form of the division of labour however was that every film became subordinated to the technological and organizational imperatives of the studio. It became the task of the actors, and above all of the director, to turn the script-writer, or script-writers', blueprint into a living scene that could be recorded by the camera. As Thalberg regularly told the directors employed under him at MGM, in what was virtually a set speech, 'I consider the director is on the set to communicate what I expect of actors. It's my experience that many directors only realise seventy-five per cent of our scenarios, and while audiences never know how much they missed, I do. You gentlemen have individualistic styles and I respect them. It's one of the principal reasons we want you here. But if you can't conform to my system, it would be wiser not to start your film at all.'[3]

It was precisely here that the system of scientific management broke down. For although the difficult actor or actress could be controlled to some extent at least, by the vicious system of studio contracts, which allowed them to be put on suspension without pay until they conformed to the studio's wishes, a director, however co-operative or amenable he, or occasionally she, appeared to be, could radically change the impact and meaning of a picture, or, worse still, diminish it artistically, if he was not sympathetically attuned to what the picture was saying. The choice of camera angle, or the particular nuance or emphasis which was elicited from a performer, could be critical in this respect. Furthermore the advent of sound meant that there was more capital tied up in the sound stages and in equipment, and if an adequate return was to be made on the capital invested there would be no time for retakes. As silent pictures gave way to the talkies, MGM's studio at Culver City lost its sobriquet of 'retake valley' and there became good economic reasons for admitting the director to the echelons of mental labour.

The producers recognized the Screen Directors Guild in February 1939, but the problem that remained for Hollywood was how to reconcile its corporate needs for a consistency of studio product with the aims and ambitions of the directors to make their own individual creative contributions to the films on which they worked, for since the director now participated both in the preparation of the script and in shooting the picture on the studio floor, his creative contribution threatened to surpass that of the producer, who had the responsibility of keeping all the studio's production programme in a coherent whole.

In the mid-twenties Irving Thalberg had already recognized that one of the major problems of a head of a studio was to generate enough suitable ideas for subjects for films, so that the studio could produce a range of product wherein each film was different enough to be distinguishable from the others but similar enough to generate a consistency of output. His strategy therefore was to inspire those around him to put their creative talents to work on ideas which were acceptable to him. Eddie Sutherland, who worked with Thalberg at MGM on both silent and sound films, recalled that 'he would inspire us to spend all night kicking around his stories – for free. He would tell the director all the thoughts he had. Then he'd look at the result on film and decide he could do it better, and do a lot of retakes.'[4] But by the end of the thirties there was neither the time nor the resources to do many retakes. Michael Balcon's genius was to devise a system of production at Ealing which inspired the creative talents around him to work on ideas that were acceptable to him in order to make films that were consistent in tone yet individually different, and at the same time to keep the studio running on an economic basis. His was a system which drew on some of the ideas of Thalberg at MGM, but which was adapted and modified to meet the different economic circumstances of a small British studio producing sound films.

Sir Michael Balcon at Ealing

When Michael Balcon took charge of production at Ealing in 1938 he had already spent several years running Gainsborough and Gaumont-British and a brief but unhappy period running the British branch of the MGM empire. Until that time the mainstay of Ealing films had been the music-hall personalities of Gracie Fields and George Formby, but the other product, which had been greatly influenced by the West End theatre, had been a failure both artistically and commercially. What Balcon wanted was a studio that would produce films which would have their roots in contemporary British life, but which did not repeat themselves and which provided a coherent view of Britain. To keep the studio busy, Balcon continued with the production of George Formby films, and in addition signed up Will Hay, the music-hall comedian who had been the commercial mainstay of the studio while he was at Shepherd's Bush. That kept the existing studio staff fully employed and generated enough revenue for Balcon's other plans, for which he had to recruit additional personnel.

Balcon was in no doubt about the need for a sympathetic rapport between himself and the new people he would be recruiting. 'I don't believe in producers who put themselves up as impresarios and try to gather around them as many well-known names as possible. I personally always look for people whose ideas coincide with mine and am always ready to give them a chance to make a name for themselves.'[5] His attitude was not surprising, for those he engaged would be co-operating with him 'in bringing to the screen the producer's film and for that reason they must be chosen not only for their technical efficiency, but for their sympathy with the producer's point of view and ideas.'[6]

For his first tranche of recruits Balcon looked to those who had worked closely with him at Gainsborough, Gaumont-British or MGM: Robert Stevenson, Penrose Tennyson, Angus McPhail and John Dighton. Stevenson stayed for only two years before leaving for Hollywood, and Tennyson was killed on active service in 1941. McPhail and Dighton however stayed at Ealing until 1948 and 1951 respectively, both working as script-writers.

For his second tranche, which was to play a major role in Ealing's development, Balcon looked to the documentary movement and to the cutting room. By far the most influential recruit, from either of these fields, during the war period was Alberto Cavalcanti, Brazilian by birth, who had been producing films at the GPO and Crown Film Units. With him came Harry Watt, who had already written and directed *Target for Tonight* (CFU, 1941). From the cutting rooms of MGM and London Films Balcon brought in Charles Frend and Charles Crichton respectively and promoted them to be directors, while from the ABC studios at Elstree, where he had been editing Hitchcock's *Jamaica Inn*, he brought Robert Hamer, first to edit and later to direct. These five, together with Basil Dearden, who had joined Ealing as an assistant before Balcon arrived, formed the main body of Ealing's film directors.

Between 1942 and 1955 Crichton, Dearden, Frend, Hamer and Watt directed forty-six of the sixty-nine films produced at Ealing, while a further three were directed by Cavalcanti, who in many ways played a far more influential role during the war years as the studio's guide and mentor in the aesthetics of realism. Only Alexander Mackendrick made a comparable impact as a director, but he did not join Ealing until the end of the war. Other directors, such as Thorold Dickinson (*Next of Kin*, 1942, and *Secret People*, 1952) and Henry Cornelius (*Passport to Pimlico*, 1949) directed occasional films, but in general the directorial team was remarkably stable. Together with the script-writers, such as T. E. B. Clarke, Angus McPhail, John Dighton and Jack Whittingham, and associate producers, such as Sidney Cole and Michael Relph, they formed Ealing's creative elite, more commonly known locally as 'Mr Balcon's young gentlemen'.

In return for permanent employment the members of the creative elite were paid lower salaries than those paid elsewhere in the industry. Alexander Mackendrick's first salary as a director working on *Whisky Galore* was £30 per week (approximately half as much as that of his cameraman)[7], and the average directorial salary was about £5,000 per year.[8] In return however Mackendrick considered that they had the advantage of being very free.[9] For Hamer 'the studio was more like a family co-operative than an employer and he admired Balcon's wisdom in giving the members of his team a free hand subject to rational safeguards.'[10] Balcon however had a different perspective; for him there were two distinct stages in planning a film – agreeing the basic theme and then fleshing it out with creative ideas.

For Balcon the basic theme of the film was not something to be agreed lightly:

It is no use a director coming to me and saying he is tremendously enthusiastic about making a film dealing with the life of, say, Neville Chamberlain, if he and I do not share the same point of view about Neville Chamberlain. We may agree that his life would make an admirable film subject, but obviously we cannot work together if he happens to be a great admirer of Neville Chamberlain and plans to make a film which would redeem or embellish that statesman's reputation, while I may happen to feel strongly the other way about Chamberlain and would therefore wish to make a film exposing his failure or weaknesses as a statesman.[11]

Since the directors and associate producers were employed on a permanent basis there was potential for conflict between them and Balcon and it was therefore necessary to find a way of bending their thinking to his. First therefore the resident associate producers and directors were encouraged to put up ideas for films to Balcon, for 'quite obviously, this is the best method of procedure since the creative man will do his best work if it is something that he is enthusiastic about'.[12] Balcon's role then was 'to encourage and stimulate these enthusiasms, but at the same time to select subjects on which he and the associate producer and the director [could] work on happily together.'[13] Because of his careful selection of directors and associate producers who were thoroughly in sympathy with his ideas, and since few if any had worked in those grades outside Ealing, he was able to say that 'rarely is a subject put forward in our studios on which an associate producer and a director are tremendously keen, which I find I cannot support'.[14]

Balcon evinced a similar attitude towards the authors of any novels which he wanted to film. The producer and the author might find themselves working together for one of two reasons. 'The author may actively want to take part in turning his story into a film because the medium may genuinely interest him or because he wants to guard his brainchild as far as possible; or the producer for equally good reasons may want the participation of the author in making a screenplay out of his book.'[15] Although Balcon recognized the need for compromise between him and the author, it was a compromise of a very special kind which involved the producer in nothing more than genuinely intending to make a film out of the book of which he had bought the rights, whereas from the author he demanded 'an acknowledgement . . . that *some* changes [his italics] are required to make a motion picture from a story written to be read'.[16] It was in the name of capital invested in the production that Balcon asserted his right to overrule the author. 'How,' he asked rhetorically, can the producer put this in jeopardy 'by allowing *anyone* (his italics), least of all someone inexperienced in film-making, to dig his toes in and say that this must be in or that must be said?'[17]

For most of Balcon's Ealing career however his claim to act as the final arbiter was determined neither by the needs of the financial investors nor indeed by the needs of the market-place, but by Balcon's own personal ideology. After several years of publicly protesting, both as an individual and as a member of the Cinematograph Films Council, which advised the British government on films policy, about

the threat posed by the monopolistic activities of the Rank Organization to the role of the independent producer, Balcon proceeded, at
the end of the war, to negotiate an extremely favourable financing and
distribution deal with the Rank Organization, after which his
criticisms were considerably more muted – if not absent. The deal
gave Ealing 'complete production autonomy and independence,
circuit release for Ealing films, favourable distribution terms and
approval of the terms on which our films were booked to cinemas'.[18]
'The Rank Organization put up 50 per cent of the finance and later
increased this to 75 per cent,'[19] and 'never at any time was it
necessary' for Balcon 'to submit any of our films to any outside sources
at all. We simply borrowed money on our assets, and our assets were
our films and our studio and its equipment.'[20]

What Balcon had devised therefore was a system which enabled
him to produce between five and six films per year, which kept the
studio personnel and its stages fully employed, which all reflected his
ideological concerns and which were brought into being by the
creative energies of the four or five teams of writers, directors and
associate producers which he employed. He formalized and developed Thalberg's ideas of group collectivity by working through the
ideas, before the films went on to the studio floor at the regular
meetings around the studio's large round table, where sixteen or
seventeen people discussed each other's projects over cups of tea – or
more informally over pints of beer in the Red Lion opposite the
studio's gates. It is not surprising therefore that, seen in retrospect,
there is a remarkable consistency in the style and subject-matter of
Ealing films. It is possible, to be sure, to discern the individual
authorial contributions of writers such as T. E. B. Clarke or of
directors such as Robert Hamer or Alexander Mackendrick,[21] but it is
important to emphasize that their concerns are but minor variations
on Balcon's aims and objectives for the distinctive type of British
cinema that he wanted to build.

There were of course disagreements between Balcon and his young
gentlemen but most of these were hammered out before shooting. For
Balcon 'the most important work on the film is done before and after it
goes on the studio floor.'[22] Charles Frend emphasized the importance
of pre-production liaison between the director and the art director,
which meant that 'the director must see in his own mind just how he
proposes to shoot each scene before he even starts work on the studio
floor'.[23] Frend himself found it helpful 'to look at the proposed plan of

the set, go through each scene that plays on it in the script and decide whether the layout is adequate'.[24] After agreeing the set design with the art director, the associate producer initialled it and the construction of the set was put in hand. 'Those initials,' added Frend, 'are to stop me from trying to alibi later that the set isn't what I wanted.'[25]

Alexander Mackendrick prepared his script in even more visual detail. Drawing on his previous experience as a sketch artist at Ealing, he used to include sketches of the camera set-ups at the same time as the script was written and these were printed opposite each page of script.[26] Robert Hamer however took an opposite view and his script for *Kind Hearts and Coronets* included little, if any detail about the camera or cutting directions. He told Freda Bruce Lockhart of his 'reactionary' refusal to go on the floor with a shooting script, preferring to begin by rehearsing the scene in full. 'In the course of the scene as the players "walk through" their parts, he believes the cuts and angles proper to the scene become clear; while at the same time the method has the huge advantage of familiarity with the action when it comes to shooting out of continuity.'[27]

Of all Balcon's young gentlemen it was Robert Hamer with whom he seemed most at odds. Hamer's interests in the impact of one character upon another,[28] in the relations between the objective world and the interior subjective worlds of his characters, in the traditions of the theatre and in the resonances of the English language set him somewhat apart from Balcon's more propagandist concerns. Balcon considered that he was 'unable to impose on himself an essential discipline',[29] and in *Kind Hearts and Coronets* Balcon stepped in himself to re-edit the trial scene in order to play down the sexual dilemma faced by Louis Mazzini (Dennis Price) in having to choose between Sibella (Joan Greenwood) and Edith (Valerie Hobson) and play up his social dilemma.

But these differences were the exception rather than the rule. 'At Ealing, we produced films; and the only thing that we took into account were the things we ourselves wanted to do and we felt that if we believed in them strongly enough we could carry that belief through to an audience,' Balcon recalled in 1974.[30]

What were the beliefs that Ealing's creative elite shared in common? In 1943, in a lecture to the Workers Film Association, Balcon made great play with two distinct trends which he perceived in films, that of 'realism' and that of 'tinsel'. The tinsel tradition, which Balcon rejected, stemmed from filming the theatrical, whereas the realist tradition – or more properly a naturalistic tradition, a word which he hated[31] – drew on the traditions of the documentary movement, the newsreel and the travelogue. What Balcon, aided by Cavalcanti, set out to do was to develop a marriage of the documentary tradition with the narrative tradition of the Hollywood feature film. The first fruits of this marriage were *The Foreman Went to France* (d. Charles Frend, 1942), *Next of Kin* (d. Thorold Dickinson, 1942), *Nine Men* (d. Harry Watt, 1943) and *San Demetrio London* (d. Charles Frend and (uncredited) Robert Hamer, 1943). These wartime films had a triple function. 'First there was propaganda, the projection of our own ideas, our strength and our resources. Second, instruction – both for the Services and for civilians. Third entertainment.'[32]

With the ending of the war, Balcon carried these functions forward into his peacetime films, with the exception, of course, of the instructional element for the services. For audiences abroad British films were to be the ambassadors of the British people. 'The man in the street in New York, Moscow, Paris, Brussels, Athens and Rome must know something more of our country than the immediate foreign policy of its present Government,'[33] he wrote in 1945 before the Labour government was elected to office. 'For it is characteristic of Britain that while its Governments and policies can be altered at the will of the people, the people and the background that has shaped them remain. Therefore it is not the party in office that must be made known to the post-war world, whichever party it may be, but the people of Britain from whom the party springs and by whom it is selected.'[34]

This commitment to portray the people of Britain and the background that shaped them was the mainspring of Ealing's post-war films, but the realism of their portrayal is more problematic. It is highly significant that Balcon hated the word 'naturalistic',[35] for, despite his evocations of 'the sort of soviet that we work in our studios',[36] and the fact that he voted for the Labour Party in 1945,[37] Balcon was not essentially a socialist but a liberal. The distinction drawn by socialists between naturalism and realism was entirely alien to his way of thinking. Engels' criticism of Margaret Harkness's novel *City Girl* is a criticism that could equally be levelled at Ealing's films. The novel, Engels wrote, was 'not quite realistic enough. Realism to my mind, implies beside truth of detail the truth in the reproduction of typical characters under typical circumstances. Now your characters are typical enough as far as they go; but the circumstances which surround them and make them act are not perhaps equally so.'[38]

Although Balcon claimed that the feature film was making more and more use of 'characters and action arising out of contemporary problems such as were handled by the documentarists; labour problems, class problems, problems of psychology'[39], the first two categories are virtually absent from Ealing films. The conflict between labour and capital is never treated seriously, and when it does appear in comic vein in *The Man in the White Suit* (d. Alexander Mackendrick, 1951) it is significant that labour and capital unite in opposition to the idealist Sidney Stratton (Alec Guinness). As for class problems, they are either non-existent or vanish in a paean of collective communal endeavour, as in *Passport to Pimlico* (s. T. E. B. Clarke, d. Henry Cornelius, 1949). Only in the films of Robert Hamer, where the conflict between the dreams of the individual and the reality of the outside world are one of his central thematic concerns, do Ealing films explore the relationships between the characters and the circumstances in which they find themselves in any depth. In *Pink String and Sealing Wax* (1945) and *Kind Hearts and Coronets* (1949) the conflicts are highly attenuated within the frameworks of the Edwardian melodrama and the stylistic comedy, but in *It Always Rains on Sunday* (1947) the documentary realism of the contemporary working-class milieu, combined with Hamer's 'pre-eminent and passionate concern with the problem of character',[40] yielded a film which has been called 'one of the few worthwhile films about working class London.'[41]

The social function of the Ealing comedy is more complex. Alexander Mackendrick, who directed *Whisky Galore* (1949), *The Man in the White Suit* (1951), *The Maggie* (1954) and *The Ladykillers* (1955), was attracted by 'a certain form of comedy because I think that it can say certain things. It allows you to put across things that are too dangerous or that parts of the public won't accept.'[42] 'I wonder,' he asked during a talk on the BBC,

what would have happened if I had proposed to Sir Michael Balcon an earnest and gripping drama exposing the viciousness of some leaders of British industry who combine with shop stewards and workers in an attempt to bribe, to morally corrupt and finally to lynch an idealistic young man who was trying to offer the benefits of his science to humanity. It is a rather brutal theme; a slander of left and right wing behaviour, and pretty insulting to the liberals too. Yet we made it, we called it *The Man in the White Suit* and because it was a comedy with Alec Guinness nobody objected at all.[43]

But are Mackendrick's claims for comedy as a vehicle to put across ideas that are socially unacceptable really tenable? It may be that certain individuals, who are predisposed to think in that way, will read the films in the way that Mackendrick intends, but, far from Mackendrick outwitting Balcon, it is more likely that Balcon outwitted Mackendrick by allowing him to go ahead with the film. For Balcon comedy was an arbitrary or fanciful interruption of the normal flow of events,[44] which allowed 'the people in them to do the things we all want to do and can't in this regimented world. We all want to kick the boss or steal a million quid or bump off horrible relatives that stand between us and a fortune. Nobody does these things, but it's a lot of fun seeing others do them.'[45] That is a more likely explanation of why nobody objected to *The Man in the White Suit*.

Although Ealing's output was essentially representative of Balcon's ideas and wishes, there is also some evidence that the Ealing films which were successful at the box-office were successful because of story, directorial or other qualities which reflected the inputs of the various writers or directors involved rather than because of Balcon's grand design. For although Balcon saw his films as being ambassadors of the British people, he seemed to have little sense of what audiences abroad looked for in their films. The most successful Ealing films were of course the comedies, but, as Balcon himself admitted, 'we never set out to create a school of comedy'.[46] Indeed, there is some evidence to indicate that Balcon was quite hostile to comedy at Ealing until it proved so successful at the box-office. In the early days the comedies of George Formby and Will Hay were of course a commercial stop-gap to pay for the wartime propaganda films. After the war the first comedy made by Ealing was *Hue and Cry* (s. T. E. B. Clarke, d. Charles Crichton, 1947) which stemmed from an idea by its associate producer, Henry Cornelius.[47] It was an immediate commercial success, but it was another two years before the studio produced any more. The year 1949 saw the release of three comedies – *Passport to Pimlico*, *Whisky Galore* and *Kind Hearts and Coronets* – but there is no particular evidence that they indicated a positive shift in studio policy. Indeed, the directors of two of the three films, Robert Hamer and Henry Cornelius, were to suffer at Balcon's hands after the films were completed. Hamer was denied the chance to follow up *Kind Hearts and Coronets* with the subject he had long been preparing, a story with a strong sexual content set in the West Indies,[48] while Cornelius never worked for Ealing again, possibly because the costs of *Passport to Pimlico* had exceeded the budget. As for *Whisky Galore*, it was only made because Ealing's publicity chief, Monja Danischewsky, who had built up the studio's reputation, wanted to resign because he was feeling bored with his work. Danischewsky was too important to Ealing to be allowed to go and Balcon refused to accept his resignation. Instead Balcon suddenly discovered that he had enough money to finance the production of an additional film of which Danischewsky could be the associate producer. The subject which Danischewsky chose was Sir Compton Mackenzie's novel *Whisky Galore*.[49] According to Mackenzie however Balcon treated Danischewsky 'like an indulgent uncle'.[50]

However, *Whisky Galore* was extremely successful, both in the United Kingdom and, more importantly, in the United States, where it was retitled *Tight Little Island* in order to satisfy the Hays Office. About two minutes had to be cut from the film for the American version.[51] More importantly however the American audiences apparently preferred the accent of the Scots to that of the English.[52] Similarly, a few early scenes were cut from *Passport to Pimlico*, but the version of *Kind Hearts and Coronets* shown in America was the same as that shown in the United Kingdom.[53] *The Man in the White Suit*, *The Lavender Hill Mob* and *The Ladykillers* were also popular in the United States, particularly at the six-hundred-seat Sutton Theatre in New York, which specialized in showing British films.

The Ealing comedies were also popular in Continental Europe, where the British were expected to produce films with stories that would 'happen only in Britain and with subjects to be found only in that environment'.[54] *Whisky Galore* and *Passport to Pimlico* each became overnight the talk of Paris.[53] The reasons for their success overseas lay particularly in the films' direction, rather than in their themes, since for a film to be successful outside its country of origin it was necessary for the action to be 'so cinematic that it can be easily understood even without the help of the soundtrack'.[56]

Ealing's most successful films in the United States however were *Where No Vultures Fly* (d. Harry Watt, 1951), *West of Zanzibar* (d. Watt, 1954) and *The Cruel Sea* (d. Charles Frend, 1953), all of which played a limited circuit run.[57] The success of *The Cruel Sea* however came about largely as a result of the tremendous success in the United States of the novel by Nicholas Montserrat from which it was adapted.[58] As for the other two films, their success came partly from

the comparative exoticism of their subject-matter but mainly from
Watt's more vigorous attitude to his material. Indeed, Watt had
always been slightly out of place at Michael Balcon's Academy for
Young Gentlemen. His first Ealing film, *Nine Men*, was made for
£20,000 on Margam Sands in North Wales, which doubled for the
North African desert. Balcon took exception to his next film, *Fiddlers
Three* (1944), a musical comedy, with Tommy Trinder and Frances
Day, in which he had tried to break away from his documentary
background, and for which Balcon ordered extensive reshooting by
Robert Hamer. Balcon's next move was to send Watt to Australia
'purely "on spec" to see if it was possible to make films there and if so
to make one'.[59] Watt and Balcon had 'no set plans, no ideas',[60] and
Watt, effectively banished from the Academy, made his first
Australian film virtually without Balcon's supervision. His next film,
Eureka Stockade (1949), was more strongly influenced by Balcon and
was heavily criticized by Lindsay Anderson for its confused good
intentions, so typical of Ealing.[61] *Where No Vultures Fly* and *West of
Zanzibar* repeated the pattern of the two Australian films, but with
Africa as their locale. Their main character is Bob Payton (Anthony
Steel), whose exploits were based on those of the Kenyan conser-
vationist Mervyn Cowie.

The success in the United States of the comedies and of Watt's
robust adventure pictures contrasts sadly with the failure of the films
in which Balcon set out to project Britain and the British character,
such as *Scott of the Antarctic* (d. Charles Frend, 1948) and *The Blue
Lamp* (d. Basil Dearden, 1950).[62] For American audiences the upper
lips of *Scott of the Antarctic* were too stiff and the behaviour too
gentlemanly, while they found *The Blue Lamp* rather bland when
compared with *The Naked City* and other 'realistic' thrillers.[63]

Despite his sheltered position within the Rank Organization, the
decline of the British cinema market, in the face of competition for
leisure time from television and the motor car, meant that Balcon had
to look for revenues from overseas in order to survive. The overseas
markets however were not looking for the documentary feature films
about the British way of life which he saw as the vehicle for the
ambassadorial role he had assigned to Ealing films. Business went into
decline. By 1952 he was borrowing money from the National Film
Finance Corporation and by 1955 Ealing Studios was closed down.
His reign there had lasted for seventeen years, but in the end it was his
refusal, or his inability, to adjust to the needs of the world

market-place – and in particular to the needs of the American market-place – that brought about his downfall.

Sir James Carreras at Hammer

If Sir Michael Balcon carved out a protected position in the United Kingdom market for his Ealing films, then Sir James Carreras developed an entirely opposite strategy at Hammer Films. His policy was to produce films for the world market at a profit, without regard for the subject-matter of the films concerned. So long as the films made a profit, he was happy. In order to understand why Hammer is associated in the public's mind with the horror film, and with the Dracula and the Frankenstein films in particular, it is necessary to look both at the relationship between Hammer and the world film market and at the space which existed at Hammer for a small team of technicians to work together to make stylistically and visually interesting pictures, whose qualities were recognized throughout the world.

In 1935 Enrique Carreras, the father of James Carreras, had formed a distribution company in partnership with Will Hinds, whose stage name was Will Hammer. The company was called Exclusive Films and during the 1940s it occasionally produced a few films based on radio characters such as Dick Barton. The company was a family affair and James worked alongside his father, together with Will's son Anthony. Later on James's own son Michael was to join the company too.

In 1947 the production activities of Exclusive were rationalized and a new company, Hammer Films, was set up. James Carreras became the managing director, Anthony Hinds became a producer and Michael became his assistant. The year 1948 was not a good time to be moving into production: the film industry was sliding into recession and between September 1948 and March 1949 over two thousand studio technicians were made redundant.[64] Thanks however to ruthless cost-cutting and a determination to treat films as commercial products, which should not be made unless it was certain that they could be sold at a profit, Hammer survived. By working in the B feature market, James Carreras had a fairly clear idea of what a film could recoup from British cinemas. The problem was to reduce production costs to an economic level without sacrificing quality.

One major cost in film production was the rental of studio space, and while all location subjects were one solution to this problem, a more promising solution was to convert a large country house into a film studio. The actual cost of buying such a house compared favourably with the studio rentals asked, and with the right story material, the decor of the house could actually provide the sets for the film; and furthermore, if it was located in the right type of countryside, the exteriors for the film could be shot in the surrounding environs. An alternative approach, that of taking the studio to the location, was tried by other film companies, such as Ealing for *Whisky Galore*, Pilgrim Pictures for *Chance of a Lifetime* (d. Bernard Miles, 1950) and Outlook Films for *Blue Scar* (d. Jill Craigie, 1950).[65]

Both methods had their disadvantages. With the Mobile Studio Unit, the sets had to be prefabricated and the art director had to be skilful at adapting these when bad weather made it necessary to transfer some of the exterior shots indoors.[66] Another problem was that of billeting the unit in places where there were no hotels – or only one hotel, with insufficient accommodation or prohibitive prices.[67] Furthermore, it was by no means easy to match shots when the cutting room and the editor were several hundred miles away from the studio[68], and in addition the budget had to bear all the costs of transporting equipment and personnel to the location and the costs of providing accommodation for the unit.[69]

The main limitations of the country house system, on the other hand, were those of space. They encouraged a tendency to use a 35mm (wide-angle) lens and to avoid panning and tracking shots which would emphasize the distortions.[70] The financial advantages however were considerable: the crew paid their own transport costs to the studio and there was no need to accommodate them, since they travelled home every night. Hammer hired Dial Close, near Cookham Green, a large, luxurious building with spacious interiors, and made four films there. Their first, *Dr Morelle* (p. Anthony Hinds, 1948), cost £15,000, and their second (*PC 49*) was budgeted at £12,000 – substantially less than the £75,000 budget of *Blue Scar*, made at about the same time.[71]

Over the next two years Hammer kept on the move, still operating the same principle. By the time it had made four films it had exhausted the possibilities of the decor of Dial Close and it went first to Oakleigh Court, in Bray, next to Gilston Park, in Essex, and finally back to Bray, where it bought Down Place. With some twenty films made, James Carreras thought it was time for Hammer to settle down and convert the buildings into a studio. And so Down Place became Bray Studios, Hammer's production base for the next seventeen years.

From the very beginning Hammer had a policy of making films about subjects that were already well known to the public, so that they would come to the films knowing what to expect. These expectations would then be confirmed by the films. Many of their films were drawn from radio shows or radio characters, such as *PC 49*, *Dick Barton*, *The Man In Black* or *The Lyons Family*. Others drew on characters of myth and legend, such as Robin Hood, Dick Turpin and later on, of course, Count Dracula and Baron Frankenstein. In 1951 Hammer Films joined forces with the American production company, Robert Lippert Productions, to get their first foothold in the United States market. Anthony Hinds and Michael Carreras now started to produce a number of films in which American stars of the second rank took part, such as *Wings of Danger* (Zachary Scott; d. Terence Fisher, 1952), *Stolen Face* (Paul Henreid; d. Fisher, 1952) and *Spaceways* (Howard Duff, Eva Bartok; d. Fisher, 1953).

According to Michael Carreras it was during this period that Hammer Films was subject to two mutually complementary influences which interacted in a very productive manner. Under the guidance of the elder statesmen, Enrique Carreras and Will Hinds, the company built itself a firm footing and a reputation in the industry. Although, for instance, it frequently borrowed money from the National Film Finance Corporation, it always repaid it on time. James Carreras, on the other hand, was an expansive driving force, a salesman with an extrovert personality, who could sell refrigerators to the proverbial eskimoes. 'Had Hammer Films not inherited the services of Sir James Carreras, it would never have grown.'[72]

James Carreras created the opportunities for the younger members of the company to learn their jobs as film producers. The deal with Lippert provided first Anthony Hinds and later Michael Carreras with the chance to learn the business of film producing from first-hand experience, turning out one picture after another. Others too benefited from the intimate family atmosphere during this period. Terence Fisher recalled, 'it was excellent for me in the early days because I was feeling my way, I was young in the game. Being in a small studio one got to know everyone connected with it. The crews didn't change from picture to picture'.[73]

By 1955 however the deal with Lippert came to an end. The Bray studio stood virtually empty during the whole of 1955. The only pictures made there were a B picture, *Women Without Men* (d. Elmo Williams), and a series of shorts, mostly featuring various showbands but including one, *A Man on the Beach*, scripted by one of Hammer's young assistant directors, Jimmy Sangster, and directed by Joseph Losey, who at that time was trying to rebuild his career after having been driven out of Hollywood by the activities of the House Unamerican Activities Committee. Times were looking bad for Hammer and its future was heavily dependent on the box-office results of the films it had made in 1954. One of them, *The Quatermass Xperiment* (titled *The Creeping Unknown* in the United States; d. Val Guest) did extremely well. Adapted from Nigel Kneale's sensationally successful television series, *The Quatermass Experiment*, broadcast in July and August 1953, and with the title changed to *Xperiment*, to emphasize the British film censor's adults-only X certificate, the film's success led James Carreras to his own brand of market research. He asked cinema managers why the film was a success. Was it the science fiction element or the horror element? The answer which came back, thanks largely to an impressive and yet pathetic performance from Richard Wordsworth in a Frankenstein-like role as the half-monster, was – horror. Immediately a follow-up was set in motion, scripted by Jimmy Sangster. The result was *X – the Unknown* (d. Leslie Norman, 1956), soon to be followed by *Quatermass II* (titled *Enemy From Space* in the United States; d. V. Guest, 1957).

Carreras immediately looked around for another horror subject. The answer he found was *The Curse of Frankenstein* (d. Terence Fisher, 1956). A month before the London opening of the film James and Michael Carreras, and the producer, Anthony Hinds, flew to New York to show the picture to the New York executives of Warner Bros. Two hours after they had seen it the print was flown to Jack Warner on the West Coast, who decided to distribute the picture in the highly lucrative American market. The major box-office success of the film on both sides of the Atlantic put Hammer into the international market-place. It signed a deal with Universal to make *Dracula* (titled *The Horror of Dracula* in the United States) and a deal with Columbia to make three pictures a year. Other deals with other big American companies followed, including one with United Artists which produced *The Steel Bayonet* (d. Michael Carreras, 1956) and *Ten Seconds to Hell* (d. Robert Aldrich, 1958). James Carreras' philosophy was simple: 'I'm prepared to make Strauss waltzes tomorrow, if they'll make money.'[74]

The subjects of the pictures that Hammer made were determined entirely by the finance sources, which were usually the major American companies. It gave up making comedy films, aimed primarily at the domestic market, such as *I Only Arsked* (d. Montgomery Tully, 1958), based on the television series *The Army Game*, and *Watch It Sailor* (d. Wolf Rilla, 1961), because it found them extremely difficult to sell abroad. According to Carreras, 'If you're going to spend x on a film and your only market is your own and perhaps Australia and South Africa, we think it's better to make subjects that every country will buy.'[75] Not surprisingly the horror film became one of Hammer's staple products. Carreras was not in any way worried that they attracted the opprobrium of the critics. 'It doesn't really concern us at all. We're a purely commercial company, we turn out films we think are fairy tales in a way and we don't think they offend anybody. We've never known anyone rush out after seeing a Dracula and help himself to a pint of blood, or rush off to do a transplant because they've seen Professor Frankenstein doing one.'[76]

And so *The Curse of Frankenstein* was followed by *The Revenge of Frankenstein* (d. Terence Fisher, 1958), *The Evil of Frankenstein* (d. Freddie Francis, 1963), *Frankenstein Created Woman* (d. Fisher, 1966) and *Frankenstein Must Be Destroyed* (d. Fisher, 1969). Similarly *Dracula* (d. Fisher, 1957) was followed by *The Brides of Dracula* (d. Fisher, 1960), *Dracula – Prince of Darkness* (d. Fisher, 1965), *Dracula Has Risen From The Grave* (d. Francis, 1968), *Taste the Blood of Dracula* (d. Peter Sasdy, 1969), *Scars of Dracula* (d. Roy Ward Baker, 1970), *Countess Dracula* (d. Sasdy, 1971), *Dracula A.D. 1972* (d. Alan Gibson, 1972) and *Dracula is Dead and Well and Living in London* (d. Gibson, 1973). Other horror cycles included the 'Mummy' cycle, the 'Werewolf' cycle, the 'Jekyll and Hyde' cycle and 'Vampire' cycle. New cycles which were developed included a series of thrillers inspired by Hitchcock's *Psycho*, including *Maniac* (1961), *Paranoiac* (1961), *Nightmare* (1962), *Hysteria* (1964) and *The Nanny* (1965); also a number of 'animal' thrillers based on Hitchcock's *The Birds*, including *The Reptile* (1965). Other cycles included the prehistoric and exotic spectaculars, such as *One Million Years BC* (1965), *Slave Girls* (1966), *The Viking Queen* (1966), *The Vengeance of She* (1967), *The Lost Continent* (1967) and *When Dinosaurs Ruled the Earth* (1968). Occasionally Hammer also produced costume dramas which were suitable for family audiences, such as *Pirates of Blood River* (1961), *The Scarlet Blade* (titled *The Crimson Blade* in the United States; 1963) and *The Devil Ship Pirates* (1963).

Carreras' method of raising production finance was to take a series of titles and posters to an American distributor who was then persuaded to commission a script. Shooting would start within six months and the film would be finished within a year.[77] Carreras had a clear idea not of the content of the picture but of the impression that would need to be created in order to get audiences into cinemas across the world. 'Before we make a picture we say to ourselves "What will it look like outside the cinema?" and "Is it international?" '[78] When he could not pre-sell a picture Carreras would use a distributor's interest in a potentially highly profitable picture to shift other potentially less profitable products. Any distributor interested in acquiring the distribution rights of the potentially highly profitable *Blood of Frankenstein* (later *The Revenge of Frankenstein*) could only get them if he also bought the rights to *The Camp on Blood Island* and *The Snorkel*, both made in the same year.[79] By devices and ruses such as these Sir James Carreras managed to keep Bray Studios filled with an average of about six films a year. By keeping down production costs and aiming for high international profits, Carreras and Hammer succeeded in pushing the contribution from overseas earnings upwards from 47 per cent of revenue in 1965 to 82 per cent of revenue in 1967. Hammer was recognized by the British establishment and in 1968 it was awarded the Queen's Award for Industry.

Sir James Carreras had built up a British studio which was turning out films designed to make profits on the world market – films which, in cultural terms, were 'British' in a very specific way. By and large they were set in a fantasy world of the past or of the future, but only rarely did they deal with the real Britain of the day. One that did, *The Damned* (titled *These Are the Damned* in the United States) (d. Joseph Losey, 1961) was not released until 1963, two years after it had been completed, as a double bill with *Maniac* (d. Michael Carreras). Even then it was released in a mutilated and abridged version, cut down from a hundred to eighty-seven minutes (later reduced to seventy-seven minutes in the United States).

According to Losey, he 'undertook *The Damned* from a novel ("Children of Light" by H. L. Lawrence) [he] thought confused and not very good and because several other projects had fallen through at that moment and it was a difficult period in [his] life'.[80] Even so, he went into the project with his eyes open:

I knew I was making it for a company distinguished for making pretty horrid horror films and I knew they were primarily interested in the science fiction aspects of *The Damned*. I, on the other hand, was interested in parallel levels of violence: the violence I saw in kids; the violence of rock and roll and leather boys on motor cycles; the violence of the world everybody lives in, of the scientists, of the governments, of the rulers of the establishments [sic], which has to accept some responsibility for the violence one saw then in the extreme young.[81]

Losey seems to have made the film in the way he wanted by taking his script-wrtier, Evan Jones, and the unit to Weymouth, where most of the film was shot, and by rewriting the script between them as they went along. Losey was apparently asked to add an additional scene which clarified the relationship between King (Oliver Reed) and his sister Joan (Shirley Ann Field) and which consisted of a conversation at a pin-ball machine in an amusement arcade. He apparently did so.[82] More seriously however, a scene showing the nuclear scientist Bernard (Alexander Knox) shooting the sculptress Freya Neilson (Viveca Lindfors) was inserted by Hammer against Losey's wishes.[83] Not only did the insert alter the complete visual structure of the film (since it made complete nonsense of the appearance at the end of the helicopter from which Freya Neilson was to have been shot), but it completely altered the meaning of the film by implying that her death was the act of a single mad scientist, rather than the logical outcome of her conflict with the pro-nuclear values of the British state, which put the interests of the nuclear lobby and the arms race above the interests of its people.

Most reviews of *The Damned* attempted to assess the film in terms of Losey's authorship, and it is quite clear from the limited evidence which we have of the production that Losey was indeed the dominant creative force working on the film. His conception challenged that of Hammer and the distributors, Columbia. 'All of them doomed by the lurking unseen evil. They were . . . *THE DAMNED*' screamed the poster which double-billed the film with *Maniac*, while over both films it admonished, 'WARNING! DON'T GO ALONE, TAKE A BRAVE NERVELESS FRIEND WITH YOU.'[84] Hammer were appealing to a market that they knew well. It was the razzmatazz of the fairground that brought the people in. Shocks and thrills were the order of the day, not passionate analyses of contemporary problems. Despite critical acclaim, the film was a commerical failure, despite, or more probably because of, the way it was marketed.

And yet, despite the way in which they maltreated a major film-maker such as Joseph Losey, it would be unfair to dismiss all of Hammer's films from a cultural perspective. The qualities of *many* Hammer films – some are quite simply atrocious – come not from their overt subject-matter, but from the skill and craftmanship which Hammer was able to bring to making them, despite the vulgarity of their themes. A number of key technicians gave the films a distinctive quality, particularly in the articulation of their *mise-en-scène*, by taking seriously their fantastic, or in many cases ridiculous, plots. Hammer built up at Bray Studios a nucleus of artists, technicians and directors who were able to give Hammer films a style and a quality that marked them out from their competitors and drew the attention of the critics as well as the crowds. What is more, they knew how to give the films a gloss and a finish without spending much money, and yet in such a way that the economies were not apparent. The most successful team was undoubtedly that responsible for the early Dracula and Frankenstein pictures – producer Anthony Hinds, director Terence Fisher, writers Jimmy Sangster and John Elder (a pseudonym for Anthony Hinds), cameraman Jack Asher, art director Bernard Robinson and make-up chief Roy Ashton.

Anthony Hinds never said why he produced pictures, but, according to an undated press release from Hammer, he made them because 'that is my job – I do it for the money. And to those who depict me as the exploiter of the basest of common tastes and desires for the sake of profit, the answer is simple: I don't drive the public into the cinemas. They go because they want to go but only when there is something to see.'[85]

Hinds' philosophy, like Hammer's, was that of the market-place. First as producer, and later as both producer and, under the pseudonym John Elder, as script-writer, Anthony Hinds was clearly the person who was mainly involved in the mental labour of bringing his films to completion. The ideas contributed to the early Dracula and Frankenstein films were neither very original nor very inspiring. At a thematic level they had very little to say and were essentially formula pictures. It was their *mise-en-scène* that gave them their quality and impact. Terence Fisher, Hammer's most talented director, recognized this. He saw himself as 'not . . . an intellectual film director but [as] an emotional film director'.[86] His great skill was to be able to unify and co-ordinate the activities of a team of creative technicians and to put together a film on a limited budget and on a tight schedule, usually of the order of thirty days.

Fisher began his career first as assistant and later as editor at Gainsborough, where he edited *The Wicked Lady* (d. Arthur Crabtree, 1946). A year later he was invited by the Rank Organization to Highbury Studios, where they were running a training scheme for potential directors and where he made his first feature film, *Colonel Bogey*. He joined Hammer in 1951 and remained as one of their regular directors, frequently directing three pictures a year there, until the early 1970s. Fisher was not employed on a permanent basis however; he was essentially freelance and was normally employed for one picture at a time. As a freelance director his view was quite simple. 'I'll do anything for anybody. . . . But I've loved working with Hammer over the years. They had a certain amount of confidence in me and they did leave me alone to get on with the job.'[87] And he clearly worked well with Anthony Hinds. 'But I had a good relationship with Tony Hinds. I think one of the greatest associations is that between a producer and a director and by producer I don't mean a promoter but a working producer. Every director wants to go and cry on somebody's shoulder and he needs encouragement and advice at times too. Tony Hinds and I understood each other and we worked well together.'[88]

Although it may have been Anthony Hinds who was the one who was strong and who was able to support Fisher with encouragement and advice, it is nevertheless Fisher's creative personality that shines through all the films for which he was the director. As David Pirie has noted, Fisher's earlier work for Hammer 'has a pictorial sensuality which completely dominates all its other components'.[89] He rejected the expressionist approach associated with the German horror films of the 1920s and with those versions produced at Universal in the 1930s. His films create a world which has an internal coherence; the story is told in a direct and linear manner and there are rarely any flashbacks or dream sequences. He uses the camera to reproduce a world which obeys the same rules as the world we live in, except at those key moments when the supernatural breaks through. The opposition of ultimate good to ultimate evil, is paralleled by other oppositions: of light to darkness, of the spirit to the flesh. The oppositions are expressed visually in a clash between images of ascetic bourgeois respectability and images of decadent or romantic aristocracy. Knowledge is power, and occult knowledge, together with the elaborate articulation of arcane ritual, can be used to destroy evil, which takes many forms – not simply monsters, werewolves, gorgons and vampires of all sorts, but the decadent world of corrupt aristocrats, sensual women – be they countesses or prostitutes – and foreigners. The values of the films are those of the Victorian bourgoise. They advocate precisely those qualities of asceticism and sexual repression which the young people of the time were beginning to reject in their everyday lives, although at the same time they show, but as manifestations of evil, many of those qualities of self-fulfilment and sensuality for which people were beginning to search within their own lives.

As the cycles of horror films progressed the manifestations of evil became more and more lurid. The horror cycles of Dracula and Frankenstein gave way to the sex-vampire cycles, culminating in three scripted by Tudor Gates: *The Vampire Lovers* (d. Roy Ward Baker, 1970), *Lust for a Vampire* (d. Jimmy Sangster, 1970) and *Twins of Evil* (d. John Hough, 1971). These were concerned more with exploitation, lesbianism and sadism than with horror. It is significant that none of them was directed by Fisher, who had gradually been directing fewer and fewer films for Hammer, while they brought in younger and less experienced directors. Fisher's most productive and creative period for Hammer coincided with the spectacular growth in the company's overseas earnings, up to the period when it won the Queen's Award for Industry. Fisher was able to reconcile the essentially Victorian morality of the films with the commercial need for a horror film. With Hammer's changing economic circumstances however that was no longer possible. The need for exploitation became stronger, partly because Hammer was suffering from the general withdrawal of the major American companies from financing British films (as a result of President Johnson's decision to cut back the tax benefits for American investment overseas, in order to finance the costs of the Vietnam war) and was therefore less protected in the market-place, and partly because of the changing climate of censorship, which was becoming more and more permissive. Younger, less competent and presumably less expensive directors were brought in to direct the films, and the inexperience showed.

The cut-back in American financing not only affected the quality of Hammer's output; it also affected their industrial base. Hammer's output dropped from six films in 1967 to two films and a television series in 1968 and only three films in 1969, one of which, *Moon Zero*

Two (d. Roy Ward Baker), despite being budgeted at $1.5 million, lost
a great deal of money. The viability of Bray Studios was called into
question. Carreras had been forced to use the EMI studios at Elstree
for several of the films which had been financed by that company.
Four of the six produced in 1964, *Hysteria*, *The Curse of the Mummy's
Tomb*, *She* and *Fanatic* (titled *Die My Darling* in the United States)
were shot there, as were two more in 1965 *The Nanny* and *One Million
Years BC*. Hammer's last film to be made at Bray was *The Mummy's
Shroud* (1966). The studios were vacated in 1968 and sold in 1970. A
few days earlier Carreras had signed a deal with EMI's Bernard
Delfont to make nine pictures in the next three years. They were all to
be shot at Elstree. Three months later Sir James Carreras became
chairman and chief executive of Hammer. His wife also became a
director and Michael Carreras joined the board as managing director.
A new generation was taking over.

Bray was an important factor which enabled Hammer to produce
cheap pictures with a fine sense of quality, and the shift to Elstree had
a marked effect on the quality of their films, which now seemed to lack
that sense of style and unifying cohesion which had marked their
earlier products. For Michael Carreras Bray was a marvellous studio.
'One thing I do like is a studio where you make one picture at a time.
That way everybody on the lot is conscientiously on that one picture,
which is good. When you move into a multiple picture studio, as we
later did, you tend to get lost . . . and everything gets more difficult.
But . . . it was the flavour of Bray. It was like a family affair.'[90]

Creativity and Context

It is now possible to point to a number of factors which are common to
the production contexts of Ealing and Hammer films, despite the
widely different philosophies of Sir Michael Balcon and Sir James
Carreras. In both cases production was centred around a studio base,
Ealing and Bray, which provided continuous employment for a team
of technicians and craftsmen. By producing between four and six
films a year, the studio was kept in use continuously, and there was
therefore optimum use of the capital invested in the buildings, the
plant and the equipment of the studio. This was the smallest size of
studio compatible with economic viability, and it also made possible
the purchase of the craft skills of the technicians at the minimum price
compatible with their skills, since regular employment in a highly

casualized industry, marked by regular periods of unemployment, ensured the loyalty of the technical staff concerned for lower rates than were available on a freelance basis.

Both studios owed their existence to special situations within the market-place of the international film industry. In the case of Ealing it was because of the privileged position which Balcon had negotiated within the heart of the Rank empire, which guaranteed a release of Ealing films into Rank cinemas and also guaranteed a regular source of production finance from the Rank Organization, which in turn was able to use its very substantial cinema holdings as security in order to raise production finance from outside the organization. In the case of Bray it was because of the special relationships which Carreras was able to establish with the big American companies, through which they frequently made a major contribution to the pre-production financing of the films and in turn marketed them in the United States, the largest market in the world.

In both studios there was a history of gradual economic decline, which culminated in the studio being sold. In both studios the costs of production rose over the years, but neither Balcon nor Carreras were able to offset these by compensating productivity gains, which could only be achieved by expanding their position in the world market. Furthermore, at a time which is difficult to determine with any precision, both studios lost their protection from the full rigours of the market-place. For Ealing it was at some point during the early 1950s; for Hammer it was probably in 1967, as a result of the changes in American fiscal policy brought about by the need to pay for the Vietnam war. Both studios then turned increasingly to other sources of production finance. Ealing turned to the National Film Finance Corporation, Hammer to EMI. Within two or three years both studios were shut down. Ealing closed in 1955; Bray closed in 1968 and was sold in 1970.

Despite the wide differences between the two studios in the types of films they were making, there were also a surprising number of similarities between them in the creative context within which the writers and directors of the films themselves were able to work. In both studios there was a family atmosphere and ordinary technicians felt a personal loyalty to the head of the studio. In both studios the head, Sir Michael Balcon or Sir James Carreras, had a strong, clear view of the type of films which the studio should be making. Balcon exerted his control through very careful selection of his creative elite and of the projects which they proposed to him. Carreras exerted his control by establishing in advance the 'look' of the picture to the outside world, by focusing very precisely, at the early stages, on the title of the film and on the poster designs, and be delegating the responsibility for production either for Anthony Hinds or to his son, Michael Carreras.

In both studios film directors who clashed with their chief suffered by getting no more work for a period of time, and by having their picture re-edited by the heads of the studio, as Robert Hamer found with *Kind Hearts and Coronets* and Joseph Losey found with *The Damned*. Film directors whose world view coincided with that of the head of the studio could look forward to being employed either continuously, as Crichton, Dearden, Frend and Mackendrick were employed at Ealing, or regularly, as Fisher was employed at Bray. Directorial skill was primarily assessed in terms of the competence of the *mise-en-scène*, and of course in terms of the ability to keep on schedule and within the production budget.

In both studios scripts were normally carefully vetted before shooting started. In those films where preplanning was less than thorough, such as *Kind Hearts and Coronets* and *The Damned*, there was frequently trouble later on. On occasion, as with *Whisky Galore*, there was not.

Ideology and Context

Despite the number of structural factors which are common to the histories of the two British film companies, it is of course quite clear that the ideological intentions of the two studio heads were completely different. Balcon wanted to make pictures that brought a form of documentary naturalism to the screen during the war, and, later on, acted as ambassadors of the British people. Carreras, on the other hand, simply wanted to turn out fairy tales – many designed to frighten, to horrify or to shock. If Balcon, to use his own terms, was turning out realism, then Carreras was turning out tinsel.

Another distinction which could tentatively be drawn between Ealing films and Hammer films is between the levels of consciousness at which they sought to operate. For Balcon, the cinema was mainly concerned with showing people what the real world was like – or should be like. It was a world where surface naturalism and empirical behaviour were important and where, with rare exceptions, such as in

Hamer's films or in the comedies, the forbidden world of the subconscious rarely surfaced. In Hammer films however the cinema was a vehicle for fairy tales which bore little, if any, relation to the empirical realities of the world. In both studios trouble occurred when there was an attempt to bridge the two approaches. Hammer could not stomach Losey's attempt to come to terms with violence in the real world in *The Damned*, and Balcon could not tolerate Hammer's emphasis on Louis Mazzini's sexual yearnings for Sibella as opposed to Edith. The only Ealing films where the worlds of the subconscious and reality interact are the comedies.[91]

These differences between Ealing and Hammer contribute to a wider debate, conducted at a more general theoretical level, about the relationship between the economy and the ideology of the mass media in general and of the British cinema in particular.[92] Broadly speaking, the question is how far the economic context of production determines the ideology of the individual products of the mass media, such as the films themselves. The films of Ealing and of Hammer can both, in their different ways, be seen as expressing the dominant ideology of capitalism. In the Ealing films, with the occasional exception in the work of Robert Hamer, there is no concern about how the behaviour of the typically British characters in them is influenced, or indeed determined, by their economic circumstances. Occasionally however these concerns do surface, in a displaced and attenuated form in the comedies. Similarly the Hammer films offer the possibility of escape into a world of fantasy, where the economic realities of life are insignificant elements in the drama. The attempt by Losey to draw parallels between the violence of the leather boys and the violence of the state in *The Damned* was ruthlessly mutilated, since it challenged too openly the class interests of both Hammer and the distributors, Columbia.

That the output of both studios reflected the class interests of their owners should come as no surprise. At Ealing Balcon used his protected niche within the Rank Organization to make films about the life and achievements of contemporary Britain, free from the market demands of the international film industry. In the dramas they portrayed, for the most part an ideal world where men and women of all classes lived and worked harmoniously together, untroubled by the economic and class differences which existed in the real world. But outside that protected niche, in the overseas market, the evidence points to the fact that his films were only successful when they ignored life in contemporary Britain and replaced it with neo-imperialist adventures in the African bush, or displaced the concerns with contemporary British life through the mechanisms of comedy. As for Hammer, it consistently shunned the problems of the contemporary world and set its horror films at the high point of Victorian capitalism, in a past which was equally displaced in all countries of the world, and where, again, economic and class conflicts were effectively eliminated from the narrative.

The common economic history of Ealing and Hammer is one of industrial decline in the face of the demands for increasing returns from a shrinking world market. The common ideological history is one of articulating the common class interests of their owners, Sir Michael Balcon and Sir James Carreras. Although at first sight the films they produced appear quite different, they both ultimately came to depend on their appeal to the American market-place, to which they offered a combination of exoticism and cathartic release. For Ealing it was the neo-imperialist thrill of adventure in Africa and the laughter of comedy. For Hammer it was the shudder of horror and fantasy.

12

The James Bond Films: Conditions of Production

Janet Woollacott

> I think that the mere fact that we were lucky to stumble upon Ian Fleming and Bond was a bit of good fortune. The rest was all hard work.
>
> Cubby Broccoli, 1976[1]

Accounts of film production have a certain 'built-in' fascination both for those interested in film generally and for those intellectually concerned with the products and organization of the mass media. The story of 'what happens behind the scenes' or behind the cameras is constructed endlessly in the popular press and in academic accounts of film-making. At the same time, studies of film production, from Lillian Ross's description of the making of *The Red Badge of Courage* onwards, have occupied a space within film studies which has been conspicuous for its lack of integration with more general theoretical approaches to the mass media.[2] Why should this be? I want to explore some of the problems associated with the discussion of film productions in relation to a particular case: that of the making of the James Bond film, *The Spy Who Loved Me*.

Moreover, I also want to consider some of the implications of analysing the making of *The Spy* in terms of its 'conditions of production'. I want to use the idea of *condition* here in the sense defined by Pierre Macherey: as the principle of rationality which makes works of fiction accessible to thought, rather than as a cause in the empirical sense. 'To know the conditions of a work is not to reduce the process of its production to merely the growth of a seed which contains all its future possibilities from the very beginning . . . ,' Macherey argues. 'To know the conditions of a work is to define the real process of its constitution, to show how it is composed from a real diversity of elements which give it substance.'[3]

Macherey's distinctive contribution to literary theory has been to develop a particular conception of the relationship between fiction and ideology whereby literary work both organizes and in a novel manner 'works over' ideological themes. The direction of Macherey's work argument operates against the notion of literary works conceived of as 'created' and 'finished' products and towards the analysis of literary texts as they are inscribed in a variety of different institutional and ideological contexts. Studying a particular text does not require elevating it and isolating it from its history of productive consumption, but looking at everything about it, '. . . everything which has been collected on it, become attached to it – like shells on a rock by the seashore forming a whole incrustation.'[4] The production of literary work, according to Macherey's argument, is a process and a labour which transform ideologies through formal mechanisms and which are further transformed by literary criticism into a body of 'works' with a particular status and meaning. Clearly, the James Bond films do not fall easily into the arena of literary theory within which Macherey has constructed his theoretical strategy. But Macherey's ideas have some interesting implications not only for the analysis of the James Bond phenomena generally, but also for the specific area of the production of the Bond films.

There have been a number of accounts of film production which focus on the institutions within which film-making takes place, the occupational ideologies of the film-makers and the specific day-to-day decision-making involved in the production of any one film. The Open University case study on *The Making of The Spy Who Loved Me* examines precisely these areas in its television programmes and accompanying booklet.[5] The Bond films and *The Spy* in particular were considered in the context of the British film industry and its interrelationship with Hollywood. The Bond films, it is pointed out, were made at Pinewood Studios in England in an industrial context characterized by constant financial crisis. The perennial problems of the British film industry have been the lack of a large enough home market to support stable and permanent film-making and the inroads made by large-scale and expensive American productions on British screens. The 1960s saw the increasing exploitation of cheap film-making facilities in Britain by Americans attracted by the conditions of the Eady Levy and favourable exchange rates. The first Bond film (*Dr No*, made in 1962) was produced in this way. The partnership of the Canadian, Harry Saltzman, and the American, Cubby Broccoli, bought up the film rights to all the Bond novels, with the exception of *Casino Royale*, and got financial backing from United Artists.

. . . here was a series of books written by Fleming that were selling, really, you know, like hot cakes and no one really had envisaged making the films. And no distributor would put up the money for it until Arthur Krim of United Artists agreed to do it. He was primarily interested in making a film with me. For years we had talked about making films. I was making films for Columbia prior to that. . . . So I flew to New York and that's where it all started and then in about forty-five minutes we had a deal. I think one of the main reasons was David Picker – who was then given the job of production. He stepped in at that time. He knew about Fleming too and he was also a James Bond afficionado. He liked the idea.[6]

The Bond films proved to be immensely profitable and United Artists continued to finance the series, even though the American involvement in the British film industry substantially decreased in the early 1970s, through major cutbacks, sales of assets and write-offs. Only in the 1980s did the Bond films cease to have a British base. *Moonraker*, for example, was made from the United States, with location work elsewhere and only the special effects produced at Pinewood.

However, the combination of a studio base at Pinewood over a number of years and the continuing success of the series ensured the development and maintenance of a team of people who worked together on the Bond films over a period of time. Although there have clearly been many changes in the members of the Bond production team, it is surprising how many people have either continued to work on the Bond films or have returned to them after working on other films. At the time of the making of *The Spy*, new members of the production team – Claude Renoir (director of photography), Christopher Wood (writer), and others – were far outnumbered by those who had worked on previous Bond films. Moreover, they experienced a conscious effort on the part of Broccoli (by this time the sole producer) and other members of his team to initiate them into the world of 'Bondian' film making. 'Bondian' was the phrase used by Broccoli and other members of the production team to mean 'in the spirit of James Bond'. To a certain extent the term 'Bondian' was used to describe the Bond films, which were seen as a distinctive formula, a specific genre of film. As Lewis Gilbert, who directed *The Spy*, said:

. . . most of the things in Bond films today have kind of grown up with the picture . . . they tend to keep it into the pattern they've had all along. For instance, they have an unknown leading lady. They don't like to change all the people who are well known like 'M' and Miss Moneypenny and there's no way in which they could be changed because the public really wants to see them . . . they like the pattern, the formula. I think that part of the charm of the Bond picture [is] you know what you're going to get. . . . You're not disappointed. . . . You see audiences in a Bond film aren't looking for great acting – they want to be overwhelmed by physical things. Well the character of Bond, you couldn't change, of course . . . but you can change his attitude to a certain extent . . . he doesn't find this girl so easy – such a pushover as the other girls have been. And so in that sense, you can change it slightly, but it's very well laid down, the law of Bond and people want you to abide by it. . . . Bond films are very very different from any other kind of film made. They've disproved every law in the cinema, they've done everything wrong and they're huge successes . . . I mean in story elements, in characterization elements, things like that – the anti-climatic bit they always have at the end which you wouldn't dare do in other pictures where they have a huge big ending and then suddenly, the film starts up again. . . . Many things they do wrong, things which you would think get a laugh in a normal picture, but it's a kind of sympathetic laugh.[7]

A great deal of discussion between members of the production team of *The Spy* centred on the provision of 'Bondian effects' within the film: on the importance of the sets, the gadgets, the foreign locations, the threatening character of the villains (which must incorporate both a physical threat and an intellectual threat to the hero), Bond's relationship with the girl in the story, the jokes and the form of the crucial pre-credits sequence. The 'formula' of the Bond film was generally understood, and to a certain extent the term 'Bondian' was used to refer to that formula. At the same time, people working on *The Spy* also used the term to refer to the process of working on a Bond picture. It was recognized and acknowledged that this was different from the process of working on other films. Claude Renoir, the cameraman, listed aspects of Bond pictures as 'a lot of people, a lot of good technicians, a lot of tricks, special effects and so on' and underlined the importance of the big budget in a Bond film, pointing out that 'it's quite rare for a French cameraman to be involved in such a big budget picture'.[8]

The importance of the big budget was stressed by many members of the production team (it is part of the 'Bondian' ethos), including Christopher Wood:

I have worked on films in which people have said to me, Chris baby, it doesn't matter. The sky's the limit. You want to shoot this in Saudi Arabia, shoot it in Saudi Arabia, we don't care, as many people as you like, just don't feel there are any constraints. So I write it and then they come back and say, well, why have we got two rooms. I mean couldn't she be his uncle and his wife at the same time. I mean, we'd save money on casting as well. With a Bond film, you do know that with anything you write, money is no restraint.[9]

Wood also acknowledged some of the frustrations of working on a Bond picture, in which slightly different conceptions of the Bondian might compete:

. . . I was very pleased with a sequence I had when we established Bond in the film, in which we'd have a scene of the sea. . . . On the raft, Bond is lying with the girl, beep, beep, beep, comes a little message. Then in his usual cursory rather boorish way, he waves her farewell leaving her sort of yelping on the raft and just steps aboard his surfboard, picks up the nearest roller, roars forward on a mind-bending shot, riding a forty-five-foot-high wave, comes straight down, up the beach, still on the board to where there's a jeep, just slips off the board . . . inside the jeep, flicks up the microphone and gets his orders . . . shoves his foot down on the jeep which raises up at a priapic angle up the side of the sand dune, just roars up into space and in about thirty seconds I thought we'd establish the persona of Bond. . . . Cubby had a better idea . . . when you see Bond's entrance in the Movie, it's better . . . which I now accept, but when it was first mooted I was rather sulkily rubbing my foot against the floor and thinking, 'Blast'.[10]

In the event, the pre-credits sequence in *The Spy* involved establishing the loss of British and Russian submarines and the contacting not only of Bond (acted by Roger Moore), but also of the Russian Special Agent, X, who is apparently a Bond-type figure making love to a beautiful woman, but turns out to be the woman herself. Bond, similarly occupied in a chalet in the Alps, skis off to answer his call – only to be attacked by Russian agents, from whom he escapes and whom he kills during an extended chase, finally leaping off an enormous cliff, only to open his parachute, which unfolds to reveal the Union Jack. The production team were satisfied that this was an effective, 'Bondian' opening to the film.

The idea of the Bondian also percolated through to those not directly involved in film production. Saul Cooper, for example, the director of publicity, argued that the only bad publicity for a Bond picture was that which 'destroys the illusion'. 'The illusion,' he suggested, 'is the thing that I have learnt from Cubby Broccoli . . .

that there are things that are Bondian and things that are not Bondian.' Cooper explained that 'Bondian is our own special word . . . everything that involves Bond has to be a little bigger, a little better, to be larger than life, it has to have a certain special flair. . . .'[11] In the publicity for the film, the whole notion of the Bondian was brought into play. Journalists, for example, were invited to a 'Bondian week-end', in which they stayed at an international hotel and were served a banquet of James Bond dishes, culled from the novels. The tanker set was much publicized as the 'biggest set' in Europe. The opening of the set was a publicity event, which involved not only the participation of the bevy of beautiful, scantily clad girls which accompanied most Bond publicity stunts, but also a visit by Harold Wilson and his introduction to Roger Moore and Barbara Bach – the new Bond girl, dressed in Russian uniform.

While the Open University case study focuses on the background in the British and American film industries of the Bond films, and of the process of the making of *The Spy Who Loved Me* in particular, it also offers a particular ideological reading of the Bond films, including *The Spy*:

. . . the film is in a sense the perfection of the SPECTRE[12] genre although SPECTRE is never mentioned inasmuch as Stromberg's ransom plan is applied indiscriminately to East and West, playing upon the tensions which subsist beneath detente. Stromberg himself being presented to us as a personification of the irrational forces which permanently threaten the delicate balance of peaceful co-existence. In this sense, particularly at this precise moment in history, Bond's adventures take on a new significance inasmuch as it is through his endeavours that the ever impending crisis which threatens the world with calamity is averted. The world is led to the brink of nuclear holocaust and back again. It is by thus effecting a purely imaginary resolution of real social contradictions, which are themselves misrepresented in the form of the fantastic and the grotesque, that the Bond films attain their ideological effect.[13]

The Spy is in effect read as a working over of contemporary ideologies around international tensions. Moreover, the pattern of coverage of the case study implicitly takes for granted the classical Marxist hierarchy of determinants. We are led as readers from the financial and economic 'determinants' of the Bond films through the institutional space within which they were made and the occupational ideologies of the film-makers to a reading of *The Spy* as realist. It is 'the product of a camera which conceals itself', in which even moments of technological and fantastic excess in the film are conceived of as part of an ideological motif in which the viewer's disbelief is played upon, only to reinforce its suspension 'and the false consciousness which that suspension promotes'.[14]

The problems of this approach, however, are clearly evident. The Marxist base/superstructure model, with its focus on the problem of determination, has provided an implicit or explicit background for many studies of culture. Raymond Williams summarizes the general proposition of Marxism in the following way:

> The whole movement of society is governed by certain dispositions of the means of production and when these dispositions – forces and relations in a mode of production as a whole – change through the operation of their own laws and tendencies, then forms of consciousness and forms of intellectual and artistic production (forms which have their place in orthodox Marxist definition as a 'superstructure') change also. Some shift in relatively direct ways, like politics and law, some shift in distant and often indirect ways – the traditional examples are religion, philosophy and aesthetics.[15]

Although few, including Williams himself, would now accept a crude form of the base/superstructure model as an acceptable theoretical framework for the analysis of culture, problems associated with the base/superstructure notion have continued to dog the analysis of culture. In the study of film and media organizations, questions of determination frequently remain in the background, but they do to a certain extent justify the many studies of professional people and organizations concerned with the media. As Philip Elliott argues, such studies in America and Britain 'provide the basis for an analysis of the production of media culture under the conditions of democratic capitalism'.[16]

In film studies, accounts of the production process are either considered in isolation or they are organized around questions of determination. Hence, John Ellis, in his admirable analysis of Ealing Studios, contends that 'to determine the possibilities of any film, the material, technological, aesthetic and ideological determinants in its production have to be examined: only here can it be decided where a film coincides with the dominant ideology and where it diverges from it'.[17] Ellis's listing of the determinants of an Ealing text includes 'the entire history of the cinema (its system of production, distribution and exhibition)', 'the specific organization of production' and 'the beliefs of the group controlling production'.[18] The difficulties of attempting to explain films in terms of this type of hierarchy of determinants is often simply that an examination of 'the entire history of the cinema', even of 'the specific organization of production' and 'the beliefs of the group controlling production', tends to establish at best a series of fragmentary connections between film texts and the views of the owners or controllers of production. Ellis, for example, suggests that although the concentration of Ealing films on the lower middle class was the result of a complex of factors, the primary factor was biographical, in that the majority of the film-makers concerned were born into middle-class families, many of them strongly imbued with lower-class liberalism, 'which expressed the class interest of the emergent lower sections of the bourgeoise'.[19] Thus Ealing is seen as the product of a generation which was 'radicalized' by the experience of the Depression and for whom the desire to show 'the people' in films was satisfied by a focus on the characters and situations of the petit bourgeoisie.

The inter-connections proposed by Ellis seem less than obvious. But the implication seems to be that Ealing films, like all films, have a number of levels of determination, that they were, in effect, 'overdetermined', but that one of the crucial elements in that over-determination was the class origins and views of the group controlling production. I find some slightly worrying gaps in the analysis here. The concentration of Ealing films on lower-middle-class characters, shopkeepers, small businessmen and the like, is explained in terms of the class position and outlook of those in charge of production. The final variable area in the hierarchy of determinants seems to be 'individuality':

This is Ealing's situation; a group of conventionally educated intellectuals, through a certain liberal radicalism, come to make films about and for 'the people', whom they think of as the lower levels of the petit bourgeoisie. Thus individuals are a vital part of the process, not as finished entities with worldviews and metaphysical preoccupations, but as social beings.[20]

Unfortunately, individuality, albeit socially formed, does not seem to explain why the Ealing film-makers' class origins are 'displaced' onto the petit bourgeoisie.

In this kind of analysis, the inevitable gaps between determining factors and the films tend to be dealt with either through a designation of 'individual' activity or, in other circumstances, through an accepted and understandable lack of knowledge about the complex interpenetration of different levels of determination, because of the absence of any detailed histories of the film industry and of the productions of different films. Edward Buscombe's interesting attempt to explore the relationship between Frank Capra's films and the ownership and control of Columbia Pictures Corporation sounds a number of warnings about categorizing the relationship between films, studios and more general social attitudes, arguing that films 'cannot be explained simply in terms of who owned the studios or in terms only of social attitudes at the time'.[21] Buscombe suggests that the history of the American film industry constitutes a kind of missing link in attempts to make connections between Hollywood films and American society. The assumption in this case is that 'many of the materials needed to forge that link are missing'.[22]

The case study on the making of *The Spy Who Loved Me* shares this familiar problem of making connections between (in this instance) the occupational ideologies and actions of the Bond production team in the process of making the film and the script of *The Spy Who Loved Me* in relation to a hierarchy of determinations. Both Stuart Hall and Dyer, in their discussion of the occupational ideologies of the film-makers, stressed the limitations of the conscious views and actions of the members of the production team. Dyer argued that the whole area of professionalism and commodity production which characterizes the Bond team permits a repression of considerations of ideology. Hall suggested that Dyer's argument involved 'a species of professional unconsciousness', that 'professionalism really means being conscious about certain foreground things in order not to be conscious about some of the ideological themes'. On the one hand, Dyer's argument eschewed the notion of simple manipulation by the Bond team, but, on the other hand, it also suggested that 'you have to recognise that there is a gap between what they [the Bond production team] think they're doing and what they're actually doing'.[23] One of the difficulties of this kind of approach is precisely that the views of the Bond production team are seen to be to a large extent either irrelevant or misleading for anyone who wishes to understand the ideological meaning of the film of *The Spy Who Loved Me*. Such views have to be taken into account, but not accepted at their face value.

A number of issues seem to be involved in this placing of the views of the film-makers within the context of production studies. The first of these is undoubtedly the over-emphasis on determination. The views and practices of film-makers are conceived of as inadequate in terms of the determination of film texts. As I have suggested, they are interesting evidence, but are not to be accepted at face value, because other determining forces (technology, ownership and so on) have not only to be taken into account but also ranked in the hierarchy of determinants. The second important assumption of such arguments is that the ideological meaning of a film can be established and that that ideological meaning is self-evidently not the meaning with which the film-makers themselves would have endowed their film. Given these premises, the realm of professional ideology inevitably becomes tinged with notions of 'false consciousness'.

I would argue that it is important to rethink this formulation of the place of production studies. Firstly, the endeavour to reinsert the script of *The Spy* into its conditions of production should not be seen in terms of the exegesis of determination, conceived of in terms of the classical Marxist hierarchy of determinants. Secondly, the script of *The Spy* has to be conceptualized as part of a group of texts, including novels, films, advertising and other cultural forms, the ideological meaning of which cannot be 'delivered' in a once and for all manner outside their conditions of production and the history of their consumption. Given these provisos, the role of professional ideologies and the labour of film production take on a rather different meaning. It becomes less necessary to take for granted that the ideological work involved in producing the Bond films takes place 'behind the backs' of the Bond production team. Rather, the opposite case could be argued. The detailed and enthusiastic discussion of the experience of working on a Bond film collected in the Open University case study provides rich material both on the production team's use and transformation of existing James Bond texts (both novels and films) and on specific ideologies, outside those texts, which they were concerned to rework in the production of *The Spy Who Loved Me*. The 'hard work' of making a Bond film is not simply a matter of anecdotal interest, nor yet another example of the organization of the mass media and of the role of professional ideologies. An examination of the process of working on *The Spy Who Loved Me* actually informs us both about the existing ideologies with which the Bond production team were concerned and about the way in which these were transformed during the making of the film.

Clearly, a key element in the making of the later Bond films was the existence and popularity of the preceding films and novels. The early Bond films tended to follow the plots of the novels quite closely, but later films, such as *The Spy*, have taken little more than the title from Fleming's work. When Broccoli talked about his 'good fortune' in finding the Ian Fleming books, he was quite right to stress that, while this was mere luck, the development of the Bond films was 'all hard work'. Even in the making of the early Bond movies, the Bond books were not simply reproduced but were consciously worked over and changed. At the time of the making of *The Spy Who Loved Me*, while the production team were well aware of the heritage of Bond and happily referred to the Bond films as 'formula' pictures, they were also concerned to update and slightly shift the emphasis of these films. It is worth touching on some of the areas on which the Bond team could be seen to be working and which have implications for the transform-ation of ideologies achieved in a film such as *The Spy Who Loved Me*. The three areas with which the latter part of this chapter is concerned are the attempts to depoliticize James Bond, to engage with ideas about the independence of women, and to construct and maintain a comic strategy around Bond's own sexuality.

The James Bond of Ian Fleming's novels written before the 1960s (such as *Moonraker*, 1955; *From Russia with Love*, 1957; *Goldfinger*, 1959) is strategically located in the Cold War tensions of the period. 'The villain,' remarks Umberto Eco of the Bond novels,

is born in an ethnic area that stretches from central Europe to the Slav countries and to the Mediterranean basin; as a rule he is of mixed blood and his origins are complex and obscure; he is asexual or homosexual, or at any rate is not sexually normal; he has exceptional inventive and organizational qualities which help him acquire immense wealth and by means of which he usually works to help Russia; to this end he conceives a plan of fantastic character and dimensions, worked out to the smallest detail, intended to create serious difficulties either for England or for the Free World in general.[24]

The later novels to a certain extent discard the more obvious trappings of Cold War hostilities, although the films have always pitted Bond against SPECTRE.[25] The producer of the Bond films, Cubby Broccoli, has been noted for his declaration that the Bond films are 'not political' but are good 'old fashioned entertainment'. What Broccoli seems to mean by this claim is that he has shown a constant desire to play down the overtly anti-Soviet views of Fleming's Bond. By the time of the making of *The Spy*, the tenth James Bond film, the plot portrays Russia as being under threat. The villain, Stromberg, threatens East and West alike with nuclear destruction, and East/

West relations become a matter of the sexual and professional subordination to the West's best agent (Bond) of Russia's 'Special Agent', X (Anya).

This type of depoliticization of the Bond myth was put vigorously into effect by the production team, with a view to 'up-dating Bond' and, possibly, serving commercial interests. Members of the Russian Embassy were invited to the opening of the tanker set at Pinewood – to which Harold Wilson, as I have mentioned, was also invited. Roger Moore and Barbara Bach were conspicuously posed together hand in hand, for publicity purposes. The production team liked to characterize the Bond films as a 'circus', as 'entertainment' in which the villain or villains have to offer both an intellectual threat and a physical threat to Bond, but there is a real sense in which the *specific* political threat embodied in the villain in the Fleming books was consciously and systematically eradicated. In a Bond film, the typical villain, and Stromberg in *The Spy Who Loved Me* is no exception, intends not merely to threaten a particular country or the Western World, but to 'destroy the world'. Stromberg is, in effect, represented as a madman, a villain who threatens to destroy the existing world in order to build another one under his control under the sea. The general nuclear threat is tied here to irrational desires for change. At the same time, however, Stromberg's character takes on the quality of parody in the 'larger than life' excesses of Bond villainy. Stromberg's assistant, whose enormous size and steel teeth constitute the main physical threat to Bond, was conceived of comically as a parody of other films. Broccoli, Wood and Michael Wilson (the assistant to the producer) saw the development of the character of 'Jaws' in terms of an elaborated joke. 'Jaws', for example, reverses popular assumptions about sharks: he kills a shark by biting it.

A crucial and important part of the Bond myth has always centred around sexuality. Indeed, the elaborate sexual coding of the novels ties together Bond's relationship to M, to the villain and to the women.[26] Women in the Bond films have always been conceived in terms of male desire and pleasure. When Ursula Andress, as Honeychile Rider, clad in a bikini and with knife in hand, walked out of the sea in *Doctor No*, the visual image of the Bond woman was resoundingly established. The scenes in which Honey makes her appearance as a latter-day Venus could be read as a textbook illustration of scophophilic pleasure, whereby the manipulation of 'looks' in the film establishes the woman as the object of sexual desire both for the hero and for the audience. The Bond films generally would seem, on one level, to conform to Laura Mulvey's analysis of scophophilic pleasure in Hollywood films. Mulvey's argument suggests that, in such films, a particular regime of pleasure is established through the 'looks' of the hero and the audience. While women are represented as erotic spectacle, the audience is led to identify with the male hero, the active performer.

The Bond films also took over and reworked the motifs of the books in which the sexual subordination of the 'Bond women' plays an important part in reordering the narrative disturbances which is the task of the hero. In the books, the Bond girl is not simply the bland but desirable and sexual creature who emerges from other peoples' reworkings of the Bond myth.[27] Rather, Bond's girls have always had some initial claim to independence. There are no clinging romantic heroines in the Bond novels. But the narrative pattern of the Bond novels establishes the women as in some manner sexually and ideologically 'out of place': too aggressive (Vesper Lynd in *Casino Royale*), frigid (Gala Brand in *Moonraker*), damaged by rape (Tiffany Case in *Diamonds are Forever* and Honeychile Rider in *Dr No*) or lesbian (Tilly Masterton and Pussy Galore in *Goldfinger*). Such women are 'out of place' in relation to men, as represented by Bond, and are likely, therefore, also to be in the service of the villain. Such a girl represents a challenge to the traditional sexual order, and Bond's answer is that of 'putting her back into place beneath him (both literally and metaphorically)'.[28] In so doing, he also pulls her into the cause of 'right', removing her from an alliance with the villain and recruiting and attaching her to his task and views.

The early Bond films contained distinct echoes of these themes of the novels, although the sexual ambiguity of the Bond girls tended to be underplayed. The lesbianism of Tilly Masterton and Pussy Galore in the film of *Goldfinger* is muted to the point that only a 'knowing' viewer would recognize it. On the whole, the films reworked the role of the Bond girls in terms of plenitude and availability. Constant references are made to Bond's success with women by characters around him, particularly Moneypenny and Felix Leiter. The Bond formula, as understood by the production team on *The Spy*, involved a plethora of beautiful women and the repeated demonstration of Bond's mastery over them. The traditional ending of a Bond film sees Bond, having disposed of the villain and destroyed his headquarters, making love to the new Bond girl of the film, in the aftermath of violence, while the credits roll, promising his return in a new Bond film. The production team working on *The Spy* were powerfully aware of that tradition and of its importance in the Bondian formula. At the same time, they were also well aware of the importance of the women's movement and of public criticisms of Bond. The team saw clearly that Bond had to fulfil certain sexist expectations revolving around male pleasure, but they also wanted to register the impact of Women's Lib. The heroine of *The Spy Who Loved Me* is Anya, a Russian agent who is Bond's professional equal. Barbara Bach, the new Bond girl of the film, was told that this was a Bond girl with a difference:

> Well, first of all, she's a spy and a serious spy. And she's really not one of Bond's girls so to speak. She's in the film doing her own bit and she meets up with Bond and it's only almost at the end of the film that there's any kind of attraction between the two of them, other than let's say, professional competition. So it's quite different. Most of the girls in the Bond films have just been merely beautiful girls that you know have small parts and come in and go out. Anya stays from the beginning to the end.[29]

In some limited formal terms, the character of Anya was given equal status with Bond. Lewis Gilbert remarked that 'Women's Lib would be rather proud of her'.[30] Nevertheless, the Women's Lib heroine is used within the Bond formula. The pre-credits sequence includes a joke, which plays on the audience's expectations of Bond, when the problem of disappearing submarines produces the simultaneous calling of the top British and top Russian agents by their respective governments. In the Russian case, the camera pans across a palatial room to a virile young man making love to a beautiful girl. She is clearly upset that he will have to leave, but when the call to Special Agent X is made, it is she who picks up the telephone and identifies herself. Anya is set up as a challenge to Bond, but one to be subordinated by Bond in the characteristic development of the Bond narrative, in the visual spectacle focused on the Bond girl in the film and in the publicity for the film.

The production team were well aware of the ambiguities attached to the use of this type of heroine and their willingness to exploit a particular notion of Women's Lib was predicated on the assumption that it would reinforce the exploits of James Bond. The exploitation was both conscious and, at one level, quite cynical. Anya was conceived as the Russian and female equivalent of Bond, but she was also intended to succumb to him in the course of the film. Outside the role of Anya in the plot, Broccoli was not prepared to hire a more experienced actress for the part. Barbara Bach was selected for the following reasons:

> She's a very beautiful girl. She's comparatively unknown which I think brings a certain freshness to a Bond film. We have explored getting various well known ladies, high priced ladies, to bring in, but in my humble opinion, there's no lady today who contributes that much success, if she's high priced or otherwise, unless we like what she does. I don't think there's any actress today that can support a picture box office wise with the possible exception of Barbara Streisand. . . . But the price doesn't distinguish the girl in our film from the success of a Bond picture. I mean we've explored a certain lady in Hollywood who commands a 500,000 dollar wage . . . and that blew her right out of the box for me because she'd contribute no more than Barbara Bach will.[31]

This view of what a Bond girl must contribute was given a particular edge in discussions about publicity for the film. Barbara Bach had worked as a fashion model and wanted to avoid the 'cheesecake' image of much accepted 'Bond girl' publicity. While members of the production team were, on the one hand, anxious to create a more interesting heroine, they were also, on the other hand, concerned to fulfil people's expectations of the traditional Bond girl. Saul Cooper, for example, had clear ideas about what a Bond girl had to be: '. . . A Bond girl is part of the whole dream world that Bond creates. She is a woman of fantastic sexual allure and promise, just as Bond is every man's dream of suddenly being able to spring into action.'[32] Inevitably, there were some clashes over this view of the Bond girl:

> You have the traditional Bond girl image, which involves having the girl photographed in a bikini, in a bathing suit. This was something that took a certain amount of hassling with Barbara at the beginning. But it was something that was absolutely required because a Bond girl must, at some point, be seen within the Bond mould.[33]

The Bondian formula, as the production team were well aware, was likely to be *strengthened* by the creation of a Bond girl whose challenge to Bond was more contemporary and more direct, and seen to be more relevant. Barbara Bach's description of Bond, quoted in *Time Magazine*, as 'a male chauvinist pig', centred on the themes which the Bond team wanted to introduce in relation to the Bondian formula.

At the same time, questions of sexuality are not just linked to the displayed charms of the Bond girls in the films. Bond's sexuality is the crucial route into the 'formula' in which the girls are sexually subordinated by the hero. Bond's sexuality has been much discussed by film-makers in the past. Sean Connery, for example, was originally chosen to play Bond by Salzman and Broccoli because 'He looked like he had balls'.[34] This aspect of the Bond films has been one which has clearly shifted over the years, partly in relation to specific perform- ances of Bond. Roger Moore's James Bond (*Live and Let Die, The Man with the Golden Gun, The Spy Who Loved Me, Moonraker*) has always had a more flippant and jokey style, particularly in relation to Bond's sexual prowess. Moreover, Bond's physical presence on the screen has increasingly come to be associated with his mastery of and use of technology. Whereas it was usual for the Bond of the novels to begin his adventures with an interview with M, it was much more necessary to the Bond films that Bond also sees Q and the recurring joke of Q's elaborate workshop, full of gadgets which would be used in the film. For the production team, concerned to establish Bond as 'family' entertainment, the hero's sexuality has been conceived of in terms both of his joking conquest of beautiful women and of the technological extensions of his role. In writing the script, Christopher Wood turned to his own children to establish what was attractive about Bond and, in response to their replies, reworked the car chase (used to great effect in *Goldfinger*), in which Bond's car is equipped with every kind of weaponry. In *The Spy*, Bond drives into the sea in his efforts to escape pursuit, equipped with a Lotus which converts into a submarine and which does battle with the villains under water. But this physical mastery of technology and nature is constantly punctured by the comic strategy of the film. After an underwater battle, Bond and Anya drive from the waves, before the startled glances of the holidaymakers on a nearby beach, and Bond casually and ostentatiously removes a small fish from the car, comically underlining the technological feat which he has just performed.

The Bond team made a conscious effort to avoid what they considered to be overt sexuality and excessive violence, largely because they wanted to win the widest possible audience for *The Spy* and partly because they perceived that the Bond films are particularly attractive to children. Their main concern was with visual style and the creation of plausible but impossible technological gadgets. Hence, the most detailed discussions took place about the development of sets and gadgets and the use of these in the action sequences, or 'bumps', in the film. But the sting in the tail of this almost obsessive concern with technology – displayed by many members of the production team, from Broccoli downwards – was that this concern was set up only to be comically deflated. Michael Wilson, the assistant to the producer, pointed out that the one-line jokes for which Bond is famous were part of a well worked out strategy. An exciting action sequence, involving some technological excess, has to be followed by a joke, both to release the audience's tension, aroused by the action, and to mitigate the considerable demands that Bond films make on the audience in terms of suspension of disbelief. Scenes which members of the team felt were worked out satisfactorily almost always followed the pattern described by Christopher Wood:

> I can remember one instance in a place in the script. . . . I'd developed the idea of having a motorcycle combination – a sidecar and a motorcycle. The motorcycle sidecar breaks away and becomes a rocket which chases Bond when he's in a car. Now the way I had written it at that stage, Bond took evasive action and drove off the road, the sidecar exploded against a wall, blew a big hole in the wall and that was the end of the sequence. Now somebody in the art department thought out the idea . . . why shouldn't the sidecar hit another vehicle . . . that made me think . . . and we investigated it hitting another vehicle or how could you build something extra into hitting a vehicle, other than just a blinding flash and bits of explosive material blowing all over the place, suppose we made that vehicle something unusual . . . a vehicle that was carrying a load of feather mattresses so that when you explode the vehicle, voom, instead of just a big bang, you get a big bang and millions and millions of feathers.[35]

The effect consciously sought is that of a parody of the 'super-hero'. The strategy of *The Spy* involved a constant comic rupturing of the illusion of the reality of the fiction – a comic rupturing which has been traditionally focused on the relationship between Bond and technology, but which was also mobilized increasingly in *The Spy* in relation to women. The film ends with Bond and Anya being rescued from Stromberg's escape capsule in the sea. This traditional ending for a Bond film is capped by Bond's flippant answer to M's inquiry about what he has been doing: 'Keeping the British end up.'

Clearly, within the bounds of a single chapter, it has only been possible to indicate very briefly some of the ideological processes at work in the making of a Bond film. I have suggested, however, that questions of determination have dominated attempts to relate production studies to the meanings of specific films to the detriment of understanding the relationship between particular films or groups of films and other texts in wider and more far-reaching ideological frameworks. I do not wish to imply that all questions of determination are irrelevant to an understanding of the ideological processes involved in film-making. The organization of the industry, financial constraints, existing conventions and genres and the particular people involved in the making of any one film, will all necessarily constrain and order the making of films. Nevertheless, I would suggest that what happens in film production in working over existing ideological tensions and controversies and turning them into a film, is crucial to our undstanding of the transformation of ideologies. To know about the conditions of production of a Bond film, it is not only important to examine current ideological discourses but also to know how a Bond film was made – that is, how those ideologies were ordered and worked upon in the film. Of course, such an analysis of the meaning of a Bond film does not exhaust its ideological currency. It is only the beginning of an examination of how ideology is mediated and continuously transformed.

13

The Post-war Independent Cinema – Structure and Organization

Simon Blanchard and Sylvia Harvey

We offer here a brief and selective account of the development, structure and organization of the 'independent' cinema in England in the post-war period.[1] We concentrate in particular on the years 1966–81, and on that limited range of practices that can be associated – from the mid 1970s – with the development of the Independent Film-Makers Association. We hope in this way to give some explanation for the emergence of a distinctive sector within English cinema and to offer a framework within which its products may be understood.[2]

What is independent cinema? How does it differ from the institutions and practices discussed elsewhere in this book? To answer this question we must first look briefly at the meanings of the word 'independent'. The historical semantics of the word make an intriguing study. Its meanings are drawn principally from two overlapping histories. The first is the repertoire of themes associated with the fortunes of English liberalism, both as a political philosophy and in its links to non-conformity in religion. Central to this tradition is the notion of autonomy, or self-direction, according to which individuals' thoughts and actions are their own, not determined by agencies or causes outside their control. For example, this emphasis can be seen in Isaiah Berlin's description of 'positive' freedom as deriving from 'the wish on the part of the individual to be his own master. . . . I wish to be a subject, not an object; to be moved by reasons, by conscious purposes, which are my own, not by causes which affect me, as it were, from outside.'[3]

Secondly, there is the tradition of English constitutional political theory and its development of a vocabulary for the discussion of political representation. Here the term 'independent', accorded a positive value by its pre-democratic and patrician defenders, and linked together with such concepts as 'agent', 'party', 'constituent', 'interest' and, crucially, 'mandate' continues to play a dominant role in contemporary struggles over the role of individual agents (their rights and responsibilities) in the representative process. Central to this continuing struggle are two opposed views of representation: for one the agent must operate independently; for the other they are subject to a mandate. So, for example, the question is asked: should MPs act as the agents of their party or constituents, carrying out their instructions, or must they be free to exercise independent judgement? For 'independence' theorists of representation such as Lord Brougham, it was clearly the case that 'It is not Representation if the constituents so far retain a control as to act for themselves. They may communicate with their delegate . . . but he is to act – not they; he is to act for them – not they for themselves.'[4] In this chapter we seek to reposition the discussion and evaluation of independent cinema in the context of these debates about political representation, and we wish in particular to draw attention to the historically subordinate tradition – the concept of the mandate – a tradition that is suppressed whenever, as in Lord Brougham's comment, the autonomy or independence of the political representative is asserted. In the cultural sphere also the emphasis upon the independence of the cultural producer suppresses the idea of the mandate – it avoids questioning on whose behalf the film-maker speaks, and what social mandate the film-maker acknowledges or refuses. Moreover, the history of the term 'independent' gives the concept a pedigree whose dominant values are 'non-partisan', if not frankly 'anti-political'. With all this in mind it is obviously essential to look, not only at the slides and stresses in the use of the word as a matter of self-description by organizations, individuals, groups, but also at the actual practices of independence as they develop and interact with the contradictions in such a rhetoric. As we show below, it is a question not of in-dependence but – as has often been remarked – of dependence and inter-dependence; of an assessment of the determinants structuring and organizing both what happens and how this is understood.

From such a perspective it becomes possible, we would argue, to begin unravelling the basic premises of 'independence': to ask not 'How independent? From what?', but rather 'Dependent on what? Reliant on whom? With what benefits/costs?' In other words it requires a shift from a concern for the heroic transcendence of social and political forces, towards the questions of alignment and commitment which are inescapably present, but are often either left unarticulated or even dismissed.

So how is the term 'independent' used in English cinema? 'Independent' is an insistently relational idea: 'independent of' something. In the present context that 'something' is the dominant products, practices and values of the mainstream film industries in England and the United States. The sector we discuss below locates itself in relation to them, articulating its differences accordingly. In fact, at its most distinctive, the sector represents more than a minor episode in the history of English cinema: rather it has developed as a movement which is concerned to rethink and reconstruct that history, to think and work over the basic questions about what the cinema and film-making amount to – historically, politically, and as a cultural inheritance.

Institutionally, a major determinant of independence was the effects of the wartime and post-war shift towards the acceptability of state intervention in support of the arts. The experience of the Entertainments National Service Association (ENSA) and the Council for the Encouragement of Music and the Arts (CEMA) paved the way for the establishment of the Arts Council in 1946 and the provision in the Local Government Act of 1948 for local authorities to raise a 6d rate for leisure and entertainments.[5] However, the Arts Council of Great Britain (ACGB) embodied a very particular resolution of the various aesthetic and political currents involved in its foundation. The possibilities inherent in wartime radicalism and populism, with their implications for recasting the artist/public relationship, were settled in favour of the now famous policy labelled 'few, but roses' – an elite conception of cultural demand management which cast the arts in the role of being a principal agent to 'maintain the grandeur of the State'.[6] Although the ACGB was not to allow film within the fold as a 'legitimate' art until much later, the council's location on the trade routes of international modernism was to set a tone of aesthetic debate and example which had a major impact on the 'independent' sector.[7]

A rather later development was the slow emergence of a structure of Regional Arts Associations. CEMA had had regional sections, but the ACGB had moved to close these down (setting up at the same time its Scottish and Welsh Committees), a process which was finished by

1955. The first Regional Arts Association (RAA) – in the South West – was organized in 1956, and others were to emerge during the late 1950s and the 1960s, being particularly spurred on by the conscious commitment to decentralization in arts policy which followed Labour's victory in the 1964 election. Drawing their funds from local government, local business, the Arts Council and the British Film Institute, the RAAs had become an important source of finance by the 1970s, as well as articulating the long-standing dissatisfaction felt outside London with the direction of the cash-flow from central sources.[8]

As for the British Film Institute, from its start in 1933 it had been under the suspicious gaze of the industry, and was expected to refrain from involvement with the film trade (whether in the production or exhibition fields), limiting itself to its initial objectives in the areas of education and information, criticism, support for film societies and archival and film-lending activity. The BFI was reorganized as a result of the Radcliffe Report in 1948, and its post-war history has been characterized by cautious advances, under a range of contradictory pressures, onto the nominally forbidden territory of the film trade. These interventions became more overt, although no less subject to conflicting logic, as the failure of the industry to keep its side of the 'bargain' (that is, to maintain a moderately thriving cinema) became steadily more apparent.[9]

Before looking at some of the more immediate conditions for the growth of an independent sector, we need to give brief consideration to the phenomenon of 'Free Cinema'. Benefiting from the establishment of the Experimental Film Fund under Michael Balcon (on which see below), and from individual connections with the National Film Theatre and *Sight and Sound*, the various film-makers associated with 'Free Cinema' managed to make a succession of pioneering films – such as *Momma Don't Allow*, *Nice Time*, and *Every Day Except Christmas* – and to raise, if only temporarily, the level of discussion about film-making in England and elsewhere. This was a continuation of the work that several of them (particularly Lindsay Anderson, Karel Reisz and Gavin Lambert) had been doing with their magazine *Sequence*. Some of this energy and concern was to find its way into film-related activity inside the early 'New' Left and the Campaign for Nuclear Disarmament (see below), but by the end of the 1950s all the key activists of 'Free Cinema' had been absorbed into the mainstream of the film and theatre industries. Those involved with it had expressed a dislike at being considered a 'movement' comparable to that displayed by the poets of the so-called 'Movement'. In the absence of sustained, programmatic and collaborative work addressed to the social and economic structures impeding the film-making for which they had argued, the ensuing dispersal was largely to be expected.[10]

We can now look at some of the more direct factors which encouraged the emergence of the independent sector. Firstly, there is the complicated mixture of social, economic and political changes which brought a degree of liberalization to British society during the period from the mid-1950s to the mid-1960s: a relatively buoyant economy, involving a major recomposition and extension of the cultural sphere under the effects of generally rising incomes, particularly among the young; and the repercussions of 1956, the 'year of the break' – which saw the Hungarian uprising, the Suez fiasco, Krushchev's secret speech to the CPSU and the spreading opposition to the H-bomb, all of which opened the political arena to new ideas and alliances, notably the 'New' Left, the Committee of 100 and CND.[11] Secondly, there were the more particular effects of the arrival of the work and ideas known as 'New American Cinema', which had been developing in the marginally more benign cinematic climate of the United States throughout the 1940s and 1950s, and which provided new organizational forms (the 'co-op' tradition of distribution and exhibition), a rich corpus of film work by Andy Warhol, Maya Deren, Stan Brakhage, Jonas Mekas and many others and, by the early 1960s, a very active component of the group who pushed the London Film-Maker's Co-op into existence.[12]

The founding of the London Film-makers' Co-operative in 1966, and its subsequent acquisition of equipment (for production, printing and processing) and premises (after the move from the back room of the 'Better Books' bookshop in Charing Cross Road), gave some organizational framework to that sector of cultural producers working within a broadly 'art school' or 'fine art' tradition. The Co-op film-makers developed techniques of production that were radically different from those of the industry and their source of income tended to be drawn from part-time teaching or other work, not from film-making; their emphasis was on formal experiment and innovation and the application of modernist principles to film.

Between 1968 and 1974 a number of new production groups were formed, which all sought to secure a production base and regular access to the means of production (cameras, editing equipment and so on). In this way there emerged the first embryonic film workshops, which were to become an important feature of independent film work in the seventies. Some of these groups were also involved in distribution and exhibition work; some had close ties with a local community or sought to work with particular and identifiable audiences, such as the Labour and Women's Movement. All were involved in production for social and cultural reasons, and few managed to make a living out of their film work. They worked at other jobs to earn money; they received donations or help 'in kind' such as film stock or access to processing from friends and supporters and the occasional grant-aid from various state or state-sponsored institutions, such as the BFI, the ACGB or the RAAs. The groups were mostly based in London, the expansion of regional production centres being more a development of the mid-1970s. Among the earlier groups were Cinema Action (1968), Berwick Street Collective (1972), Amber Films (Newcastle-upon-Tyne, 1969), Liberation Films (1972), London Women's Film Group (1972), Four Corner Films (1973), and the Newsreel Collective (1974). In general these groups owned at least some of the necessary means of production and worked as collectives, in a co-operative manner, around a shared production base. Often they made their knowledge and equipment available to others, and both their ownership of equipment and their methods of working distinguished them from some of the production centres established later in the decade, where the equipment was owned and administered by an RAA and made available as a local 'resource' to film-makers in the region. The early groups sometimes rotated jobs, refusing the traditional craft distinctions of the industry, and were committed to the difficult principle of a parity of both technical and conceptual involvement in the film project. For a variety of reasons – some principled, some pragmatic – their films tended to be made over a long period of time, departing from the schedules which normally obtained in the industry. This had effects on the formal means of expression developed, and also allowed potential audiences to look at and contribute to the unfinished film. Thus the screening of rushes for audience groups (Cinema Action, for example, showed unfinished material to trade unionists), and the development of alternative exhibition circuits, built the principle of 'production for use' firmly into the production process itself.[13]

Many of these groups contributed to the development of the politics of the New Left in England, opposed the Vietnam war and supported current critiques of American and English imperialism. The positive aspect of the anti-imperialist stance included a new commitment to internationalism, support for and an insistence upon the cultural significance of, national liberation movements and civil rights campaigns, and a desire to learn about and draw upon other national experiences and struggles, from Eastern Europe to Africa, from Alabama to Havana and Hanoi. From the late 1960s an awareness of sexual discrimination and of the struggle for women's liberation became increasingly important; this struggle consistently emphasized the role of cultural forms in contributing to and perpetuating the oppression of women.[14] There was an openness also to post-war developments in French culture and politics; this receptiveness can be traced through the interest in, for example, the work of Althusser in journals like *New Left Review* and *Screen*, back to English versions of the angry utopianism of the events in Paris of May 1968,[15] and beyond that to the presence of 'Left Bank' models in the early development of the New Left.

The film groups were both products and producers of a climate that laid increasing stress upon the importance of culture and ideology for the development of any serious strategy for social change, and their practical activities contributed to the shaping of a new theory and practice of cinema. In contradistinction to the mainstream industry, with its commitment to profitable entertainment, the search for a mass audience and a primarily 'box-office', or market, orientation towards that audience[16] this other sector developed in partial, contradictory and hesitating ways the 'conditions of possibility' for a more socially responsible recasting of the institutions of cinema.

The aspirations, and the political and aesthetic interests of the members of the London Film-makers' Cooperative were in many respects quite different from those of the other production groups discussed above. But they did hold in common the project of developing different modes of production, and of achieving a qualitatively different relationship with their audiences. Both the Co-op and the other groups sought, whether through formal and aesthetic means or through political radicalism, to transform the existing practices of cinema, from the point of production, through the processes of distribution and exhibition, to the point of viewing or 'consumption'. Some of the film-makers worked (through the adoption of new formal means) for the development of a more active role for the audience in producing the meaning of the film, believing that the film should function as a kind of 'open text', only to be closed or completed by the active response and the intellectual participation of the spectator. Others worked to develop new forms of exhibition, which sometimes involved film-makers in direct discussions with their audiences and led to the combination of production centres with exhibition spaces in order to facilitate this dialogue.

The development of the relationship between producers and 'consumers', the recognition of the responsibility of the former to investigate and meet the cultural needs of the latter, and the dedication of both to the creation of socially useful cultural forms, has begun, insofar as this is possible within a market economy, the process of breaking down film as a commodity form, an object for sale. In general this development leads to an emphasis on the quality of the social processes of making, and of 'consuming', and to questioning the extent to which the product meets contemporary social and cultural needs.

However, the political implications of this development have not always been perceived or highlighted, and not all production groups have asked themselves the question, 'Whose social and cultural needs should be given priority?' Or, if they have asked the question, they have not all answered it in the same way. For the film-makers of the aesthetic avant-garde the scope of the cinema was being reworked, used and subverted for an audience that was actively built up in the late 1960s but drawn largely from the ranks of those already interested in developments in the visual arts. By contrast, groups like Cinema Action and Liberation Films sought trade union and community involvement, and the development of methods of exhibition relevant to more directly political movements and concerns.

One of the organizations most concerned with the development of more explicitly political forms of film exhibition was The Other Cinema, which was founded in 1970 as a non-profit-making film-distribution company. It emerged from the work of other movements or organizations, such as Angry Arts and Politkino. The Other Cinema stated its commitment to distributing the work of film-makers who 'seek to change people's perceptions of political, social or personal situations, often with the aid of new film forms',[17] and set out to create an alternative exhibition circuit for broadly 'progressive' films by building new audiences and new ways of using cinema, often in clubs, pubs, local halls, art centres and colleges quite outside the mainstream cinema circuits. By importing films from Africa and Latin America, they also helped to give an international dimension to this new kind of exhibition work. In 1976 they opened a public cinema in London with an ambitious screening programme, and although the campaign to obtain BFI funding for this initiative failed, and the cinema closed in December 1977, much was learnt in the process. The new practices developed around this cinema remain to be assessed as constituting one of the most advanced experiments with progressive intervention in public film exhibition – an experiment that struggled to develop outside the cultural ghetto of the art cinema.[18]

In 1974 the diverse strands of the independent film production sector outlined above, together with radical distributors, critics and teachers, came together to set up the Independent Film-makers' Association (IFA), a process that was to take some two years before the organization effectively emerged as a public entity. Internally, the structuring principle was, for much of the time, an agreement to disagree about a variety of aesthetic and political questions, but to unite in the creation of a new organizational identity capable of providing a national voice for the sector. The size of the membership fluctuated between about seventy-five and three hundred and was drawn in general from the very restricted social base of those who had received some form of higher education. The association attempted to discriminate positively in favour of women, but drew few members from working-class or black communities. It has a formal structure, including an executive body composed of delegates from the various regional sections of which there were twelve by 1981. However, it had no paid administrator, and no funds beyond its low membership fees (low, that is, in comparison with trade union subscriptions) until, in 1980, grant-aid was obtained from the BFI. It suffered from all of the obvious problems of a voluntary body: the expense of travelling to meetings, the difficulty of finding time to develop policies and to mount and sustain campaigns. While there was a small and relatively permanent core of active members, the constant gravitational pull of individually perceived needs and individual projects made the development of sustained collective activity continually difficult. In the context of a society whose dominant institutions are deeply hostile to collective and co-operative values, celebrating always the achievements of individuals emerging from the struggle of competition, this difficulty is not a surprising or unique one. It was compounded in the IFA by the effects of libertarian conceptions of association which emphasized the independence of the associating individuals rather than their collective responsibilities, and by a sometimes voluntarist approach to the making of alliances, which, despite its positive aspect of emphasizing conscious, willed activity, sometimes failed to assess the underlying determinants, the actual material interests of the groups entering the alliance. Although the principle of seeking to establish, and work for, the common good was certainly upheld in the IFA, the problems always remained both of recognizing differences of interest within the association and of specifying the relationship between the 'common good' of its members and their broader social and cultural responsibilities. It has been here that the larger questions of 'constituency' and 'representation', in the cultural and political spheres, have become most pressing.[19]

What the IFA did achieve over a number of years was the development of policies and campaigns affecting a wide range of issues (though without the ability to hold evenly 'in focus' a range of issues at any one time), the dissemination of information about funding sources and some concrete advances in the provision of state finance. In this last respect, the association contributed to the various lobbies and the diverse pressures that led, by 1981, to a considerable increase in the production funds available through the BFI, a smaller increase within the RAAs, and the setting-up of a fund for independent production by the Channel Four Television Company. Annual conferences were held in London in 1976 and 1977, in Nottingham in 1980 and in Birmingham in 1981, and there was a special Film Workshops Conference in Bristol in 1979.[20] Major questions for discussion were repeatedly those of organization and finance, and relationships with state funding bodies and with the film technicians' union, the Association of Cinematograph, Television and allied Technicians (ACTT).

Since the IFA membership included writers and teachers as well as film-makers, distributors and exhibitors, it was able to maintain productive relationships with developments in film education, such as the BFI's Education Department, the work of the Society for Education in Film and Television and its journals *Screen* and *Screen Education*, and with the newer film journals such as *Afterimage*, *Framework* and *Under Cut*. But there were few connections with the film critics of major newspapers or journals, and this gap seriously limited the circulation of the policies and polemics developed within the association. There were, however, links with the organizers of the Edinburgh Film Festival which provided a valuable forum both for screening and discussing new work.[21]

The major questions of organization and finance can perhaps best be considered in terms of three sets of relationships: with the state (BFI, ACGB, RAAs, Department of Trade and Industry), with the film technicians' union (ACTT) and with the Channel Four Television Company.

Like the mainstream of the industry, the state-sponsored film sector in England has been characterized by a diversity of institutions and purposes and an absence of rational planning. We can only note here in passing the existence of the National Film Finance Corporation (established by the Labour government in 1949) and of the Arts Council of Great Britain, which has funded two sorts of films: those about artists and (from 1972) those by artists. The Experimental Film Fund was established at the BFI in 1952 under the chairmanship of Michael Balcon. It received a block grant of £12,500 from the Eady Levy.[22] At this stage the BFI itself provided neither finance nor permanent administrative or production assistance. By 1966 the fund had been reconstituted as the British Film Institute Production Board, and the BFI provided for the first time an annual budget of some £10,000, in addition to the Eady money. It also appointed a full-time head of production.[23] By 1974 the production monies available from this source were just over £100,000 and by 1980 just over £600,000.[24]

The Board's monies were received, directly or indirectly, from a wide variety of sources; in 1981 (apart from any specific co-production money) the list included the Department of Education and Science, the British Film Fund Agency, the Independent Television Companies Association and the Channel Four Television Company. The causes of the increase in available grant-aid can be traced only partly to the lobbying activities of the independent film-makers, or to the interest and tenacity of individual cultural administrators. Perhaps more importantly, these increases need to be understood in the context of major and minor shifts in the structure and function of the mainstream film and television industries. At the same time those film-makers who, for aesthetic or political reasons, avoided or were excluded by the industry sought strategies for survival which increasingly included the demand for a proper allocation of funds for wages in the making of films. The state's cultural policy of providing only grants for materials, on a 'one-off', project-by-project basis, allowed only those with private means, those with access to regular part-time employment or those willing to live at the barest subsistence level to enter the arena of cultural film production. While the wages principle was established by the mid-seventies in consultations between the BFI Production Board and the ACTT, the rates paid were considerably lower than those established by the union in the feature film industry, and throughout the decade there was considerable debate about the advisability of the Board's involvement in low-budget feature film production. By the end of the seventies the union was taking an increasing interest in what it provisionally defined as the 'grant-aided' sector, and in the terms and conditions under which money was made available for production. Meanwhile, the IFA had sought representation on the decision-making committee of the Production Board and two IFA nominations to the Board were accepted in 1977. It also entered into negotiations with the Production Board on the questions of copyright and editorial control, in particular the BFI's role as producer and the division of returns from distribution income to the BFI and to the film-maker. In general the IFA's approach to the Production Board could be characterized as one that saw the Board as one of the bases for the creation of an alternative, state-sponsored industry (to be organized according to cultural, not commercial, criteria), an industry which combined workers' control with an interest in and respect for the needs of the cultural consumer. It thus differed from the approach that sees the board solely as the experimental, research or 'nursery' wing of the mainstream film and television industries. Such differences of approach are entirely predictable if we see the culture industry as one of many in England that are the sites of the ideological and economic conflicts of the mixed economy.

The demand for an adequate wage component to be included in the costs of production was principally developed by the IFA in relationship to the development of policies for the RAA-supported film sector. The Northern Arts Association was among the first to make grants to local film-makers, allocating £1,500 for this purpose in 1968. Others followed suit as the BFI encouraged the development of RAA-supported film production and exhibition work.

A chain of Regional Film Theatres, financed jointly by the BFI and the RAAs, had been established by the mid-1970s in most major cities. By the late 1970s the discrepancy between the levels of production finance available to film-makers working through their RAAs and those working through the production board was clear. In 1978–9, for example, the highest typical RAA budget for a feature-length film was about £5,000, when the highest production board budget was about £90,000.[25] It was in response to this situation that a group of independent regional film-makers within the ACTT took the initiative of asking the union to establish a 'Code of Practice', in collaboration with those RAAs that were willing to enter into an agreement to regulate the wages component of films being produced with RAA money. The code was introduced in 1980. This 'regional dimension' of the campaign for state finance brought with it a complex cluster of concerns that included, on the one hand, questions of devolution, democracy and local accountability, and, on the other, an advocacy of new regional workshop bases for production, where the film-makers, working collectively, retained full control over all aspects of the production, beginning in this process to transform the social relations of production.

Although this code of practice was only selectively adopted (in general by those RAAs with the larger film production budgets), it can be seen, together with the 1980–81 campaign to establish a Regional Production Fund, to have initiated a significantly new way of conceptualizing the establishment of an infra-structure for non-profit-making film production and distribution. This initiative grew out of the proposals for a state-supported film industry contained in the IFA's paper, *The Future of the British Film Industry* (1978). The paper emerged in response to the public debate on the Terry and Wilson Committee reports (1976 and 1978) on the film industry, and from diverse discussions on the future of audio-visual culture, which included a consideration of the Annan report (1977) and of the proposals for an Open Broadcasting Authority and a British Film Authority. It was submitted to the Department of Trade and discussed with the then Under-Secretary of State for Trade, Michael Meacher. The fall of the Labour government in April 1979 brought an end to this initiative, referred to as the 'Meacher Proposal'. Much of the work of the IFA was subsequently devoted to the development of policies connected with the new fourth television channel. The 1978 paper remained the nearest thing to a 'hegemonic bid', addressing in ambitious terms the question of the transformation and re-establishment of a whole industry.[26]

This brief history of developments in funding both at the BFI

Production Board and through the RAAs indicates the de facto involvement of the film technicians' union (ACTT) in these developments. From its 1976 conference the IFA had been involved in discussions about, and was often deeply divided in the attitudes of its members towards, the ACTT. Some independent film-makers feared absorption into a body that had historically and necessarily been developed to protect its members through organizational structures such as the craft sections that were themselves the mirror image of the practices of the industrial mainstream. Others argued that it was the union alone that had the necessary power to provide a sound material basis for those seeking, at many different levels, to break with the existing practices of the industry. A kind of resolution of this debate was reached when, at the 1980 annual conference, the association agreed to 'unconditionally support the union's drive against low wages and casualization', welcomed 'alliance between the memberships of the IFA and the ACTT . . . to defend the independent film production sector against the devastation of the public spending cuts' and approved the ACTT's initiative on the Code of Practice for regional production.[27] The following two years (1980–82) saw important changes in the union's attitude towards and understanding of the independent sector. The setting up of a Committee for Independent Grant-Aided Film within the union provided a forum for discussion and the development of policies which included the unionization and regularization of the sector, based on an advocacy of 'workshop' production centres and the principle of a regular annual wage.

The establishment of the fourth television channel in autumn 1982 provided the grounds for the independent sector's first sustained attempt to grapple with the host of specific problems which television raises. Committed by statute to 'encourage innovation and experiment in the form and content of programmes', the Fourth Channel was the object of a public campaign by the IFA.[28] The campagin began formally at the 1979 Edinburgh Television Festival and led, via a number of detailed arguments and proposals, to the appointment by the Channel Four company of a commissioning editor for independent film and video.[29] This editor has responsibility for a 'slot' in the channel's schedules, and has been able to develop a mixture of support funding, direct commissioning and programme purchase mechanisms appropriate to the varied history and ways of working of the independent sector. The funds committed by the channel for these purposes amounted to just over £2 million in the first year.[30]

A number of factors have made this development possible. Firstly, the members of the IFA have been able to make common cause with a varity of interest groups who pushed the Conservative government hard to ensure that the fourth channel was required to 'say new things in new ways'. Dissatisfaction with the performance and structure of the existing television networks had been widespread for some time, and the IFA benefited from this mood. Secondly, the IFA was able, in some respects, to benefit from the legal obligation placed on the Fourth Channel Television Company to commission a substantial proportion of its programmes from sources other than the existing independent television companies or their subsidiaries. Thirdly, the IFA was assisted in making its case to the channel by the inter-change of personnel between the Channel and the BFI, since the director of the BFI had been appointed to the board of the Fourth Channel Television Company and the chief executive/programme controller of the channel had recently been chairperson of the BFI Production Board.[31] Fourthly, the Association had presented an extensive and carefully thought out case, drawing upon the previous decade and more of practical experience of the sector, and had lobbied hard in support of its arguments both in Parliament and then directly with the channel itself, once this had been established. At the time of writing the independent sector's engagement with television has only just begun; money has been made available, but the problem that now arises is that of making the transition from the ideas and practices of independent cinema to working with a means of communication whose operations are quite different.

Beyond Independence

Throughout the period 1966–81 the independent sector has struggled in various ways to establish the conditions of its own existence and growth. This struggle has taken place in the context of major changes in the English film and television industries and their markets (the drastic reductions in film production, the decline of cinema-going, the establishment of the fourth television channel), and of significant new developments in the audio-visual field (satellite, cable, video cassette – all media devoted primarily to the private and domestic market). But it would be wrong to see these changes only in economic and technological terms, or simply to assume the fact of the historical demise of cinema, for the changes involve social habits, and questions about cultural provision that are also, fundamentally, political questions. In this respect while independent film-makers must increasingly be concerned with developments in cassette, cable and satellite, a case must be argued through concerning the value of the cinema as a means of *public* communication. Moreover, in a situation not only of major technological changes but also of major economic and political shifts in England (mass unemployment, coupled with an aggressively confident right-wing assertion of the virtues of private enterprise), independent film-makers and those who work with them have two related issues to confront.[32] Firstly, they need to build on those theoretical and practical gains made by the sector in order to assist a much wider social movement, whose key objective (in the sphere of communication, as in all else) will be the mobilization of support for the principles of public, collective and democratic provision as against the principles of independence and the free market. But before it can hope to make this contribution effectively the independent film sector needs to examine the reasons for its general invisibility within the arena of public debate, as compared with, for example, the more obvious cultural presence of radical theatre and progressive popular music.[33] As we have tried to show, the term 'independence' has made it difficult to confront these urgent issues. Indeed, it has served at times as a convenient expression of the sector's vacillation over the question of which social forces it wishes to serve and be sustained by in the long term. We do not doubt that the non-partisan presence of the independent sector has allowed it to win significant though sectional gains for its members. But we would argue that it must now develop longer-term strategies, and seek alliances with and a mandate from those democratic forces that seek to represent and to further the interests of the majority in economic, political and cultural terms.[34]

Part Four

British Films: Ideology and Culture

'Patriotism with Profit': British Imperial Cinema in the 1930s

Jeffrey Richards

The importance of films as a medium of propaganda was widely appreciated by the 1930s, a fact fully reflected in parliamentary debates, government reports and the large number of local and national enquiries into the effect of films on the mass audience. The prevalent view is summed up perfectly in the 1936 report of the Board of Trade Committee which, under the chairmanship of the former Minister of Agriculture, Lord Moyne, investigated the working of the 1927 Cinematograph Films Act. It declared,

The cinematograph film is today one of the most widely used means for the amusement of the public at large. It is also undoubtedly a most important factor in the education of all classes of the community, in the spread of national culture and in presenting national ideas and customs to the world. Its potentialities moreover in shaping the ideas of the very large numbers to whom it appeals are almost unlimited. The propaganda value of the film cannot be overemphasized.[1]

The direct consequence of this widely held view was that throughout the 1930s there was a vociferous demand, both inside and outside parliament, and particularly in the press, that the British film industry should more truly and fully reflect the life, policies and values of Britain in its films. Sir Stephen Tallents – who, as secretary of the short-lived Empire Marketing Board, sought to do just that through the now celebrated EMB Film Unit – encapsulated the argument in his influential pamphlet, *The Projection of England*.[2] He asserted that 'No civilized country can today afford either to neglect the projection of its national personality or to resign its projection to others.' Declaring that 'the greatest agent of international communication at the moment is unquestionably the cinema', he called for films which would project England to the outside world.[3] The nub of his argument – and it was one repeated whenever film matters were debated in parliament – was that

> In the cause of good international understanding within the Empire and without it; for the sake of our export trade; in the interests of our tourist traffic; above all, perhaps, in the discharge of our great responsibilities to the other countries of the Commonwealth of British peoples, we must master the art of national projection and must set ourselves to throw a fitting presentation of England upon the world's screen. The English people must be seen for what it is – a great nation still anxious to serve the world and to secure the world's peace.[4]

A major part of Britain's activities, interests and responsibilities centred on the British Empire and there was similarly a repeated call for positive propaganda on its behalf. The government's view was expressed by Sir Philip Cunliffe-Lister, President of the Board of Trade, in the House of Commons in 1927, when, referring to the unanimous resolution of the 1926 Imperial Conference that imperial film production should be increased, he stated,

> I believe that that resolution expresses a sentiment which is prevalent in the House and the country and throughout the Empire. It is based on a realization that the cinema is today the most universal means through which national ideas and national atmosphere can be spread, and even if these be intangible things, surely they are among the most important influences in civilization. Everybody will admit that the strongest bonds of Empire – outside of course, the strongest of all, the crown – are just those intangible bonds – a common outlook, the same ideas and the same ideals which we all share and which are expressed in a common language, and a common literature. . . . Today films are shown to millions of people throughout the Empire and must unconsciously influence the ideas and outlook of British people of all races.[5]

But films propounding imperial ideals were not needed simply to strengthen bonds: they were also needed to counteract the deleterious effect, particularly in Africa and the East, of films featuring white men indulging in sex, violence and criminal activities. As the former Chancellor of the Exchequer, Sir Robert Horne, said in the same debate, voicing another often-canvassed view, 'I do not suppose that there is anything which has done so much harm to the prestige and position of Western people and the white race as the exhibition of films which have tended to degrade us in the eyes of peoples who have been accustomed to look upon us with admiration and respect.'[6]

A need, then, was clearly seen to put over in an easily assimilable way a positive message about the Empire and its value – at home, within the Empire itself and in countries outside it. At home, despite Empire Day, the Prince of Wales's highly publicized tours of the Empire, Lord Beaverbrook's newspaper crusades on behalf of the Empire and an unending stream of books about the Empire and Imperial problems, there was considerable ignorance about and no very great interest in the Empire. H. G. Wells estimated that nineteen Englishmen out of twenty knew no more about the British Empire than they did about the Italian Renaissance. The chairman of the Empire Day movement admitted that in Britain in the 1920s there were 'many dark corners where the rays of our Empire sun have not been able to penetrate'.[7]

Abroad, the propaganda pumped out by the efficient and expanding propaganda machines of the Fascist dictatorships depicted Britain as a decadent and rapidly dwindling force in world affairs, with a slave empire ruthlessly exploited and cruelly repressed. There was also considerable antipathy to the British Empire in the United States, with its deeply ingrained elements of isolationism and Anglophobia. As early as 1919 Sir William Wiseman, head of British Intelligence in the United States, had said that there was a need 'to find means of explaining to the Americans the meaning of the British Empire'.[8]

Despite this, there was considerable reluctance on the part of the British government to become directly involved in propaganda, and, even when this reluctance was overcome in the late 1930s, it still neglected the most potent means of conveying a message to the mass audience – the cinema. As Philip Taylor has shown in his important book *The Projection of Britain*, government reluctance stemmed in part from a deep hostility to the whole concept of propaganda, the feeling that it was somehow ungentlemanly, unsportsman-like and unEnglish, and in part from the Treasury's reluctance, at a time of depression and financial stringency, to sanction the expenditure. The Empire Marketing Board, axed in 1933, was a victim of just such a mentality. Taylor concludes,

> In so far as propaganda in the Empire was concerned, the Board's demise was more significant because despite the efforts of the BBC's Empire service from 1932 and despite the work of the Colonial Empire Marketing Board from 1937, the projection of the British Empire went largely unpractised until the 2nd World War.[9]

This failure was not for want of trying on the part of a dedicated group of officials and civil servants centred around Reginald (Rex) Leeper and Sir Robert Vansittart of the Foreign Office. Pressure from them resulted in, for instance, the setting up of the British Council. But all the overseas propaganda activities of the British government, like those of the British Council, were aimed at influential elites. When, in 1938, the government finally approved a committee to co-ordinate propaganda, under the chairmanship of Vansittart, it called for the use of feature film to influence a mass audience. The committee issued a report advocating the creation of a National Film Council and a National Film Unit, proclaiming the particular importance of feature films because 'they strike subconscious chords and reinforce or modify prejudices or opinions already held, and thus in the long run make a more lasting impression' than newsreels or documentaries.[10] But the government remained unconvinced and there was no official use of feature film until the Second World War.

At home, the government's involvement in feature film took the essentially negative form of censorship. Although the British Board of Film Censors was not a state-run organization, it maintained close links with relevant government departments, to ensure that nothing undesirable reached the screen. The bulk of their work was moral censorship, the preservation of middle-class standards of propriety and decorum. But in political matters they enforced a policy of 'No controversy', thus virtually excluding from the screen any discussion of such current issues as fascism, pacifism and industrial unrest. The maintenance of the political status quo was the aim.[11]

It is clear from the operation of this policy that the government's primary interest was not the constructive use of feature film to put over their policies, but the negative approach of fear – fear of causing offence or inflaming public opinion. When it came to the Empire the government was on the whole content to leave things to the BBFC. The board operated according to a strictly defined code, which expressly prohibited films which reflected adversely on the British Army, British colonial administration or the white race. On the basis of this, it was able to reject all but six of the twenty Imperial projects submitted to it at script stage.[12] The government was, however, prepared to intervene when it was politically necessary, as when two films in which it was proposed to deal with the Indian Mutiny were banned by the BBFC after consultation with the India Office. Sir Samuel Hoare, the Home Secretary, defended the decision in the Commons in 1938, saying, 'to produce a film depicting scenes of the

Indian Mutiny would be undesirable at this time when we are just embarking on a new chapter in the constitutional development of India, and when we want to get rid of the differences which there have been between us in the past'.[13] The government's concern was not without foundation, as there had been riots in Bombay and Madras when Alexander Korda's film *The Drum* (1938), was shown there.[14]

There was, nevertheless, a flourishing cinema of Empire in the 1930s, powerfully advocating a view of the British Empire as beneficent and necessary. There is little evidence that the government was directly involved in them. They could hardly have been involved in the stream of Imperial epics produced in Hollywood, from *The Lives of a Bengal Lancer* (1935) to *Sundown* (1940).[15] The reason for the appearance of these films and of the appeal of them to America was summed up in 1939 by Margaret Thorp in her book *America at the Movies*:

> The immediate explanation of this burst of British propaganda is a very simple one. As continental audiences dwindled Britain, which had always stood high, became an even more important section of the American movies' foreign public. It was highly desirable to please Great Britain if possible, and it could be done without sacrifice, for the American public, too, seemed to be stirred with admiration for British empire ideals. Loyalty as the supreme virtue no matter to what you are loyal, courage, hard work, a creed in which *noblesse oblige* is the most intellectual conception; those ideas are easier to grasp and very much easier to dramatize on the screen than social responsibility, the relation of the individual to the state, the necessity for a pacifist to fight tyranny, the nature of democracy, and the similar problems with which the intellectuals want the movies to deal.[16]

It is clear that foreign countries fully appreciated the extent of Imperial propaganda contained in these films. Mussolini's Italy banned the Hollywood films *Lives of a Bengal Lancer*, *Charge of the Light Brigade*, *Clive of India* and *Lloyds of London* because of their pro-British sentiment.[17]

In Britain, the major Imperial films of the 1930s were the trilogies produced by Alexander Korda and Michael Balcon. Korda produced *Sanders of the River* (1935), *The Drum* (1938) and *The Four Feathers* (1939) for his London Films; Balcon produced *Rhodes of Africa* (1936), *The Great Barrier* (1936) and *King Solomon's Mines* (1937) for Gaumont-British, where he was production chief. Why were these commercial producers moved to spend so much money on Imperial topics? One reason was given by Paul Holt in the *Daily Express* in 1938 when he announced,

> Mr Korda plans to make a lot of films about the Empire in the future. That is good news to this newspaper. It is also good business for Mr Korda. He knows that films about the Empire make money. He knows that films of his like *Sanders of the River* and *Elephant Boy* and *The Drum* have been far more successful at the box offices of the country than any equal amount of sophisticated sex nonsense. Korda knows too that Hollywood knows it; that Hollywood has British producers fazed about British Empire films; can beat them any day they choose with Cavalcades, Mutinies on the Bounty, Houses of Rothschild, Bengal Lancers, Lloyds of London. *Patriotism goes with profit.* [my italics][18]

'Patriotism with profit' might well be the slogan of these producers of Imperial epics and a good reason why the government would be content to leave to ordinary commercial interests the projection of the British Empire. But it is important to stress that there was patriotism. Both Korda and Balcon were intensely patriotic, and both were concerned with the creation of a flourishing British film industry and the favourable promotion of the national image abroad. Both were in due course to be knighted. It is also now known that in the 1930s both of them advised the Conservative Party Film Association on the making of its propaganda films.[19] There were particularly close links with Korda, as Sir Joseph Ball, deputy director of the National Publicity Bureau, reported to the Prime Minister, Neville Chamberlain in 1938. But Gaumont-British, the biggest British film company and the one for which Balcon worked, was also close to the government – and, indeed, in 1935 Isidore Ostrer, the company's chairman, made a secret agreement with the government to place his entire organization at its disposal. The fact that the scripts of the Gaumont-British Imperial epics were all vetted and passed by the BBFC, and that the Korda epics were produced with the full co-operation of the Army and the colonial authorities in India, Nigeria and the Sudan, confirms that the government was happy with the Imperial image that was being projected.

In Korda's case there were also close links with key figures who were not in favour with the government but whose views on propaganda and the Empire clearly harmonized with Korda's own. That unrepentant old Imperialist and master of propaganda, Winston Churchill, was on Korda's payroll during his wilderness years, hired to write a script for a Jubilee film (that was never made) on the reign of King George V.[20] Even more significantly, Sir Robert Vansittart, having failed to persuade the government to initiate its own propaganda film programme, set about using the commercial cinema. Under the heading, 'Britain to put the Empire on the screen', the *Daily Express* reported in July 1938,

He has signed a contract with Alexander Korda to write dialogue and scenarios for a series of new films. Films will glorify the British Empire. Story Sir Robert was working on yesterday was Edward Thomson's *Burmese Silver* which will have little Sabu and Conrad Veidt in it. After he's finished that he moves over to help with *Four Feathers*, although the main work on that is already shared between R. C. Sherriff and A. E. W. Mason. Surprising that a key man of the government should turn to scriptwriting? Not at all. He is co-author of *Sixty Glorious Years*, the new Neagle epic. Sir Robert has the sense to know that the film is a great potent propaganda medium.[21]

Sixty Glorious Years (1938), the second of Herbert Wilcox's two films about the life of Queen Victoria, made a powerful impression both at home and abroad on its release. Typical of the reviews it received, and which show that Vansittart was doing his work well, was the one in *Today's Cinema*, which declared, 'Herbert Wilcox has excelled himself in the direction of a tremendous page of our history that quietly and unobtrusively acclaims the greatness of the British Empire and its peoples.'[22]

But what was the image of the Empire enshrined in these British Imperial epics? The similarity of the British and American films in terms of content and visual imagery is a strong indicator of the extent to which popular culture on both sides of the Atlantic had become saturated with the myths and images of British Imperialism. Popular novels and poems, picture postcards and exhibitions, ballads and musical comedies had, since the last decades of the nineteenth century, sedulously promoted the concept of a glorious and beneficent British Empire, an empire on which the sun never set.[23] No-one had done more for this image than Rudyard Kipling. Louis Cazamian assessed his impact thus in 1926,

While statesmen grasped the possibilities included in a fact which their conscious will had never contributed to create, and were anxious to strengthen and develop it; while scientists explored it, studied its resources or told its progress, it was given to a man of letters to make it supremely and most deeply actual by implanting it among the familiar and intimate ideas of all men. It is from Kipling that, to the majority of the English, the existence of the Empire dates back.[24]

It was Kipling's concept of 'The White Man's Burden', the God-given destiny and duty of the British race to bring peace, order and good government to the world, that found its way onto the screen. In Hollywood, several films (*Gunga Din, Wee Willie Winkie, The Light that Failed*) were direct adaptations from Kipling. Others, (*Lives of a Bengal Lancer, Charge of the Light Brigade*) clearly drew on the Kipling ideology. In Britain it was the Kiplingesque Imperial adventure stories of A. E. W. Mason and Edgar Wallace that provided Korda with his source material.

The fact that the idealized view of the Empire put forward in films is essentially a late nineteenth-century one is borne out by the fact that none of the films sought to tackle the contemporary issues. There is no reflection of the fact that the Empire was in a constant state of flux in the interwar years, evolving towards something quite different – the Commonwealth, the concept of a world-wide community of nations in free and voluntary association. The emergence of the Dominions, the successive reforms in India and the colonial development acts find no place in the films. Instead, we see in Korda's films a timeless and unchanging Empire, whose government and defence are firmly and permanently in the hands of the British.

The plots of all three Korda films are strikingly similar in outline.[25] In *Sanders of the River* the District Commissioner Sanders puts down a native uprising in Nigeria and rescues his African ally, Chief Bosambo, from the evil King Mofalaba. In *The Drum* Captain Carruthers joins forces with the Indian boy, Prince Azim, to put down an uprising on the North-west Frontier, led by his uncle, the wicked Ghul Khan. In *The Four Feathers* a disgraced British officer, Lt Harry Feversham, redeems his honour (assisted at the end by the pro-British chieftain, Karaga Pasha) by helping to put down the revolt of the Khalifa in the Sudan.

These three films unquestionably championed the continuation of the British Empire. In each of them, the exercise of power by the British is supported by the consent of the governed, as represented by Bosambo, Prince Azim and Karaga Pasha, and is defined by the opposition of self-seeking, power-hungry native despots, who, if left alone, would prey unmercifully on their own people – King Mofalaba, Ghul Khan and the Khalifa. The films offer no concrete political, economic or constitutional justification for the Empire's existence. The Empire is justified in the apparent moral superiority of the British, demonstrated by their adherence to the code of gentlemanly conduct and the maintenance of a disinterested system of law, order and justice.

So the key to understanding these films is their exaltation of British Character. It is this which set the British, and particularly their imperial administrators and soldiers, apart from other peoples and justified their ruling a quarter of the globe. As *The Times* declared in the mid-nineteenth century;

That which raises a country, that which strengthens a country, and that which dignifies a country – that which spreads her power, creates her moral influence, and makes her respected and submitted to, bends the heart of millions, and bows down the pride of nations to her – the instrument of obedience, the fountain of supremacy, the true throne, crown and sceptre of a nation; this aristocracy is not an aristocracy of blood, not an aristocracy of fashion, not an aristocracy of talent only; it is an aristocracy of Character.[26]

It is this aristocracy of character that shines forth from Korda's films and the objectives of these sterling characters are those defined by Sir Stephen Tallents, showing that Britain is still 'a great nation anxious to serve the world and to secure the world's peace'. The key sequences in the Korda films are based on the charismatic strength of the British heroes, who are invariably quiet, pipe-smoking, good-humoured and authoritative. When Sanders summons King Mofalaba to palaver, Mofalaba comes with his warriors, who out-number the British forces ten to one. Yet Sanders curtly reads the riot act to the King, warning him to behave, and then dismisses him with an abrupt, 'The palaver is finished.' Mofalaba and his men could easily have fallen on the British and slaughtered them. Instead, they obediently go home. The rapid crumbling of the situation when Sanders goes on leave and revolt flares up indicates just how essential the personal charisma and character of Sanders are to the government. The missionary priest, Father O'Leary, cables the Colonial Office: 'Send 4 batallions or Sanders.' Sanders returns and rapidly puts down the unrest.

Captain Carruthers in *The Drum* is a blood-brother of Sanders. In order to ensure the establishment of a British protectorate in the border state of Tokot, he is prepared to risk his life by going to a banquet which he suspects may be a trap. He tells his wife, 'A not unusual preliminary to our establishing law and order is the murder of one of our representatives.' 'Our establishing law and order' is the key phrase. That is the reason why British control in Tokot must be established, not so much in the interests of the Empire as in the interests of the Tokotis. Carruthers' decision to attend the banquet and the reasoning behind it is one of the emotional high-points of the film, the counterpart of Sanders' decision, when racked by malaria, to sail up to the Old King's country to rescue Bosambo. In both cases, the British representatives scorn their numerical inferiority and place their trust in their moral superiority.

The triumph of character, training and breeding over baser instincts is at the centre of *The Four Feathers*. Harry Feversham resigns from his regiment rather than sail with Kitchener's army to the Sudan. He talks of his duty to his tenants and estates, but is in fact afraid of being afraid and thus letting down the family name. His fiancée, Ethne, the one person he had expected to understand, expresses her horror at his decision and explains that they are not free to act as they might wish. They were born into a tradition, a code which they must obey because the pride and happiness of everyone around them depends on it. The rest of the film details Harry's redemption, as he goes to the Sudan in disguise and, at the climax of the action at the height of the Battle of Omdurman, seizes the arsenal and raises the Union Jack. Thus both the over-all political objective – the restoration of British rule and all it implies in terms of law, order and justice – and Harry's personal redemption are achieved in a final symbolic act. Judging by the reviews, audiences both at home and abroad took away the obvious and intended messages from these films. The *Sunday Times* declared that *Sanders* provided 'a grand insight into our especial English difficulties in the governing of savage races, and providing us with a documentary film of East African [sic] nature in its raw state, a picture which could not be improved upon for the respect it displays to British sensibilities and ambitions'.[27] The *New York Times* wrote of *The Drum* (titled *Drums* in the United States),

This is British propaganda week at the Music Hall and the British are the world's ablest propagandists. In the new *March of Time* chapter entitled 'The British Dilemma', they had a matinee crowd on the verge of declaring war against Germany yesterday. But an even more effective instrument for cementing the democratic axis, it seemed to us is Alexander Korda's *Drums*, a gorgeously High Anglican sermon for peace in the inconsistent but swirlingly dramatic terms of Imperialist warfare. . . . In Technicolor, the British are especially persuasive, with those red coats, those regimental toasts to the King, that look of high moral purpose.[28]

The same newspaper, describing *The Four Feathers* as 'an imperialist symphony', declared, 'The news this morning – in spite of what you hear about British colonial difficulties – is that Alexander Korda has retaken the Sudan. In fact, Mr Korda, the Kipling of the kinema, has retaken the already twice filmed *Four Feathers* of novelist A. E. W. Mason – and a fine, stirring, gorgeously Technicolored job he has made of it too. In a week rich in action epics, African locales and good remakes, Mr Korda has managed to plant the British flag higher than all the rest.'[29]

While Korda's films celebrated the administration and defence of the Empire, Balcon's films dealt with a chronologically earlier period – that of exploration and exploitation. In other words, they tackled the other side of the patriotism profit equation. Reviewers tended to see the films merely as exciting adventure stories. But they have a larger significance. Adventure is the powerful and beguiling legitimization of the imperial economic impulse.[30] The building of the Canadian Pacific Railway in *The Great Barrier* may be depicted as a 'Romance of Engineering', and the trek across the Dark Continent in search of fabled wealth in *King Solomon's Mines* as a 'Romance of Exploration'. But at the final count they add up to the 'Romance of Profit'.

But this profit is always justified by placing the events of the films squarely in an imperial context. The Canadian Pacific Railway is built in order to keep British Columbia within Canada. Rhodes acquires his diamond mines in pursuit of an Africa united under British rule. The English adventurers in *King Solomon's Mines* help the rightful chief, Umbopa, to overthrow the tyrannical Twala and restore good government to the Kukuanas.

It is also validated by its demonstration of character. The building of the railway is the making of the two worthless central figures: the American gambler, Hickey, and the English remittance man, Carson. Both are initially parasites but both become real men by hard work and sacrifice. *King Solomon's Mines* faithfully transcribes Rider Haggard's picture of the small and outnumbered band of white men (Sir Henry Curtis, Captain Good, RN and Allan Quatermain) as gods, courting the Africans with their innate charismatic strength, buttressed by superior technology (guns) and knowledge (of eclipses).

The film-makers were on rather more difficult ground with the life of Cecil Rhodes, because of his deep involvement in power politics and profit-making. But they succeeded in mythifying him by playing down the disreputable and playing up the heroic aspects of his story.

Firstly, they constantly emphasized his dream – an Africa united under British rule and peopled by British settlers. For this, he acquires the De Beers Diamond Mines and, once in charge, explicitly rejects the directors' obsession with profit in favour of his own expansionist plans. Secondly, his love of the African is emphasized. The Africans love him, call him 'Great White Father' and salute him on his death with the royal Matabele valediction. In return, he loves and cares for them. The film acquits him of responsibility for the Jameson Raid and the Matabele and Boer Wars. He emerges as a heroic figure, battling with death to make his dream a reality. At the end, he achieves the immortality accorded to all the great men of Empire. 'Living he was the land,' declares the narrator, 'and dead his soul shall be her soul.'

If *Rhodes of Africa* is the least satisfying of all the imperial epics, it is partly because it lacks the sweep and gusto of its counterparts, but also because it is fatally flawed by the central performance of the imported American star, Walter Huston. As James Agate tartly observed, 'It is a pity that Mr Walter Huston's Rhodes should look so exactly like Mr Ramsay Macdonald. As he also makes him act like President Lincoln and look as though he might at any moment burst into Drinkwater, I for one must vote this impersonation a failure.'[31] This sort of confusion of image was something the ordinary cinema-goer did not want. But in general the image of the Empire projected onto the screens of Britain and the world was one of benevolence and timelessness, of a framework for character-forming adventures and of an outlet for a deep-seated need to serve. Above all, the films hymned a decent, honourable people, shouldering the burden of Empire with disinterested single-mindedness and selfless dedication. It was a simple, satisfying and coherent view and it was one which the government felt able to leave to a commercial cinema which, in the 1930s, was able to achieve a successful blending of patriotism and profit.

15
Comedy, Class and Containment: The British Domestic Cinema of the 1930s
Tony Aldgate

Commentators invariably agree upon the role of the cinema in British society during the 1930s. In the course of his book *English History 1914–1945*, for example, A. J. P. Taylor states that 'The cinema was the essential social habit of the age'.[1] Similarly, C. L. Mowat notes how pervasive 'the flicks' were, adding that 'the cinemas took in some £40 millions annually'.[2] 'The cinema was in its heyday,' comment John Stevenson and Chris Cook during a more recent account of the period, and 'by 1939 the cinema was easily the most important form of mass entertainment with 20 million tickets being sold and 3 new cinemas being opened each week. . . . Admission cost only a few pence and provided probably the cheapest form of mass entertainment in most towns and cities.'[3]

In particular, the cinema was a constant source of attraction for the working class in Britain. This fact was amply demonstrated in *The Social Survey of Merseyside* (which was published in 1934), in several other social surveys that were conducted during the period, and in Simon Rowson's 'A Statistical Survey of the Cinema Industry in Great Britain in 1934' (published in 1936).[4] A Ministry of Information Wartime Social Survey, *The Cinema Audience*, showed how little this had changed by 1943. It commented that 'cinemas reach a wider public than other media' and that the cinema audience was made up predominantly of 'the lower economic and education groups'.[5]

The cinema, furthermore, cost very little to enjoy. Walter Greenwood's novel *Love on the Dole* (1933), painted a picture of working-class life, which for young Harry Hardcastle consisted, before the dole threatened, of 'a threepenny seat in the picture house twice a week' and 'a ninepenny or shilling dance of a Saturday night'. If Harry were to marry, Greenwood makes it clear, then, even though the dances might stop altogether, Harry would still expect to afford the luxury of visiting the cinema.[6] Indeed, Simon Rowson's survey went on to establish that 43 per cent of cinema admissions were in respect of seats for which the charge did not exceed 6d and that another 37 per cent did not pay more than 1s – in other words, that 'Nearly four out of every five persons visiting the cinema did not pay more than 1s (including duty) for admission.'[7]

The ravages of unemployment seem to have had little effect upon cinema admissions, particularly among those who were most affected by it. The consumption of alcohol declined during the 1930s and, though gambling was kept up more than drinking among the unemployed, since smaller bets could be placed, the cinema reigned supreme as 'a leisure pursuit'.[8] E. W. Bakke's study of the unemployed in Greenwich found, for instance, that the cinema was considered to be 'the most exciting event of the week'.[9] Similar studies of different cities ascertained that 52 per cent of the unemployed in Cardiff still managed to get to the cinema once a week (and half of their number went twice a week), and that in Liverpool and Glasgow as many as 80 per cent of the unemployed went at least once a week.[10]

The cinema, then, was a great attraction; it commanded a huge following and it was an inexpensive medium of 'entertainment' in the eyes of its patrons. It is perhaps worth adding also that in comparison with, say, gambling on the horses and the dogs (though not, of course, the football pools), or going to sporting events like soccer, cricket and boxing matches – which, again, experienced a boom period during the 1930s – the cinema was a medium which was enjoyed by both sexes alike. The cinema industry was well aware of this and in their review columns, trade magazines often designated films as having 'feminine appeal' or as being 'a woman's film'. Sidney Bernstein, who owned a chain of cinemas and conducted a regular questionnaire on cinema-goers' preferences, certainly paid a great deal of attention to women's opinions when deciding what films to book for his cinemas – their likes and dislikes with regard to particular film stars, their tastes as far as certain genres of film were concerned. No matter how crude the investigation, it is clear that the cinema provided one arena where women's votes were openly canvassed.[11]

But what other characteristics have been attributed to the mainstream British cinema of the 1930s?

Most observers, historians and film historians alike, agree that if 'the institution of cinema' attracted a considerable following in Britain during the 1930s, it was hardly on account of any British films which might have been shown in that period. Looking back upon those years, the film critic, Dilys Powell, argued in 1947 that 'with a few exceptions British films aroused no critical interest among the serious public, while to the masses who swarmed to the popular cinemas they were an inferior substitute for the American made film'.[12] A. J. P. Taylor endorses the argument and believes that 'Few British films made their mark.' According to his account two film directors enhanced their reputations and reached 'the front rank' – the expatriate Hungarian, Alexander Korda, and Alfred Hitchcock – thereby providing a handful of films which were the occasion of some success. But, otherwise, 'the Americans had it all their own way.'[13] 'Audiences stayed away from British films in droves,' it has been suggested of late, and 'British audiences also felt more at home with Hollywood films.'[14] The Americans 'colonized' the British cinema during the 1930s, we have been repeatedly told; there was no tradition of British films and little evidence of 'a national cinema', and, as a consequence, British films had no significant part to play in 'the national life' until the advent of the Second World War.[15]

Thereafter, so the argument goes, the British cinema was essentially 'a dream factory'. For the many thousands who flocked to it week by week it represented, as George Perry puts it, 'an escape from reality into a fantasy world', which produced 'little that could be interpreted as comment'. Perry advances two reasons for this 'silence' – a silence which he implicitly sees as in some way reflecting 'the spirit of the times', since he talks of it being inextricably bound up with the climate set by the 'close-lipped . . . appeasers' and a habit shared by the other media of communication.[16]

To begin with, he states that 'Undoubtedly, commercial presures prevented a more serious cinema emerging and the feeling that messages were for Western Union was applied as vigorously to British output as to that of Hollywood'.[17] And then he places great emphasis upon 'the repressive form of censorship imposed at that time by the British Board of Film Censors'.[18] It is a theme to which Perry consistently returns throughout the course of his book, and which has often found its echoes elsewhere.[19]

More recently, as a result of valuable new research into the work of the British Board of Film Censors, the role of censorship has been increasingly stressed; it has assumed paramount importance and been held to account almost entirely for the carefully delineated, well bounded, and strictly policed 'vision of the world' that was prevalent in the British cinema of the 1930s.[20] Cinema-goers were quite simply prevented from being subjected to 'the powerful impact of images and stereotypes designed to undermine their faith in the intentions of their rulers and in the beneficial effectiveness of the political system under which they lived', one commentator has observed, and 'harmony and hope of better days, arising from the innate strength and justice of the system in which they lived . . . were most successfully and effectively fostered.' This happy state of affairs for cinema-going audiences was achieved through 'the exclusion of any alternative viewpoint from the medium which they regarded as their chief escape into the world of dreams', and the process of 'Censorship ensured that dreams were not turned into nightmares of doubt and distrust, and that there were no alluring visions of alternative new orders'.[21]

It is a compelling argument, but, like the argument that an American 'colonization' of the British cinema existed (and like its concomitant theory that British films were decidedly 'unpopular'), it is in need of some modification. It is to these arguments that we now turn briefly in order to help locate the British cinema within the cultural life of the country at large.

It is difficult to determine with confidence the relative 'popularity' of British and American films with British audiences of the day. This is a problematic area: the evidence is scanty and invites speculation and generalization. Clearly, many commentators have concluded that British films were largely disregarded by British cinema-goers, who preferred instead the American product. And indeed it would be foolish to pretend that American films did not have immense appeal in this country. At one level, such evidence as there is available bears this out. There was a considerable number of American films, for a start – even at the peak of British film production, British films still only accounted for about 30 per cent of the films on offer to the home market – and American films starred some of the most 'popular' film personalities of the decade. The Bernstein questionnaires of 1934 and 1937 – in effect, glorified popularity polls – show the latter to be the case, though sometimes for the most unlikely of reasons (James Cagney, for example, invariably topped the poll for 'the star that everybody loved to hate').

Yet the argument that American films were dominant is by no means as clear-cut as all that. For it is also generally agreed that the

George Formby films were well received – in box-office terms, if not by the critics – thereby making Formby the top British box-office draw of the late 1930s and early 1940s, as were the films of Gracie Fields (winning her a Hollywood contract and a salary effusively described as 'the highest salary ever paid to a human being'). Were these, along with the Will Hay films and such notable successes as Korda's *The Private Life of Henry VIII* (1933) simply the exceptions that prove the rule?

Perhaps not. One could marshal a certain amount of anecdotal evidence, for instance, to suggest that at the beginning of the 1930s, at least, some British audiences did not like American films. In general, it has been argued that 'The public at first found the American accents bewildering and missed much of the dialogue'.[22] More specifically, it has been suggested that there was both a class and a regional reaction, as 'the English working class, and the Northern working class in particular, exercised a strong suspicion, not to say hatred, of the American idiom'.[23] In fact, it would appear that John Maxwell's British International Pictures sought to capitalize upon such responses for a while, by putting the slogan, 'Spoken with all the charm and purity of the English voice', on the advertising for their product – on films which varied as much in their appeal as the 1930 version of Ian Hay's and Stephen King-Hall's West End hit *The Middle Watch* and Leslie Fuller's 1931 provincial comedy, *Poor Old Bill*.

No doubt, though, this antipathy soon disappeared, just as the apparent hostility to talking pictures quickly evaporated in its turn. And perhaps one might get a better indication of the new-found changes and reactions, and the subtle variations in cultural response which ensued as the thirties progressed, from Winifred Holtby's fictional account, *South Riding* (1936). For there Holtby describes one of her characters, the maid Elsie, in the following terms: 'Like most of her generation and locality, Elsie was trilingual. She talked BBC English to her employer, Cinema American to her companions, and Yorkshire dialect to old milkmen like Eli Dickson.'[24]

Yet it is not necessary to dwell upon anecdote alone to argue the case for British films. Simon Rowson's surveys are especially useful in this respect. His 'Statistical Survey' of 1934, for instance, gave a clear indication that British films were winning considerable ground and that they were more popular with British audiences than they were given credit for.[25] The Americans, for their part, had noticed the trend even earlier. Indeed, an article in the American trade magazine

Variety, for 3 January 1933, went so far as to state that 'The one outstanding fact of the British film field of 1932 was the complete stranglehold the home-made picture established on the local box office'. While admitting that 'No one could suggest the studio output, as a whole, anywhere approaches Hollywood in originality or quality', it maintained that 'The huge success of the British film can only be ascribed to temperamental affinity to the home audience'.[26]

With somewhat less hyperbole, Simon Rowson made the same basic points once again in the testimony and tables he presented to the Moyne Committee of 1936.[27] There he went on to argue that in his opinion British films had demonstrated their 'superior attractiveness over foreign competitors', as far as British audiences were concerned, in the four years prior to 1936. To substantiate his claims, he pointed out that in every one of those years the exhibitors' quota had been greatly exceeded – in other words, that the cinemas were showing of their own volition (and no doubt because the demand was there) a good deal more British films than the 1927 Act required of them. Then, more significantly, he produced tables to show that, on average, British films had been screened about 6 per cent more frequently than foreign films. In particular, he commented, the statistics revealed that British films 'have been showing more times in this country than the American pictures'. There may have been more American films than British films in circulation, but the basis of his arguments was that, on average, a British film was screened more often.

Rowson did go on, however, to add that the difference in the number of screenings, in favour of British films, was rapidly disappearing. In fact, he concluded that by 1936 it had gone; and of course within two years of Rowson's evidence film production in this country suffered a slump. Some 212 British films were registered in 1936 and 228 films in 1937; but only 76 films were registered in 1938.

But why was there a sudden decline in British film production if it could be demonstrated that there was a demand for British films from exhibitors, based upon the assumption that they were popular with home audiences? The answer to that may lie in the fact that the decline in film production bore little or no relationship to the popularity of British films. It had more to do with the nature of the film industry in this country and the conditions surrounding film production and finance.

This is not the place to go into these matters at length, but it seems clear, for instance, that the production system was geared towards the extensive use of 'short-date capital', as Rowson put it, and 'such finance is very dear money'. 'Apart from serious other inconveniences,' he continued, it 'represents a further charge on the cost of production'. It was a dangerous spiral which meant that the ultimate cost of making a film in this country could often reach a prohibitive figure that was never likely to be recovered, no matter how popular the film turned out to be in the domestic market. This dawned on many people, not least the financiers, when serious losses were incurred on films despite a production boom in 1936 and 1937.

When one also considers the administrative inefficiency in the industry, the excessive cost of studio space, the over-long production schedules and inordinately slow releases practices, to name but a few additional factors, it is not difficult to see why many were prompted to conclude that the 'methods of production in the industry had outrun the dictates of financial prudence'.[28] Nor is it difficult to understand why the financiers largely withdrew from film production, thereby precipitating the slump in the British industry.

Yet just as there is no reason to assume that the slump in British film production in the later years of the 1930s bore any relation to the popularity of British films, so indeed one must not assume that British films in the period necessarily lost their popularity just because there were fewer of them on show. An impressionistic survey of sixty-six exhibitors conducted by the trade magazine, the *Daily Film Renter* (published in a special edition on 1 January 1937), confirmed that British films had a considerable 'box-office appeal' at the beginning of the second half of the decade.[29] And, more significantly, the *First Report of the Cinematograph Films Council* (relating to the year ended 31 March 1939) reiterated the point that Rowson had made earlier. It concluded that 'there was an insistent demand by exhibitors for British films which was not limited by the extent of their statutory quotas and as a result any satisfactory British picture had an eager market in this country'.[30]

The undoubted popularity of American films, then, should not be allowed to blind one to the existence of an essentially British cinema. Nor should one be so quick to conclude that the so-called American 'colonization' of the British cinema necessarily threatened cultural domination under the hegemony of the United States, at least during the 1930s. It is all too easy to forget that, as one study has observed, 'Britain remained a relatively cohesive and insular society in which there were still a large number of shared assumptions',[31] or to underestimate the insularity of that society and the stability of its social arrangements. As a British Board of Film Censors' reader put it so succinctly, when commenting upon an American *March of Time* release in 1938, 'I suggest that conditions are by no means similar in the United States and in England, 3000 miles of Atlantic Ocean is a useful buffer,' before going on to add with supreme confidence (or characteristic arrogance), 'The cinemagoing public in England seek amusement, not political guidance, from the screen, and are quite likely to resent such guidance especially if it comes from an alien source.'[32]

To what extent, though, did the British Board of Film Censors, as a body, ensure that all that cinema-goers got was harmless, escapist amusement?

Its successes in controlling the content of films, and in setting the moral, social and political code by which the cinema must be judged, have been admirably and convincingly charted. Yet the extent of this success should not be exaggerated. It depends greatly upon the proposition that the censorship process exercised by the BBFC was monolithic and that it had a uniform effect upon local censorship authorities, film producers and audiences alike. It has already been suggested, for instance, that 'it would be misleading to ascribe a fictitious unity to the fundamentally different types and levels of "censorship" during the period by lumping them together under the generalized heading "the censor" or "censorship measures" '. ' "Censorship" was not, and never has been, the activity of one centralized institution, but a network of interrelated and contradictory institutions', it has been rightly stressed, and 'The anomalies in the legal situation showed that no single group had responsibility for "censorship".'[33]

Some contradictions were plainly evident in the realms of film production. There, as Victor Saville recounted, producers 'were always battling with censorship. . . . My friend, the story editor of Gaumont-British, and I worked out that if we were to obey every restriction set by the British Board of Film Censors . . . you wouldn't be able to make *Cinderella*.'[34] Yet films were made. Furthermore, it is clear that the advice proferred by the BBFC script-readers – those 'ex-Colonels and maiden aunts in long flowered frocks', as Thorold Dickinson described them from experience,[35] who commented upon the pre-production synopses and scenarios presented for their consideration – did not naturally command either deferential or wholehearted respect. The various reactions to the filming of *Once in a New Moon*, for example, show that to be the case.

The pre-production scenario for the film, under the title *Lucky Star* (it was based upon the novel of that name by Owen Rutter), was submitted to the BBFC by Fox British on 9 July 1934 and was immediately adjudged by one script-reader to be 'a fantastic story worthy of Jules Verne or H. G. Wells'.[36] The plot recounts the adventures of a typical English village after it has been cast into space as the result of a collision between earth and a dead star. Once the village awakens to its plight, the gentry form a government, under the lord of the manor, and seek to rule the community to their own advantage. But the mass of the villagers soon grow discontented, two 'violently opposing parties' emerge, and a general election is held, from which the villagers emerge victorious. They are preparing to take the manor by force when their village is returned to earth. Peace, stability and the old social order are restored.

The two BBFC examiners who were reading the scenario highlighted numerous details which they wanted to see either removed altogether or suitably modified. Matters of 'taste' were noticeably to the fore in the suggestions to delete remarks such as 'Nothing like corpses for manure,' 'Lousy,' 'Hands off motherhood,' 'Plenty of No. 9's, doctor?' (the latter being accompanied by a heartfelt comment to the effect that 'I do not know what it means but coming from an ex-sergeant major, I suspect the worst'), and in calls to 'Avoid vulgarity in scenes of handling baby' and to 'Delete man and woman in bed together'. In addition, both readers noted 'various references to birth control' throughout the script. In this context they were of the unanimous opinion that 'all references to birth control and subsequent dialogue', and the mention of 'family limitations', should be excised.

They were not, however, of the same opinion in their overall assessments of the piece. The reader who had likened it to Verne or Wells felt that it was 'Quite well worked out, and the story is free from objection'. On the other hand, the reader who had agonized over 'No. 9's', considered that 'This story is in my opinion unsuitable for production', giving as the major objection the fact that 'there is far too much class controversy'.

In the event, Fox British continued into production on the film, retitling it *Once in a New Moon* in the process. Anthony Kimmins

266 / British Cinema History

directed it at the Sound City Shepperton studios, and the completed film was submitted for viewing by the censors on 11 October 1934. It was passed as a 'U' with no further deletions.

Yet, interestingly, for all that efforts had obviously been made to allay some of the concern expressed by the censors (the birth control references were dropped completely, as were all potentially 'offensive' remarks and scenes), the resulting film still persevered with its 'controversial' theme of 'class' conflict.

The film was naturally bound by limitations. It was a fantasy comedy, after all, and an opening prologue made clear its primary intentions when stating at one point, 'If Shrimpton's story is not exactly true, that does not make it any the less good fun.' But thereafter a fair amount of latitude was found for wry comment, particularly in the scenes which mark the growing 'discontent' between the villagers and the gentry.

Class divisions and social barriers are well set at the beginning and remain distinctly underscored throughout. A sub-plot concerning the relationship between the village postmaster's daughter and the lord of the manor's son helps to do this with the postmaster deferentially counselling his daughter, early in the film, to 'remember who we are and who they are' (though such sentiments are of course finally undermined, at the film's end, when, in the best tradition of mainstream narrative cinema, 'love conquers all' and 'boy gets girl').

But it is in the main plot, with its theme of 'What the people want is equal rights and equal bites . . . and if they don't get it, there'll be trouble' (as it is jocularly put at one point by Wally Patch, who continues the comic touch by persistently mispronouncing 'ruling clique' as '. . . click'), that the class divisions ultimately emerge in conflict, even if this is regularly tempered with doses of humour.

As the BBFC reader's 'two violently opposing parties' are formed, most of the leading characters are given a gibe or two. 'That's always the way with the British public. The more you give them, the less thanks you get,' the lord of the manor remonstrates on hearing of his rejection by the villagers, before concluding, 'I never knew a government yet that someone wasn't fed up with. The British workman will be against the government of heaven . . . if he ever gets there.' Meanwhile his wife (described in the BBFC synopsis as 'a rabid anti-socialist') argues, 'Give these people an inch and they take a mile. This is what comes of having a government of butchers and bakers . . . it's rank socialism.' To which their son retorts, 'What if it is? Just because it doesn't work in England, doesn't mean it can't work here.'

By far the majority of such lines, however, are reserved for the character, played by John Clements, whose tone and fervour leave no doubt that he was meant to be construed as the 'rabid socialist' counter to the 'rabid anti-socialist' lady of the manor, and which clearly prompted the BBFC reader to talk of there being 'too much class controversy'.

In seeking to win the affection of the postmaster's daughter for himself, he describes the lord's son as 'a young capitalist pup who's living off the fat of the land while the rest of the community's starving'. 'This is the age of the worker, Stella, it's the man who works that matters, now more than ever,' he declares; then he asserts, 'You belong to the people, so do I. It's up to us to see these damned capitalists turned off their pedestals.' And his arguments reach their climax in an impassioned speech to the villagers in which he demands, 'We want fair play in the future and a proper retribution for our treatment in the past.' Whereupon he goads the villagers into taking forceful action and suggests 'a revolutionary army' be formed: 'We've got the numbers . . . train 'em to fight.'[37]

Subsequently, the film reverts to the light-hearted vein which predominates throughout. Training the 'army' proves makeshift and turns into a comic romp. The Clements character fades into the background. The lord of the manor and the postmaster meet, regret the animosity which has arisen, lament their new-found positions and look forward to the day 'when peace is restored'. And, on being returned to earth, albeit off the Scarborough coast, everybody happily assumes their old roles and proudly boast, 'We've not been anything but British during our absence.'

In the final analysis, it is not difficult to see why the BBFC was quite content to pass the film with a 'U' certificate, despite one of their readers' undoubted reservations. The 'construction of reality' which it advanced was hardly radical or even especially trenchant. Indeed, the consensus which it evoked could be attuned quite neatly to the consensus which the BBFC sought to evoke. But it is important to note that this consensus arose as naturally from 'below' (from the forms and conventions adopted in the general practice of film production – those 'various pleasure-producing and identification mechanisms inherent in the mainstream narrative cinema, codified into genre categories and mobilizing apparently "a-political", "innocent" emotions', as they have been aptly described),[38] as it did from any attempt by the BBFC to impose a measure of content control from 'above'.

It is illuminating, in this respect, to observe the 'reality' represented in a film which did not come before the censors until after completion. Like Korda, Basil Dean was comparatively unconcerned about submitting his projects to pre-production scrutiny by the BBFC, and it seems that he rarely availed himself of the facility. 'We asked Mr Dean to submit this script to us. . . . He never co-operates with us and now he's got to face up to it,' the censors threatened Thorold Dickinson on his being ushered into their presence for the purpose of defending one of Dean's films, a task which he nevertheless successfully fulfilled.[39]

It was Dean's Associated Talking Pictures, more than any other production company, which provided the majority of films in that 'whole school of working class comedy that existed in the thirties'.[40] These films proved to be vehicles for the exploitation on a national scale of comic talents like those of Formby and Fields, whose origins were largely in regional variety. And they offered an outlet for 'populist' writers like J. B. Priestley, who scripted two of the Gracie Fields films, and Walter Greenwood, who wrote the first of Formby's films for ATP. (Similarly, Fields's first film, *Sally in Our Alley* (1931), was based upon a stage play, *The Likes of 'Er*, by Charles McEvoy, whom Harold Brighouse ranked alongside the Manchester Playwrights, producing what he described as 'realistic comedy'.)

A film like *Sing As We Go* (1934) was typical of this sort of production. It was written by Priestley, directed by Dean and starred Gracie Fields. Priestley used the depression in the Lancashire cotton industry as the framework for the story – something, as Dean put it, 'solid enough to support its broad humours without loss of credibility'.[41]

Interestingly, it would appear that Priestley wanted to make more of the initial 'establishing' scenes, in which the Greybeck Mills are closed down, than finally appeared in the film itself. An earlier draft of the script envisaged a scene there in which an elderly woman 'wearily' and 'tearfully' accepts her insurance cards and the 'small sum of money' owing to her from a cashier's counter.[42] But it was not used. Clearly the inclusion of such a scene, with its emphasis upon the blight of depression and its sense of personal plight ('We're beaten,' said the cashier), would have been greatly at odds with the rest of the film that followed. Priestley himself commented in *English Journey* upon the sturdy refusal to give up on the part of the unemployed in the Lancashire cotton towns, and noted their stoical insistence that there were 'Lots worse off than them'.[43]

And *Sing As We Go*, as released, is essentially an optimistic film, as its beginning makes abundantly clear. Depression threatens, the mills are closing down and unemployment looms. 'It's a damned bad day for Greybeck,' everybody agrees. On being told by the manager's son, Hugh Phillips, that the mills won't reopen 'unless we can find a new cheap process', the foreman laments, 'Aye, and just when we wor getting a damned good football team together again.' The mass of the workers bemoan the loss of the mill concert party and send Grace to see 'young Mr Phillips' on their behalf, since 'He's been rehearsing with us'.

When she is in Mr Phillips's office Grace seems intent upon cracking jokes, making plain her affection for him and displaying her indomitable spirit. 'If we can't weave, we can still sing,' she says, and, 'We'll be able to practise while we're all queuing up for the dole.' It is quickly established that Hugh will also be thrown out of work by the mill's closure and that he too will have to look for a job elsewhere. Then their conversation peters out with some more light-hearted banter. 'I think I shall miss you, Grace,' reflects Hugh. 'Yes, well, I'd rather you missed me than hit me, lad,' she retorts.

The script direction for that last piece of Grace's dialogue reads 'carrying it off bravely'. And that is precisely the spirit – 'bravery and fortitude in the face of adversity' – which is engendered in the subsequent scene when Grace reports back to the workers. On being told 'It's no good. We'll have to pack up,' an older man jeers, 'Well Grace, this lot's knocked the song and dance out of you.' 'No, it hasn't, long face,' she replies sharply. And then, turning to the crowd, Grace utters, 'Come on girls, come on lads. Let's leave the owd place in style. Give it a chorus. "Sing as we go." ' Linking their arms together, the workers march out with a rousing chorus of the theme song to the film.

By this point, the scene has been well and truly set: depression and unemployment are unfortunate occurrences; they deprive people of their livelihood and their social life; but they threaten both workers and bosses alike. Furthermore, such setbacks need not take away personal dignity or pride in one's local culture. And it is possible to overcome adversity. Most of the rest of the film shows Grace doing just that. She finds a variety of jobs in seasonal employment at Blackpool and in the process treats the audience to a rich array of comic escapades.

Only at the end of the film do we return to the problems of the mill. Yet it too is saved, by a miracle of technological innovation, the sort of 'new cheap process' Hugh was talking about. Consequently, the mill reopens and Grace is promoted to the position of welfare officer. Thereafter, Grace leads the workers back in triumphant procession, at the head of a column which now includes a brass band. Everyone boisterously sings the theme song and some are waving the Union Jack. The band marches off and the workers follow on behind Grace until a new shot singles her out and brings her to the forefront of the screen. Gaily she continues singing; someone rudely brushes past her, but she now confidently calls after him, 'Who do you think you're shoving?' She fades from view, to reveal the logo of Dean's Ealing Studios, yet another Union Jack, which fills the entire screen as the film comes to an end.

Clearly, *Sing As We Go* was a joyful film, which amounted to a stirring and patriotic reassurance that all will be well in the end. On the face of it the film does simply use the depression in the Lancashire cotton industry as the framework for the story and little else. It distances whatever social comment it has to make, and the bulk of the film is reserved for Grace's humorous jaunt in Blackpool. That is obviously why the *Observer* film critic was moved to comment in 1934, 'We have an industrial north that is bigger than Gracie Fields running round a Blackpool funfair.' But it has also been suggested, more recently, that 'The fact that the film is set in Blackpool and not Greybeck Mill does not invalidate its reality', and that to the predominantly working-class audiences who would have seen the film 'Gracie's escapades among the familiar scenes of the "Wakes Week" excursionists were only heightened versions of their own remembered exploits.' In short, that 'They were thus a part of reality rather than a substitute for it'.[44]

In such circumstances, bodies like the BBFC had little to fear from the British cinema of the 1930s. And it is perhaps not surprising that the British cinema was, for its own part, and without much prompting, a further significant factor in contributing to the remarkable stability of British society during this period. It reflected and reinforced the dominant consensus and sought to generate adherence to the idea that society should continue to remain stable and cohesive as it changed over time. British films did indeed have an important part to play in 'the national life'.

Women, Realism and Reality in British Films, 1943–53

Sue Aspinall

Looking back in 1948, one film critic noted with dissatisfaction that British films had failed to reflect certain important aspects of reality. She contended that

> Our epoch has produced probably the most fundamental changes in the relationship between men and women ever known, changes which have not yet attained stability and which are still conflicting with the more long-standing traditions of the past. . . . New ethics are in the making. Every day we encounter the drama and complexity of it all: the woman who wants it both ways, expecting protection from the men with whom she now competes in politics, professions and (on unequal terms) in industry; the man who wants it both ways, expecting to be served by the wife who shares the fatigue and hazards of bread-winning – points such as these are assiduously avoided.[1]

This critic, Catherine de la Roche, associated the films' failure with the loss of that 'urgent sense of reality' produced by the war years. Unlike many film critics of the 1940s, for whom formal realism was a panacea for all cinematic ills, Catherine de la Roche was more concerned that films should interpret contemporary life, using all the resources of allegory, satire, documentary, comedy, realism or fantasy. Although she was concerned about the representation of reality, she did not reduce her concern to the simplistic equation for 'realist = progressive' or 'non-realist = reactionary'.

The way in which the British films of 1943–53 registered changes in gender roles in this period certainly cannot be accounted for simply in terms of form or genre. These years were a time of transition for women – from the possibility of a relatively independent working and sexual life during the war, to a renewed emphasis on their subordinate domestic and feminine role in the 1950s. This transition was accomplished primarily at an ideological level – since, despite fluctuations and certain changes in employment practice, women continued to go out to work in ever greater numbers in the fifties. In this chapter, I want to ask how and why films contributed to this process of transition.

When one recalls the films of the 1940s and 1950s, two contrasting images spring to mind: the dignified woman of the 1940s, with her tailored suit and well modulated upper-class accent, and the pouting young blonde of the 1950s, with her noticeable breasts and lack of concern for class formalities. This shift in image aroused my curiosity: it seemed to involve questions of class, gender and sexuality. As I began to look at the films of the period, it became clear that the shift did involve questions of cinematic form; but it seemed to me that a particular style of realism was in fact closely allied to a traditional, conservative attitude to women and marriage, while the unrealistic costume dramas and melodramas, which were more widely seen and enjoyed, were more unstable in their attitudes to women's sexuality and role in life. My original image of the *Brief Encounter* type of woman had then to be modified by the existence of another submerged layer of films: the popular women's pictures of the 1940s, which are no longer exhibited.

My discussion will be focused primarily on the films which were designated as having a special appeal for women, because of their depiction of (hetero)sexual relations. These films can be loosely divided into three types. Firstly, there are the 'quality' films, such as *The Way to the Stars* (G-B, d. A. Asquith, 1945), *Brief Encounter* (G-B, d. D. Lean, 1945) or *Fame is the Spur* (G-B, d. Boulting, 1947), which catered for well bred tastes by presenting images of well bred women. Secondly, there are the unserious entertainments, abounding with gypsies, peasants and Regency aristocrats – with anything, in fact, which is removed from the class realities of the present. Thirdly, there is a category which includes a few films which found a place sandwiched between the first two classes; these are neither in the 'quality' market nor in the realm of unashamed fantasy. A film such as *They were Sisters* (G-B, d. A. Crabtree, 1945) shares many features with the 'quality' realist films: it was shot partly in authentic locations (in this case, a large middle-class residence and garden and in the countryside) and it deals with experiences of marriage that are recognizable and realistic, if exaggerated. Even though both the characters and the actresses are middle-class, they represent a female experience that cuts across class divisions. The sisters of the film are firmly rooted in their upper middle-class environment, but their experiences of marriage itself could be translated to a working-class environment: the maternal woman who cannot have children, the hedonistic woman whose marriage is one of convenience, not commitment, and the woman who has lost her identity and allows her husband to terrorize herself and her children. Films such as this were clearly marked as 'women's pictures' – which is to say that they were made with a female audience in mind, their narratives are focused on women's experience and they have no obvious 'message', in the sense of saying something about great issues or moral problems, as a 'quality' picture would do.

Brief Encounter is a rarity in combining women's picture material with 'quality' in its writer (Noel Coward), director (David Lean) and actors (Celia Johnson and Trevor Howard). I find it a powerful film; it states the contradiction between sexual desire and stable child-rearing arrangements with quiet force. Laura Jesson is a housewife who is caught unawares by sexual desire – 'I'm an ordinary woman – I didn't think such violent things could happen to ordinary people', she says. The violent emotions which are commonplace in melodrama achieve a different sort of power when placed in the context of the restrictions of everyday working life, and in drab settings like railway stations and cheap tea-rooms; refusing the costume drama's vicarious enjoyment of sin and passion, this realist film tries to convey a sense of the painful choices of real life. It was unusual for a realist and a 'quality' film to base its narrative on a woman character at all – and, even more so, to make that narrative the story of her sexual feelings. 'Quality' was in a sense synonymous with restraint, good taste and the higher moral values.

Although *Brief Encounter* does return its heroine to her dull, dependable husband in the end, her choice is presented as an ambivalent one. The film makes Laura's return to her husband convincing only by emphasizing the material side of her married life. She has a clean, spacious house, a maid to do the cooking, no apparent financial anxieties. She also has a position in the community – established by her familiarity with the staff of the railway station and by her meeting a social acquaintance there. She has two healthy, well educated children whom she cannot leave because 'the feeling of guilt, of doing wrong, is a little too strong, isn't it? Perhaps too great a price to pay for the few hours of happiness we get out of it' – not because she loves them too much to leave them. The relationship between husband and wife is also not presented as a site of conflict – he is reliable, sympathetic and a good provider. The film clearly states the dilemma for a contented middle-class housewife between the established 'good life' she has and her need for sexual and emotional fulfilment. Despite its conventional ending, *Brief Encounter* does not completely succeed in closing off sexual freedom in a convincing way: ultimately, Laura rejects her lover out of a fear of the unknown and because her middle-class sensibilities are offended by the sordidness of adultery; she chooses social approval and security because the alternative seems to offer no clear role in life.

The film might have been read differently by a working-class female spectator, who might merely have envied Laura her prosperity, leisure and security; or might have wondered why Laura was so squeamish about making love in a borrowed flat. For whatever reason, the film was not popular with working-class audiences.

Love Story (G-B, d. L. Arliss, 1944), on the other hand, was a women's picture which dealt with wartime feelings about sex implicitly from a working-class woman's point of view. It is a low-key melodrama about a woman, Lissa (Margaret Lockwood), who knows she is going to die in six months' time. Unlike Laura, Lissa has nothing to lose by expressing her sexuality freely. She does attempt to repress her feelings for the sake of her lover – so that he can form a relationship with another woman who is devoted to him – but in the end she gives in to her emotions. The film concludes with the message that 'the happiness we have is *worth* grasping – if only for a day or an hour'. This clearly echoed the experience of thousands of women who found new sexual freedom during the war. As one book noted disapprovingly in 1946, 'the dangers and excitement of war often stimulate these instincts and inflate them to quite an abnormal extent. Add to this the general loosening up of restraints due to the idea that if one doesn't take one's chances when one can, one may never have them again, and the stage is set for many mistakes.'[2] Similarly, speaking from a less critical standpoint, a northern woman in domestic service during the war remarked that 'Once all the boys and girls around us seemed to tell dirty stories and jokes and kiss and cuddle in every corner as soon as it was dusk; but now it's as if they *do* things and don't talk about them . . . it's as if people don't *think* it's wrong any more. . . .'[3] *Love Story* was released in 1944, at a time when husbands and fiancés were still in danger of being killed; *Brief Encounter* was released in late 1945 when the war was over, and it provided a bridge between wartime indulgence and traditional restraint, hovering as it does between the two.

The Wicked Lady (G-B, d. L. Arliss, 1945) was a popular costume drama which approached the subject of female freedom through the filter of the rich, aristocratic world of the past, when extravagant clothes and extravagant passions went hand in hand. On one level the film reproduces the staple diet of large numbers of low-budget entertainments: the conflict between the good, faithful, loving woman, generally socially respectable, and the sexy, opinionated, unprincipled woman. Stereotypes of good and bad women are used to express a more fundamental conflict between marriage, affection and stability, on the one hand, and hedonism and self expression on the other. *The Wicked Lady* enjoyed enormous popularity, not because good ultimately triumphs over evil, but because the case for pleasure is made so convincingly. Although the heroine, played by Margaret Lockwood, dies saying she wants 'a home and children, things I never thought mattered before', telling her True Love, 'if I'd met you sooner I'd never have done these things,' the images of the film that persist are those of Lockwood as a defiant wife, an energetic highway robber, an enthusiastic lover, an instigator of action. These images are more powerful than the pat ending.

Unlike other actresses in British films of the 1940s, Lockwood stood out as the image of a woman who was not part of the upper-class establishment. Although she was by no means working-class she did not possess the kind of poise which comes from knowing one's place in the world and from expecting respect. There was an edge of bravado and insecurity to her personality as she appeared on film. Early in her career she had been typecast as the silly, selfish, opinionated woman in films such as *The Lady Vanishes* (G-B, d. A. Hitchcock, 1938), and *The Stars Look Down* (G-B, d. C. Reed, 1939). Although she resented getting what were deemed to be 'bad' parts, she nonetheless succeeded in establishing herself as one of the most popular British film actresses of the 1940s, consistently being voted top in numerous polls and questionnaires.[4] Other favourites were Phyllis Calvert and Anna Neagle, followed by Patricia Roc and Jean Kent. Lockwood's success reached its peak in 1945 with *The Wicked Lady*, which finally translated her bitchiness and bravado into a positive celebration.

In this film, Lockwood offered a way of being female that was not dependent on attracting male protection. Yet her aloofness and self-determination did not produce much sexual charisma – as the critics noted in decrying the idea that she could play the *femme fatale*. She was too robustly cheerful to be a convincingly unattainable and mysterious sex object. In fact, she gave out too much energy to be considered an object at all, being essentially active, not passive. Many interpreted her lack of orientation to men as sexlessness, and she was certainly not in the same league as Garbo, Bergman or Hayworth. But she did have something in common with the most popular American stars of the war years: Bette Davis, Joan Crawford, Barbara Stanwyck, Katharine Hepburn – a certain kind of strength based on the active principle. The American stars, however, were often cynical and manipulative as well, whereas Lockwood lacked their sophistication. In fact, she was probably the least sophisticated of all the British stars of the 1940s – Anne Crawford, Phyllis Calvert or Anna Neagle were all much closer to the Hollywood model of a film star. But it was probably Lockwood's naiveté and her lack of pretension that endeared her to her thousands of women fans.

British film actresses were not at this time produced as 'stars' to anything like the same extent as their American counterparts. There was no star system until the Rank 'charm school', the 'Company of Youth', was set up when Sydney Box joined Rank in 1946; it was closed down in 1949 because 'we couldn't find even another Margaret Lockwood'.[5] Both Phyllis Calvert and Margaret Lockwood, two of Britain's most popular actresses, were uninterested in glamour. Calvert confessed that she detested the paraphernalia of 'immaculate hairdos', 'toothpaste smiles' and 'aching feet in ridiculously high-heeled shoes'.[6]

Hollywood was a problem for these actresses. Lockwood could not cope with the unfamiliar press and publicity, wore the wrong clothes and said the wrong things on her visit shortly before the outbreak of war.[7] Phyllis Calvert and Deborah Kerr were reluctant to go at all, resisting all offers until 1947, when the war could no longer be offered as a valid excuse for declining. Calvert's patriotism did not help her career; she admitted that 'When I heard the way they talked about America's war effort and sacrifices and so on, I just couldn't keep quiet. I'm afraid I let them have it.'[8] Kerr was more restrained, putting up with the 'duchess' roles, which were all she was offered, until 1953, when she found herself a new agent, had 'sexy' photographs of herself taken, and landed the starring role in *From Here to Eternity* (United States, 1953, d. F. Zinneman). Perhaps Kerr was more aware that her long-term career prospects depended on pleasing the American market. She was certainly unusually receptive to Hollywood, claiming in one interview that it had 'taught me to act for the screen'.[9]

The rising British film actresses of the late 1940s and early 1950s were only too aware of the necessity of pleasing Hollywood. Joan Collins and Diana Dors, for example, were desperate to reach the mecca of fame and fortune. Unlike their predecessors, they were both sexually precocious and fashion-conscious; they wanted to be 'stars' not actresses. They were well informed and willing to accept Hollywood standards: for example, Dors remarked in her auto-biography, 'When I went to do a film with George Gobel, I had never even seen him, let alone met him, but I did know that he was one of America's top TV names, and that was good enough for me.'[10]

These pliable lower-middle-class women of the 1950s accepted that they were a commodity to be marketed in a way that the respectable 'nice' generation of Lockwood, Calvert, Kerr, Roc and Neagle would not have tolerated. To a certain extent, the personalities and image of the latter group of actresses limited the scope and the resonance of the films that could be made in the 1940s. They came from middle-class backgrounds, were often trained in the theatre and regarded them-selves as actresses. Many films of the forties were based on plays and shared the same class values as West End plays. The shift in the cinema's image of women was partly attributable to the move away from this theatrical tradition caused by the increasing dominance of Hollywood mass production criteria.

Because women in Britain were more clearly marked by their class origins than in America, this shift towards American standards also involved a shift in the class status and background of actresses. Catherine de la Roche complained about these new 'types' in 1949, claiming that they gave 'a deceptive picture of the part women play in modern society, or ignore it altogether'.[11] These new 'types' of the late 1940s and early 1950s were exemplified in Britain by actresses such as Dors and Collins, whose personalities were primarily a projection of their sexuality. Simone de Beauvoir accounted for this development in terms of the new status of women, which required a new form of sex appeal: 'In an age when woman drives a car and speculates on the stock exchange, an age in which she uncer-emoniously displays her nudity on public beaches, any attempt to revive the vamp and her mystery was out of the question.' Instead, films 'tried to appeal, in a cruder way, to the male's response to feminine curves. Stars were appreciated for the obviousness of their physical charms.'[12] Her assumption is that the more independent women of the war years had had no sexual appeal; women must either return to the coyness and mystery of the pre-war vamp or must develop a new brashness and vulgarity in order to revive men's sexual interest.

As the actresses were changed, so were the films. The early part of the forties has been seen by critics of the time, and since, as the golden age of British film; and, indeed, British films in this period were actually dominating the popularity polls. There was a tendency for the critics to ascribe this to the uniquely British form of realism which had emerged in films such as *In Which we Serve* (G-B, d. N. Coward and D. Lean, 1942) – thus projecting their own preferences onto the British public at large. Although some of these 'realist' films were top box-office successes, more often than not it was the Gainsborough dramas and melodramas that were consistent winners. However, for the critics, realism was the great white hope of British cinema. It was assumed by them to be progressive, because it dealt with social rather than individual reality and because it began to break down class taboos. War films such as *In Which we Serve* were among the first to portray working-class people as serious fictional characters, not merely as comedians or servants. This important development took place against the background of the work of the British documentary movement of the 1930s, with its romantic reverence for the working man – but its main impetus was the necessity of forging a wartime alliance between classes, which until then, had been rigidly segregated.

However, the unfamiliarity of middle-class writers, directors, producers and actors with working-class life militated against any radical change in the images they produced. Instead, they drew on familiar stereotypes from comedy or music-hall, such as the cheeky Cockney, the seedy spiv or criminal and the steady family man. These stereotypes seemed to function in terms of the working man's relationship to work, while the stereotypes of working-class women defined them in terms of their sexual function: the tart, the motherly type or the naive young thing. In the absence of serious working-class actors or actresses, their middle-class counterparts gave poor imitations of working-class accents and manners. Despite all these limitations, a breakthrough in realism did take place; working-class men and women were at least beginning to be represented as significant individuals in the social world. However, the mere presence of fictional working-class characters – or female characters – in a film was (and is) no guarantee of the presence of a working-class – or female – point of view.

The realist films of the early 1940s were trying to provide a more faithful reflection of common experiences than British fictional films had hitherto attempted. The impulse was short-lived; in the post-war period, British film-making returned to its traditional path of making entertainment – implicitly understood to be about exceptional situations or people, made to 'take you out of yourself' rather than to reflect on common situations and ordinary people. This slide from realism to entertainment values can be examined more closely in the work of Frank Launder and Sidney Gilliat. In 1937, Launder wrote, 'We are seeing the end of unbelievable puppets shooting smart lines into the air at machine-gun pace. In its place, we are going to meet real people – people we know – people that live next door to us – that travel with us on the bus.'[13] At the time of writing, Launder was a young script-writer; he did not get a chance to put his aspirations into practice until 1943, when he made *Millions Like Us* (G-B, d. Launder and Gilliat, 1943), a wartime story about young women working in a munitions factory. This film was realist in its central concern with working-class characters and in its documentary background – it was shot in actual factories and hostels, and on real gun-sites. It remains something of a landmark by its placing of working-class women at the centre of its narrative. However, although its authentic locations and working-class characters gave it the appearance of 'real life', its values were not new, particularly in relation to women. Dad is manly, while his daughters weep. Without women to take care of him, Dad lets his home become a pig-sty of unwashed dishes. The heroine wants to select the area of war-work where she is most likely to meet eligible young men. She is disappointed to find herself in a factory – but, fortunately, a group of young pilots are given a guided tour round the factory and she manages to fall in love with one of them. Their marriage is brief – a dreamy look comes into her eyes when she thinks of babies, while men in the honeymoon hotel corridor snigger over her impending loss of virginity – but she is given the strength after his death to face her important drudgery by the sound of other brave men leaving in their aeroplanes overhead, knowing that, as a woman, her task is to continue to 'back up' the real heroes.

Waterloo Road (G-B, d. Gilliat, 1944), made the following year, took up more wartime emotional problems: this time, dealing with a working-class soldier's anxiety about his wife's sexual fidelity while he was away. Unlike the heroine of *Brief Encounter*, the wife is seen primarily as the property of her husband; *Waterloo Road* shows her from the husband's point of view, through the suspicions of her husband. Her sexual desires do not concern us – she does not seem to possess any very clear feelings, except resentment at not being able to live with her husband. She toys with the idea of an affair with the local spiv, but rejects his advances only because 'if she did something wrong Jim might not return from the war', not because of what she herself wants. The problem of female uncontrollability is finally resolved by the husband making his wife pregnant – thus ensuring that she is sexually out of action and irrevocably dependent on his return.

Whatever their limitations from a feminist point of view, these two films are centrally concerned with working-class experience. In making them, Launder and Gilliat faced opposition from their producer, Maurice Ostrer. Although both films did well at the box-office, the directors were put under pressure not to continue in the same vein. In 1945, Launder and Gilliat dropped two other projects they had intended to make into films: a pictorial biography of Karl Marx and a film on the Industrial Revolution. They claimed in a later interview that this was because the material was insufficiently anecdotal to make good films. Then, in an interview in 1946, they said they were turning to light entertainment thrillers as a 'timely change' before returning to 'serious' pictures. But they never did return, except to make *Captain Boycott* (G-B, d. Launder, 1947), which turned the struggle of Irish peasantry against a greedy and callous landowner into a *Boy's Own*-type adventure. Although its political themes are initially raised with some seriousness, the film allows its humour to become farce and its politics to become a clichéd account of mob violence.

By 1948, Launder and Gilliat were making *The Blue Lagoon* (G-B, d. Launder, 1948), a fantasy about two children growing into sexual awareness on a desert island (recently remade). In the 1950s, light-hearted sexism became their trademark, in films about beauty queens, bigamists and muscle men, such as *Lady Godiva Rides Again* (G-B, d. Launder, 1951) and *The Bridal Path* (G-B, d. Launder, 1959). They also made the St Trinian's School farces. The struggle to depict 'real people – people that live next door to us' had ended in this kind of representation of 'ordinary' people in silly situations – no longer the common experiences binding people together, but, instead, the extreme or ridiculous experience or character which was good for a laugh. Entertainment had thus reasserted its precedence over realism – but a particular style of entertainment. The influence of audiences on this trajectory is hard to determine. Certainly, *Millions Like Us* and *Waterloo Road* were popular; but when Launder and Gilliat strayed away from topical issues to the costumed politics of *Captain Boycott* they lost their audience. Perhaps their final turn towards the formula of sex plus humour was a means of holding on to the kind of box-office success which *The Blue Lagoon*'s sexual fantasy had brought them.

The alternative might have been to play the realist card with more commitment and vigour. Although the realist films of the early 1940s were topical in relation to the war itself, very few films were made that attempted to deal with other aspects of contemporary reality. In particular, the most painful experiences of women during these years were not represented: the struggle to eat reasonably on rations, the long hours of work, the terror of air raids, prolonged separation from small children, the death of friends, acquaintances and loved ones, the shame of venereal disease and the emotional trauma involved in unwanted pregnancy were not shown on the screens. Between 1940 and 1945, the rate of illegitimate births had almost doubled, rising to an unprecedented one-third of all births.[14] Nearly a third of these children were born to married women. Unmarried mothers, on the other hand, often lost their jobs and were evicted by landladies who could not tolerate the 'shame' of lodging them. Abortion was a criminal offence; nonetheless, about 20 per cent of illegitimate pregnancies were terminated by back-street abortionists.[15]

Only a couple of films dealt with illegitimacy at all, and these skipped lightly over the suffering of thousands of women. In *Piccadilly Incident* (G-B, d. H. Wilcox, 1946), the man is able to marry the mother of his illegitimate child after his wife's convenient death. In *Woman to Woman* (G-B, d. M. Rogers, 1946), an upper-class 'society' wife refuses to grant her husband a divorce, apparently making it inevitable that the other woman would have to 'surrender' her illegitimate child. In both cases, the problem is presented both as a conflict between women and as a problem primarily of legitimacy – not as the problem of deep emotional turmoil which it must always be, particularly for a married woman who already has a family and husband, nor as a problem which could ruin the life of a single woman. A look at these films of the 1940s often suggests that it is their omissions which are most ideologically significant.

Sexual freedom may have been practised because of the conditions of the war, but it was neither openly approved nor consciously posed as an alternative to monogamous marriage. Neither the family nor the institution of marriage were ever questioned. However, women's new experiences had perhaps changed their attitudes *within* marriage. Nella Last wrote in her diary for Mass Observation, 'pants are more a sign of the times than I realized. . . . Why this "lords of creation" attitude on men's part? I'm beginning to see I'm a really clever woman in my own line. . . . I feel that, in the world of tomorrow, marriage will be – will have to be – more of a partnership, less of this "I have spoken" attitude.'[16]

Perfect Strangers (G-B, d. A Korda, 1945) was one of the few British films to deal explicitly with these changes in women's consciousness wrought by the war. Deborah Kerr plays a drab, listless housewife called Kathy, who develops into a confident and attractive member of the WRNS. The problems this might generate in her relations with her husband are neatly sidestepped by the film, which reveals that her husband has also been metamorphosed from a timid clerk into a manly, authoritarian naval officer – restoring their compatibility, so it seems, at a stroke. When Kathy joins the WRNS, she tells a fellow Wren that 'My husband doesn't like me to smoke. . . . My husband doesn't like me to use lipstick,' with traditional deference to the absent patriarch. By the end of the film, her husband is joking about her new personality: 'Kathy mend your socks? *This* Kathy?' Although the film does go some way towards investigating these changes, its humour and its playful comparison of the development of husband and wife are evasions of the real incompatibilities, conflicts and tensions created between men and women because of women's new consciousness.

If women had achieved a new self-confidence, it must have been attributable largely to their experience of 'men's work' and to the sense that their activities were at last of some social significance. Even middle-class women, who had previously been expected only to manage households and servants, were unable to avoid involvement in the 'war effort'. By 1943, every woman under forty was expected to work, unless she had an exceptionally large family or billeted war workers in her home. Younger unmarried women between twenty and thirty years of age were treated as 'mobile' and could be sent to work in any part of the country. However, women's new work experiences were always contained within the rhetoric of war. They were characterized as 'an exceptional and valiant effort', not as a permanent change in women's status.[17] Men 'tolerated' women in their jobs only because of the war and were reluctant to allow them to join their unions; women's pay never represented an independent income – in government training centres, for example, women received just over half the pay of men.

During the war, film-makers reproduced these attitudes both in films like *Millions Like Us* – which skilfully managed to combine an appreciation of women's contribution to the war effort with a sense that, nonetheless, women's true role in life was to be a wife and mother – and through their continued reliance on images of women as glamourous, feminine dancers, pianists, secretaries and servants. This was less true of American films, where women could be seen in more diverse roles; in a number of films made between 1944 and 1946, for example, women took the parts of a spy, a hospital administrator, a taxi driver, a photographer, a congresswoman and a pilot. British films made little attempt to depict women's new experiences and working lives, other than as the background to their involvements with men. *My Ain Folk* (G-B, d. Burger, 1944), for example, despite its unusual factory setting, shows Moira Lister winning the admiration of her fellow-workers for her singing. She wins their admiration because she carries on, even when her fiancé is reported missing. Her moral qualities are then rewarded by the return of her fiancé at just the moment when she is singing at a workers' concert. Her actions are thus depicted primarily in the light of the impression they will make on her boy-friend.

Narratives not only depicted women primarily in terms of their sexual relations with men; after about 1945, they seemed increasingly to delight in reducing 'strong' women to size. In this post-war period, there was a slight trend comparable to the American *film noir*, of portraying women as manipulative and selfish – in films such as *The Rocking Horse Winner* (G-B, d. A. Pelissier, 1949), *So Well Remembered* (G-B, d. E. Dmytryk, 1947) or *This was a Woman* (G-B, d. T. Whelan, 1947). However, unlike the American films, the British counterparts did not depict such situations as arising from the exercise of female power through sexuality. The strong female characters in

British films were upper-class women, such as Wendy Hiller, in *I Know Where I'm Going* (G-B, d. M. Powell and E. Pressburger, 1945), or Googie Withers in *The Loves of Joanna Godden* (G-B, d. C. Frend, 1947). These narratives prove that even self-sufficient women cannot manage without men. However, many American *films noirs* perform the same ideological work of returning women to normal heterosexual coupledom – yet, as films, they are infinitely more complex, and their images of women are often fascinating and compelling (for example, Joan Crawford in *Mildred Pierce* or Rita Hayworth in *Gilda*). British films did not combine the (women's) melodrama with (men's) thriller in the same way.

British thrillers rarely placed women at the centre of the narrative. Most often, they appeared as the girl-friends of criminals. If they were bad, it was because they were in bad company – not because of any evil inherent in womanhood. *Good Time Girl* (G-B, d. D. Macdonald, 1948) shows Jean Kent as a working-class girl who runs away from home and from the beatings of her father. Although she defiantly asserts, 'I'm *not* a victim', she is plainly just that. Bad girls are immature in British thrillers – not powerful, mature women, as they so often are in American thrillers. The cynical girlfriend of *They Made me a Fugitive* (G-B, d. A. Cavalcanti, 1947) characteristically bursts into tears when she is told, 'You're not really tough – you just try to be because you think it's the smart thing to do.'

Work on the American *film noir*[18] has suggested that the films of this period expressed a *male* loss of identity and security, faced with the unstable nature of female roles in the immediate post-war period; these films needed to set up the strong woman in order to knock her back into her traditional, subordinate place. However, there were few memorable images of strong women in British films; any such impulse, if it existed, was expressed through British films in a more diffused way. The widespread assumption that such films reflected 'the post-war impulse to punish the independent female image as a reflex of the economy's need to push women back into the home'[19] would have to be slightly qualified in any case; in Britain, a campaign was launched in 1947 to *increase* women's employment to meet the needs of increased production. The government had even considered introducing conscription for women. In the event, their appeal was phrased in guarded terms, suggesting that the government 'was not asking women to do jobs usually done by men, as had been the case during the war. Second, the labour shortage was only temporary, and women were being asked to take a job only for whatever length of time they could spare, whether full-time or part-time.'[20] Clearly, women were not so much being pushed *out* of the economy as being pushed *back* to their former subordinate role in it as a pool of cheap, unskilled labour.

Films did not, of course, directly advocate this trend. But within their depiction of heterosexual relationships, there was a way of letting women know what their priorities should be. Any gains in female self-confidence produced by wartime experience could not be consolidated in the face of the eternal choice between love and career. But this was love on men's terms: it inevitably involved feeding, clothing and caring for him and his children. Given these expectations on the part of men, the ability of women to enjoy paid employment was greatly diminished. A 1947 survey[21] shows the clear trend of young working-class women to give up work on marriage. Clearly, for most women, work was tiring, badly paid, manual work; creating a domestic life, caring for men who had been absent for so long, must have seemed an attractive alternative, if it was financially possible.

Some films of the post-war period expressed these conflicts, as they existed for middle-class career women, in such a way as to affirm the necessity for women of finding happiness only through a man's love. *Root of All Evil* (G-B, d. B. Williams 1947) shows Phyllis Calvert as a businesswoman whose relationships with men are unsuccessful as long as she is successfully making money. But once her oil refineries are destroyed, she is freed to make the right choice, which is to find happiness with her childhood sweetheart. Such films provided a subtle form of propaganda for women's true role in life. However, there were films which expressed the conflict as a more profoundly ambivalent one. *The Red Shoes* (G-B, d. Powell and Pressburger, 1948) shows Moira Shearer as a young dancer struggling to fulfil her talent in a male-controlled world. When the man she loves forces her to choose between her career and her role as a supportive wife, she simply cannot choose; in refusing that choice, she has nowhere left to go – so she dies.

The year 1947 has been described as a year of 'mental and physical freeze-up'.[22] A bitter winter of power cuts, increases in rationing and moral exhortations to increase production provoked a demand for pleasure. The New Look came over from Paris, emphasizing women's hips and breasts with padding. *Picture Post* began a series on glamourous actresses. The Conservatives overtook the Labour Party in opinion polls,[23] and the magazines which had been critical of conspicuous wealth and exotic life-styles throughout the 1930s and during the war began to 'insert the reader by proxy into that lifestyle of wealth and glamour'.[24] Women became symbols of sexual pleasure, one of the only pleasures available in these harsh post-war years. Women's glamour signified a missing wealth and abundance. Concurrently with this trend, increasing numbers of films in 1948 and 1949 placed male characters in the leading role, marking a turning-away from 'women's pictures' – which, in however distorted a fashion, had attempted to project the narrative from a female point of view. *The Fallen Idol* (G-B, d. Reed, 1948), *The Guinea Pig* (G-B, d. R. Boulting, 1948), *Scott of the Antarctic* (G-B, d. Frend, 1948), *Brighton Rock* (G-B, d. J. Boulting, 1948), *The Third Man* (G-B, d. Reed, 1949), *The Winslow Boy* (G-B, d. A. Asquith, 1948) and *The Small Back Room* (G-B, d. Powell and Pressburger, 1949) initiated a trend which gathered momentum in the 1950s. Masculine adventure came to dominate the box-office with successes such as *The Cruel Sea* (G-B, d. Frend, 1953), *West of Zanzibar* (G-B, d. L. Norman, 1954), *The Dam Busters* (G-B, d. M. Anderson, 1955), *Colditz Story* (G-B, d. G. Hamilton, 1955), *Battle of the River Plate* (G-B, d. Powell and Pressburger, 1956) and *The Bridge over the River Kwai* (G-B, d. David Lean, 1957).

From 1949, the attendance of women at the cinema began to decline more rapidly than that of men, within an overall pattern of decline. While in 1948, women were still attending on average 0.60 times a week, compared to men's 0.59, by 1949 women's attendance had dropped to 0.55, while men's attendance had only dropped to 0.58. By 1954, women were attending 0.40 times, while men were attending 0.44 times and also constituted a higher percentage of regular attenders than women. Thus, men were replacing women as the most frequent and regular cinema-goers.[25]

This change may be accounted for in several ways. The birth-rate had risen to a peak between July 1946 and June 1947, presumably tying hundreds of thousands of women to the home while their babies were small; approximately 300,000 more babies were born in this year than in each of the previous four years.[26] In 1947, there was a sharp decline of 3½ millions in cinema attendances, which may have been due to the embargo on American films, imposed in that year, which lasted until May 1948 and was prompted by the government's imposition of a 75 per cent tax on them. As John Spraos has pointed out, in a different context, 'mass picture-going was built up on a continuous flow of new films';[27] when this flow was stemmed, and only British pictures and re-runs of American ones were available, perhaps the habit of seeing the latest film was lost. It is also likely that there was some change in the composition of cinema audiences. The youthful audience on which the cinema had always depended had shrunk. For there were fewer young adults in the population; by 1951, there were 18.5 per cent fewer women between the ages of fifteen and twenty-four, and 18.8 per cent fewer young men, than there had been in 1931.[28]

It is hard to disentangle cause and effect here: did women go less often to the cinema because of their new duties to their husbands and children; because there were other entertainments to enjoy, now that the war was over; or because there were fewer films that appealed to them? The decline in the number of new 'women's pictures' did not start until about 1949; in startling synchronization with the decline in the female audience. By the early 1950s, fewer melodramas and serious dramas with central female characters were being made. Emotions were increasingly treated with a lightness bordering on comedy. The year 1949 also saw the return of American films to popularity, after several years in which British films had topped the polls. The successes of 1949 were *Johnny Belinda* (United States, d. J. Nequlesco, 1948), *The Paleface* (United States, d. N. McLeod, 1948), which celebrated Jane Russell's breasts, and *Red River* (United States, d. H. Hawks, 1948). In 1950, musicals such as *Annie Get Your Gun* (United States, d. G. Sidney, 1950) were top-box office successes, together with other American comedies and westerns. These films supposedly appealed to 'all the family'. Although there is some evidence of adolescent group attendance at the cinema during the war,[29] I am uncertain as to whether the concept of family entertainment, or Rank's hostility to 'X'-rated films, on the grounds that they broke up 'family viewing', had any basis in changing patterns of viewing practices.

British film-makers may have been induced by the decrease in young spectators to lessen the quantity of films which relied on strong identification with a central character. Nevertheless, in 1955, Roger Manvell noted that, although the average age of audiences had risen, 'younger people in the audience still predominate'.[30] Film-makers may also have simply returned to the practices of pre-war film-making, when British fiction films were 'equally uninterested in world politics or social problems. Their whole intent was for our delight. Most of them were gay and they slipped easily into song and dance . . .';[31] and may have seen wartime film-making as a temporary aberration, caused by the demands of propaganda and the needs of the wartime audience. Rank's post-war strategy must also have been decisive. Increasingly, he had monopolized studios and budgets for a small number of super-productions, hoping to compete with Hollywood. But British film-makers could not beat Hollywood at its own game. Despite strenuous efforts by Rank, British films failed to capture the American market (see Chapter 10). The advice of critics like Paul Rotha, still arguing in 1949 that 'Britain has neither the resources nor the flair for the mass-manufacture of popular entertainment movies à la Hollywood. Thank God she hasn't. But she has got the intellectual and emotional resources, and she is undergoing the experiences, which could make her a leader of the film of reality', had long since been ignored.

In the early 1950s, films continued their tradition of categorizing women in terms of their functions for men. These stereotypes were by no means new, but this kind of reductive characterization became more common, even in serious films, giving them a superficiality and a comic touch that had been present only in the costume dramas of the 1940s. *Turn the Key Softly* (G-B, d. J. Lee, 1953) described the release of three women prisoners into the outside world. Yvonne Mitchell played a well bred lady who had been led astray by a seductive bad man; her basic decency and marriageability are restored when she rejects the man and settles down to a job. Joan Collins was the reckless tart, who could not resist the temptation of buying jewellery instead of putting down a deposit on a flat; she could only retrieve the situation by granting men her 'favours'. Kathleen Harrison played a poor old lady with a heart of gold, whose attachment to her dog led to her death.

Steve Neale has argued that stereotyping should be seen as part of a process of 'differentiation', not merely of repetition; each instance of 'the dumb blonde', for example, is 'always new, always different'. He suggests that these 'restricted and repetitive modes of character' are 'a means by which specific forms of difference can be marked and re-marked in accordance with the racial and sexual distinctions and discriminations constructed by the discourses that traverse and articulate the texts being analysed'.[32] Certainly there are distinctions and discriminations to be drawn from a comparison of the immoral woman of the forties and the immoral woman of the fifties, and they reveal subtle shifts of attitude. There are differences between the 'good wife and mother' stereotype played by the same actress, Phyllis Calvert, in *They were Sisters* in 1945 and in *Mandy* (G-B, d. A. Mackendrick, 1952) seven years later. Although, in both films, motherhood is presented as natural and unproblematic for the motherly woman – not necessarily for all women – *Mandy* is a much richer and more complex film, because it suggests that beneath the placid surface of even a good marriage there are conflicts and tensions. When the husband is challenged to decide whether or not he believes that his wife has been unfaithful, he replies, 'No – Kit's not like that.' In fact, the film suggests that Kit *was* very nearly 'like that': her relationship with the headmaster of her child's school was on the brink of development when her husband's intervention forced her to return home. In many ways the film implies criticism of the husband's stifling and rigid attitudes.

Yet in noting the differences, and in welcoming them when they are due to a greater depth of characterization, and not merely to a change of styles, one should not ignore the fact that these particular stereotypes are reproducing the basic structural positioning of women. In both 1945 and in 1952, Phyllis Calvert represents an idealized view of motherhood, of endless spontaneous devotion and warmth. If the effect of films – as one form of social reproduction among many – is to 'provide models for identification, confer status on people and behaviour, spell out norms, define new situations, provide stereotypes, set frameworks of anticipation, and indicate levels of acceptability, tolerance and approval',[33] the presentation of women in such a restricted range of modes of being, as objects either of desire, contempt or idealization, must become particularly crucial when ways of living and being female are in transition. Precisely because 'private' life is otherwise hidden from public scrutiny, films offer evidence which may play an important role in the choices made by individuals – particularly, perhaps, for younger spectators, whose definitions are less rigid and whose experience is less extensive than adults'. Spectators aged fourteen to seventeen were, in fact, the most frequent cinema-goers throughout the 1940s.

Similarly, the resolution of narratives often performs the task of restoring the status quo and reintegrating women into the patriarchal order. However sensitively emotional conflicts are described, if they are always resolved in favour of the existing order of things, that order begins to seem immutable. If Kit had left her husband for the school-teacher, if Laura had run away with Alec, if Kathy had gone to live with her WRNS friend instead of falling into the arms of her bullying husband – a climate of opinion might begin to be created in which real women would be freer to make such choices. This, however, would have required film-makers to take up a conscious position. Instead, they defended and adapted the old stereotypes and images of women's lives. While the early 1950s saw the largest increase in working women since 1881, due to the expansion of the economy into 'service' areas, such as health, education and administration, film-makers joined advertisers in assuring women that their *real* identity still lay in 'home-making'. *Something Money Can't Buy* (G-B, d. P. Jackson, 1952) shows a husband and wife each starting their own business and being successful. Rivalry and jealousy develop, until eventually the woman acknowledges her husband as the breadwinner and 'returns to being a wife again'.[34] *Dance Hall* (G-B, d. C. Crichton, 1950) assumes that, once she is married, a working-class girl will give up work. The heroine is also required by her husband to give up dancing, which makes her cry rebelliously, 'You just want me to stay at home and be bored bored bored.' Reconciliation is achieved when the husband overcomes his possessiveness and allows his wife her little interest.

Most producers, directors and script-writers were middle-class men. While the 'ideological effect' of the cinema cannot, as John Hill argues, 'be seen necessarily to correspond to a maker's personality or intentions, nor likewise his or her social and political beliefs', British films were on the whole weak in the 'specific effectivities' of signifying practices.[35] With some exceptions, the *mise en scène* of the majority of British films of the forties was literal and lacked resonance. British films were only beginning to emerge from their position as the poor relation of the theatre and of music-hall, and to make a fuller use of cinematic language. Their makers were still reliant to a large extent on recycled West End plays, novelettes, and films built round personalities, such as Tommy Trinder or Gracie Fields, who had made a name in another medium. Films were not taken seriously as a form of individual or collaborative expression. Although the pressures of war allowed more young men access to film-making, and provoked a more serious attitude to films because of their propaganda value, once these pressures were removed it was felt that films could revert to their true function of light entertainment.

Few women had access to film-making in the 1940s. Muriel Box and Jill Craigie were the only directors; Betty Box the only producer. Muriel Box faced many obstacles in her attempts to become a director in the 1940s, from the documentary producer Arthur Elton (who thought a documentary on 'Road Safety for Children' was not suitable for a woman to direct) to Michael Balcon (who 'wasn't sure a woman had the qualities necessary to control a large feature unit').[36] She and her husband, Sydney Box, had to start an independent company before she could try her hand at directing.

There was no feminist movement to capitalize, in an organized fashion, on the changes wrought by the war. Although it seems that there was a shift in consciousness, caused by the experiences of the war, this shift was not consolidated through political action, legislation or cultural representations. This was not just an oversight on the part of film-makers. Balcon, for example, was quite capable of demanding that films perform a political and cultural function in the post-war period, to restore Britain's international prestige,[37] but only Catherine de la Roche demanded that films should contribute to the new 'ethics' of sexual relations.

In the event, neither happened. The industrial nature of film-making for a mass audience had given rise to formulae and stereotypes which film-makers updated and adapted in order to perpetuate their success. In this way, film-makers played their part in reinforcing and reproducing existing modes of life, without necessarily being aware of it. However, when social upheavals produce more than minor changes in existing modes of life, 'updating' the formulae proves more problematic. The changes produced by the war were still 'conflicting with the more longstanding traditions of the past'[38] – yet film-makers did not openly dramatize these conflicts. Instead, films obliquely reinforced traditional values by dealing with problems in marriage as if they were ones of readjustment to an obvious norm. *I'll Turn to You* (G-B, d. Faithfull, 1946) suggests that marital conflict is due to the difficulty of adjusting to the humdrum nature of married life after the excitement of the war, during which the husband was a pilot and the wife had a rich boy-friend. Interestingly, *The Years Between* (G-B, d. C. Bennett, 1946), written by Muriel Box, does take a different line. Here, the wife has become an MP and has fallen in love with another man, believing her husband to be dead; when he returns, the marriage can only be saved (and, even then, somewhat unconvincingly) by his acceptance of the changes in his wife. Most films refused to endorse new modes of behaviour: more typical than *The Years Between* was *A*

Girl in a Million (G-B, d. F. Searle, 1946), in which a man is freed by divorce from a 'relentlessly nagging wife'[39] and chooses as his new partner a young girl whose lack of brains is supplemented by her beauty and domesticity. So much for the new partnership of equals.

By 1949, life was very much back to 'normal', even though some of the rigidity of both the class and sexual hierarchy had melted. As one 1949 survey of adolescent cinema-going concluded, 'Films dealing with human relationships are more popular among girls than among boys who seem to prefer films of strenuous adventure, war and horror.'[40] The sentimental education which films provided for many young people continued to reproduce sex and gender roles which had barely changed throughout the decade.

Films had helped to resolve an ideological crisis in the post-war period. The war had opened up new possibilities for women as it did for the working class: 'What some regarded as pragmatic measures for the emergency, others saw as the embryo of a superior social system.'[41] The ideological task had been to ensure that new developments were contained in this rhetoric of transience, the sense of 'only for the duration'. Film-makers fell in with this way of thinking; they acted positively to create morale and to unite classes, but added no encouragement to women to create a permanent new way of life. The subsequent development of British life produced few radical changes. The welfare state was probably the most far-reaching, yet it left intact, or even reinforced, women's traditional roles. The sense of women as 'comrades', felt by some in the Labour and Communist parties, was lost.

Those involved in making films contributed to this containment partly because of their own class and gender allegiance and experience, but also because of unstated pressure from those who 'regulate the production and distribution of their age'.[42] This was not power crudely exercised, but a general awareness, permeating the industry, of what was or was not acceptable to the owners of the film companies and their representatives. Vetos could be and were exercised at the stages of both production and distribution.[43] While such control was ultimately possible, the owners rarely chose to intervene actively in the production of films; they left the 'complex orchestration of consent'[44] in the capable hands of the film-makers themselves.

Ealing: in the Comedy Frame

Ian Green

The conflation of Ealing and comedy is important for a study of British cinema and popular culture. It is one made by most critics and most audiences. The phrase, 'Ealing comedy', is so familiar in British popular culture that, ironically, films *not* made at Ealing can be dubbed 'Ealing comedies' because of some intuitive feeling that the ideas and/or style contained within them connote Ealing. An example is *Geneviève* (s. William Rose, d. Henry Cornelius, 1953). Similarly, a comic idea or notion brought up in conversation, or some absurd news item, might be remarked upon as 'sounding like an Ealing comedy'.

Comedies made at Ealing Studios shifted from their initial position, before and during the war, as musical comedy or 'music-hall comedy' (star vehicles for George Formby, Gracie Fields and Will Hay) to their transformation after the war; the change from *Champagne Charlie* (s. Austin Melford, Angus Macphail, John Dighton, d. Alberto Cavalcanti, 1944), to *Hue and Cry* (s. T. E. B. Clarke, d. Charles Crichton, 1947) marks this transformation. The comedies remained a constant product that ran through Ealing's work. The other genres in Ealing's output seemed to be exploited less consistently and with less assurance. The war and its effects marked the studio's output considerably, but only in the field of historical subject-matter: they were not used consistently as material for the construction of a reasonably stable sub-genre. The war was not moulded into a conventional narrative context in ways that the Hollywood studios were elaborating at the same time after the war. Other Ealing policies on the subject-matter suitable for films or concerning the type of product desired, for instance the films about social professions and the 'prestige' productions, have at best a rather hazy relationship to notions of genre, or at least they fail to follow a consistent and developing thread of formal and thematic concerns.

On the other hand, it was felt by those within Ealing, and by those who made and still make up its audience, that the comedies have a consistency, a logic or form which are somehow recognizable, that they embody a series of conventions that set up or meet expectations, that they have a function or functions. In other words, they made up a paradigm within which producers and audience could, or were made to, 'recognize' their respective places. If we 'feel' that there is such a genre, or sub-genre as the 'Ealing comedy', this is above all because some of the comedies were felt to work; they were successful and they have lasted. It is the comedies that are remembered: *Passport to Pimlico* (s. Clarke, d. Cornelius, 1949), *Whisky Galore* (s. Compton Mackenzie, Macphail, d. Alexander Mackendrick, 1949), *Kind Hearts and Coronets* (s. Robert Hamer, Dighton, d. Hamer, 1949), *The Lavender Hill Mob* (s. Clarke, d. Crichton, 1951), *The Man in The White Suit* (s. Roger Macdougall, Mackendrick, Dighton, d. Mackendrick, 1951) and *The Ladykillers* (s. Rose, d. Mackendrick, 1955). Even the less successful or tired ones that preceded or (mostly) followed these, when televised, produce groans of *recognition* and a grudging, nostalgic and even chauvinistic response in British viewers: *The Titfield Thunderbolt* (s. Clarke, d. Crichton, 1953), *The Maggie* (s. Rose, d. Mackendrick, 1954), *Barnacle Bill* (s. Clarke, d. Charles Frend, 1957).

The axis of Ealing and comedy is productive in thinking about British popular culture and, using Ealing as an example, one might ask of comedy, what are its functions, what themes can it explore, what are its parameters, and what problems and resistances does it negotiate? Balcon writes,

> We had great affection for British institutions: the comedies were done with affection, and I don't think we would have thought of tearing down institutions unless we had a blueprint for what we wanted to put in their place. . . . The comedies were a mild protest, but not protests at anything more sinister than the regimentation of the times.[1]

Mackendrick, in an interview published in *Positif*, remarks, 'Personally, I am very attracted by comedy. . . . It lets you do things that are too dangerous, or that a certain audience can't accept.'[2] When T. E. B. Clarke, in his autobiography, describes being arrested by the police, the following exchange takes place:

'Says he wrote *The Blue Lamp*,' the man on the beat concluded. 'Then aren't you the same one that wrote *The Lavender Hill Mob* – the film that takes the piss out of the police?' The frying pan had given way to the fire. I had to admit it. 'Just a bit of good-humoured fun,' I equivocated. 'Now don't you play it down! – it was great. It's a long time since I enjoyed a picture like that last one of yours. Just what was needed – somebody to take the piss out of the job!' I knew then that I really had reason to feel proud, for I had not let my old force down.[3]

These remarks pinpoint several arguments about comedy and what its function might be, both as filmic and a non-filmic form. The *framing*, or *enveloping*, to use Freud's term, of an idea or substance within a comic or joking form might serve several functions.

As Mackendrick's words imply, comedy might be used as a framework or as a disguise that allows the overcoming of inhibitions, so that, within the context of comedy, the rupturing of the moral or political conventions of a society becomes possible. Others have argued that because such a supposed rupturing can only be achieved within the context of comedy, the function of comedy is therefore to negate any possibility of significant realignment or effect upon a society's conventions and practices. This is implied in Clarke's anecdote – the policeman accepts and even condones Clarke's 'piss-taking'. The undercutting of the police in *The Lavender Hill Mob* stands in an acceptable opposition to the eulogizing in *The Blue Lamp*. But if *The Blue Lamp* (s. Clarke, d. Basil Dearden, 1950) or another drama about the police (the television films *Law and Order*, perhaps) had made criticisms, perhaps the reaction would have been different. Thus Balcon defines the comedies as 'real people in impossible situations'. The comic framework that negotiates the differences between real and unreal, possible and impossible, seems all-important here. Similarly, the 'Festival of Light' argument about *Law and Order* was not so much that it might be slanderous fiction as that it masqueraded as fact in its coded signification of reality that is, the framework was not acceptable. Television series, like *The Professionals* and *The Sweeney*, have acceptable *fiction* frameworks, even connoting impossibility, but a further taboo is raised here: violence. Discussions about current television treatment of the police revolve around the possible framings for such treatments. The spectrum of possibilities allows different play with various degrees and types of fantasy and various degrees of signifying the real world. If the makers of *The Sweeney* and *The Professionals* insist on 'real situations' (location photography) they are careful also to exoticize and romanticize the narratives and their protagonists ('unreal' people, fictional police institutions – CI5 –

dynamic editing, and so on), and here the gross violence (taboo in one respect) acts as a safeguard of the narratives' fiction through its particular play with fantasy. The TV tradition of drama-documentary treatment of the police, as in *Z-Cars* and *Softly Softly* – a tradition that one can trace back, via *Dixon of Dock Green*, to Ealing's *The Blue Lamp* – admits the 'documentary' framing due to its supportive and 'affectionate' treatment. For some viewers, *Law and Order* (deliberately) transgressed the 'possible' combinations by signifying documentary within a fiction framing and evoking criticism of the relationship between law and society.

This becomes relevant to the issues raised by Ealing comedy when one notes how important the realist base is to some Ealing comedies – *Hue and Cry, Passport to Pimlico, Whisky Galore, The Man in the White Suit* – from which the comic fantasy takes off into impossible situations; in these cases comedy allows criticism of contemporary institutions as a conscious strategy on the part of the film-makers themselves, and this criticism can be seen to slide between the affectionate and the subversive.

The problem, or the inbuilt contradiction of the comic framework then, is that it can be seen simultaneously (1) to overcome censorship, both in the straight social meaning of the term and in the Freudian sense of the censorship of conscious and pre-conscious processes, and thus can treat sensitive issues of varying natures; and (2), through its mechanism, to avoid, repress or displace the treatment of sensitive issues by, so to speak, drowning them in laughter. The first process negotiates, and the second avoids, possible unpleasure through a comic form. Both, of course, aim to give pleasure: the first through lifting inhibitions; the second through displacing inhibitions into laughter, or some other issue.

For instance, as Freud points out,[4] obscene jokes circumvent repression; they allow pleasure and cause laughter over something not to be admitted as enjoyable or acceptable. However, it has been argued that jokes about race, homosexuality or gender difference, for instance, raise 'problems' in society that are then repressed or 'resolved' through laughter; pleasure displaces the need to think or rethink one's attitude to these issues in society. Such jokes are thought to reinforce the status quo and to hinder serious debate. They are thought of as reactionary by those who seek to question and change accepted or dominant views on race, homosexuality and gender difference. Similarly, when an issue is raised in conversation which

298 / British Cinema History

might be personally threatening if it were to be considered seriously, the evasive strategy probably adopted is one of 'laughing it off' by twisting the issue into a comic mode – in other words, by reframing it.

This double function of the comic framework – of overcoming censorship and then, or alternatively, reimposing it – can be seen at work in the Ealing films, both in terms of individual comic pieces of business, jokes or actions, and of the narrative framework or development as a whole. *Passport to Pimlico* uses several devices that frame the comic fantasy of the main substance of the plot in order that what goes on can be read as possible only within that context of comic fantasy. Take the frame away and you have the possibility – or in this case the impossibility – of direct criticism, unacceptable anarchy, rebellion, real conflict. These framing devices are used. The first is the extraordinary and unusual heatwave, the summer madness in which anything is possible and which also connotes a foreign environment – at first Latin America and then France. The second is the bomb explosion, producing a shock, a second separation from ordinary reality; when Pemberton ascends from the pit he remarks, 'I thought I was seeing things again.' The third device is the bomb crater itself – a dark, mysterious pit in which the treasure and the charter of independence are found. It is from within this frame, and perhaps only this frame, that genuinely funny jokes arise. There is little that is 'independently' funny about the dialogue and antics of *Passport to Pimlico*. None of the jokes could stand alone for example, Professor Hatton Jones's remark, 'I am now able to change the course of history,' PC Spiller's, 'Blimey, I'm a foreigner,' or the ultimate irony, 'It's just because we *are* English that we are sticking up for our rights to be Burgundians.' All the antics to do with the siege: the airlifting, the abandonment of rationing ('This is Burgundy'), which is then reinstated from within – all the humour of these ironies and events depends on the framing of the story as a comic fantasy and on the logic that is then permitted to develop within it. Finally, the framing is taken away by the negation of the context of the fantasy: the heatwave ends in rain and a drop in the temperature; the thunder negates the explosion; the bomb-site is transformed into a playground and swimming pool. The framing device is analogous to a game – an imitation of reality or a training practice for it. When a monkey practices fight behaviour with a fellow monkey it frames its actions with a gesture, a grimace, which, as a message, means 'Everything I do from now on is play, pretence. When I bite you it is not a *real* bite.'

In other words, the framed event is rendered harmless and a genuinely aggressive response is inappropriate: 'It's only a game.' On the other hand, play *is* some kind of activity. It is a learning process.

Similarly, *Hue and Cry*'s comic fantasy is framed by devices – the choir of respectable and regulated boys. A comic magazine is thrown out of the window and falls to the less respectable boys in the street below. The story in the comic marks the switch in to fantasy. Significantly, Joe, who reads the comic avidly, does not go off and subjectively fantasize a story inspired by it. On the contrary, now that the framing has occurred, the story itself is 'defictionalized' and becomes concrete, acceptable fact within the framework of the comic fantasy. It is Joe's job in the narrative to convince everybody else that this situation is not a product of his mind but an externally verifiable sequence of events, subject even to predictability. In this context a comment by Charles Barr is worth bearing in mind: 'Ealing's form of cinema, like its whole mentality, is a profoundly empirical and naturalistic one, at home with people, not ideas, with the solidly realistic, not the abstract or stylised.'[5] In *Hue and Cry*, within the frame of the fantasy as set up in the film, the fantasy of the comic magazine can then become fact. Significantly, the children discover this new level of reality, which the adults attempt to disguise or conceal from them, by accusing Joe of fantasizing. Meanwhile, the author, the creator of the stories, remains unaware of the real world he has helped to form and does live in a world of unreality. The pantomime villains, the adults, are apprehended by the boys, who however, are returned to the normality of the choir.

The framing devices used in *The Lavender Hill Mob* have similarities with those used in both *Hue and Cry* and *Passport to Pimlico*: the exotic feel of the opening and closing scenes of the film, the flashback device; the thriller that Holland reads from in the rooming house, the childlike characteristics and glee of the main protagonists. And children, again, are instrumental in exposing the criminals, if unknowingly. No doubt these similarities are accounted for in the main by the facts that T. E. B. Clarke wrote the scripts for all three films and that his type of comic fantasy leaves its mark on Ealing's output. But overall similarities in narrative devices and structure to other Ealing films, in which Clarke took no part, should not be ignored. Moreover, Clarke's authorship does not necessarily account for the films' significances, nor for the ways in which the narratives operate.

Most of the comic fantasies in the Ealing comedies are well marked out and so are most of the narratives. Flashback and voice-over techniques predominate in Ealing's output. To the best of my knowledge, the flashback is not used to question in any way the point of view or subject-matter presented, but, on the contrary – like the voice-overs – to anchor the narrative firmly in fact and explanation. Flashbacks are used to explain a sequence of events that have already happened and that are therefore closed. A framing structure that circles back to the same event or context has a similar function of enclosing its material. Perhaps *Kind Hearts and Coronets* and *The Man in the White Suit* are the only exceptions in the way flashback is used. At the conclusion of the former the hero, Mazzini, who is narrating the story, is left to make a crucial choice between his two lovers, Sibella and Edith. In addition, his 'real' murders have gone un-punished; but the narrative leaves us in doubt about whether or not he will be caught, through the agency of his own memoirs. Perhaps these two ambiguities are related. In the latter film the voice-over narrative is related not by the hero, Stratton, but by Birnley, a fatherly but (*vis à vis* the hero) ambiguous figure. Birnley concludes his narrative confident that the status quo which Stratton disrupted has been firmly restored. However, as Stratton, like Mazzini, is released into the world, we are offered the possibility that Stratton's disrupting force has not in fact been neutralized. In addition, *Kind Hearts and Coronets* can be separated from the other comedies mentioned in that it is set in the past and thus automatically 'distances' itself. It can be compared to the drama, also directed by Hamer, *Pink String and Sealing Wax* (s. Diana Morgan, 1945). This, likewise, is set in the past and involves family disruptions, murder, and issues of class and sexuality. The film opens and closes with a journalist dictating a story, the opening story being of a woman who is about to be hanged (as in the later film Mazzini, who is also about to be hanged, writes his own story). This framing device is 'imposed' by the news editor; its function seems quite 'arbitrary' in that it signifies no more than the opening and closing of a film narrative – stating that what is to follow, and what has been related is, precisely, a story.

In these examples I have stressed the vaguely generic term 'fantasy' as much as I have the term 'comedy', in order to emphasize that Ealing comedies seem to proceed along a realist path, well marked by camera style, sets and settings, narrative devices (flashback and voice-over) that anchor and naturalize the point of view conveyed and the events related. A disruption occurs at some point in the marking of the framing device, and the logic of the comic fantasy is then followed through from the initial fantastic premise/disruption. But the realist base is always there beneath, until finally the frame of fantasy is taken away and 'full reality' is restored. Of course, all films can be seen as fantasies, according to one interpretation, but in the sense which I am implying here fantasy must be distinguished from the signified reality that is also part of the same film. Not all comedies make such a distinction.

Ealing's concern, seems to dictate that the problems it explores through comedy should be the problems of living in the real world; the network of inhibitions and censorship that it is necessary, or seems necessary to set up and *accept* for people to live contentedly. Balcon, in *Realism or Tinsel*, quotes approvingly from an issue of *The Documentary Newsletter*: 'The way in which we make the real world seem exciting does not matter. . . . But whatever method is used it must be to the point that men and women welcome the idea of living in a real world. It is only by knowing it truly and honestly that they can work and play in it happily.'[6] 'You never know when you're well off till you aren't,' says Mrs Pemberton in *Passport to Pimlico* and this is the point, the function, of Ealing's comic model. To show that the real world is worth living in you have to show that an unreal world is not, and you have therefore to resolve the problem of the plot in the comic narrative by restoring that real world. The 'decadent' Ealing comedies, such as *The Titfield Thunderbolt* and *Barnacle Bill*, cope with change in the real world by restoring an old world of rural tradition and total escapism – by making a desperate attempt to restore the balance, so to speak.

In a sense the films about the Second World War offer a model that struggles with the same problem, ('You never know when you're well off till you aren't'), though some of the protagonists prefer the unreal real world of war to the real world of peace, like Ericson in *The Cruel Sea* (s. Eric Ambler, d. Charles Frend, 1953), whereas, in the same film, Lockhart finds a purpose in the real world, and something worth planning for, when he discovers love in it. In *Passport to Pimlico* the models of war are temptingly offered again (siege, airlifting – 'He really misses that old white hat of his,' says Mrs Pemberton of her husband), but these imaginary or nostalgic solutions are rejected. *Scott of the Antarctic* (s. Walter Meade, Ivor Montagu, d. Frend, 1948) offers a neurotic twist to this model, as the main protagonists escape from the real world to the unreal world of the Antarctic wastes – they feel well off *when* they aren't. Just prior to the landing on barren, snowcapped soil, Scott's voice-over journal recounts, 'Wonderful to be free at last from problems so difficult for me to handle. Whatever lies ahead I am now on my own ground' – a statement of the total escapism that the comedies release but then resolve. In *Scott of the Antarctic* it is resolved by death.

Thus, when considering the main theme of the Ealing films – their concern with the real world and with the repressions and inhibitions that living in it involve, it is instructive to separate the comedies, as a generic form, from the multiple generic forms of the serious, or dramatic, films, in order to map out what devices both sets use to negotiate this concern. However, perhaps the dramas can be further divided into those that find disruption abroad, in an enemy without (the Germans, or the elements – the sea or the Antarctic) and those that face disruption from within society (villains, delinquents, bureaucracy, corruption). This further division might then involve a spectrum of models that negotiate the problems of the real world, from the adventure of conflict abroad to serious social drama at home and to the comic social fantasy, in which comedy itself is of specific importance in that it acts as a framing device for a particular type of fantasy – a game, the bite that is not a bite.[7]

Working-class Realism and Sexual Reaction: Some Theses on the British 'New Wave'[1]

John Hill

> When *Room at the Top* hit the screen in 1959, it signalled the beginning of one of the most exhilarating bursts of creativity in the history of the British cinema. During the following five or six years new film-makers with fresh ideas brought to the screen a sense of immediacy and social awareness that had people queuing again after nearly a decade of decline.[2]
>
> Nina Hibbin

There can be little doubt that the conventional perception surrounding British cinema of the fifties has been that of a period of decline and stagnation, dramatically rescued towards its close by a breakthrough of new films and new talents. It is not, of course, that it was novelty per se which was significant, but rather the way in which the 'new' cinema sought to break with the habits of the 'old' by inserting a whole area of social experience hitherto suppressed or treated as marginal. That is to say, what crucially defined the breakthrough was the new cinema's determination to centre upon the lives of the industrial working class, and to do so, moreover, in a way that would break with the false theatricality of conventional commercial cinema by developing a style that was in some way more 'authentic' and befitting of the novelty of its subject-matter. Raymond Williams has suggested[3] that a concern with social extension (the inclusion of persons of 'lesser' rank) and contemporaneity has consistently marked the terrain on which 'realist' innovations have worked themselves out. If this is the case, the British 'new wave' is clearly no exception.

Now, having said all this, it would clearly be a perversity to argue that this period of British cinema was not a significant one after all (it clearly was, if only in terms of the legacy it has bestowed upon our sense of cinematic history and judgement) or to deny that a breakthrough of sorts did occur. What I do want to suggest, however, is that the breakthrough was not as important as has often been suggested and certainly cannot be accepted as an unproblematically 'Good Thing', as Sellars and Yeatman might have put it. The doubts here are of two kinds. The first has to do with the adequacy of the realist form fashioned for the expression of those social experiences with which the films sought to deal (I shall discuss this in the 'Addendum'; see below). The second, and for my present purpose more important doubt, arises from the way in which the handling of issues of class in such films has characteristically produced a representation of women and female sexuality which works against and ultimately undercuts their claims to be 'progressive'.

What I mean by this might best be illuminated by reference to one of the few contemporary observers to have noted such a process. Writing in 1962 on *A Kind of Loving*, Penelope Gilliatt had this to say: 'The sad thing is that with an ounce more courage it could have been a genuine, affronting original: for if it had the candour to say so its real theme is not social discontent . . . but the misogyny that has been simmering under the surface of half the interesting plays and films since 1956.'[4] Although Ms Gilliatt does not push her point very far, it does nonetheless seem that she is by and large correct. Indeed, misogyny is not only 'simmering under the surface', but is embedded in the very structures of the films themselves. The narrative patterns adopted in such films not only revolve around characters who are working-class but who are also male and whose progress 'along' the narrative is characteristically worked out in terms of their relations with the other sex. Questions of the hero's identity in relation to a class thus never appear 'pure', but are crucially 'overdetermined' in relation to questions of sex.

This is clearest in those films based on works by writers of the Movement, like Kingsley Amis and John Braine, and their 'Angry Young Man' successor, John Osborne.[5] In practically all such cases (*Lucky Jim, Only Two Can Play* (after Amis' novel *That Uncertain Feeling*), *Room at the Top, Look Back In Anger*) the central theme and organizing principle of the narrative is that of social mobility, of a working-class or lower-middle-class character coming to terms with an upper-middle-class milieu. And central to this process of upward social mobility is the seduction of or marriage to a woman from a higher social class.[6] Indeed, Blake Morrison suggests, in a discussion of the relevant literature, how the combined connotations of the word 'class', as both social status and physical attractiveness ('She's got class'), work to produce a sense of the ambivalent social/sexual involvements of the male hero.[7] And so, even in those films where the hero remains within his class (*Saturday Night and Sunday Morning*, *A Kind of Loving*, *This Sporting Life*) a contrast is still to be found between the 'rough' and 'respectable' working class with the woman representing a social refinement or 'classiness' desired by the male hero (for example, Doreen in *Saturday Night and Sunday Morning* or Mrs Hammond, whose 'noble suffering' in *This Sporting Life* stands in contrast to the 'ape-like' qualities of Frank).

The two groups of films, moreover, share a particular way of working out their heroes' sexual involvements – according to what might justifiably be called the patriarchal principle.[8] By and large, women function either as elusive objects of desire or as threats to the conventional social/sexual order (mainly via adultery), and, either way, must be brought under some kind of male control. Laura Mulvey's notion of films having a sadistic structure is helpful in this respect.[9] Mulvey, in fact, introduces such a notion in the context of a discussion of the responses of the male unconscious to the threat of castration (alternatively fetishism and sadism), and although I have reservations about both the psychoanalytic model employed and the procedures whereby it might be applied to an understanding of the cinema, it does nonetheless have at the very least a clear metaphorical value in describing those films whose narratives are centred on the devaluation and punishment of women. Mulvey herself suggests the example of *film noir*, in which excessive and disruptive female sexuality is often either punished or destroyed and male control reasserted. What I hope to indicate is its further application to most of the apparently very different films of the British 'new wave'.

Indeed, although it is clear that the British 'new wave' and American *film noir* are very different in their choice of narrative and stylistic conventions, there are nonetheless some illuminating points of similarity. What has been made much of, for example, in the case of *film noir*, is the absence, noted by Sylvia Harvey, of 'normal' family and marital relations.[10] And, in many ways, what is also a central characteristic of the British 'new wave' is the fragility of the families that it portrays. Crucial here is the absence or weakness of fathers. Joe Lampton's parents are dead in *Room at the Top*, while Colin in *The Loneliness of the Long Distance Runner*, watches his father die. Jimmy Porter remembers his father dying in *Look Back In Anger*, while

Archie Rice's father dies after collapsing on stage in *The Entertainer*. Doreen in *Saturday Night and Sunday Morning*, Ingrid in *A Kind of Loving* and Jo in *A Taste of Honey* all live with their widowed or separated mothers, while Mrs Hammond's husband in *This Sporting Life* is also dead. Arthur Seaton in *Saturday Night and Sunday Morning* does have a father, but he is effectively impotent (introduced sitting catatonically in front of the television set), as is Joe Lampton's surrogate father, his uncle (preoccupied with his modelling and silent). What might be suggested, indeed, is that, while so much of the British cinema hitherto had been characterized by its deference to strong father figures, what is notable about the new British cinema is precisely their absence, and the search, as a consequence, for the re-establishment of the 'law of the father'.[11] And this, in turn, has consequences for the treatment of women. By and large, the British 'new wave' offers its own modest equivalents to *film noir*'s femme fatale and nurturing woman, and part of the plot in such films focuses on the making of a choice between them. Thus, in *Room at the Top*, *Only Two Can Play* and *Saturday Night and Sunday Morning*, for example, the three adulterous women (Alice, Liz and Brenda) are rejected, while the hero returns to or enters into marriage. As such, the triumph of the hero is not unequivocal. For he too must adjust to marriage and family. Paul Hoch has distinguished 'two major conceptions of masculinity': the 'puritan' (committed to an ethic of production and family), and the 'playboy' (more orientated to consumption and sensual indulgence).[12] And although the word 'playboy' carries with it associations of an aristocratic life-style, in Hoch's extension of its meaning it has a clear application to the heroes of the films under review. Precisely because of his lower social status, the working-class, or 'rough' working-class, hero is characteristically compensated by the 'caste of virility' and thus becomes defined in terms of his sexuality and preference for a 'good time' (Arthur Seaton in *Saturday Night and Sunday Morning* is archetypical here).[13] Therefore his ultimate rejection of extra-marital sex must go hand in hand with a transition from 'playboy' to 'puritan' masculinity. And thus, while the 'patriarchal solution' of the movies works in favour of the male hero, it also in part works against him, for it is also containing and repressing *his* sexual desires.

Two examples should help clarify the argument. *Look Back In Anger* (a 1958 film after the 1956 play), for example, draws a number of such threads together: the transposition of questions of class onto those of sex, the need for an assertion of male sexual control, the association of this with absent or impotent father figures and the partial depression of the male hero's 'virility'. Jimmy Porter (Richard Burton), the archetypical 'angry young man', is married to an upper-class woman, Alison (Mary Ure), the daughter of a retired colonel. As such, she stands as the representative of a particular social order and Jimmy's 'anger' thus becomes reduced to an abuse of her (a process considerably helped in the film by its excision of most of the play's direct political references). As Stuart Hall has put it, 'Alison becomes for him the embodiment of their society . . . and the sexual and human relationship between Jimmy and Alison is a metaphor for the social relationship between Jimmy and the world.'[14]

But what then is striking about the relationship is its clear association with loss – the memory of Jimmy's father's death, the trauma of Ma Tanner's death and the failed power of Alison's father. The death of the imperial era thus becomes dramatized in terms of loss to the family (as it does, even more clearly, in *The Entertainer*). Lucy Bland and her two co-authors have noted, in relation to the *Wolfenden Report on Homosexuality and Female Prostitution* (1957), how 'debates over national decline and Empire are linked to the proliferation of "perverse" and "degenerate" sexual practices',[15] and something of an analagous process occurs here. In *Look Back In Anger* the failed confidence in colonial certainties goes hand in hand with a failed confidence on the terrain of sexuality, and, in the process, becomes a struggle for the reassertion of 'manhood' and the patriarchal principle (as Jimmy puts it to Alison, 'I want to be there when you grovel').

Without wishing to labour the comparison with *film noir*, I think that the process here seems interestingly similar to that described by Pam Cook in relation to *Mildred Pierce*.[16] Cook suggests that the ideological work of such a film should be understood in the context of the need to reconstruct a failing patriarchal order. And part of this process, she argues, is the undermining of the 'matriarchy' represented by Mildred's relationship with Ida and the 'castration' of Mildred by an enforced separation from her daughter, Veda, which is tantamount 'to an act of physical mutilation'.[17] This is also what occurs in *Look Back In Anger*. The 'matriarchal' defence found by Alison in Helen (Claire Bloom) collapses as the latter sexually submits to Jimmy (and thus has her threat defused), while Alison herself makes her own submissive return to Jimmy, 'castrated' by the loss of her unborn child (a result Jimmy had himself wished upon her). It is

308 / British Cinema History

perhaps not surprising, then, that the style and setting of Alison's return to Jimmy at the railway station should be so replete with associations with *Brief Encounter*, with its similar reinsertion of female sexual desire into the 'normality' of the family.

Such a process also seems central to the apparently very different *A Kind of Loving* (1962). One sequence here is crucial. This begins with Vic (Alan Bates) in the kitchen with his wife and mother-in-law. He has been sent two tickets for a brass band concert in which his father is performing, and an argument then ensues about whether he and Ingrid (Julie Ritchie) will be attending. The scene ends with Vic deciding, 'We're going anyway,' but he is hemmed in in the middle of the frame by Ingrid (rear left) and his mother-in-law (foreground right). We then cut to a long shot of the brass band, followed two shots later by Vic's father playing a trombone solo. His wife and younger son are watching, while the camera tracks past them and his sister and brother-in-law onto two empty seats. A cut to a close-up of a television set follows, with a question-master beginning the show, 'Spot Quiz'. A competitor is introduced whose hobbies include 'gardening' and 'looking at people' before we cut to a three-shot of Vic, Ingrid and her mother, all watching.

Although Peter Cowie has cited this as a prime example of the film's meretricious realism (its calculated effect and 'non-natural' use of space),[18] at another level it brings together a number of basic themes. First, and most noticeably, it contrasts the old traditional working-class culture of the brass band (corresponding to declining imperialism in *Look Back In Anger*) with the new, trivial and facile mass culture represented by television.[19] But, second, this juxtaposition of values is effected in terms of a contrast between men and women. While the brass band is all-male, the superficial values of the new 'affluence' are linked inextricably with women, whose obsession with house, television, clothes and physical appearance is persistently emphasized throughout the film.[20]

This opposition is most decisively worked out in terms of the presence or absence of a father. While the brass band soloist is father to a family in the audience, the family watching television has no father, a change from the novel. The corresponding domination of Vic by womenfolk is tantamount to 'castration' (Vic and Ingrid cease to make love in the house). In this context the film reasserts the 'natural order': Vic has to take up his 'proper' role as father and husband. Structurally, this involves the son re-uniting with his father to break up the relationship between mother and daughter. Vic returns to his father for advice, and from the 'natural' base of his allotment the father counsels assertive control: 'She'll live where she's bloody put.'

And thus, as with so many of these films, the ending of *A Kind of Loving* works to endorse the normality and naturalness of the patriarchal family, though not perhaps without a certain amount of irony. The moral centre of the film is represented by Vic's sister and her husband – the 'ideal marriage' which has eluded him. But the couple seem heavily weighed down by an aura of containment and repression. The husband is bespectacled and balding, and they live in an ugly modern flat, with a solitary tree outside, strapped and fenced in. It is more than a little reminiscent of the opening imagery of *No Trees In The Street* – a film aptly denounced by Raymond Durgnat for its appeal to 'gormless conformism'.[21]

So it is within this context that the achievements of the British 'new wave' have to be assessed. As we have seen, it has often been represented as a 'breakthrough' in the British cinema, not only because it came to terms with the lives of ordinary working-class people but also because it did so through an honest treatment of adult sexuality. (The two factors are not unrelated, insofar as the association of sexuality with socially defined subordinate groups has been historically quite common, as, for example, in the case of the sexual mythologies surrounding black peoples.)[22] Indeed, 'sexuality' in such films was something that cinema could offer and television could not, and thus became crucial to the films' box-office exchange-value. But this is not to assume that such an increasing explicitness in sexual content represented some unproblematic march forward to sexual liberation and 'permissiveness'. Indeed, I am suggesting the opposite – namely, that the films' handling of sexuality in fact constitutes what Marcuse would call a 'pseudo-liberation' – that is to say, it is ostensibly liberating but actually repressive.

This is especially so if we consider the context in which such films appeared. For in many ways British society was undergoing a 'boundary crisis' in relation to the role of women and attitudes to sexuality.[23] Indeed, the Birmingham Feminist History Group have argued that 'the expansion of the number of married women working, the "compressed fertility" typical of the period and the increasing importance of home consumption all called for a new view of the role of women and their place in the family'.[24] Increasing female participation in the labour force was prompting reassessments of the role of the family, while the increasing availability of methods of contraception made not only such participation possible but contributed to an increasing acceptance of non-procreative sexuality ('sex as pleasure'). Perhaps it is not surprising that the Royal Commission on Marriage and Divorce set up to reflect on Britain's increasing divorce rate, should have called for less permissiveness when reporting in 1955.

So far from being 'progressive', then, the ideological work of the British 'new wave' can be assessed. By and large, such films end by reproducing an ideology of marital and procreative sexuality which punishes extra-marital and non-procreative sexuality. Indeed, films like *A Kind of Loving* find it difficult to concede the possibility of such activity at all: extra-marital sex, it is assumed, always leads to pregnancy. These films also reaffirm the need for male regulation of female sexuality within the marriage institution, against a vision of a world where such an institution is under threat. The 'new wave' can therefore be seen to be reactionary both within the context of the ideological tensions of the period and in its relation to earlier British cinema. Charles Barr, for example, draws on Ernest Bevin's notion of a 'poverty of desire' as a metaphor for British cinema in general and the work of Ealing in particular – a cinema quintessentially characterized by a dampening of energy and the repression of emotional and sexual desires.[25] If my analysis is accepted, the conclusion must be that the 'new' British cinema of the late fifties and early sixties is not so very different from the old.

Addendum

Although I have primarily focused on what I have called the 'sexual reaction' of the British 'new wave', I should also like to pass a few comments on the aesthetic strategies adopted in such films and the type of working-class experience which these allowed to be projected. In doing so, I should like to consider another implication of Mulvey's idea of sadism. For she also suggests that there is a strong association between sadism and most narratives, insofar as it is male heroes who are the main protagonists of the action and in the development of the plots. And, insofar as the makers of the British 'new wave' films have adopted tightly developmental narrative forms, carried by sharply accentuated male heroes – witness, for example, how the translation of *Saturday Night and Sunday Morning* from novel to film effected a tightening-up of the cause-effect narrative chain and a removal of 'redundant' auxiliary characters – so they have embedded a type of 'masculinization' in the very structures of the films (underwritten, of course, by the powerful, charismatic performances of the rising young working-class actors, like Albert Finney).

Two points are suggested by this. First, running alongside the films' concern to deal with the working class as a group, there is an ideology of individualism cemented into the narrative form which in turn is often picked up thematically – the male hero is treated as an 'outsider', set apart from the rest of his class. Thus, in *Saturday Night and Sunday Morning*, Arthur Seaton is clearly counterpointed to the 'poor beggars' around him who have all been 'ground down'. Second, this has led to a failure to develop what we might call a 'collective aesthetic'. Whenever the British cinema has attempted to project a sense of collectivity on the screen, as in wartime, this has tended to generate a loosening of narrative form in favour of a more episodic structure and a multiplication of characters. The makers of the 'new wave' films, on the other hand, precisely because of their adoption of tightly wrought narrative and of a dominating central character, tended to experience difficulty in projecting a sense of collective working-class experience.[26] As a result, this sense of the collectivity of working-class life tended to become exteriorized into iconography and 'atmosphere'.

Two devices become particularly noticeable. First, the use of 'surplus' establishing or linking shots. Thus, before an action is initiated a series of contextualising shots will be employed, not so much to denote a locale for action as to connote the environmental ambience in which the action is occurring (for example, *Saturday Night and Sunday Morning*). Likewise, an action will be extended over a number of shots – again, not so much to provide information necessary to the narrative as to offer 'atmospheric' information about its context (for example, *A Kind of Loving*). The second device is a development of this whereby such 'surplus' shots are extended to form a complete sequence (the equivalent of Metz's 'descriptive syntagma'). Once again, typical shots of a place or locale are presented without any particular narrative function. Such examples are to be found particularly in the films of Tony Richardson. In both cases, the effect is the same: the creation of 'images' of working-class life – which, nonetheless, lack integration with the narrative as a whole.

Carry On . . . Follow that Stereotype

Marion Jordan

The 'Carry On' films have had a good run for their, in any case exiguous, money. Produced with astonishing regularity from 1958 to 1980, they have never achieved anything of the critical acclaim of, say, the Ealing films, but they have often done well at the box-office, frequently topping the figures for British films in the period from 1958 to the mid-seventies. Moreover, though some of the later films have been less successful, the series has had a new life both in the television spin-off series and in television screenings of the originals (usually running, incidentally, during the early evening or weekend afternoon 'family viewing' time), and the earliest video-tape lists of films for hire all included some example of the series.

The fact that the films were produced so cheaply, that they were often ignored by critics, or mentioned only in passing by reviewers, and that they have made no claim to be Art, has meant that they have not in general been seen as part of British film history, selective (as all histories are) of those things that it regards as important. The series gains no more than a passing mention even in standard works of reference, and is given only an occasional nod of acknowledgement, variously patronizing or dismissive, in works of critical assessment. Such a split between popularity and critical or academic evaluation is, of course, charactertic of our culture.

After this implied criticism of the arbitrary principle of selection which omits the 'Carry On' films from consideration, it is seemly to acknowledge that the present account too is arbitrarily selective, both in its concentration on the 'Carry On' films at all and in its specific focus on the existence of stereotyping in the films, at the expense of many other factors. The choice of stereotyping as the focus has been made partly on the intrinsic grounds that it is a central feature of the films, partly on the extrinsic grounds that this allows a direct confrontation with those who would dismiss the films chiefly on the grounds that they are stereotyped – and are thereby rendered cheap, vulgar and beneath consideration.

However positive may have been the original implications of the word 'stereotype', there is little doubt that today the word is usually derogatory. Walter Lippmann's original conception was that the stressing of similarities within a group was a way of asserting the value of that group: 'It is the guarantee of our own self-respect; it is the projecting upon the world of our own sense of our own value.'[1] The use of the first person here is revealing. It implies that the characteristics emphasized as shared will be both positive and non-prescriptive. If the ascription of shared characteristics to any group is made from outside, however, then it is likely that the shared features will be both less positive and more crudely inescapable – and it is with connotations of this kind that the word is commonly used today in criticisms of fiction. Richard Dyer, for example, suggests that the stereotype is commonly a device to 'maintain sharp boundary distinctions',[2] and the context makes it clear that the boundary which he has in mind is that between 'them' (the stereotypical) and 'us' (the interestingly varied and self-defining).

Yet all fictional characters exist (at least in a limited sense) as stereotypes. This is to say no more than that the units of information about characters which we are given in fiction are necessarily larger and more discrete than the continuous elements of which actual people are constituted, since, contrary to artistic cant, it is art which is short and life which is long. The two hours of a play or a film will typically purport to deal with much longer periods of real life for a diversity of characters: a day, say, in *Ivan Denisovich*, a love affair of some weeks (in *Brief Encounter*, for example), longer even (as in *Tom Jones*). Without the use of synecdoche (whereby the part must be read as the whole) and metonymy (whereby character is read from associated objects and surroundings), there can be no fictional recognition. So Ivan Denisovich's crust of bread hidden in a mattress (quite apart from the information it gives us about the physical circumstances of Denisovich's life) says not only that here is a man who has saved a crust of bread, but, more broadly, that here is a man who ekes out his food, and, even more expansively, that here is a man who ekes out his life. (It is perhaps salutary to remember that in life too we are forced by the incompleteness of our information to make judgements in similar ways about our acquaintances.)

The artistic necessity for this (what we may think of as limited) degree of stereotyping often goes unrecognized, and the word 'stereotype' is customarily restricted to the derogatory description of characterization which uses 'blocks' of information that the critic or audience finds obtrusive or distasteful. Such judgements are not, of course, simply matters of personal fastidiousness, as their pro-pounders would often have us believe. With regard to stereotypes, they are affected by (among many other factors) both the tacit recognition of the degree of stereotyping to be expected of any genre and the critic's attitude to the genre in question. Generally speaking, those genres (farce, say, or the school story, the romantic novelette or the gangster film) which depend heavily upon a recognizable, though not customarily an openly stated, use of stereotypes have not traditionally been thought of as particularly worthy of critical attention. When they have been discussed in film studies they have usually been introduced under the guise of studies of individual stars or individual authors, since (again for a variety of reasons) criticism is thought more respectable when it concerns itself with named individuals).

It is one of the ironies of the 'Carry On' series that what must be the largest group of feature films to be produced by recognizably the same, very small, number of people (twenty-eight films made over a period of twenty years, all produced by Peter Rodgers and directed by Gerald Thomas, with only two screen-writers for the first twenty-one and a small, repeatedly engaged band of performers) is not seen as an individual oeuvre, but as very much a genre product. This is, at any rate partly, because the exaggerations of stereotypes in the films depart from realism into the world of the genre proper, where (in Jonathan Culler's term) 'we allow works to contribute to a semi-autonomous world,'[3] and even, after the first three or four films, to go beyond this to a realm where it is previous 'Carry On' films which provide the chief point of reference against which the stereotype can be measured.

The 'Carry On' films are, in fact, part of a strong (though not always acknowledged) line in British cinema. One description of the 1940s and 1950s British films suggests, 'The members of each class conform to a rigid stereotype. This stereotyping was (and still is) a common feature of British films.'[4] What the 'Carry On' films do at their best (which here often means 'at their most self-conscious') is to display by means of grotesque exaggeration and repetition their own use of stereotyping, and, in so doing, mock the similar, but hidden, stereotyping elsewhere. Their effect is not, then, to say, 'Look, this is what such people are like,' but rather, 'Look, this is what we claim such people are like – and it is so farcical it cannot be true.'

Of course, the situation is not as simple as I may seem to be suggesting. To begin with, there is no firm dividing-line between these two points of view, and because they *are* points of view what is seen in the films depends upon the position of the observer as well as on the position in which the object to be viewed is placed. Furthermore, the sheer pleasure given by a performance of one of the films (by the script and production as well as by the acting) may be such as to promote rather than to deride the stereotype. It is for reasons of this kind that my own view of the characters in the 'Carry On' films is an ambivalent one.

There have, of course, been changes in the 'Carry On' films during the twenty years during which they have flourished, but the power of the developing formula has been such that these changes have not been, as one might have expected, the outcome of the change of script-writer from Norman Hudis (who wrote the scripts for the first six films) to Talbot Rothwell (who wrote the scripts for the next twenty). The first film, *Carry On Sergeant* was not envisaged as the first of a series when it was made in 1958, and it is, if only for this reason, the least typical. It is a fairly straight comic treatment of the training of national servicemen, with no more than the mildly farcical scenes customary for a light realist comedy, the farce being concerned either with the inappropriate behaviour of men not yet schooled as soldiers (physical ineptitude, obtrusive individualism, pride in irrelevant achievement) or with the mismatching of sexual desire and sexual opportunity. The main theme (the sentimental desire of an ostensibly hard-bitten sergeant to end his career in muted glory by training the star squad of the intake) is seriously presented. The sergeant himself is never mocked, and he does gain his star award – and that not by means of a series of farcical accidents (which is the typical way in which later 'Carry On' films flaunt the falsity of their 'happy endings'), but by the genuine good-will and strenuous effort of the group of recruits, who have come to admire him – and who present him in all misty-eyed seriousness, with a gold cigarette-lighter before being driven off into the future at the end of their training.

The film would have been a small-budget, money-making, forgettable success, had not the director and producer decided that what they would continue with would be not the conventional sentimental story-line (though *Carry On Teacher* tries to tack on an even more sentimental ending, it is too close to the immediately preceding farce to be taken seriously, even in the film's own terms), but the music hall farcical elements which had obviously been what the audience enjoyed.

Many of what became the staple elements of the series are present, though they are not emphasized, in this first 'Carry On' film – from the outrageous, usually rude, puns (as in the description of an inept recruit, who has a collection of chits excusing him from most duties, as 'just a load of chits'), through the locked-in-the-lavatory episodes, to the comic frustrations of a honeymoon night, with the bride and groom a hundred miles apart – and all this happening in the setting of a large and theoretically impersonal institution. The combination of these elements became the formula for all the films which followed. Not that such a formula is peculiar only to these films: other British film series used it, such as the *Doctor in the House* sequels, for example (1953–64), or the Saint Trinian's films (1954–66). The 'Carry On' films differed only in being both cruder and cheaper to make, and in their not claiming even a marginal verisimilitude for their eccentrics by having them play ostensibly the same characters, as happened in these other series. The 'Carry On' films present supposedly different stories, but settings, characters and plot all conform to stereotypes.

The most important shared feature of structure of the 'Carry On' films is the setting, which is typically that of the large-scale, impersonal institution – the army barracks, the hospital, the school, the camp-site, the tourist hotel – and the moment of concern is the moment at which newcomers are taken from their homes and introduced to the institution. The source of the humour, then, is to be found in the contrast between the impossibly repeated, identical, stereotypical human beings for whom the institution's rules are devised, and the diverse and unpredictable 'real' people who arrive there. (The play made of the fact that these 'real' people are also stereotypes, though of a different kind, is discussed below.) What the institution typically fails to cater for is the animal nature of human beings: their sexuality (the institutions are typically segregated by sex), their excretory functions, their preference for idleness as opposed to pointless physical strain. In this way the bureaucratic institution is clearly shown as a substitute for a society which is represented as trying to produce conveniently biddable plastic clones.

The interest lies in the way in which people constantly reassert their animal natures in the face of the institution which denies them. Life, as the institution enforces it, would be, as the Sid James character puts it in one film (and the overtones are not lost on his audience), like having an itch and not being allowed to scratch.

The institution most often chosen is the hospital (the setting for five of the films), and one can see why this was so. Benny Green points out that one reason why the vulgar comic postcard is most commonly set at the seaside is because the seaside 'necessarily features people in various states of undress';[5] another reason is that it allows at least a dream of unbuttoning (the figure is again revealing) when away from home. Just as the 'Carry On' films are the British cinema's equivalent of the rude postcard, so the hospital is 'Carry On's' equivalent of the seaside, in its exact reproduction of the tense equivocation of nakedness (or rather undress) between the promise of sexual pleasure and the fear of indignity (or, in effect, of sexual rejection). The two possible responses are seen side-by-side in the earliest 'Carry On' film proper (that is, the earliest one to be presented as part of a formula), *Carry On Nurse*, in which a nurse's forcible removal of the reluctant Kenneth Connor's trousers is followed by a dismissive downward glance, 'What a fuss about such a little thing,' whereas Terence Longden's resistance to being undressed (he is admonished by Joan Sims' 'Don't be a baby') is followed, when his pyjamas are removed for pubic shaving, by an admiring, 'And to think I called you a baby.' The female equivalent of this is so common as to be seen in almost every film, when Barbara Windsor's (or earlier, Joan Sims') undress is meant to be read as a promise of pleasure, whereas Hattie Jacques' attempts to strip evoke shudders of horror from whichever man she is currently pursuing.

The fact that almost all the films involve people removed from their home background has another effect which is similar to that of the comic postcard, in that the promise (in any case not usually fulfilled) of sexual freedom when away from home is presented not as a possible world of promiscuity but as the possibility of a fleeting aberration in a world that remains solidly monogamous. George Orwell pointed out the postcard's equivalent of this in an article on the art of the postcard artist Donald McGill: 'Whereas in papers like *Esquire*, for instance, or *La Vie Parisienne*, the imaginary background of the jokes is always promiscuity, the utter breakdown of all standards, the background of the McGill postcard is marriage.'[6]

In terms of plot this is even more true of the 'Carry On' films. For, if the common physical setting is that of some *physical* institution, then the commonest theme is that of the *social* institution of marriage. Marriage, as seen by the 'Carry On' films, demands the same uniformity and conformity as the army or the school, but in a much stronger form, for its *primary* (not as in the other cases *incidental*) aim is regulation – the regulation of sexual desire, and, by extension, in these films, of all other pleasures of the flesh (notably eating, drinking and repose). Typically, too, as school-girls resist the school's demand that they remain conveniently pre-pubertal, and patients resist the hospital's demand to have them all pee by the clock, so married people (here, since most things are seen from a man's point of view, this means husbands) resist, at least in their vividly active fantasy, both the forbidding of their desire for other women and the enforced service of their own wives.

If the characters for whom the institution caters so misguidedly are the stereotypes which the institution finds desirable – law-abiding, mechanical, without sensuality or emotion, metaphorical extensions of the well drilled soldier whose very limbs move to the word of command – the characters who actually appear are *literary* stereotypes of the anarchic/human refusal to conform to the institutional stereotype. Essentially these are the stock characters of the most demotic types of fiction – the comic postcard and the bar-room joke. The implications of this latter comparison are borne out in some detail in the films, for not only are the jokes often obscene, they also express a very masculine view of the world. This is true even of literal interpretations: mothers-in-law are mothers of wives; all the babies born (there are quite a few) are male (though children, again, in a typical masculine view, are usually girl-women); sexual desirability (however much parodied) is most commonly female, sexual desire and potency most commonly male.

That the characters are essentially those of the comic postcard is virtually beyond dispute. The following descriptions, taken from two analyses of the comic postcard, could equally well form part of an analysis of the 'Carry On' films: 'Every man is plotting seduction and every woman is plotting marriage.'[7] 'Pictures of randy swains pursuing busty grinning girls down the labyrinth of bachelor days.'[8] 'The amorous honeymooning couple reappear as the grim-visaged wife and shapeless mustachioed red-nosed husband, no intermediate stage being allowed for.'[9] 'There is no intermediary stage between saucy girl-friend and irascible wife. . . . The young blade of courting days shrinks into the brow-beaten dish-washer of middle-age.'[10] It is the *sharpness* of divisions of this kind which most clearly marks the caricatures in the films, so that the members of the different groups which are set up – male/female, married/single, working-class/ middle-class – are treated as members of different species.

The first of these suggested groups is the most signal one, and the sharpness of the male/female division is emphasized by the frequency of appearances in 'drag', not reduced, as it might have been by some treatments, since in the drag of these films 'the stress is on grotesquerie, not attractiveness',[11] on the impossibility of the swap. Typically, Bernard Bresslaw is dressed as a pregnant woman in *Carry On Matron*, or characters in drag are forced into situations where they must undress. Moreover, the jokes made about these changes of clothing (like the frequent jokes about going into the public convenience for the wrong sex) emphasize this sexual/social in- compatibility. So when Kenneth Cope, trying in the same film to escape from the embarrassment of the woman nurse's clothing which Sid James has induced him to put on, suggests that he should be allowed to disguise himself as a male orderly, he is admonished as mad: 'Whoever heard of a male orderly wearing black lace knickers?'

Such sex-swap clothing changes are, in keeping with the male orientation of the films, almost always of male to female. Women may adopt 'unfeminine' clothing – typically, Hattie Jacques as army officer or starched matron – but this is not *men*'s clothing.

Men are divided among themselves almost equally sharply. Apart from the token 'nice young men' who appear unmemorably in each film, they are divided into the unmarried, the sexually voracious (here, interestingly, they are scarcely ever young, but rather in raddled middle age) and the impotent (who are represented as either born effeminate or neutered by marriage). The impassability of the barrier between these types is stressed by the fact that members of the same group are often played by the same actors throughout the whole series of films: Jim Dale, say, and Kenneth Connor are the nice young men; Sid James and Bernard Bresslaw the randily single; Kenneth Williams and Charles Hawtrey the effeminate; Terry Scott the castrated husband. Moreover, both this immutability and the fact that they exist as types rather than as rounded characters are stressed by the names of the film characters, which may retain the actor's own first name and add to it a comic surname stressing the stereotype chosen:

so, for example, Sid James appears as Sid Boggle, Gladstone Screwer, Sir Rodney Ffing and Sidney Fiddler. The cumulative effect has a wry flavour: on the one hand, characters are fixed for ever in their roles; on the other, we are forcibly reminded that these roles are performed by known actors.

The films leave little doubt about which of these character types are supposed to win our approval. The nice young men are bland but forgettable. The effeminate – homosexual scarcely seems the right word (though it is often used) for characters so bereft of sexuality that Kenneth Williams is described in one film as looking as though he has not got much to lose – are presented as sickly, or even mentally deficient. In a typical scene Kenneth Williams' Julius Caesar sighs, 'I feel a little queer,' as he sits in his Roman mini-skirt ('Julie' to his friends), with his feet in a mustard bath, trying to cure his cold. Or Charles Hawtrey is presented as a charmingly whimsical, middle-aged, pre-pubertal child-innocent. Indeed, the domination of male heterosexuality is such that the two actors are often given, amid the cissy simpers, crudely lecherous lines of the kind, 'Wouldn't mind putting my cart down before her.' The castrated husbands are despised, except in their moments of reawakened sexuality. It is the sexually rampant males who are approved. In Sid James they surely find their most jaunty exponent. His best lines are jokes about the ubiquity of his sexual readiness:

Nurse: 'What do you want?'
James: 'That's very nice of you but I haven't got the time.'

A slightly more plaintive Bernard Bresslaw, in any case an alter ego for James, is the only one to rival him in similar exchanges:

Bresslaw: 'I dreamt of you last night, nurse.'
Nurse: 'Did you?'
Bresslaw: 'No. You wouldn't let me.'

The divisions among the women are equally sharp and equally dependent upon attitudes to sexuality. Here too the expected 'nice young women', technically the heroines of a mild romance, fade away. The types which remain prominent are young women, who are to be read as sexually desirable, or obsolete, wives. (Benny Green sums up their comic postcard equivalents in the phrase 'dream breasts and nightmare bosoms'.[12]) Both types are shown in caricature form. We know the young women are meant to be desirable because of the stress on their breasts or bottoms, but there is little attempt otherwise to make them a sexual enticement for audience consumption. (In this sense the films could scarcely be described appropriately as 'sex comedies'.) The grossness of the exaggeration forbids any such pornographic effect, quite apart from the indignity with which even the notionally desirable picture of female nudity is presented. We know that we are to laugh at male nudity when it is represented at the beginning of *Carry On Camping* by a paunchy middle-aged man on a bicycle, but female nudity is no more erotic when Barbara Windsor's bikini top flies off during her keep-fit exercises, or when glimpses of bare female flesh are seen through undignified peep-holes in the communal showers. Nonetheless, we know that this female body is supposed to be read as attractive, because the reactions of people in the film tell us so. Essentially, such young women are sexually knowing (and appreciative), but forced by their circumstances (as school-girls, say, or members of a harem) to pretend innocence. They are embodied with giggling sugariness in Barbara Windsor's predictable roles, or, more astringently, in the primly provocative Lady Jane Ponsonby of *Carry On . . . Follow that Camel*. She is subjected to the attentions of a sequence of male officials who, after ascertaining that she is travelling alone, draw the blinds, and variously punch her ticket, check her port-hole, or see if her accommodation is satisfactory, until at the last enquiry, as to whether she is alone, she wearies of pretence and, with a mock-resigned, 'All right, I'll do it', draws the blinds herself. Typically, by the end of the film she has returned to the knowing innocence of all the films' ingénues, assuring her protective parents, 'Everyone was terribly kind. They couldn't do enough for me.'

There is no continuity at all between such women and the nightmare bosoms of the wives that they presumably become. It is interesting to see the progress of the actress Joan Sims in the light of the implied changes in women, since she starts as the provocative piece of the early films – Miss Allcock, indeed, in one of them, with her shorts splitting over her plump bottom – and becomes by the middle period the actress of choice to depict the middle-aged harridan. The nagging wives of the films are presented equivocally (if such a word can be used for films which pride themselves on their blunt vulgarity). They are at one and the same time deniers of sexual indulgence within (and also, of course, without) their marriages, and demanders of it from failing husbands. Since the denial is customarily presented in the form of husbands being put off by their wives' unattractiveness (there is no need, according to these films, for *men* to be attractive), the two apparently contradictory attitudes can exist together, as in exchanges of this kind:

> Wife (to husband): 'You need a repellent.'
> Husband: 'I married one.'

or

> 'Dr Goode, I am not interested in your wife.'
> 'That's funny, nor am I.'

Perhaps the most objectionably cruel of the stereotypes of the unattractive woman is that of the aging (or in some other way non-pin-up) spinster, aping a coy girlishness in the hope of catching a man. The most frequent exponent of this is Hattie Jacques (acting characters with such names as Miss Haggerd, Grace Short, or even Frost-faced Sister, and in any case carrying echoes of castrating roles as Captain Clark or the earlier matron). In *Carry On Camping* her acceptance of every double entendre from Kenneth Williams ('Surely we can keep control') is presented as grotesquely repellent in one too old, too plain and above all too fat for sex. Yet repeatedly throughout the films men older and plainer (Terry Scott's Dr Prodd, say, in *Carry On Matron*) are set up as successful sexual adventurers. Where the aging wives are unattractive, but emasculating in their power, these women are unattractive and comically, cruelly powerless.

A variety of not always compatible effects arises from the choice of such types. In one sense, they advertise a sexuality which does not have to be tied to great romantic ideals, passions or abnegations. The films celebrate with fertile innuendo the ingenuity with which the common language, so subjected to bowdlerization, nonetheless throws up sexual connotations, and, in so doing, they celebrate the liveliness of sexual interest. The ubiquity, the gaiety, the cheeky street resilience, of such sexuality is cheering. At least as far as men are concerned, the films serve as a jokey but palatable antidote to the sentimental cant that only the young, the well formed, the un-bespectacled, the standard English, may be interested in sex. And for some women, at least (the young, buxom and unintellectual), a hearty sexual awareness and appetite are allowed. More negatively, for women who are in any way less (or more) attractive than the magazine cover-girl and who lack the typically generous endowments admired in the 'Carry On' films' – that is to say, for the plain, the fat, the thin, the middle-aged, the competent, the responsible, the married – sexual desire is grotesque. Such stereotypes may perhaps be read positively, as giving a humorous but fair critical picture both of the cruel incompatibilities which may exist within marriage and of the extremely limited and widely differentiated roles which society forces upon women. Yet this is scarcely the feel of the films. Too often, too expectedly, too smugly, such women are set aside. It is only the power of performances such as those given by Hattie Jacques, Joan Sims, or the more fleeting June Whitfield that allows any questioning of the unvarying dispositions of the plots.

Alongside the 'ordinary people' gender stereotypes in these films there also exist class stereotypes. The occasionally mocked picture of the working-class couple is that of a sexually irresponsible and work-shy husband and a vulgarly prolific wife. *Carry On Nurse* has a father of eleven lying in hospital mourning the missed opportunity to beget a twelfth; *Carry On Matron* has Kenneth Connor's railwayman say: 'I gotta be back work Monday. We start the strike then.' Such a desire to avoid work, however, is more commonly (and untypically for films in general) presented as sensible and salutary. We are on the side of the wide boy Sid James when he sees his son's desire for steady work rather than thieving as unhealthily deviant: 'He wants to go straight before he's even been crooked.' In this way too these films echo the comic postcard's sensible recognition that, the nature of industrial work being what it is, 'most people, given the choice, would rather not do any work at all. . . . With the worldly wisdom of the townee, they have seen through the sham of the puritan work ethic and are reacting accordingly.'[13]

Class stereotypes of a derogatory kind are more commonly ones of the middle classes. The educated classes fare badly in comparison with the stereotypical common-sense masses. An injured working man's refusal or inability to fill in a form is shown as a sensible attitude to bureaucracy: 'Look, I fell off a scaffolding and broke my leg. . . . What else do they expect to know – my father's chest measurement?' Education might teach one to avoid the cliché view of the nuclear physicist 'pressing buttons, making explosions, giving everybody awful weather in the summer' – but the same education has unfitted Kenneth Williams' nuclear physicist for life (that is, in this context, for sex). Men whose education is stressed are commonly presented as sexually incompetent, if not impotent. Kenneth Williams B.Sc., does not have sufficient nous to look up a girl's skirt; Kenneth Williams MA, refuses all sexual advances; Kenneth Williams MD, has to consult his textbooks to find out about sex; Sid James authenticates his impersonation of a parson by pretending not to know the demotic euphemisms for (and by implication, therefore, the pleasures of) sex; Charles Hawtrey's middle-class twit never recognizes (or at least can successfully pretend not to recognize) the abundant innuendo of being shown (inter alia) how to put the pole up. The apotheosis of such upper-class enervation is seen in the Khasi of Khalabar's refusal of a proffered seduction: 'No, I do not make love . . . I am extremely rich. I have servants to do that sort of thing for me.'

It is of interest that the films' consistent refusal of the realism of character-acting means that it is the performer, not the supposed role, that carries the marks of class.[14] So, a knighted Sid James, even a King Sid James, remains a working-class, street-wise twentieth-century Londoner, sexually voracious as ever. The regularly occurring visiting performers are used in the same way to deny any realist illusion. When Phil Silvers appears as Sergeant Nocker in *Carry On . . . Follow that Camel* he is recognizably still Sergeant Bilko. In this way the films work like short comic acts from music-hall, radio and television, in which the comedian will supposedly play another role while trading on being recognizably his own (stage) self.

This constancy of performance is a major part of the 'Carry On' approach. For if the films are stocked with stereotypical characters they also find another source of humour in their parodies of film genres which have become so rigid in their forms that they are themselves unacknowledged stereotypes. Features of the fictional worlds of these films are then mocked: the essential human niceness theme of the Doctor films; the awed respect demanded for Shakespeare spectaculars or travel epics; the cleverness (of plot or gimmickry) of spy films; the historical truth and romance of costume dramas. Cheeky visual reminders are given in credit titles, as with the early use of the BBC test-card, or the parodies of the sultry Elizabeth Taylor posters for *Carry On Cleo*. As with the drag performances in the films, there is no attempt here at fidelity to such genres; the style is that of crude parody, not elegant pastiche. The real joke lies in the 'Carry On' spoofs' display of what such genre films may disguise – the fact that such films too are in their own way variants of the gender dramas and modern commentaries that 'Carry On' films (and others of the type) openly show themselves to be.

The rejection of any realism in these parodies is marked. If someone is to fall through the floor (as in *Carry on Abroad*) one can see the cut-out in the floor long in advance; if a tent is to fall down (as in *Carry On Camping*) there is no attempt to make it look as though it is even temporarily secure; if that customarily typical young-man-in-the-street, Jim Dale, plays an upper-class adventurer (as in *Carry On up the Khyber*) he makes no more than a token attempt at the class and accent of his time; if a psychiatrist turns up in a maternity hospital nobody bothers to write in an excuse for his presence.

Sometimes such lapses in realist style look merely shoddy, as with howls of pain from a hammered thumb which is clearly never struck. Usually, however, they are carried purposefully to a zany extreme in the frequent anachronisms (or photographic equivalents of anach-ronism) of the films. So the nineteenth century epic, *Carry On Up the Khyber*, has Bernard Bresslaw's triumphant tribesman exult, 'That'll teach 'em to ban turbans on the buses.' A knock on a tent flap in *Carry On Camping* makes a sound as though on a wooden door. The door of an ordinary terrace house is opened in *Carry On Cabby*, to reveal a field with a lavatory pan in it. Such jokes almost always work well. It is through them that the only directly political commentary of the films is made – usually in the form of outdated references to the period twenty years earlier. So Kenneth Williams mimics a pompous Churchillian voice in the middle of *Carry On Cleo*, or Sid James remarks of a polo-playing officer called Philip, 'That lad'll go far if he marries right.'

A similar effect is achieved by the insertion of already familiar jokes (usually rude), often from music-hall, radio or comic magazines. The jokes quoted above about the randy male's readiness to see a sexual invitation anywhere are variants on traditional music-hall routines, as in a Max Miller sketch:

> Bus conductress: 'Do you want to get me into trouble?'
> Max Miller: 'What time are you off duty?'

Similarly, the films use the comic postcard's stock joke of the unlooked-for baby ('Can you change this lucky charm for a baby's feeding bottle?'), as in

> 'The wedding party's arrived.' (*sounds of a new baby crying*).
> 'Yes, I can hear they have.'

No excuse is given in terms of plot for the insertion of such jokes. The mere fact of being in the countryside (in any case very artificially presented) is enough to allow the use of the old chestnut of the farmer's daughter taking the cow to the bull:

'Couldn't your father do that?'
'No. It has to be the bull.'

Similarly, the puns are appreciated precisely because they are familiar. 'Matron's round.' 'I don't care if she's triangular,' capped by 'It's matron's round.' 'Mine's a pint,' depends on the ingenuity of its insertion, not on its newness. We know that the word 'ball' will never be used unambiguously. Joan Sims' brothel-keeper's offer of transport: 'I have a good ass, no?' looks forward to the supposed nudist camp's notice: 'ALL ASSES MUST BE SHOWN' (the owner has gone for a P). In this way the films are a part of the tradition of English working-class humour, which Orwell claims (in his analysis of picture postcards) is 'as traditional as Greek tragedy, a sort of sub-world of smacked bottoms and scrawny mothers-in-law which is part of Western European consciousness.'[15]

Despite the claim that there are more 'Carry On' films to come, the series is virtually at an end. Films so dependent on repeated types are changed beyond repair by the change of personnel which time inevitably brings. Moreover, the fact that the films have always seemed old-fashioned does not mean that they are not subject to fashion. They depend on looking back only so far – on a self-conscious assertion that neither they nor their attitudes are governed by modern gimmickry – and on the tolerant affection that this degree of backward-looking can engender for them. Their dependence too on the view they take of the visible social relations between the sexes means that they are very subject to changes in sexual and social mores, the more especially as they treat the moral climate as permanent rather than historically determined. The distorted cartoon world which they mock is one which would deny sexuality and physicality, and insist on pudeur, reticence, a romantic view of love and an imposed order-liness. They oppose this world with the deliberate bad taste of rude words and farting elephants. But bad taste changes too. When films can now speak openly of the private parts there is little fun to be won from the prurient schoolboy ambiguities of a meeting at the Old Cock Inn. (Bad taste – deliberate or otherwise – still exists, of course, in sexual discourse, but it is worn with a difference, in, say, the mention, à la Woody Allen, of masturbation, which the makers of the 'Carry On' films would certainly find shocking rather than titillating.)

Perhaps it no longer seems worth-while today to sit through ninety minutes of narrative in order to hear twenty naughty words. Indeed, the films, with honourable exceptions, like *Carry On Spying* have always seemed long-drawn-out in terms of plot; the point at which the repeated comparisons with rude postcards and music-hall sketches breaks down is precisely this one of length, which is a by no means unimportant factor. Where the postcards and sketches *imply* a background by means of a few simple lines, the choice of an accent, the set of a collar, a 'Carry On' film labours to establish 'a story' about which no-one cares. There is an intermittent danger that, though one might find the point amusing, one wearies on the way to it. Yet in their day, and despite their denying any place to women in their pantheon – portraying them, indeed, as gaolers, sexual objects, or unnatural predators – they nonetheless asserted by their themes, and by the gusto with which they were presented, a lower-class, masculine resistance to 'refinement'; an insistence on sexuality, physicality, fun; on the need for drink in a kill-joy world, for shiftiness in an impossibly demanding industrial society, for cowardice amid the imposed heroism.

Notes

Chapter 2

1 This chapter is a much abbreviated version of a longer original text. In particular the references have been severely pruned; readers should supplement those given in the notes by consulting the Bibliography at the end of the book. I have also drawn upon the following articles, written by myself or by myself in collaboration with other authors: '[Re] Making it New', *Undercut*, 1 (1981); 'What is the Subject of [a] Cultural Production?', *Undercut*, 3 (1982); 'The Orders of Experience', *Social Text*, 6, 1982; with M. Barrett, A. Kuhn, J. Wolff, 'Representation and Cultural Production', in our collectively edited book, *Ideology and Cultural Production* (London, Croom-Helm, 1979); with Paul Willis, 'Cultural Forms and Class Mediations', *Media, Culture and Society*, 2 (1980); I am most grateful to the book library of the British Film Institute for their assistance.

2 Griffith on his audience is quoted by R. Manvell, 'The Place of Film in the Age of Television', *Journal of the Royal Society of Arts*, 103 (1954), p. 79. A relevant and similar comment on early television is made by Gerald Cock, the first Director of BBC Television, and quoted by G. Ross, *Television Jubilee* (London, W. H. Allen, 1961), p. 44. For BBC television during Cock's directorship see P. R. D. Corrigan, 'The Moment of English Television', unpublished dissertation, 1981 (copies in BFI and PCL libraries).

3 See S. Heath, *Questions of Cinema* (London, Macmillan, 1981), especially pp. 221–35; C. F. Altman, 'Towards a Historiography of American Film', *Cinema Journal*, 16 (1977); N. Carroll, 'Film history and film theory', *Film Reader*, 4 (1979); G. Perry, *The Great British Picture Show* (London, Paladin, 1975); A. Wood, *Mr Rank* (London, Hodder and Stoughton, 1952), and sources cited in the notes below.

4 H. R. Jauss, 'Literary History as a Challenge to Literary Theory', *New Literary History*, 2 (1970).

5 L. A. Handel, *Hollywood looks at its Audience* (University of Illinois Press, 1950), table 2, p. 22.

6 D. Atwell, *Cathedrals of the Movies* (London, Architectural Press, 1981).

7 A. B. Walkley, *Pastiche and Prejudice* (London, Heinemann, 1921), p. 226.

8 C. Belsey, *Critical Practice* (London, Methuen, 1980), p. 125; my italics.

9 H. E. Browning and A. A. Sorrell, 'Cinemas and Cinema-going in Great Britain', *Journal of the Royal Statistical Society*, 117 (1954), table 2, p. 135.

10 Ibid, table 3, p. 136.

11 P. Hohendahl, 'Introduction to Reception Aesthetics', *New German Critique*, 10 (1977); J. Wolff, *The Social Production of Art* (London, Macmillan, 1980); N. Pearson, *The State and the Visual Arts* (Open University Press, 1982).

12 S. Suleiman and I. Crossman, (eds), *The Reader in the Text* (Princeton University Press, 1980); B. Sharratt, *Reading Relations* (Harvester, 1982).

13 R. Barthes, 'The Death of the Author', in S. Heath, ed., *Image–Music–Text* (London, Fontana, 1977), p. 148.

14 B. Nichols, *Ideology and the Image* (Bloomington, Indiana University Press, 1981), p. 4.

15 R. Barthes, *The Pleasure of the Text* (New York, Hill and Wang, 1975), p. 59.

16 A. Briggs, 'The Language of "Mass" and "Masses" in Nineteenth-century England', D. E. Martin and D. Rubinstein, ed., *Ideology and the Labour Movement* (London, Croom Helm, 1979), pp. 62–83; B. Waites, 'Class and Class-consciousness in Early 20th century England', *Literature and History*, 2 (1977).

17 N. Burch, 'Porter, or Ambivalence', *Screen*, 19 (1978–9), and 'Charles Baudelaire versus Doctor Frankenstein', *Afterimage*, 8–9 (1981); B. Salt, 'The Early Development of Film Form', *Film Form*, 1 (1976); and 'Film Form 1900–1906', *Sight and Sound*, 47 (1978); D. Vaughan, 'Let there be Lumierè', *Sight and Sound*, 50 (1981). For earlier recognition that audiences had to learn how to look at and 'get into' pictures see R. Manvell, *A Seat in the Cinema* (London, Evans, 1951), pp. 28–9. More generally, see H. M. Mendelsohn and H. T. Spetnagel, 'Entertainment: a Sociological Enterprise', Chap. 2 in P. H. Tannenbaum, ed., *The Entertainment Functions of Television* (Lawrence Erlbaum Associates, 1980); R. Williams, ibid., chap. 1, and 'Social Environment and Theatrical Environment' in his *Problems in Materialism* (London, New Left Books, 1980); J. L. Smith, *Melodrama* (London, Methuen, 1973).

18 D. Gomery, 'Writing the History of the American Film Industry: Warner Brothers and Sound', *Screen*, 17 (1976), and 'The Coming of the Talkies', in T. Balio, ed., *The American Film Industry* (University of Wisconsin Press, 1976). A very important article by Gomery appeared too late to be absorbed into the argument of the text: 'Economic Struggle and Hollywood Imperialism: Europe converts to Sound', *Yale French Studies*, 60 (1980). This shows (p. 82) that cinemas in England, Scotland and Wales converted to sound very rapidly: in 1929 22 per cent of cinemas in the United Kingdom were wired for sound; in 1930 the figure was 63 per cent.

19 E. Branigan, 'Color and Cinema', *Film Reader*, 4 (1979).

20 E. Buscombe, 'Notes on Columbia Pictures Corporation, 1926–1941', *Screen*, 16 (1975); T. Balio, *United Artists* (University of Wisconsin Press, 1976); C. Barr, *Ealing Studios* (Newton Abbott, David and Charles, London, Cameron and Tayleur, 1977); Perry and Wood, cited in note 3, are also relevant.

21 P. Kerr, 'Out of what Past? Notes on the B Film Noir', *Screen Education*, 32–33 (1979–80), pp. 50–51.

22 See, for example, Handel, *Hollywood audience*. P. Espinosa, 'The Audience in the Text', *Media, Culture and Society*, 4 (1982).

23 The point is made by C. Chaplin, 'Does the Public know what it wants?' *Adelphi*, January 1924, pp. 706 ff.; see also 'Flops' in D. Pirie, ed., *Anatomy of the Movies* (London, Windward, 1981).

24 V. Strauss (in *Harvard Business Review*, 1930), quoted as Table 1 in J. Woollacott, *Media Organizations 2: Hollywood, a Case Study* (Milton Keynes, Open University Press, 1977), p. 19. Apart from the texts cited in note 26, see J. Staiger and D. Gomery, 'The History of World Cinema', *Film Reader*, 4 (1979), J. Tunstall, *The Media are American* (London, Constable, 1977); D. Kellner, 'Network Television and American Society', *Theory and Society*, 10 (1981).

25 S. Rowson, 'A Statistical Survey of the Cinema Industry in Great Britain in 1934', *Journal of the Royal Statistical Society*, 99 (1936), Table XX, p. 105.

26 R. Manvell, *Film* (Harmondsworth, Penguin, 1946), rev. ed. after L. C. Rosten, *Hollywood* (New York, Harcourt Brace, 1941). The 'Big Five' were Paramount, Twentieth Century Fox, MGM, Warners and RKO, of which the first four took 95 per cent of all Hollywood profits in 1939.

27 M. Balcon and others, *Twenty Years of British Film* (London, Falcon Press, 1947), pp. 9, 82–3.

28 British Film Institute, *British Film Industry* (London, British Film Institute, 1981), pp. 2–3. See also V. Porter, 'British Film Culture and the European Community', *Sight and Sound* (Summer 1978; V. Porter, 'Film Policy for the 80s', *Sight and Sound* (Autumn 1979); J. Hill, 'Ideology, Economy and the British Cinema', in M. Barrett *et al.*, ed., *Ideology and Cultural Production* (London, 1979).

29 The list here is extensive: I have found useful C. L. Mowat, *Britain between the Wars* (London, Methuen, 1955); A. Calder, *The People's War* (London, Panther, 1971); P. Forster, 'J. Arthur Rank and the Silver Screen', in M. Sissons and P. French, ed., *Age of Austerity* (Harmondsworth, Penguin, 1964).

30 R. Manvell, *The Film and the Public* (Harmondsworth, Penguin, 1955), pp. 50 ff. See also M. Chanan, *The Dream that Kicks* (London, Routledge, 1980), Chaps. 13, 16.

31 I follow Atwell, *Cathedrals of the Movies*; Chanan, *The Dream*, and, as a good local study, P. Wild, 'Recreation in Rochdale, 1900–1940', in J. Clarke *et al.*, ed., *Working-class Culture* (London, Hutchinson, 1979). See also A. Field, *Picture Palace: a Social History of the Cinema* (London, Gentry Books, 1974) and the work of Mayer cited in note 65.

32 Atwell, *Cathedrals*, p. 38.

33 Chanan, *The Dream*, p. 234; Atwell, *Cathedrals*, pp. 5 ff.

34 Chanan, *The Dream*, pp. 228 ff. and all of Chap. 15.

35 Atwell, *Cathedrals* pp. 23, 6; Wild, 'Recreation in Rochdale', p. 143.

36 R. Manvell, *A Seat in the Cinema*, p. 21. *Picture Palace*, pp. 46–47, suggests that by 1916 'annual attendances had greatly overtopped the billion mark'.

37 Chanan, *The Dream*, pp. 258–9. A. H. Halsey, 'Leisure', in A. H. Halsey, ed., *Trends in British Society since 1900* (London, Macmillan, 1972), Table 16, 19, suggests a figure of 3500 cinemas in 1914.

38 S. Meacham, *A Life apart* (London, Thames and Hudson, 1977), pp. 17, 93; R. Roberts, *A Classic Slum* (Manchester, Manchester University Press, 1971), pp. 140–41.

39 Atwell, *Cathedrals* p. 50 (for 1921); Rowson, 'Statistical Survey', tables IV–VII; Halsey, 'Leisure', Table 16.19 (for 1926).

40 Rowson, 'Statistical Survey', Table V; Atwell, *Cathedrals*, p. 59.

41 Wild, 'Recreation in Rochdale', p. 157; Atwell, *Cathedrals*, passim, but especially pp. 157, 162; Manvell, *Film*.

42 Browning and Sorrell, 'Cinemas and Cinema-going; p. 153.

43 Montagu, *Film world*, Chap. 6.

44 British Film Institute, *British Film Industry*, p. 1. See also the Cinematograph Films Council Reports.

45 Atwell, *Cathedrals*, p. 168.

46 Chanan, *The Dream*, pp. 160 ff., 254 ff.; Atwell, *Cathedrals*, pp. 10, 18 ff.; Field, *Picture Palace*, pp. 18 ff.

47 Various disasters, involving children, preceded both the 1909 Act and, for example, the Cinematograph Regulations (SR & O, 1930: 361).

48 As amended and extended by the Cinematograph Films Acts of 1960 and 1970; see also Rowson, Statistical Survey, pp. 102 ff., V. Porter, 'End of the road for Quota?', *Sight and sound* (spring 1979).

49 Since amended by the Cinematograph Films Act (1975); From 26 January 1979 onwards, details of individual levy earnings have been made public in *Trade and Industry* (later *British Business*).

50 See also D. Macpherson, ed., *Traditions of Independence* (BFI, 1980) Part 2, and Montagu, *Film World*, chap. 8.

51 Apart from the sources mentioned above, the crucial texts are N. Pronay, 'The First Reality', in K. R. M. Short, ed., *Feature Films as History* (London, Croom Helm, 1981), and J. Richards, 'The British Board of Film Censors . . .', *Historical Journal of Film, Radio and Television*, 1 (1981) and 2 (1982).

52 The 1929 Local Government Act also gave additional administrative powers to County Councils.

53 Reprinted in N. M. Hunnings, *Film Censors and the Law* (London, Allen and Unwin, 1967), pp. 408–9.

54 The board alternated between 'rules' and 'exceptions'. I quote from the 1931 version taken from Pronay, p. 120; see his text for others.

55 Quoted by Manvell, *Film*, p. 173; a fuller extract from the same speech is given in Richards, 'British Board of Film Censors', p. 98. Of course these closures were never complete; seeing films like Dearden's *The Bells go down* (1943), Launder and Gilliat's *Waterloo* Road (1944) and Harry Watt's *Siege of Pinchgut* (1959) shows the limitations.

56 The figure for 1914 has been grossed up from Manvell, *A Seat in the Cinema*, p. 21; later figures are from Browning and Sorrell, 'Statistical Survey', or British Film Institute, *British Film Industry*. See also Patricia Perilli, this volume, p. 372.

57 The 1947–53 figures are from Briggs, *Sound and Vision* (Oxford, 1979), p. 240; 1955 and 1965 from Halsey, 'Leisure', Table 16.12; 1971–6 from *Social Trends*, 7, 1976, Table 10.20.

58 E. Buscombe, *Films on Television* (SEFT, 'Screen Pamphlets', 1, n.d.). See also T. Darvas, 'Old Films on Television', letter to *The Times*, 7 May 1981, p. 17; BARB ratings, *The Times*, 8 January 1982, for ratings for the December 1981 screening of *Gone with the Wind*. For the latter's cinema audience see Handel, *Hollywood*, p. 96; G. Morgan, *Red Roses every Night* (London, Quality Press, 1948), pp. 76–7; Pirie, *Movies*, pp. 204–5. In 1976 1200 films were shown on British television, the nearest European figure being 1008 for West Germany (*The Focus Report*, Appendix 6).

59 Manvell, 'The Cinema and the Public', p. 12; Social Survey, *The Cinema Audience* (NS 37b, 1943).

60 For television audiences see R. Silvey, *Who's listening?* (London, Allen and Unwin, 1974) and the work of B. P. Emmett and R. Silvey, also the BBC's *Annual Review of Audience Findings* (from 1973). For the United States see R. E. Frank and M. G. Greenberg, *The Public's Use of Television* (Sage, 1980).

61 P. Norton Shand, 1930, quoted in Atwell, *Cathedrals*, p. 176; O. Deutsch, 1937, quoted in ibid., p. 159; T. Komisarjevsky, quoted in ibid., p. 130. For American cinemas see M. F. Thorp, *America at the Movies* (London, Faber and Faber, 1946); D. Naylor, *American Picture Palaces* (Van Nostrand, 1981). Even a statistician recognizes the phenomenology involved (Rowson, 'Statistical Survey', p. 71, as does an entrepreneur S. Bernstein, 'Walk up! Walk up!! – please', in C. Davy, ed. *Footnotes to the Film*, Lovat Dickinson, 1937) and a writer E. Bowen, 'Why I go to the Cinema', in Davy. For an excellent phenomenology, written for the young, see A. Buchanan, *Going to the Cinema* (London, Phoenix House, 1947), Chap. 1.

62 Montagu, *Film World*, pp. 219 ff.

63 Manvell, *The Cinema and the Public*, p. 4; M. Hinxman, 'The Passing of the Picture Palace', *Daily Mail*, 10 April 1982, p. 6. On categorizing films and audiences see Manvell, *A Seat in the Cinema*, Chap. 3; the Bernstein surveys; the Cinema Advertising Association, *Cinema Audience Research* (Carrick James, 1980), Section 6.3. For a different view see Bowen, 'Why I go to the Cinema', pp. 214–6, and J. Mayer, *British Cinemas*, p. 239 and all of Pt. II.

64 See the statement by a 1970 graduate quoted in H. Saloman, *Interaction of Media, Cognition and Learning* (Jossey Brass, 1979), p. 117.

65 J. P. Mayer, *The Sociology of Film* (London, Faber and Faber, 1943); *British Cinemas and their Audiences* (Dobson, 1948).

66 Mayer, *British Cinemas*, p. 154, claims a readership of a million for this magazine. Of the 110 documents he used, 78 were from women and 32 from men.

67 Calder, *The People's War*, is excellent; see also Morgan, *Red Roses every Night*, especially pp. 67–77. Manvell (in Balcon *et al.*, *Twenty Years of British Film*) sees 1942–3 as the high point for English films with wartime subjects.

68 S. Chaneles, *Collecting Movie Memorabilia* (London, Arco, 1977); on 'Fan' magazines see Dyer, *Stars* (BFI, 1979); on 'star ratings' see the Bernstein surveys.

69 One analysis is N. Alexander, 'Frustrated, Lonely and Peculiar', in J. Sutro, *Diversion* (London, Max Parrish, 1950), pp. 70–78. Only 20 per cent of the letters to Richard Attenborough, mentioned by Sutro, were from men.

70 This information is widely scattered; see the extensive bibliography (pp. 229–366) in I. C. Jarvie, *Towards a Sociology of the Cinema* (London, Routledge, 1970).

71 Sidney Bernstein started these surveys in 1928; the British Film Institute library holds those for 1934 and 1937; Morgan, *Red Roses every Night*, Appendix A, gives that for 1946–7.

72 Manvell, *Film*, p. 154(n) and *Marketing Trends* (1963, Pt IV, pp. 38 ff.

73 Bernstein, 'Walk up! Walk up!! – please', p. 225.

74 Marketing Trends (1963).

75 *Patterns of British life* (London, Hulton Press, 1950). Section 12 is based on a survey of 13,000 adults in 1949.

76 Browning and Sorrell, 'Statistical Survey', p. 165. Their comments on television were criticized by L. T. Wilkins *et al.*, pp. 166 ff.

77 Rowson, 'Cinema Industry'; Social Survey, *The Cinema Audience* (1943), Table 11. See also Social Survey, *The Cinema and the Public* (1946); Gallup Poll, *The Cinema Habits of the British* (n.d., [1948?], typescripts in the British Film Institute book library); Browning and Sorrell, 'Stat-

istical Survey', pp. 148 ff.; Screen Advertising Association, *The Cinema Audience* (1960); P. Houston, 'Looking for an Audience', p. 174.
78 Rowson, 'Cinema Industry', pp. 79 ff.
79 Browning and Sorrell, 'Statistical Survey'.
80 *Marketing Trends* (1963).
81 I.P.A. Readership surveys, 1966.
82 *Marketing Trends* (1963), Pt. IV, pp. 20 ff. The categories of class employed in such social surveys are drawn from those of the Registrar General: AB indicates securely upper- or upper-middle class; C categories of non-manual workers and manual workers with skills; DE, the remainder.
83 Pearl and Dean Ltd, The West End Cinemagoer, (1971).
84 *Cinema Audience Research* (London, Carrick James, 1980), vol. 2. This volume is full of important differentiating statistics.
85 JICNAR survey for 1976, quoted in *Variety*, republished in *The Focus Report*, Appendix 12.
86 *Marketing Trends* (1963), Pt. III, Chart 3.
87 Social Survey, 1943, Pt. II, Table 12.
88 See also R. Low 'The Implications behind the Social Survey,' *Penguin Film Review*, 7, 1948, pp. 107–2.
89 *Marketing Trends* (1963), Pt. III, Chart 2.
90 Social Survey, 1943, Table 2 and Table 23. See also the Gallup survey for 1948 and compare Gallup's findings for 1963, 1966, 1970 and 1976.
91 Bernstein surveys, 1928–47; *Cinema Audience Research*, vol. 2.
92 P. Harcourt, *Movies and Mythologies* (Canadian Broadcasting Corporation, 1977), pp. 95 ff. See also R. Samuel's articles on the Social Democratic Party, *New Society*, 22 and 29 April 1982 and my letter in the same magazine, 18 May 1982.
93 Social Survey, 1943.
94 Low, the 'Implications behind the Social Survey', p. 109.
95 *Patterns of British Life*.
96 Screen Advertising Association, 1960, 1961.
97 *Marketing Trends* (1963); IPA, 1966.
98 *Focus Report* (1978), Appendix 12.
99 Pearl and Dean Ltd, *The West End Cinemagoer* (1971), Table 5.
100 *Cinema Audience Research* (1980), vol 2.
101 Dyer, *Stars*, p. 182.

Chapter 3

1 Peter Bachlin, *Histoire Economique du Cinéma* (Paris 1947).
2 *Kine Weekly*, April 1919.
3 George Orwell, *The Road to Wigan Pier* (London 1938).
4 See, for example, Armand Mattelart, *Multinationals and the Control of*

Culture (Brighton Harvester Press, 1979). The point is discussed in Michael Chanan's forthcoming history of cinema in Cuba.

5 Bachlin, *Histoire Economique du Cinéma* p. 12.
6 A. C. Bromhead 'Reminiscences of the British Film Trade', *Proceedings of the British Kinematograph Society*, No. 21 (11 December 1933).
7 Cecil Hepworth, *Came the Dawn, Memoirs of a Film Pioneer*, (London, Phoenix House, 1951).
8 See Michael Chanan, *The Dream that Kicks* (London, 1980), p. 245.
9 Bachlin, *Historie Economique du Cinéma*, p. 21.
10 Rachael Low, *The History of the British Film* (London, Allen & Unwin, 1948), Vol. 2.
11 *Bioscope*, 18 March 1920.
12 *Bioscope*, 20 November 1908.
13 Moyne Report, 1936, para 17.
14 Politics and Economic Planning, *The British Film Industry* (London, Political and Economic Planning, 1952), p. 38.
15 Adrian Brunel, *Nice Work* (London, Forbes Robertson, 1949).
16 Low, *The History of the British Film*, London, 1970), p. 50).
17 *Kinematograph Year Book* (1925), p. 15.
18 Thomas H. Guback, *The International Film Industry* (Bloomington, Indiana University Press, 1969), pp. 7–8.
19 Sidney R. Kent, 'Distributing the Product' in J. P. Kennedy, ed., *The Story of the Film* (Chicago, A. W. Shaw & Co., 1927), pp. 225–6.
20 *Report on Market for Cinematograph Films in Cuba*, furnished by His Majesty's Consul General in Havana, 13 March 1923 (typescript, library of the British Film Institute, London).
21 Isidore Ostrer, *The Conquest of Gold* (London, Cape, 1932).
22 Paul Rotha, *Documentary Diary* (London, Secker and Warburg, 1973), p. 44.

Chapter 4

1 *Hansard*, vol. 185, col. 2084 (HMSO, 1925).
2 F. D. Klingender and Stuart Legg, *Money Behind the Screen* (London, Lawrence and Wishart, 1937), pp. 19–20.
3 *Minutes of Evidence*, Committee on Cinematograph Films (HMSO, 1936), p. 1.
4 Klingender and Legg, *Money Behind the Screen*, p. 13.

Chapter 5

1 Board of Trade figures.
2 *Documentary News Letter*, no 2, 1944, p. 14.

3   Board of Trade files, BT 64 95 2974, January 1943.
4   Board of Trade, *Tendencies to Monopoly in the Cinematograph Industry*: report of a committee appointed by the Cinematograph Films Council, Chairman Albert Palache (HMSO, 1944).
5   Ibid., para 60.
6   Ibid., para 65.
7   Ibid., para 81.
8   Ibid., para 7.
9   'A State Film Industry?' *Cine Technician*, May/June 1941.
10 Paul Rotha, *The Government and the Film Industry (1945)*, reprinted in Paul Rotha, *Rotha on the Film* (London, Faber and Faber, 1958).
11 Ralph Bond, *Monopoly: The Future of British Films* (London, Association of Cinematograph Technicians, 1946).
12 F. Mullally, *Films; An Alternative to Rank, an Analysis of Power and Policy in the Film Industry* (London, Socialist Book Centre, 1946).
13 Board of Trade, Cinematograph Films Council, *Recommendations of the Cinematograph Films Council for New Legislation on Cinematograph Films* (1947).
14 The Cinematograph Films Act (1948).
15 Board of Trade, *Report of the Film Studio Committee*, Chairman, G. H. Gater (1948).
16 Board of Trade, *Report of the Working Party on Film Production Costs* Chairman Sir George Gater (1949).
17 Board of Trade, *Distribution and Exhibition of Cinematograph Films*: Report of the Committee of Enquiry appointed by the President of the Board of Trade, Chairman Rt. Hon. Viscount Portal, succeeded by Professor Arnold Plant, Cmnd 7837 (1949).
18 Political and Economic Planning, *The British Film Industry* (London, 1952).
19 Cinematograph Film Production (Special Loans) Act (1949).
20 Paul Rotha, 'A Plan for British Films', *Leader*, November 1949; reprinted in *Rotha on the Film*.
21 See the interview with Wilson in *Screen*. Vol 22, No. 3, 1981, pp. 9–22.
22 Figures from Board of Trade, *Tendencies to Monopoly in the Cinematograph Industry*; Monopolies Commission, *Films, A Report on the Supply of Films for Exhibition in Cinemas*, H.C. 206 (1966); Economic Intelligence Unit Retail Business 177. *The Cinema Industry* (November 1972).
23 Figures from Political and Economic Planning and from Association of Cinematograph Television and Allied Technicians *Nationalising the Film Industry* (1973).
24 National Film Finance Corporation (NFFC), Cmnd 4402, p. 5, para 17, 1970.
25 See Monopolies Commission, 1966.
26 See, for instance, NFFC, Annual Report, 1966, Cmnd 3066, p. 6.

27 *The Future of the British Film Industry*: (1976), p. 8. Report of the Prime
   Minister's Working Party. Chairman: John Terry. London: HMSO
   1976 (Comnd 6372). Terms of Reference p. 8.
28 ibid. Terms of Reference p. 2.
29 ibid.
30 Proposals for the setting up of a British Film Authority: Report of the
   Interim Action Committee on the Film Industry. Chairman: Sir Harold
   Wilson. London: HMSO 1978 (Comnd 7071).

Chapter 6

1 Forsyth Hardy, ed., *Grierson on Documentary* (London, Faber and Faber
  1946), p. 78.
2 Forsyth Hardy, *John Grierson, A Documentary Biography* (London,
  Faber and Faber, 1979).
3 Hardy, ed., *Grierson on Documentary*, p. 78.
4 Ibid., p. 149.
5 Hardy, *John Grierson*, p. 42.
6 Hardy, ed., *Grierson on Documentary*, p. 35.
7 Ibid.
8 Ibid., p. 49.
9 Ibid.
10 Ibid.
11 Ibid., p. 172.
12 Ibid.
13 Ibid.
14 Ibid.
15 Ibid.
16 Paul Rotha, *Documentary Diary* (London, Secker and Warburg, 1973),
   p. 125.
17 Rotha, p. 155.
18 Rotha, p. 157.
19 Ibid.
20 Hardy, ed., *Grierson on Documentary*, p. 48.
21 Elizabeth Sussex, *The Rise and Fall of the British Documentary* (London,
   University of California Press, 1975), p. 15.
22 Sussex, p. 77.
23 Hardy, *John Grierson*, p. 80.
24 Sussex, p. 1.
25 Hardy, ed., *Grierson on Documentary*, p. 49.
26 Hardy, ed., *Grierson on Documentary*, p. 49.
26 Sussex, p. 60.
27 Ibid.
28 Ibid., p. 9.

29 Eva Orbanz, ed., *Journey to a Legend and Back – the British Realistic Film* (Berlin, Verlag Volker Spess, 1977) p. 78.

30 Sussex, p. 29,

31 Sussex, p. 9.

32 Sussex, p. 50.

33 Hardy, ed., *Grierson on Documentary*, p. 36.

34 Ibid., p. 37.

35 Ibid.

36 Ibid., p. 36.

37 Ibid., p. 41.

38 Ibid.

39 Ibid., p. 42.

40 Ibid., p. 43.

40 Ibid., p. 43.

41 Sussex, p. 19.

42 Obituary on Tom Harrison in *The Times*.

43 Hardy, ed., *Grierson on Documentary*, p. 32.

44 Sussex, p. 110.

45 Orbanz, ed., p. 124.

46 Sussex, p. 101.

47 For a fuller discussion see Ryan in this volume.

48 Hardy, *John Grierson*, p. 93.

49 Ibid., p. 112.

50 Roger Manvell, *Films and the Second World War* (London, Dent, 1974), p. 77.

51 Ibid.

52 For a discussion of the production relations of the EMB and GPO Film Units to their respective organizations, to the Treasury and to the film industry, see Annette Kuhn, ' "Independent" Film-making and the State in the 1930s'. *Edinburgh '77 Magazine*, No. 2, 'History Production Memory'. Here she suggests that 'a measure of "independence" came from being outside the industry, so that the commercial criteria of cost-effectiveness did not determine relations of production . . . [and that] the organizational character of the film unit system . . . ensured that production work was carried on without immediate determination from the sponsor, the State'.

Chapter 7

1 See the record of a meeting of the Labour Party Press Department, 'Film Propaganda', *Labour Party National Executive Committee Minutes* 18 December 1919; also a circular issued by the party, 'Labour Cinema Propaganda', ibid., March 1920. The question of film was reconsidered in 1928. See Research and Publicity Committee, ibid., 25 September

1928, 17 December 1928. For the Workers' Inter-national Relief, see *Soviet Russia Pictorial*, no. 4, August 1924, p. 11.

2   *Close Up*, November 1929, p. 438.

3   Alfred Williams, interview with Seona Robertson. The recorded interview can be consulted at 'Manchester Studies', Manchester Polytechnic.

4   See, for example, 'Regulations for Bureaus for the Directing of Educational Work, Initiated by the Trades Councils of Revolutionary Trade Union Organizations', *Trade Union Propaganda and Cultural Work*, no. 1, October 1928, pp. 2–3. This journal was the bulletin of the Agitprop Department of the Red International of Labour Unions.

5   See 'Tasks of the Communist Party of Great Britain. The 10th Plenum and the International Situation', *Communist Review*, September 1929, pp. 532–4. A communist organization which played a key role in this propaganda work was the Friends of Soviet Russia, which started showing films publicizing the USSR in October 1928.

6   *Manchester Guardian*, 4 April 1932, referring to a statement by the Council of the Federation in the second issue of *The Workers' Cinema*, the official bulletin of the FWFS. No copies of this bulletin are known to have survived.

7   R. Bond, 'Workers' Films: Past and Future', *Labour Monthly*, January 1975, p. 29.

8   For a comprehensive account of the legal and administrative development of censorship in Britain, see N. M. Hunnings, *Film Censors and the Law* (London, Allen and Unwin, 1967).

9   See 'First Steps Towards a Workers' Film Movement', *Close Up*, January 1930, pp. 66–9.

10 For some members of the Federation there were even greater restrictions. The difficulties encountered by workers' film societies in satisfying the requirements of local licensing authorities are revealed in the wrangle between the London County Council and the Independent Labour Party's Masses Stage and Film Guild. See, 'Report of the Theatres and Music Halls Committee', *London County Council. Minutes of Proceedings*, 11 March 1930, 14 May, 17 and 28 October 1930; 'Sunday Cinematograph Exhibitions – The Masses Stage and Film Guild – Application for Permission to give Cinematograph Exhibitions on Sunday Afternoons', *London County Council. Verbatim Reports*, 11 March 1930.

11 Under the terms of the Cinematograph Act of 1909 such premises could be used 'occasionally and exceptionally', but not for more than six days in any one year, and local licensing authorities were empowered to attach appropriate conditions to this category of exhibition.

12 Descriptions of these films are provided in B. Hogenkamp, 'Workers' Newsreels in the 1920's and 1930's', *Our History* (pamphlet), no. 68 (1977), and R. Bond, 'The Production of Working Class Films', *Experimental Cinema*, no. 4 (February 1933), p. 42.

13 *Turksib*, according to one report, was shown in over 200 different cinemas: see D. Knowles, *The Censor, the Drama, and the Film, 1900–1934* (London, Allen and Unwin, 1934), pp. 213–14.

14 See 'Control of Cinematograph Exhibitions in England and Wales. Summary of Replies to a Questionnaire Addressed from the Home Office in February 1931, to all Licensing Authorities,' *British Board of Film Censors Verbatim Reports* (n.d. [1931]).

15 The available prints of *Soviet Russia: Past and Present* quickly became unusable, due as much to careless handling as to constant use.

16 Kino Films, *First Annual Report*, 1936. *Battleship Potemkin*, for example, would have cost approximately £25 to import and £40 to print on 16mm film (pre-war values), apart from any distribution rights payable.

17 As a direct result of Kino's activities attempts were made by the Home Office to introduce amending legislation, bringing 16mm film within existing censorship regulations. Both police and licensing authorities were particularly vigilant and were quite prepared to prevent shows from taking place by intimidation, or, failing that, to interrupt them by conducting 'inflammability' tests. While the Home Office gradually adopted a less alarmist view, these practices continued. See the numerous files on the subject in *Home Office Papers*, Public Record Office, HO 45 17067/671873 and 17068/671873. Correspondence in the files of the National Council for Civil Liberties is also very revealing.

18 A meeting on Spain, for example, was held in Manchester, during which *China Strikes Back* was shown specifically to raise funds for Spanish Relief (*Daily Worker*, 12 February 1938, p. 6).

19 *Daily Worker*, 5 August 1939, p. 3.

20 The League's activities were not confined to the labour movement however: it had strong connections with the amateur film movement generally, and sought both to provide 'progressive' material for cine groups and to establish links between these groups and sections of the labour movement which were keen to use film.

21 David Brotmacher (formerly the League's treasurer) in conversation with the author, 16 November 1977.

22 'Minutes of Meeting of New Production Unit', 26 October 1938, Film and Photo League Collection (hereafter, FPL); *Amateur Cine World*, January 1939, p. 544.

23 Workers' Film and Photo League, circular to members, n.d. [June 1935], FPL; circular to members, 28 February 1936, ibid.

24 *Leftfilmfront*, no. 1, July 1937, p. 2; *Left News*, June 1937, p. 392, August 1937, pp. 479–80.

25 H. Cuthbertson to Sol Freedman, 19 July 1938, FPL.

26 H. Cuthbertson to Mrs Sinker, 14 May [1938], ibid.

27 I. Montagu, interview with the author, 14 April 1978.

28 I. Montagu, letter to the author, 6 May 1979; *Daily Worker*, 28 February 1935, p. 2.
29 Most of the independents of course used circuit material. For details of the cinema industry see S. Rowson, 'A Statistical Survey of the Cinema Industry in Great Britain in 1934', *Journal of the Royal Statistical Society*, vol. 99 (1936) (hereafter, 'Statistical Survey'); H. E. Browning, A. A. Sorrell, 'Cinemas and Cinema-Going in Great Britain', ibid., vol. 117 (1954).
30 The Tatler Theatre in Leeds, for example, showed many PFI films. It gave the first public performance in Britain of Luis Bunuel's *Land Without Bread* (original title, *Las Hurdes*), showing the film for a week in March 1938.
31 Herbert Marshall, interview with the author, 24 May 1978. Marshall was involved at various times with the PFI, Kino and the Workers' Film and Photo League.
32 *Reynolds News*, 8 May 1938, p. 1; H. Marshall, interview with the author. See also I. Montagu, interview with P. Wollen *et al.*, *Screen*, (13) no. 3, winter 1972, p. 90.
33 For details of the committee and Muenzenberg, see A. Koestler, *The Invisible Writing* (London, 1954), pp. 194 ff; C. H. Rolph, *Kingsley: The Life, Letters and Diaries of Kingsley Martin* (London, 1978), pp. 193–4; B. Gross, *Willi Muenzenberg: A Political Biography* (Michigan, 1974), pp. 235 ff.
34 I. Montagu, interview with the author. See I. Montagu's letter in *Sight and Sound*, 49, no. 2 (spring 1980), pp. 130–31.
35 For accounts by various member of these expeditions, see I. Montagu, interview with B. Hogenkamp, *Skrien*, no. 51 July/August 1975; S. Cole, 'Shooting in Spain', *Cine Technician*, May–June 1938, pp. 1–2; A. E. Graham, 'Pictures in War-time', ibid., July–August 1938, pp. 56–8; T. Dickinson, 'Experiences in the Spanish Civil War, 1938', notes written in 1976 at the request of the Archivio Nazionale Cinematografico della Resistanza, Turin.
36 B. Megarry, interview with the author, 22 September 1977. Mr Megarry was a member of the PFI and at various times worked for Kino.
37 I. Montagu, interview with the author.
38 *International Peace Campaign*, October 1936, pp. 8, 12; February 1937, p. 15, June 1937, p. 19; Frank Jackson, 'A People's Cinema Grows', *Daily Worker*, 9 August 1938, p. 2. Jackson was a key member of Kino.
39 V. Gollancz, 'The Left Book Club – Its Past and Future', *Daily Worker*, 28 January 1938, p. 2; *Left News*, September 1938, p. 981, April 1939, p. 1220.
40 *Daily Worker*, 12 January 1938, p. 2; *Left Review*, March 1938, pp. 857–9.
41 See, for example, F. Jackson's letter in the *Daily Worker*, 4 January 1939, p. 2.

42 This 'informal' world has been briefly sketched by Aluṅ Howkins in 'Class Against Class: The Political Culture of the Communist Party of Great Britain 1930–35', in F. Gloversmith, ed., *Class, Culture and Social Change: A New View of the 1930's* (Hassocks 1981).

43 A Kino school, for example, was held at High Beech, Epping Forest, in July 1934, and lectures were given by Herbert Marshall (*Daily Worker*, 11 July 1934, p. 4). See also *Cinema Quarterly*, winter 1934–5, p. 127.

44 See *Kino News*, no. 2, n.d. [May 1936]; 'Can Twenty Million People Be Fooled?', *Daily Worker*, 11 June 1936, p. 4. Issues of *Kino News* appear to have been published at least until the end of 1937, but unfortunately only the first two are known to have survived.

45 'The New Road to Progress', *Kino News*, no. 1 (winter 1935); ibid., no. 2 (May 1936).

46 Basil Burton, Memorandum, 'Popular Film Societies and Associations', 9 February 1938. Burton was Kino's dynamic chairman. Copies of this and other Kino documents were kindly given to the author by Herbert Marshall. *La Marseillaise* was released in France in January 1938: for details of its production, see G. Fofi, 'The Cinema of the Popular Front in France, 1934–38', *Screen*, winter 1972–3, pp. 35–7.

47 Nottingham Labour Party, for example, produced a forty-minute silent film in 1934 about which virtually nothing is known.

48 An interesting collection of such films is to be found in the film archive of 'Manchester Studies', Manchester Polytechnic.

49 Workers' Film Association, *Annual Report*, 1939.

50 S. Rowson, 'Statistical Survey', *Journal of the Royal Statistical Society*, op. cit., p. 73.

51 'Memorandum of Evidence to be submitted to the Cinematograph Advisory Committee to the Home Office on the subject of sub-standard films, by Messrs Kino Films (1935) Ltd, and Progressive Film Institute Ltd', submitted to the committee, 3 February 1939, *Home Office Papers*, PRO HO 45 21109/695383/67 (hereafter, 'Memorandum of Evidence').

52 Kino Films, *Annual Report*, 1936.

53 *Report of the Fourteenth Congress of the Communist Party of Great Britain: It Can Be Done*, 1937, p. 251. Advertisements in the left-wing press suggest that this was not an exaggerated claim. The experience of one Communist Party district organizer gives an indication of the level of local party involvement in the showing of this and many other Kino films. See D. Hyde, *I Believed: The Autobiography of a Former British Communist* (London 1952), p. 58.

54 See, for example, *Daily Worker*, 26 October 1935, p. 6; *Left News*, November 1938, p. 1053, January 1939, p. 1136.

55 These estimates are based on information in Kino's *Annual Report*, 1936; on 'Kino Films Ltd, Statement of Accounts as at 4th March 1936', *FPL*; and on the two surviving issues of *Kino News*.

56 'Memorandum of Evidence' *Home Office Papers*, op. cit.

57 J. Reeves, *Film And Education* (Stoke 1937), p. 3. Reeves was a leading figure in the London labour movement.

58 See S. Rowson, 'Statistical Survey', *Journal of the Royal Statistical Society*, op. cit., p. 70.

59 D. Sharp, *The Picture Palace and other Buildings for the Movies* (London 1969), pp. 140–43. Examples of this type of cinema are the Dreamland, Margate, and the Gaumont, Bradford.

60 'The Position of British Films', *Trades Union Congress*, 1936, p. 221; *Plebs*, September 1934, pp. 193–4.

61 See W. W. Hill, presidential address to the Annual Conference of the National Union of Teachers, cited in *The Times*, 9 April 1928, p. 16; Memorandum of the TUC Trades Councils' Joint Consultative Committee, 'Trades Councils – Their Industrial Functions and Activities', 17 November 1936, reproduced in the *Report of the Annual Conference of Trades Councils*, 1937, pp. 27–30.

62 See, for example, the views of Gary Allighan, the Independent Labour Party's film critic, writing under the pen-name 'Benn', 'The Cinema as an Instrument of Class Rule', *Plebs*, April 1931, pp. 90–91.

63 See R. Bond, 'Labour and the Cinema', ibid., August 1931, p. 186; I. Montagu, 'Their Films and Ours', *New Red Stage*, June–July 1932, p. 5; F. Jackson, *Left Review*, December 1937, pp. 679–81.

64 Compare Harold Laski, *Democracy in Crisis* (London 1933), p. 74, with Harry Pollitt, *Report of the Fifteenth Congress of the Communist Party of Great Britain*, 1938, pp. 86–7.

65 See 'Benn', 'Why Not a Socialist Newsreel?', *New Leader*, 31 May 1929, p. 2; R. Bond, 'Labour and the Cinema', *Plebs*, August 1931, p. 186.

66 Despite the Soviet and German connections of Montagu, Bond and Marshall, the aesthetic debates raging in Germany and the Soviet Union prior to 1933 made little impression in Britain, in keeping with the insular, empiricist intellectual tradition in this country.

67 These themes are explored in the following: S. Hall, 'The Social Eye of Picture Post', *Working Papers in Cultural Studies*, no. 2 (spring 1972); S. Hynes, *The Auden Generation: Literature and Politics in England in the 1930's* (New York 1977); D. Mellor, 'Patterns of Naturalism: Hoppé to Hardy', *The Real Thing: An Anthology of British Photographs 1840–1950* (London 1975); D. Macpherson, 'Nation, Mandate, Memory', *Camerawork*, September 1978.

68 This influence was apparent in other areas of activity. See, for example, H. Gustav Klaus, 'Socialist Fiction in the 1930's: Some Preliminary Observations', in J. Lucas, ed., *The 1930's: A Challenge to Orthodoxy* (Hassocks 1978).

69 See, for example, 'M.B.', letter in *Daily Worker*, 10 September 1938, p. 7. Herbert Marshall, in an interview with the author, voiced similar complaints.

Bibliography

For further details of the labour film groups discussed in this chapter, and of others active during the 1929–39 period, the following should be consulted:

B. Hogenkamp, 'Film and the Workers' Movement in Great Britain, 1929–1939', *Sight and Sound*, 45, no. 2 (spring 1976).

'Workers' Newsreels in the 1920's and 1930's', *Our History*, no. 68 (1977).

V. Wegg-Prosser, 'The Archive of the Film and Photo League', *Sight and Sound*, 46, no. 4, (autumn 1977).

T. Dennett, 'England: The [Workers'] Film and Photo League', in T. Dennett and J. Spence, eds., *Photography/Politics: One* (London 1979).

T. Ryan, 'Film and Political Organizations in Britain, 1929–39', in D. Macpherson, ed., *Traditions of Independence: British Cinema in the Thirties* (London, British Film Institute, 1980).

P. Marris, 'Politics and "Independent" Films in the Decade of Defeat', in D. Macpherson, ed., *Traditions of Independence*.

Details of most of the films handled by these film groups can be found in a filmography, compiled by the present author, in D. Macpherson, ed., *Traditions of Independence*.

Chapter 8

1 R. Donald, 'Films And The Empire', *Nineteenth Century*, C, p. 596 (October 1926), p. 497.

2 'Minority Report by Sir Hesketh Bell', *Report of the Colonial Films Committee*, Cmd 3630 (London 1930), p. 24.

3 See R. Smyth, 'The Development of British Colonial Film Policy, 1927–1939, With Special Reference To East And Central Africa', *Journal of African History*, 20, 3 (1979), pp. 437–50.

4 Public Record Office, Kew: C.O. 323/990/26096, L. S. Amery, 8 January 1927.

5 Appendix XVIII, 'Cinematograph Films (A) Memorandum prepared in the Colonial Office', *Colonial Office Conference, May 1927. Summary of Proceedings and Appendices*, Cmnd 2883–4 (London 1927), pp. 243–44.

6 H. Vischer, 'The Educational Use of Cinematograph Films', Annex I, *Colonial Office Conference, May 1927, Summary of Proceedings*, p. 28.

7 C.O. 323/1252/30125/1, J. S. Huxley, 'Report on the Use of Films for Educational Purposes in East Africa' (1930), p. 4.

8 See Smyth, op. cit. p. 441.

9 J. Merle Davis, *Modern Industry and the African: An Enquiry into the Effect of the Copper Mines of Central Africa upon Native Society and the Work of the Christian Missions* (London 1933).

10 L. A. Notcutt and G. C. Latham, *The African and the Cinema* (London 1937), p. 183.

11 Ibid., pp. 103–4.

12 In 1931 the open-air native compound cinema at Luanshya had an average weekly attendance of 2000; the open-air cinema at Nchanga, 1200. C.O. 323/1122/80160/2, enclosure in Maxwell to Cunliffe-Lister, 20 November 1931.

13 Zambia National Archives, Lusaka: SEC/E/7, vol. III, 'Report of Central Advisory Board on Native Education, N. Rhodesia, 1937', p. 8.

14 Public Record Office, Kew: INF. 1/200 F/237, C. Eastwood to A. G. Highet, 4 December 1939. The Colonial Marketing Board, founded in 1937, ceased to function in 1939, and responsibility for *Men of Africa* was taken over by the Ministry of Information in consultation with the Colonial Office.

15 From the sound track of *Men of Africa* (copy at Imperial War Museum, London), and from the script in INF. 1/200 F/237.

16 *Palaver*, made in Northern Nigeria by British Instructional Films, was about the vicissitudes in the life of a District Officer. See N. Barkas, *Behind the Camera* (London 1934). *Sanders of the River*, a London Films Production, was a hymn of praise to the wise rule of the British official, Sanders: Paul Robeson, playing a collaborating chief, sings of 'Sandy the Strong, Sandy the Wise, Righter of wrongs, Hater of lies'. See J. Koyinde Vaughan, 'Africa and the Cinema', in Langston Hughes, ed., *An African Treasury* (New York 1960), p. 87. *Rhodes of Africa*, a Gaumont-British film, glorified the empire-builder. See N. Barkas, *Thirty Thousand Miles for the Films* (London 1937) and M. Perham, ed., *Ten Africans* (London 1936), pp. 63–64, 76–79 and pictures.

17 See W. Sellers, 'Making Films in and for the Colonies', *Journal of the Royal Society of Arts*, 101, 1952–3, pp. 829–37; also G. Pearson, 'The Making of Films for Illiterates in Africa', *The Film in Colonial Development; a Report of a Conference* (London, British Film Institute, 1948), pp. 22–27.

18 The title used by Stephen Tallents for his pamphlet, *The Projection of England* (London 1932), in which he urged the use of the film in a national advertising campaign.

19 *Mass Education in African Society* (London, HMSO, 1944), Col. no. 186, pp. 40–46.

20 For example, *Education in England, Blind People, The Story of Cotton*.

21 'Films for East African Soldiers', *Colonial Cinema*, 4, 2 (1946), pp. 30–35.

22 'The Instructional Film In The United Kingdom Dependencies', COI. No. R. 3161 (October 1955).

23 Rhodes House, Oxford: MSS. AFR. s 1159, 'An Experiment in Mass Education: Nyasaland and Northern Rhodesian Tour of the East Africa

Command Mobile Propaganda Unit', Captain A. Dickson, March 1944.

24 W. V. Brelsford, 'Analysis of African Reaction to Propaganda Film', *NADA: The Southern Rhodesia Native Affairs Department Annual*, no. 24 (1947), p. 21.

25 Personal communication from Louis Nell (Harare, Zimbabwe, 8 January 1981). Nell joined the Northern Rhodesian Information Office to produce films for Africans in 1943. In 1948 he joined the Central African Film Unit.

26 *Colonial Cinema*, 1, 2 (1942) p. 3.

27 Mass Education in African Society, op. cit, pp. 45–46.

28 Examples of films considered by the Kenya censorship board to be unsuitable for African exhibition in 1940–41 included: *Gone with the Wind, Return of the Scarlet Pimpernel, Son of Frankenstein, Blackmail, Angels with Dirty Faces, The Four Just Men, The Last Train from Madrid, Murder in the Museum, The Oklahoma Kid, North West Frontier* and *The Four Feathers*; and the following films in which white women appeared in 'undignified' roles: *Naughty but Nice, Girl in a Taxi, Love and Kisses, Glamorous Night* and *Bachelor Mother*. Northern Rhodesia followed the ruling of the Kenya censors at this time (ZNA, SEC/NAT/368, Chairman of Nairobi Film Censorship Board). In 1948 Northern Rhodesia indicated that it banned all scenes in films which had: '(a) Women in scanty attire, including bathing costumes. (b) Undue exhibition of parts of the naked body. (c) Women of easy virtue. (d) Manhandling of women. (e) Prolonged embraces. (f) Fights between women' (ZNA, SEC/NAT/368, W. V. Brelsford, Acting Director of Information Department, 17 June 1948).

29 T. Dickinson, 'Making a Film in Tanganyika Territory', in P. Noble, ed., *The British Film Yearbook 1947–48* (London 1948). The story was developed from an idea of E. Arnot Robertson, of the MOI Films Division and Noel Sabine, of the Colonial Office public relations branch. The dialogue was by Joyce Carey, author of *The African Witch*.

30 J. Koyinde Vaughan, 'Africa and the Cinema', in L. Hughes, ed., *An African Treasury*, p. 88. In 1943 the West African Students' Union in Britain (WASU) took exception to the filming of *Men of Two Worlds* because of this characterization of the witch doctor, which they found 'unrealistic' and 'harmful'. PRO, C.O. 875/17/9105/4, L. Solanke, Sec. Gen. WASU to Under Secretary of State for the Colonies, 11 September 1943.

31 'The Instructional Film In The United Kingdom Dependencies'.

32 G. Pearson, 'The Making of Films for Illiterates in Africa', p. 26.

33 N. F. Spurr, 'Some Aspects of the Work of the Colonial Film Unit in West and East Africa', *Visual Aids in Fundamental Education* (Paris, UNESCO, 1952), p. 37.

34 Editorial, *Colonial Cinema*, 8, 2 (1950), pp. 27–28.

35 *Fifth Report from the Select Committee on Estimates* (HMSO, 1950), John Grierson, 15 June 1950 (evidence).

36 C. Y. Carstairs, 'The Colonial Cinema', talk given at the International Conference, 'New Directions in Documentary Films', Edinburgh Festival, 1952, *Corona*, 5, 2 (1953), p. 54.

37 'Showing Films in the Villages', *Colonial Cinema*, 6, 3 (1948), p. 63.

38 C.O. 875/08988, Northern Rhodesian analysis of answers to CFU questionnaire, 1943.

39 P. Morton-Williams, *Cinema in Rural Nigeria: A Field Study of the Impact of Fundamental-Education Films on Rural Audiences in Nigeria* (Ibadan n.d. 1953), p. 46.

40 Ibid, pp. 38–47.

41 W. Sellers, 'The Production and Use of Films for Public Informational and Educational Purposes in British African Territories', *Rencontres internationales: Le cinéma et l'Afrique au Sud du Sahara*, Brussels Exhibition, 1958, pp. 36–38.

42 F. Aig-Imoukhuede, 'The Film and Television in Nigeria', *Présence Africaine*, 30, 58 (1966), p. 89.

43 'The Instructional Film In The United Kingdom Dependencies'.

44 Ibid.

45 See H. Franklin, *The Saucepan Special: The Poor Man's Radio for Rural Populations* (Lusaka 1950).

46 ZNA, Central African Film Unit Report for 1954.

47 *Fifth Report from the Select Committee on Estimates* (HMSO, 1950), Annex 16, 'Memorandum by the Colonial Office', p. 230. See also *Overseas Information Services*, Cmnd 685 (HMSO, 1959), p. 3.

48 Colonial Office, *The Colonial Territories 1952–1953*, Cmd 8856. (HMSO, 1953), p. 76.

49 After the Second World War community development and fundamental education became more fashionable terms for what had previously been designated mass education.

50 *Corona*, 1, 7, 1949, p. 36.

51 See K. W. Blackburne, 'Colonial Office Information Department', *East Africa and Rhodesia*, 18 December 1947.

52 'Film and Television in Africa', *World Screen*, 4, 1 (1962), p. 29.

53 *Fifth Report from the Select Committee on Estimates*, Annex 16 'Memorandum by the Colonial Office', 231; Alan Izod, 'History of the Central African Film Unit', July 1960 (unpublished MSS.); 'The Development of Broadcasting in the United Kingdom Dependencies', COI, No. R. 2644, 31 July 1953.

54 See *Rencontres internationales*; Vaughan, 'Africa and the Cinema'; S. Feldman, 'Viewer, Viewing, Viewed: a Critique of Subject-Generated Documentary', *Journal of the University Film Association* 29, 1 (1977), pp. 23–26; G. Hennebelle, ed., *Les Cinémas Africains en 1972* (Dakar

1972), p. 253; L. de Heusch, *The Cinema and Social Science: a Survey of Ethnographic and Sociological films* (Paris, UNESCO, 1962), pp. 40–49.
55 T. Bishop, 'Film-Making In Udi', *Spectator*, 1 April 1949, p. 431.

Chapter 9

1   *Programme for Film Propaganda*, PRO INF 1/867 c. December 1939.
2   For censorship in general see Paul O'Higgins, *Censorship in Britain* (London, 1972); for the development of film censorship in legal and institutional terms: Neville March Hunning, *Film Censors and the Law* (London, 1967); for the political censorship of film: N. Pronay, 'The First Reality: Film Censorship in Liberal England', in K. R. M. Short, ed., *Feature Films as History* (London, Croom Helm, 1981); N. Pronay, 'The Political Censorship of Film in Britain', in N. Pronay and D. W. Spring, ed., *Propaganda, Politics and Film 1918–1945* (London, 1982); Jeffrey Richards, 'The British Board of Film Censors and Content Control in the 1930s: Images of Britain', *Historical Journal of Film, Radio and Television*, vol. 1, no. 2, 1981, and vol. 2, no. 1, 1982.
3   The Categories and Exceptions are listed and discussed in Pronay, 'The Political Censorship of Film', pp. 102–7; the relationship between them and those operated by the Lord Chamberlain's Office in Pronay, 'The First Reality: Film Censorship in Liberal England', pp. 119–2.
4   Tyrell was, in fact, a pioneer of, and by the 1930s the government's chief expert on, matters concerning 'cultural propaganda'. For Tyrell see P. M. Taylor, *The Projection of Britain, British Overseas Publicity and Propaganda* (Cambridge, 1981).
5   J. C. Robertson, 'British Film Censorship Goes to War', *Historical Journal of Film Radio and Television*, vol. 2, no. 1 (1982) p. 58.
6   Public Records Office, [Kew] INF 1/189, 20 October 1939.
7   For the control of newsreels and the relationship with Central Office, including an account of Lord Trenchard 'teaching the newsreels a lesson', see T. J. Hollins, 'The Presentation of Politics, the Place of Party Publicity, Broadcasting and Film in British Politics, 1918–39', unpublished Leeds University Ph.D. thesis, 1981 pp. 616–78.
8   For the development of pre-war plans for news-control and for the story of the MOI and War Office attempts to operate them during the phoney war, see N. Pronay, 'The News Media at War', in N. Pronay and D. W. Spring, *Propaganda, Politics and Film*, pp. 181–6.
9   PRO, INF 1/92, 20 August 1940.
10 PRO, INF 1/178/3. The order was revised and reissued on 14 February 1942. Admiral G. P. Thomson, the chief censor of Press and Censorship, in his own book on censorship, *Blue Pencil Admiral* (London, 1947), stressed that the censor's *only* duty was security censorship and that political censorship was emphatically neither a part of his duties nor even

allowed to colour his judgement in any way. Francis Williams, the Controller of Press and Censorship, stressed the same in his own several post-war accounts. It was on their printed testimony that the generally held 'security only' view of wartime film censorship was based. This, however, was not the view of either Thomson or Williams while in office. Thomson wrote to Williams, for example, in December 1941, 'Apart from seeing film does not contain information of value to an enemy, the censor must be able to recognize when a sequence of film may be undesirable because it runs counter to some policy of the government and give and obtain for the producer the necessary guidance.' (PRO, INF 1/92, 10 December 1942). In fairness to Admiral Thomson it should be pointed out that his book was itself subject to censorship (in peacetime under the Official Secrets Act). The file dealing with the censoring of Thomson's book appears on the list of Admiralty files for 1947; but it is closed to researchers.

11   PRO, INF 1/178, A, 13 September 1940.
12   Thomson, *Blue Pencil Admiral*, p. 66.
13   Robertson, 'British Film Censorship goes to War', (p. 58).
14   PRO, INF 1/178, Admiral Thomson to Francis Williams, 13 October 1942. A letter containing this list was also sent on behalf of the Films Division to the British Film-Makers Association. Robertson, p. 54.
15   Richards, *'The British Board of Film Censors'*, vol. 1, no. 2, pp. 112–3.
16   Ibid., vol. 2, no. 1, p. 42.
17   Ibid.
18   *Mission to Moscow* was made by Warner Brothers on, for all practical purposes, the personal orders of President Roosevelt. It is about the work of his close political and personal friend and Special Envoy to the USSR, Joseph R. Davies, who also appeared in person at the start of the film, delivering a prologue. The script was personally vetted, and in places written, by Davies himself, and – at least according to Davies – with Roosevelt's knowledge and approval of what it contained. What Stalin said to Davies in the film was, 'England and France have allowed Hitler to take Austria without a struggle. They will probably allow him to do the same with Czechoslovakia. They have repudiated their pledges to the League and are throwing the defenceless countries on the mercies of bandits.' Davies: 'It is clear what they are doing. What I don't understand is *why* they are doing it.' Stalin: 'I will tell you why, Mr Davies, and I will tell you frankly because this is a time for plain words – the reactionary elements in England, represented by the Chamberlain government, have determined upon the deliberate policy of making Germany strong. And at the same time they shout lies in their press at the weakness of the Russian army and disorder in the Soviet Union. . . . In my opinion the present governments of England and France do not represent their people. Finally the Fascist dictators will drive too hard a

bargain and the people will call their governments to account – but by then it may be too late.' The close relationship between Davies and Roosevelt, as well as Roosevelt's glowing approval of Davies' book about his mission – based on his official dispatches to Roosevelt, which he was allowed to cite by special presidential dispensation – were common knowledge in Washington and perfectly well known to Brendan Bracken, the Minister of Information. To ban such a film at a time when all depended on Roosevelt's goodwill towards Britain was out of the question in the interests of Anglo-American relations. Moreover, the film also contained a dialogue with Churchill, who was introduced as one man in England who spoke out against Chamberlain's policies and who 'kept *his* word' (italics in original). Thus Bracken – who was out of favour with Churchill at the time – had no reason whatsoever to want to suppress the film, which was excellent personal propaganda for Churchill, and of a kind which it would have been politically impossible to have made in Britain. It is against this background that the well-known story of Bracken curtly rejecting a Central Office request to suppress the film needs to be interpreted. See David Culbert, *Mission to Moscow* (Wisconsin, 1980).

19 Thorold Dickinson, *A Discovery of Cinema* (London, 1971), p. 72. In a subsequent paper, 'A Film-Maker Contributes to the War Effort', delivered at the conference, 'Film Propaganda and the Historian', at the Inter-University History Film Consortium/Imperial War Museum, Conference, 1973, Professor Dickinson elaborated on the subject of stock control and dated it to 'early 1940'. Other film-makers of the period all appear to have the same recollection. No documentary evidence has, however, been found for the operation of a formalized scheme of this sort before March 1942. The documentation concerned with working out details of the arrangement once Hugh Dalton had taken over the Board of Trade does however, appear to pre-suppose that something like it had been in operation already. For these negotiations, occasioned specifically by the acute shortage of film stock supply, owing to shipping losses in the Atlantic, see the Minutes of the discussions of the Legislation Committee (PRO CAB. 75/14, HPC (42) 107). In committee the MOI expressed the hope that 'The Board of Trade would not give a licence [for film stock] in cases where the Ministry objected to their so doing', to which the Parliamentary Secretary to the Board of Trade replied 'that while the BoT could not give a firm undertaking to this effect, they would pay due regard to the views of the Ministry.' A few weeks later Dalton summed up the nub of the matter, and laid down future policy, in a personal memorandum to Bracken: 'In deciding cases under the Regulation the Board of Trade will, of course, pay due regard to the advice of the Ministry of Information, but this cannot for constitutional reasons be stated in the order. . . .' (PRO INF 1/627, July 1942).

20   PRO, INF 1/627, Exhibitors' Quota.
21   Dickinson's phrase ('A Film-Maker Contributes to the War Effort', p. 8).
22   Ibid., p. 4; see also Dickinson, *A Discovery of Cinema*, p. 77: 'The Films Division was given control of all negative film which was made available to producers only after approval of each script. This veto, intelligently applied, raised the quality of the British product without removing the element of competition. . . .'
23   PRO, INF 1/199, Abandoned Films Projects, 1942–1944.
24   PRO, INF 1/864, Anderson to Bracken, 6 March 1943, quoted in Ian McLaine, *The Ministry of Morale* (London, 1979), p. 181. Jackson told his side of the story in Elizabeth Sussex, *The Rise and Fall of British Documentary* (London, University of California Press, 1975), p. 156. For the 'blanket' decision see the Minutes of the Reconstruction Secretariat, INF 1/683, and also McLaine, p. 183.
25   House of Commons Debates, 1918, vol. 109, cols 1000–1001.
26   'Propaganda in Motion Pictures: Hearings before a Senate Sub-committee of the Committee on Interstate Commerce,' United States Senate, 77th Congress, 1st Session, September 1941. The sub-committee was set up in consequence of the motion before the Senate, which claimed that: 'Whereas the motion picture screen and radio are the most potential instruments of communication of ideas, and whereas numerous charges have been made that the motion picture and radio have been extensively used for propaganda purposes designed to influence the public mind in the direction of participation in the war, and whereas all this propaganda has been directed to one side . . . be it therefore resolved that the committee on interstate commerce . . . make and report to the Senate the results of the thorough investigation of any propaganda disseminated by motion pictures . . . to influence public sentiment in the direction of participation of the United States in the present European war.' The motivating spirit of the enquiry was Senator Gerald P. Nye. For the strength of American suspicions during the inter-war years, engendered by the disclosures about British propaganda operations in the United States during the First World War see H. C. Peterson, *Propaganda For War: The Campaign Against American Neutrality* (New York, 1939); for the degree to which this forced the utmost caution upon British officials in rebuilding information services in the United States after the war see Philip M. Taylor, *The Projection of Britain, British Overseas Publicity and Propaganda 1919–1939* (Cambridge, 1981).
27   Ian Christie, ed., *Powell, Pressburger and Others* (London, 1978), p. 35.
28   After discussions between Rank and Powell and Pressburger, Rank established a new company, Independent Producers (Production Managers (BFM)) Ltd, to handle the financial and legal aspects of

established a new company, Independent Producers (Production Managers (BFM)) Ltd, to handle the financial and legal aspects of production by independent producers using the Rank studios on a contract basis – producers whose films would be distributed by Rank. The management board of Independent Producers (Production Managers (BFM)) Ltd consisted of Rank himself, Powell, Pressburger, Leslie Howard and two others. The first 'independent' company to be formed and to make use of the services offered was The Archers, Ltd, wholly owned by Powell and Pressburger. It was formed after the aforementioned discussions between Rank and Powell and Pressburger (Christie, p. 30).

30 PRO, PREM 4 14/5, 8 September 1942, quoted in Christie, p. 106.
31 Ibid.
32 Christie, *Powell, Pressburger and Others*, p. 107.
33 PRO, PREM 4 14/5, quoted in Paul Addison, *The Road to 1945* (London, 1977), p. 132.
34 There were two films, *Personnel Selection in the British Army – Officers* (40 minutes) and *Personnel Selection in the British Army – Recruits* (58 minutes). For production details and synops. see F. Thorpe and N. Pronay, *British Official Films in the Second World War* (Oxford 1980), p. 192. The films became available in Britain after 1945.
35 PRO, War Cabinet 126 (42), 21 September 1942, quoted in Christie, p. 108.
36 PRO, War Cabinet 67 (43), 10 May 1943, quoted in Christie, *Powell, Pressburger and others*, p. 108.
37 *Evening Standard*, 28 June 1943, quoted in Christie, *Powell, Pressburger and others*, p. 108.
38 *The Volunteer* (The Archers, 1943).
39 *A Canterbury Tale* (The Archers, 1944) – another film focusing on American attitudes towards Britain theme – and *I Know Where I'm Going* (The Archers, 1945).
40 Interview with Powell and Pressburger quoted in Christie, *Powell, Pressburger and others*, p. 106.
41 PRO PREM 4 14/5, 15 September 1942, quoted in Christie, *Powell, Pressburger and others*, p. 107.
42 Ibid.
43 Defence Regulation 39 B made it an offence 'to endeavour, whether orally or otherwise, to influence public opinion (whether in the United Kingdom or elsewhere) in a manner likely to be prejudicial to the defence of the realm or the efficient prosecution of the War'. It was this Regulation on which the ministry operated its censorship machinery and which was used, for example, in suppressing *Tobacco Road*.
44 'Dear Rowan, – I am returning your file about the release of "Colonel Blimp" which somehow or other came into my hands while we were in

America. . . .' PRO PREM, 4 14/5, 21 September 1943, quoted in Christie, p. 111.

45 Andrew Boyle, *Poor Dear Brendan* (London, 1974), p. 300.
46 'Churchill has been credited with the phrase: 'Truth is so sacred that in war it must be surrounded by lies.' No better minister than Brendan Bracken could have been found, for that very reason to succeed, where his distinguished predecessors had failed. . . .' (Boyle, *Poor Dear Brendan*, p. 306.
47 Ibid. p. 297.
48 This should not be taken, of course, to mean that in the technical sense the Film Censorship Section had little to do. Between June 1940 and the date of Japan's surrender it examined 26,274 films of all kinds. See Thomson, *Blue Pencil Admiral* p. 67.

Chapter 10

1 *Kine Weekly*, 11 April 1937, p. 8.
2 Thomas Guback, *The International Film Industry* (Indiana 1969), p. 69.
3 Alan Wood, *Mr Rank* (London, 1952), p. 124.
4 *Kine Weekly*, 4 December 1941, 5 December 1946.
5 *Time*, 5 June 1944, p. 77.
6 Tino Balio, *United Artists: The Company Built by the Stars* (Wisconsin, 1975), pp. 144, 197.
7 Balio, 'United Artists', pp. 197–200.
8 *Kine Weekly*, 16 March 1944, p. 8.
9 *Motion Picture Herald*, 29 July 1944, p. 31.
10 *Balio*, 'United Artists', p. 202.
11 *Variety*, 23 March 1945, p. 8. Road-showing' originally meant an engagement whereby a film was played on a two-showings-a-day reserved-seat basis at increased prices, but on a continuous-run policy; it came to mean any special distribution handling.
12 *Variety* 6 June 1945, p. 28, 11 July 1945, p. 3.
13 The history of UWP, International and the subsequent Universal-International merger is very adequately dealt with by Allen Eyles in 'Universal-International', *Focus on Film*, 30, pp. 22–27.
14 *Time*, 10 December 1945, p. 32.
15 Variety, 12 June 1946, p. 1.
16 Ibid., 10 July 1946, p. 21.
17 Ibid., 12 December 1945, p. 20.
18 Don Miller, 'Eagle Lion – The Violent Years', *Focus on Film*, 31, pp. 27–33, is primarily concerned with E-L as a production company, but provides some useful background information.
19 Variety, 16 January 1945, p. 11, 21 November 1945, p. 19, 27 March 1946, p. 4, 19 March 1947, p. 16, 23 April 1947, p. 5.

20 Ibid., 23 April 1947, p. 5.
21 Ibid., 21 May 1947, p. 5.
22 Ibid., 6 March 1946, p. 5.
23 Ibid., 30 October 1946, p. 3.
24 Ibid., 5 November 1947, p. 4.
25 Ibid., 11 June 1947, p. 1.
26 Ibid., 23 May 1947, p. 4.
27 See ibid., 3 May 1949, p. 15, for Rank's claims for Canadian box-office receipts and for Hollywood's claims that he would do better if he 'laid off long-hair themes aimed at attracting intellectuals'.
28 Ibid., 16 July 1947, p. 4.
29 Wood, *Mr Rank*, p. 226.
30 *Variety*, 29 January 1947, p. 3, 20 March 1947, p. 3.
31 Ibid., 6 October 1948, p. 8.
32 Ibid., 5 May 1948, p. 15.
33 *Economist*, 16 March 1947, p. 290.
34 Political and Economic Planning, report, *The British Film Industry* (London, 1952), p. 95.
35 *Economist*, 20 December 1947, p. 1914.
36 *Variety*, 17 May 1948, p. 9.
37 Ibid., 9 June 1948, p. 5.
38 Ibid., 1 September 1948, p. 6.
39 Ibid., 16 June 1948, p. 5.
40 Ibid., 27 October 1948, p. 3.
41 Ibid., 9 November 1949, p. 14.
42 PEP, p. 109.
43 R. Griffiths, 'Where are the Dollars?', *Sight and Sound*, December 1949, January and March 1950.
44 See R. Roud, 'Britain in America', *Sight and Sound*, 26, no. 3, Winter 1956–7.
45 *Variety*, January 1948, p. 27.
46 Ibid. Political and Economic Planning, report, p. 109.

Chapter 11

1 Janet Staiger, 'Dividing Labor for Production Control: Thomas Ince and the Rise of the Studio System', *Cinema Journal*, XVIII, no. 2, (1979), p. 16.
2 See, for example, Bob Thomas, *Thalberg: Life and Legend* (New York, 1969), especially Chapter 13, and Samuel Marx, *Mayer and Thalberg: The Make-Believe Saints* (London, 1976); for a valuable 'fictional' insight see F. Scott Fitzgerald, *The Last Tycoon*, – the character of Monroe Stahr was based on Thalberg.
3 Quoted in Samuel Marx, pp. 96–7.
4 Kevin Brownlow, *The Parade's Gone By* (First Abacus ed. London, 1973), p. 488.

5   Francis Koval, 'The Studio: Sir Michael Balcon and Ealing', *Sight and Sound Films in 1951* (1951), p. 9.
6   Michael Balcon, *The Producer* (London, 1945), p. 4.
7   Kenneth Tynan, 'Ealing's Way of Life', *Films and Filming*, 2, no. 3 (1955), p. 10.
8   John Ellis, 'Made in Ealing', *Screen*, 16, no. 1, (1975), p. 92.
9   Bernard Cohn, 'Entretien avec Mackendrick', *Positif*, 92 (1966–7), p. 41.
10 Freda Bruce Lockhart, 'Interview with Hamer', *Sight and Sound*, 21, no. 2 (1951), p. 74.
11 Balcon, *The Producer*, p. 5.
12 Ibid.
13 Ibid.
14 Ibid.
15 Sir Michael Balcon, 'An Author in the Studio', *Films and Filming*, July (1957), p. 7.
16 Ibid.
17 Ibid., p. 34.
18 Sir Michael Balcon, *Michael Balcon Presents: A Lifetime of Films* (London, 1969), p. 154.
19 Ibid.
20 Sir Michael Balcon, unpublished interview with John Ellis (1974), filed in the library of the British Film Institute. A shortened and edited version has been published as ' ". . . das war der Ealing-Film" Interview mit Sir Michael Balcon', in Geoff Brown, ed., *Der Produzent* (Berlin, W., 1981), p. 23.
21 See, for instance, Charles Barr, *Ealing Studios* (London and Newton Abbot, 1977).
22 Balcon, *The Producer*, p. 3.
23 Charles Frend, *The Film Director* (London, 1945) p. 5.
24 Ibid., p. 7.
25 Ibid.
26 Anon., 'In the Script', *Sight and Sound*, 21, no. 2 (1951), p. 57.
27 Lockhart, 'Interview with Hamer', p. 75.
28 Ibid., p. 74.
29 Balcon, *Michael Balcon Presents* p. 163.
30 Balcon, 'Interview with John Ellis'.
31 Michael Balcon, *Realism or Tinsel* (London, 1943), p. 4.
32 Ibid., p. 6.
33 Michael Balcon, 'Let British Films be Ambassadors to the World; a Cogent Plea from the Head of Ealing Studios', *Kinematograph Weekly*, 335, no. 1969, (1945), p. 31.
34 Ibid.

35 Balcon, *Realism or Tinsel*, p. 4.
36 Balcon, *The Producer*, p. 5.
37 Balcon, 'Interview with John Ellis'.
38 Friedrich Engels, 'Letter to Margaret Harkness' in David Craig, ed., *Marxists on Literature: an Anthology* (Harmondsworth, Penguin, 1975), p. 269.
39 Michael Balcon, 'The Feature carries on the Documentary Tradition', *Quarterly of Film Radio and Television*, VI, no. 4 (1952), pp. 352–3.
40 Lockhart, 'Interview with Hamer' p. 74.
41 Editorial comment in *Screen*, 13, no. 2 (1972), p. 49.
42 Cohn, 'Entretiens avec Mockendurck', p. 41.
43 Quoted in John Cutts, 'Mackendrick Finds the Sweet Smell of Success', *Films and Filming*, 3, no. 6 (1957), p. 8.
44 Sir Michael Balcon, 'Film Comedy', in Peter Noble, ed., *British Film Yearbook 1949–50* (London, 1949), p. 25.
45 Lawrence Earl, 'The Mighty Balcon', p. 4, *John Bull*, 10 May 1952, at p. 20.
46 Ibid., at p. 22.
47 T. E. B. Clarke, 'Just an Idea', in Roger Manvell and R. K. Neilson Baxter, eds, *The Cinema 1951* (Harmondsworth, Penguin, 1951), p. 150.
48 Barr, *Ealing Studios*, p. 119.
49 Monja Danischewsky, *White Russian – Red Face* (London, 1966), pp. 152–3.
50 Compton Mackenzie, *My Life and Times: Octave Nine 1946–1953* (London, 1970), p. 182.
51 Michael Truman, 'The Cutting of British Films in the United States', *Film Industry*, 17 November 1949.
52 Ibid.
53 Ibid.
54 Jean George Auriol, 'The British Film Abroad', in R. Manvell, ed., *The Year's Work in the Film 1949* (London, 1950), p. 53.
55 Francis Koval, 'British Films in Europe', *Sight and Sound*, 20, no. 1 (May 1951), p. 11.
56 Ibid.
57 Richard Roud, 'Britain in America' *Sight and Sound*, 26, no. 3 (Winter 1956–7), p. 119.
58 Ibid.
59 Harry Watt, 'You Start From Scratch in Australia', *Penguin Film Review*, no. 9 (May 1949), p. 10.
60 Ibid.
61 Lindsay Anderson, 'British Films: the Descending Spiral', *Sequence*, no. 7 (Spring 1949), p. 6.
62 Roud, 'Britain in America', p. 120.

63 Ibid.
64 Peter Baker, 'Over 2,000 Studio Employees Have Lost Their Jobs', *Kinematograph Weekly*, 31 March 1949 (British Studio Supplement Section), p. 9.
65 Baynham Honri, 'Mobile Studio Units for Feature Films', *Cine Technician*, September–October 1950, p. 146.
66 Sir Michael Balcon, *Film Production and Management* (London, 1950), p. 17.
67 Honri, 'Mobile Studios for Feature Films', p. 154.
68 Balcon, *Film Production and Management*, p. 17.
69 Ibid.
70 R. Howard Cricks, 'The Country House as a Film Studio', *Kinematograph Weekly* 31 March 1949 (British Studio Supplement Section), p. 16.
71 British Film Academy, *The Film Industry in Great Britain* (London, 1950), pp. 9–10.
72 Allen Eyles *et al.* ed., *The House of Horror* (London, 1973), p. 9.
73 John Brosnan, *The Horror People* (London, 1976), p. 109.
74 *Variety*, 28 May 1958 (press cutting in British Film Institute).
75 Colin Heard, 'Hammering the Box Office, *Films and Filming*, June 1969, p. 18.
76 Ibid.
77 Ian Brown, 'The Hammer Horrors', *Photoplay*, September 1969, p. 42.
78 Lucy Abelson, 'The Man Who Makes Millions Out of Monsters', *Sunday Express*, 30 May 1971.
79 David Pirie, *Hammer: A Cinema Case Study* (London, 1980), Item 19, p. 2.
80 Tom Milne, ed. and introd., *Losey on Losey* (London, Thames and Hudson, 1967), p. 32.
81 Ibid., p. 33.
82 Editorial note, *Movie*, no. 9 (May 1963), p. 34.
83 Ibid.
84 See, for example, *Movie*, no. 9 (May 1963), p. 1.
85 Brosnan, *The Horror People*, p. 116.
86 Ibid.
87 Ibid., p. 116.
88 Ibid.
89 David Pirie, *A Heritage of Horror: the English Gothic Cinema 1946–1972* (London, 1973), p. 57.
90 Brosnan, *The Horror People*, p. 109.
91 For a more extensive discussion see Chapter 17.
92 See, for example, G. Murdock and P. Golding, 'For a Political Economy of Mass Communications', in R. Miliband and J. Saville, ed., *The Socialist Register* (London, 1974); Ian Connell, 'Monopoly Capitalism

and the Media' in Sally Hibbin *et al.*, *Politics, Ideology and the State* (London, 1978), John Hill, 'Ideology, Economy and the British Cinema' and Peter Golding and Graham Murdock, 'Ideology and the Mass Media: The Question of Determination in Michèle Barrett *et al.* ed., *Ideology and Cultural Production* (London, 1979).

Chapter 12

1 Cubby Broccoli, interview. All the interviews cited in these notes were given in the course of work on the case study, *The Making of The Spy Who Loved Me*, carried out by staff of the Open University in 1976.
2 Lillian Ross, 'Picture', *Reporting* (London Mayflower Books, 1964).
3 Pierre Macherey, *A Theory of Literary Production* (London, Routledge, 1978), p. 49.
4 Pierre Macherey, interview, in *Red Letters*, no. 5 (Summer 1977), p. 17.
5 T. Bennett *et al.*, *The Making of the Spy Who Loved Me* (Milton Keynes, Open University, 1977).
6 Cubby Broccoli, interview.
7 Lewis Gilbert, interview.
8 Claude Renoir, interview.
9 Christopher Wood, interview.
10 Ibid.
11 Saul Cooper, interview.
12 Special Executive for Counterintelligence, Terrorism, Revenge and Extortion: the villainous organization, created by Fleming in his later novels, with which Bond has to contend.
13 Bennett *et al.*, *The Making of The Spy Who Loved Me*, p. 29.
14 Ibid., p. 31.
15 Raymond Williams, *Problems in Materialism and Culture* (1980).
16 Philip Elliott, 'Media Organization and Occupations; an Overview', in J. Curran, M. Gurevitch and J. Woollacott, ed., *Mass Communication and Society* (London, Arnold, 1977).
17 J. Ellis, 'Made in Ealing', *Screen*, 16 (1975), no. 1, p. 80.
18 Ibid., pp. 80–81.
19 Ibid.
20 Ibid., p. 81.
21 E. Buscombe, 'Notes on Columbia Pictures Corporation 1924–41', *Screen*, 16 (1975), no. 2, p. 82.
22 Ibid.
23 Open University radio programmes 14 and 15, DE 353, 'Mass Communication and Society' 1977.
24 U. Eco, 'The Narrative Structure in Fleming', in O. Del Bueno and U. Eco, ed., *The Bond Affair* (London, Macdonald, 1966).
25 See note 12.

26 T. Bennett, 'James Bond as Popular Hero', in Open University Course U203, *Popular Culture* (Milton Keynes, Open University, 1982).
27 F. Colombo, 'Bond's Women', in O. Del Bueno and U. Eco, ed., *The Bond Affair* (London, Macdonald, 1966).
28 Bennett, 'James Bond as Popular Hero'.
29 Barbara Bach, interview.
30 Lewis Gilbert, Interview.
31 Cubby Broccoli, interview.
32 Saul Cooper, interview.
33 Ibid.
34 Alexander Walker, *Hollywood England*, London, Michael Joseph, 1974, p. 187).
35 Christopher Wood, interview.

Chapter 13

1 On the Anglocentrism of 'British' history, see J. G. A. Pocock, *The Limits and Divisions of British History*, 'Studies in Public Policy, no. 31 (Centre for the Study of Public Policy, University of Strathclyde, Glasgow, 1979). Material on developments outside England can be found in M. Grigor, ed., 'Scottish Cinema?', *New Edinburgh Review*, no. 34 (August 1976); C. Harvie, *No Gods and Precious Few Heroes* (London, Arnold, 1981); K. Rockett, 'Film and Ireland: A Chronicle', *A Sense of Ireland* (Festival Booklet, London, 1980), and Irish Cinema – Notes on Some Nationalist Fictions', *Screen*, 20, no. 3/4 (winter 1979–80); M. Stephens, ed., *The Arts in Wales 1950–75* (Cardiff, Welsh Arts Council, 1979); K. Morgan, *Rebirth of a Nation: Wales 1880–1980* (Oxford University Press, 1981). The relationship between English nationalism and the trajectory of the 'British' film industry is a crucial issue not discussed here, but see P. M. Taylor, *The Projection of Britain* (Cambridge University Press, 1981).
2 We have not had space to discuss the films themselves. For discussion of those films funded by the British Film Institute see the three Production Board Catalogues published to date : J. Ellis, ed., *Catalogue British Film Institute Productions 1951–1976*; E. Cowie, ed., *Catalogue British Film Institute Productions 1977–1978*; R. Stoneman and H. Thompson, ed., *The New Social Function of Cinema. Catalogue British Film Institute Productions 1979–1980* (all published by British Film Institute, London, 1977, 1978 and 1981 respectively). Articles about the films have appeared in a number of periodicals, including *Afterimage, Screen, Framework, Under Cut, Monthly Film Bulletin, Wedge, Cinetracts, Camera Obscura*.
3 From *Four Essays on Liberty* (Oxford University Press, 1969), quoted in S. Lukes, *Individualism*, chap. 8, 'Autonomy', p. 55 (Oxford, Blackwell, 1973).

4   From *The British Constitution* (1861), quoted in H. F. Pitkin, *The Concept of Representation*, chap. 7, 'The Mandate-Independence Controversy', p. 150 (London, University of California Press, 1967).

5   See A Calder, *The People's War* (London, Jonathan Cape, 1969); J. S. Harris, *Government Patronage of the Arts in Great Britain* (London, University of Chicago Press, 1970); R. Hewison, *Under Siege* (London, Weidenfeld and Nicolson, 1977).

6   J. M. Keynes, quoted in J. A. Sutherland, *Fiction and the Fiction Industry* (London, Athlone Press, University of London, 1978), p. 131.

7   Something of the tensions inherent in the formative stage of the Arts Council's history can be seen in Jack Lindsay's interview with Mary Glasgow (the Council's first secretary-general), in *Our Time*, 7 (January/February 1948), no. 5, pp. 107–8. For a much fuller account, See R. Hutchison, *The Politics of the Arts Council* (London, Sinclair-Browne, 1982).

8   See Harris, *Government Patronage of the Arts in Great Britain*; also *The ACGB and the RAA's – Towards A New Relationship* (*Report of an Informal ACGB/RAA Working Group* (London, ACGB, May 1980).

9   See I. Butler, *To Encourage the Art of Film* (London, Robert Hale, 1971). For a useful typology and discussion of 'fringe bodies', including the BFI, see Outer Circle Policy Unit, *What's Wrong with Quangos?* (London, July 1979).

10 See A. Lovell and J. Hillier, *Studies in Documentary* (London, Secker and Warburg, 1972); B. Morrison, *The Movement: English Poetry and Fiction of the 1950s* (Oxford University Press, 1980).

11 See M. Horovitz, ed., *Children of Albion – Poetry of the 'Underground' in Britain* (Harmondsworth, Penguin, 1969); C. Booker, *The Neophiliacs* London, Fontana Books, 1970); D. Widgery, *The Left in Britain 1956–68* (Harmondsworth, Penguin Books, 1976); '1956 and After', in *The Socialist Register, 1976* (London, Merlin Press, 1976); R. Hewison, *In Anger: Culture in the Cold War 1945–60* (London, Weidenfeld and Nicolson, 1981); R. Bradshaw, D. Gould, C. Jones, *From Protest to Resistance – The Direct Action Movement against Nuclear Weapons* (Peace News Pamphlet No. 2, Nottingham, Peace News 1981).

12 See in particular Deke Dusinberre's unpublished M.Phil. thesis, '*English Avant-Garde Cinema, 1966–74*', University College, University of London (1977). See also S. Dwoskin, *Film Is – The International Free Cinema* (London, Peter Owen, 1975); D. Curtis, 'English Avant-Garde Film: An Early Chronology', in D. Curtis and D. Dusinberre, ed., *A Perspective on English Avant-Garde Film* (London Arts Council of Great Britain, 1978).

13 See, for example, D. Elliott, *The Lucas Aerospace Workers' Campaign* (Young Fabian Pamphlet, London, 1977).

14 See, for example, J. Mitchell, *Woman's Estate* (Harmondsworth, Penguin, 1971); S. Rowbotham, *Women Resistance and Revolution* (Harmondsworth, Penguin, 1972); S. Rowbotham, *Woman's Consciousness Man's World* (Harmondsworth, Penguin, 1973); S. Allen, L. Sanders and J. Wallis, ed., *Conditions of Illusion. Papers from the Women's Movement* (Leeds, Feminist Books, 1974); S. Rowbotham, L. Segal and H. Wainwright, *Beyond the Fragments. Feminism and the Making of Socialism* (London, Merlin Press, 1979).

15 See J. Pines, 'Left Film Distribution', *Screen*, 13 (winter 1972–3), no. 4, pp. 116–27; Newsreel Collective, 'Five Years on' *Wedge*, no. 3, pp. 38–43; D. Glyn and P. Marris, 'Seven Years of Cinema Action', *After Image*, no. 6 (summer 1976), pp. 64–83; S. Harvey, *May '68 and Film Culture* (London, British Film Institute, 1978). For further information about the film groups see the three British Film Institute Production Board Catalogues; 'Problems of Independent Cinema, A Discussion between Marc Karlin, Claire Johnson, Mark Nash and Paul Willemen', *Screen* (1980–81), no. 4, pp. 19–43.

16 In the context of this characterization of the industry it is important to recognize both the dedication of some individuals within it to a consideration of the social and cultural needs of audiences (conceived of in social and human, rather than in market, terms) and their constant struggle to obtain finance for their projects, as well as some measure of control over the content and subsequent distribution of their films.

17 The Other Cinema, 'Why an Other Cinema?', in *Film Catalogue* (summer 1972), p. 2.

18 See, however, J. Clarke and R. Elliott, 'The Other Cinema: Screen Memory', *Wedge*, no. 2 (1978). There were, of course, other distributors who could justifiably be referred to as independent: ETV, Contemporary, Connoisseur and Concord (the last of these emerging from the early history of CND). Subsequently there were important developments in feminist distribution, which included the setting up of the Sheffield Film Co-op, Cinema of Women and Circles.

19 See R. Williams, *Culture* (London, Fontana, 1981), chap. 3, 'Formations'.

20 The IFA has produced a number of duplicated documents. These include 'Independent Film-making in the '70s: A Discussion Paper for the Founding Conference of the IFA' (May 1976) and 'Notes Towards a Social Practice of Production/Distribution/Exhibition/Criticism' (1977). For information on the Film Workshops Conference in 1979 see R. Stoneman, ed., *Independent Film Workshops in Britain 1979* (Torquay, Grael Communications, 1979). The association can be contacted at its National Office: 79 Wardour Street, London, WIV 3PH.

21 See G. Bruce, *Festival in the North* (London, Robert Hale, 1975) and 'An Edinburgh Woman – Simon Perry interviews Lynda Myles', *Sight and*

Sound, 50 (winter 1980/81), no. 1.

22 For details of the Eady Levy see Association of Cinematograph, Television and allied Technicians, *Nationalising the Film Industry. Report of the ACTT Nationalization Forum 1973* (London, ACTT, 1973); also in this volume, chapter 5.

23 For details of the history of the Production Board see A. Lovell, ed., *Production Board* (London, British Film Institute, 1976); J. Ellis, ed., *Catalogue British Film Institute Productions 1951–1976*.

24 It is difficult to estimate these figures exactly. For details see the *Annual Reports* of the British Film Institute.

25 The debate about the funding of regional production came to a head at the BFI's Annual Regional Conference in September 1980. For details see the collected papers of the conference, British Film Institute, *Independent Cinema and Regional Film Culture* (University of London, Institute of Education, 1981), Media Analysis Paper 2; also J. Curling F. Oppe, 'Interim Report on Regional Film Production', duplicated research paper, British Film Institute Production Board, London, 1980.

26 For an account of the IFA's paper, *The Future of the British Film Industry*, see S. Hartog, 'The Perils of Film Policy', in R. Stoneman, ed.; *Independent Film Workshops in Britain 1979*, pp. 58–62; P. Houston, 'Independent Voice', *Sight and Sound*, 47 (autumn 1978), no. 4, pp. 223–4.

27 The ACTT/RAA 'Code of Practice' is printed in Association of Cinematograph, Television and allied Technicians, *Minutes of Evidence taken before the House of Commons' Education, Science and Arts Committee*, 4 March 1981, Supplementary Memoranda, House of Commons Paper HCP 106–IV (London, HMSO, 1980/81).

28 For brief details of the campaign see S. Blanchard, 'Broadcasting, Independent Cinema and the Future', *Undercut* no. 1 (March–April 1981), pp. 48–51.

29 Video work in the independent sector is outside the scope of this chapter. See, however, the brief history and useful bibliography in G. Wade, *Street Video – an account of 5 video groups* (Leicester, Blackthorn Press, 1980). For video and television see S. Herman, *The Broadcasting of Low Gauge Video – A Research Report* (London, Community Communications Group, 1980).

30 See the Guidelines for Independent Film and Guidelines for Independent Video issued by the Channel Four Television Company in December 1981 and April 1982 respectively.

31 For Jeremy Isaacs' reflections on his experiences as BFI Production Board chairperson, see 'Winning the Pools', *Sight and Sound*, 50 (winter 1980/81), no. 1.

32 For further discussion of these shifts, see K. Middlemas, *Politics in Industrial Society* (London, Deutsch, 1979); E. Hobsbawm *et al.*, *The*

Forward March of Labour Halted (London, Verso/New Left Books, 1981); B. Rowthorn, 'The Past Strikes Back', *Marxism To-Day*, January 1982.

33   For an example of the effects of this general invisibility, see the comments on independent cinema in J. McGrath, *A Good Night Out* (London, Eyre Methuen, 1981).

34   We should like to thank the following people who helped us in writing this article: David Curtis, Andrew Davies, Margaret Dickinson, Vincent Porter, Jan Worth, as well as the many members of the IFA and others who read and commented on the first draft. Nonetheless, we would stress that the account offered here in no way constitutes an 'official history' of either the IFA or of the independent sector generally.

Chapter 14

1   *Cinematograph Films Act, 1927*: report of a committee appointed by the Board of Trade, Cmnd 5320 (1936), p. 4.

2   S. G. Tallents, *The Projection of England* (London 1932), p. 12.

3   Ibid., p. 29.

4   Ibid., pp. 39–40.

5   *Hansard*, vol. 203, col. 2039.

6   Ibid., cols 2059–60. Cf also a speech by Ramsasy Macdonald (col. 2051–2).

7   James Morris, *Farewell the Trumpets* (London, 1978), pp. 299–305.

8   P. M. Taylor, *The Projection of Britain* (Cambridge, 1981), p. 69.

9   Ibid., p. 110.

10   Ibid., p. 232.

11   For full details of the activities of the BBFC, see N. Pronay, 'The First Reality: Film Censorship in Liberal England', in K. R. M. Short, ed., *Feature Films as History* (London, 1981), pp. 113–37; J. Richards, 'The British Board of Film Censors and Content Control in the 1930's: images of Britain', *Historical Journal of Film, Radio and Television*, 1 (1981), pp. 95–116.

12   There will be a full discussion of the censors and the cinema of Empire in my forthcoming book, *The Age of the Dream Palace* (London, 1983).

13   *Hansard*, vol. 342, col. 1306.

14   J. E. Harley, *Worldwide Influences of the Cinema* (Los Angeles, 1940), pp. 35, 148–9, 183, 186.

15   The American cinema of Empire is discussed in Jeffrey Richards, *Visions of Yesterday* (London, 1973), pp. 2–202.

16   Margaret Farrand Thorp, *America at the Movies* (New Haven, 1939), pp. 294–5.

17   Colin Shindler, *Hollywood Goes to War* (London, 1979) p. 2.

18   *Daily Express*, 9 July 1938.

19   T. J. Hollins, 'The Conservative Party and Film Propaganda Between

the Wars', *English Historical Review*, 96 (April 1981), pp. 359–69.
20 Karol Kulik, *Alexander Korda: the man who could work miracles* (London, 1975), pp. 254–6.
21 *Daily Express*, 9 July 1938.
22 *Today's Cinema*, 14 October 1938.
23 This aspect of the projection of the Empire will be discussed in detail in John Mackenzie's forthcoming book *Propaganda and Empire* (London, 1983).
24 Quoted by Brian V. Street, *The Savage in Literature* (London, 1975), p. 10.
25 For a full discussion of the Korda trilogy, see J. Richards, 'Korda's Empire', *Australian Journal of Screen Theory*, 5–6 (1979), pp. 122–37.
26 Quoted by Samuel Smiles, *Self-Help* (London, 1911), p. 449.
27 *Sunday Times*, 7 April 1935.
28 *New York Times*, 30 September 1938.
29 *New York Times*, 4 August 1939.
30 This interpretation is discussed in detail in Martin Green, *Dreams of Adventure, Deeds of Empire* (London, 1980).
31 James Agate, *Around Cinemas* (Second Series, London, 1948), p. 128. The review originally appeared in the *Tatler*.

Chapter 15

1 A. J. P. Taylor, *English History 1914–1945* (London, Oxford University Press, 1965), p. 313.
2 C. L. Mowat, *Britain Between the Wars 1918–1940* (London, Methuen, 1955), p. 501.
3 John Stevenson and Chris Cook, *The Slump. Society and Politics during the Depression* (London, Jonathan Cape, 1977), p. 27.
4 See, in particular, D. Caradog Jones, ed., *The Social Survey of Merseyside* (Liverpool, 1934), vol. III, pp. 280–82, and S. Rowson, 'A Statistical Survey of the Cinema Industry in Great Britain in 1934', *Journal of the Royal Statistical Society*, vol. XCIX, 1936, pp. 67–129.
5 Wartime Social Survey, *The Cinema Audience* (London, 1943), p. 22.
6 Walter Greenwood, *Love on the Dole* (Harmondsworth, Penguin, 1976), p. 42.
7 Rowson, 'A Statistical Survey', p. 71.
8 Stevenson and Cook, *The Slump*, pp. 89–92.
9 E. W. Bakke, *The Unemployed Man* (London, Nisbet, 1933), p. 178.
10 Mowat, *Britain Between the Wars*, p. 485.
11 The *Bernstein Questionnaires* (1934 and 1937, held in the British Film Institute Library, London).
12 Dilys Powell, *Films since 1939* (London, Longmans, 1947), p. 64.
13 Taylor, *English History 1914–1945*, p. 315.

14 Don Macpherson, ed., *Traditions of Independence. British Cinema in the Thirties* (London, British Film Institute, 1980), p. 127.

15 Powell, *Films since 1939*, pp. 64–5. Rachael Low's *History of the British Film* has yet to be published on the feature film of the 1930s, but for her comments upon the 'colonization' argument see *The Movie*, Partwork (London, Orbis, 1979), pp. 41–4 and 261–3. See also Peter Stead, 'Hollywood's Message for the World: the British Response in the 1930s', *Historical Journal of Film, Radio and Television*, vol. 1, no. 1 (March 1981), pp. 19–32.

16 George Perry, *The Great British Picture Show* (London, Paladin, 1975), p. 85.

17 Ibid.

18 Ibid., pp. 12–14, 85–6.

19 See, for example, The Arts Enquiry, *The Factual Film* (London, Political and Economic Planning, Oxford University Press, 1947), pp. 210–17; Ernest Betts, *The Film Business* (London, Allen and Unwin, 1973), pp. 142–6, 280–81.

20 Nicholas Pronay, 'The First Reality: Film Censorship in Liberal England', in K. R. M. Short, ed., *Feature Films as History* (Croom Helm, London, 1981), pp. 113–37; Jeffrey Richards's two articles on 'The British Board of Film Censors and Content Control in the 1930s', *Historical Journal of Film, Radio and Television*, vol. 1, no. 2 (October 1981), and vol. 2, no. 1 (March 1982).

21 Pronay, 'The First Reality', p. 125.

22 John Montgomery, *Comedy Films* (London, Allen and Unwin, 1954), p. 179.

23 Jeff Nuttall, *King Twist. A Portrait of Frank Randle* (London, Routledge, 1978), p. 14.

24 Winifred Holtby, *South Riding* (Glasgow, Fontana/Collins, 1981), p. 35.

25 Rowson, 'A Statistical Survey', pp. 103, 113–15.

26 'British-mades Best Box Office at Home', *Variety*, 3 January 1933, p. 13.

27 Board of Trade, *Minutes of Evidence Taken before the Departmental Committee on Cinematograph Films* (HMSO, London, 1936), pp. 109–26.

28 *First Report of the Cinematograph Films Council* (HMSO, London, 1939), p. 15; also, for a review, pp. 16–18. For later comment see Political and Economic Planning, *The British Film Industry* (London, 1952), pp. 55–78.

29 'Exhibitors Talk', *Daily Film Renter*, 1 January 1937. The results of this survey were grossly over-simplified in a summary contained in *World Film News*, February 1937, pp. 6–7.

30 *First Report of the Cinematograph Films Council*, p. 9.

31 Stevenson and Cook, *The Slump*, p. 276.

32 *British Board of Film Censors Scenario Reports*, 1938, p. 19 (bound

volume, British Film Institute Library).

33 Macpherson, ed., *Traditions of Independence*, pp. 96, 103.
34 Quoted in Cyril B. Rollins and Robert J. Wareing, ed., *Victor Saville* (London, British Film Institute, 1972), p. 14.
35 Quoted in *Film Dope*, no. 11 (1977), p. 6.
36 *BBFC Scenario Reports*, 1934, pp. 315, 315a. A print of *Once in a New Moon* is held by the National Film Archive.
37 This was Clements's first feature film role of any importance and he was clearly 'typecast' for a time as a result of it. In *South Riding* (1938, Victor Saville) he appeared as a similar, if less vindictive, character.
38 Macpherson, ed., *Traditions of Independence*, pp. 127–8.
39 *Film Dope*, no. 11, pp. 5–6.
40 John Russell Taylor, 'Lords, Ladies and Cockney Sparrows', *The Movie* Partwork (London, Orbis, 1979), p. 533.
41 Basil Dean, *Mind's Eye* (London, Hutchinson, 1973), pp. 204–5.
42 See the Blue Script for the film, dated 15 May 1934, p. 2 (British Film Institute Library).
43 J. B. Priestley, *English Journey* (London, Heinemann, 1934), p. 281.
44 Jeffrey Richards, 'Gracie Fields. The Lancashire Britannia', pt 2, *Focus on Film*, no. 34 (1979), p. 36.

Chapter 16

1 C. de la Roche, 'The Mask of Realism', *Penguin Film Review*, 7 (1948), p. 38.
2 L. and P. Bendit, *Living Together Again* (Gramol, 1946), quoted in R. Minns, *Bombers and Mash* (London, Virago, 1980).
3 R. Broad and S. Fleming, eds., *Nella Last's War: a Mother's Diary* (Falling Wall Press, 1981), p. 161.
4 See, for example, the British Film Institute Library's compilation, 'Box office winners', from *Kinematograph Weekly*, 1942–52; the *Daily Mail* polls of British films and players in *Film Review*, 1946, 1947, 1948 (ed. M. Speed); the Bernstein Questionnaire, 1946–7.
5 Eve Perrick, *Daily Express*, 3 December 1949.
6 P. Calvert, interview with Jympson Harman, *Evening News*, 3 April 1950.
7 M. Lockwood, *Lucky Star* (London, Odhams, 1955), p. 71.
8 P. Calvert, interview with *Sunday Dispatch*, 1953.
9 D. Kerr, interview with *Time*, February 1947.
10 D. Dors, *Swingin' Dors* (London, World Distributors, 1960), p. 156.
11 C. de la Roche, 'That Feminine Angle', *Penguin Film Review*, 8 (January 1949), p. 33.

12 S. de Beauvoir, *Brigitte Bardot and the Lolita Syndrome* (London, New English Library, 1962), p. 10.

13 G. Brown, *Launder and Gilliat* BFI Monograph (London, 1977), p. 9.

14 R. Minns, *Bombers and Mash*, p. 182.

15 Ibid., p. 184: estimate of Interdepartmental Committee on Abortion, 1939.

16 Broad and Fleming, eds., *Nella's Last War*, p. 255.

17 D. Riley, 'Pronatalism and Working Women', *History Workshop Journal*, spring 1981, p. 109.

18 E. A. Kaplan, ed., *Women and Film Noir* BFI Monograph (London, 1978)

19 Ibid., p. 12.

20 E. Wilson, *Only Halfway to Paradise* (London, Tavistock, 1980), p. 44.

21 G. Thomas, *Women and Industry* (London, 1948).

22 Alan Ross, *The Forties* (London, Haycock Press, 1950).

23 R. Eatwell, *The 1945–51 Labour Governments* (London, Batsford Academic, 1979), p. 80.

24 J. Leman, ' "The advice of a real friend". Codes of Intimacy and Oppression in Women's Magazines 1937–1955', in H. Baehr, ed., *Women and Media*, vol. 3, no. 1 *Women's studies international quarterly* (Oxford, Pergamon, 1980), p. 76.

25 Hulton Readership surveys, 1947–54 (available in the British Library).

26 Census of Registrar General, 1931 and 1951.

27 J. Spraos, *The Decline of the Cinema* (London, Allen and Unwin, 1962), p. 42.

28 Census, 1931 and 1951.

29 P. Jephcott, *Rising Twenty* (London, 1948), p. 156.

30 R. Manvell, *The Film and the Public* (London, 1955), p. 219.

31 C. Lejeune, *Thank you for having me* (London, Hutchinson, 1964), p. 135.

32 S. Neale, 'The Same Old Story', *Screen Education*, 32/33 (autumn/winter 1979/80), p. 36.

33 J. Halloran, *The Effects of TV* (London, Panther, 1970), p. 19.

34 *Monthly Film Bulletin*, 1952.

35 J. Hill, 'Ideology, economy and the British Cinema', in Barrett *et al.*, eds., *Ideology and Cultural Production* (London, Croom Helm, 1979), p. 115.

36 M. Box, *Odd Woman Out* (London, 1974), p. 162.

37 M. Balcon, 'Let British films be ambassadors to the world: a Cogent Plea from the Head of Ealing Studios', *Kinematograph Weekly*, vol. 335, no. 1969 (1945), p. 31.

38 C. de la Roche, 'The Mask of Realism', p. 38.

39 *Monthly Film Bulletin*, 1946.

40 W. D. Wall and E. M. Smith, 'The film choices of adolescents', *British Journal of Educational Psychology*, Vol, XIX part 2 (June 1949).
41 P. Addison, *The Road to 1945* (London, Quartet, 1975), p. 115.
42 K. Marx, *The German Ideology* (London, 1974), p. 64.
43 For example, the case of *Chance of a Lifetime*, which faced distribution problems. See accounts in the *Evening Standard* (22 February 1950) and the *Daily Worker* (26 February 1950).
44 C. Mercer, 'After Gramsci', *Screen Education*, 36 (autumn 1980), p. 8.
45 With thanks to Jane Clarke, Richard Collins, John Ellis, Paul Kerr and Robert Murphy for their helpful comments on a draft of this article.

Chapter 17

1 Quoted in John Ellis, 'Made in Ealing', *Screen*, vol. 16, no. 1 (spring 1975), p. 119.
2 Quoted in ibid., p. 113.
3 Quoted in ibid., p. 117.
4 S. Freud, *Jokes and Their Relation to the Unconscious* (London, Penguin, 1976).
5 Charles Barr, *Ealing Studios* (London, Cameron and Tayleur/David and Charles, 1977), pp. 52–3.
6 In Monja Danischewsky, ed., *Michael Balcon's 25 Years in Film* (London, World Film Publications, 1947), p. 13.
7 I should like to thank Vincent Porter and Christopher Williams for their support. I am thoroughly indebted to the writings on Ealing of John Ellis and Charles Barr. I hope this piece serves as a modest complement to their work.

Chapter 18

1 The ideas in this paper are very much the distillation of a larger project on the British cinema 1957–63 to be published by the British Film Institute as 'Class, Sexuality and the British Cinema'.
2 Nina Hibbin, 'The British "New Wave" ', in *The Movie*, Partwork, chap. 57. London, Orbis, 1981.
3 Raymond Williams, 'A Lecture on Realism', *Screen*, vol. 18, no. 1 (spring 1977).
4 Penelope Gilliatt, *Observer*, 15 April 1962.
5 The exact delineation of the Movement, and of the 'Angry Young Men', is of course complicated. I use them both here as labels of convenience.
6 This was a process noted by Geoffrey Gorer in his essay, 'The Perils of Hypergamy', (in Gene Feldman and Max Gartenberg, *Protest* (London, Quartet, 1973). However, the political sophistication of the piece can be judged from the following conclusion: 'In this English pattern, there is a

much better fit with female hypergamy, for both sexes feel themselves indulged: and, as far as I know, chorus girls were happy, and made their well-born husbands happy, in the old Gaiety days' (p. 333).

7 Blake Morrisson, *The Movement: English Poetry and Fiction in the 1950s* (Oxford University Press, 1980).

8 Because of the confusions surrounding the concept of 'patriarchy' I use the term with a certain amount of hesitation. For a discussion of these confusions, and a conclusion with which I largely agree, see Michele Barrett, '*Women's Opppression Today: Problems in Marxist Feminist Analysis*', (London, New Left Books, 1980).

9 Laura Mulvey, 'Visual Pleasure and Narrative Cinema', *Screen*, vol. 16, No. 3 (autumn 1975).

10 E. Ann Kaplan, ed., *Women in Film Noir* (London, British Film Institute, 1978).

11 In his survey of British cinema, 1945–58, 'the climax period of a middle class cinema', Raymond Durgnat concludes as follows: 'The feeling for military-style paternalism, for the system and for the police, are special forms of a general acquiescence to father figures of a quietly heavy kind'. (*A Mirror for England*, London, Faber and Faber, 1970, p. 140).

12 Paul Hoch, *White Hero Black Beast: Racism, Sexism and the Mask of Masculinity* (London, Pluto, 1979).

13 'The literature of the past thirty years provides a staggering number of incidents in which the caste of virility triumphs over the social status of wealthy or even educated women' (Kate Millett, *Sexual Politics*, London, Virago, 1977, p. 36). It is perhaps not merely coincidental, then, that in 1960 a film of *Sons and Lovers* should have been made and *Lady Chatterley's Lover* be published by Penguin (an event followed by the now notorious trial).

14 Stuart Hall, 'Jimmy Porter and the Two-and-Nines', *Definition*, February 1960, p. 100.

15 Lucy Bland, Trisha McCabe and Frank Mort, 'Sexuality and Reproduction: Three 'Official' Instances', in Michèle Barrett *et al.*, ed., *Ideology and Cultural Production* (London, Croom Helm, 1979), p. 84.

16 "Duplicity in Mildred Pierce" in Kaplan, ed., *Women in Film Noir*, pp. 68–82.

17 Ibid., p. 79.

18 Peter Cowie, *The Abortive Renaissance* (Axle Publications, 1963).

19 Such an opposition is central to nearly all the 'new wave' films. I discuss the subject further in 'Ideology, Economy and the British Cinema', in Barrett *et al.*, *Ideology and Cultural Production*.

20 In his essay, 'Looking Back On Anger', in Vernon Bogdanor and Robert Skidelsky, ed., *The Age of Affluence* (London, Macmillan, 1970), D. E. Cooper sums up an attitude tailor made to fit *A Kind of Loving*: 'What these writers really attack is . . . effeminacy . . . the sum of those

qualities which are supposed traditionally, with more or less justice, to exude from the worst in women: pettiness, snobbery, flippancy, voluptuousness, superficiality, materialism' (p. 257). Of course, the basis of such an attitude is not just 'traditional' but embedded within the contemporary critique of the 'affluent society'. Viewed as the prime beneficiaries of the explosion in consumer durables ('gadgets for the home'), women can thus be made to carry the responsibility for a process whose dynamic (social and economic) is clearly something rather more than an expression of 'feminine qualities'.

21 Durgnat, *A Mirror for England*, p. 59.

22 'What seems to be at stake . . . is the attribution of certain dark and unclean, even animalistic, practices – especially sexual practices – to rebellious, outsider or subordinate groups' (Hoch, *White Hero Black Beast*, p. 54). Hoch suggests an explanation for this in terms of a ruling group's projection of their own forbidden sexual desires: '*Someone* had to serve as the source of the repressed desires, and the men of the lower classes and castes were (and are) the obvious targets' (ibid.)

23 See Kai T. Erikson, *Wayward Puritans* (London, Wiley, 1966).

24 Birmingham Feminist History Group, 'Feminism as Femininity in the Nineteen-Fifties', *Feminist Review*, 3 (1979).

25 Charles Barr, *Ealing Studios* (London, Cameron and Tayleur, 1977), p. 17.

26 *The Kitchen* (1961) is probably unique in this respect, with its concern to project work as a collective process. However, in order to achieve this the film was forced into an attenuation of narrative and dialogue in a central sequence which stands at odds with the rest of the film.

Chapter 19

1 W. Lippmann, *Public Opinion* (London, Macmillan, 1956; 1st ed. 1922), p. 96.

2 Richard Dyer, 'The Role of Stereotypes', in J. Cook and M. Lewington, *Images of Alcoholism* (London, British Film Institute, 1979), p. 19.

3 Jonathan Culler, *Structuralist Poetics* (London, Routledge, 1975), p. 145.

4 Vicki Eves, 'Britain's Social Cinema', *Screen*, 10, no. 6 (November/ December 1969).

5 Benny Green, *I've Lost My Little Willie* (London, Elm Tree Books, 1976), p. 29.

6 George Orwell, 'The Art of Donald McGill', in *My Country Right or Wrong* (London, Secker and Warburg, 1968; 1st ed. 1941), p. 159.

7 Ibid., p. 157.

8 Green, *I've Lost my Little Willie*, p. 120.

9 Orwell, 'The Art of Donald McGill', p. 157.

10 Green, *I've Lost my Little Willie*, p. 23.
11 Raymond Durgnat, *A Mirror for England* (London, Faber and Faber, 1970), p. 187.
12 Green, *I've Lost my Little Willie*, p. 23.
13 Ibid., p. 68.
14 It is perhaps of use in estimating the relative power of performer over role to list the number of appearances of the chief performers in the 28 films: Kenneth Williams (24), Joan Sims (23), Charles Hawtrey (23), Sidney James (19), Kenneth Connor (16), Peter Butterworth (15), Hattie Jacques (14), Bernard Bresslaw (14), Jim Dale (10), Barbara Windsor (9), Terry Scott (7). Joan Sims was the only one of these actors to achieve any significant change in character type.
15 Orwell, 'The Art of Donald McGill', p. 138.

Appendix
Statistical Survey of the British Film Industry
Patricia Perilli

Table 1

	Cinema admissions (millions)		Television licences Total	Monochrome	Colour
1935	907				
1940	1027				
1945	1585				
1950	1396	1950	343,882	343,882	
1955	1182	1955	4,503,766	4,503,766	
1960	501	1960	10,469,753	10,469,753	
1965	327	1965	13,253,045	13,253,045	
1970	193	1970	15,882,528	15,609,131	273,397
1975	116	1975	17,700,815	10,120,493	7,580,322
1980	96	1980	18,284,865	5,383,125	12,901,740

The figures for cinema admissions are those issued by the Department of Trade. According to the Cinema Commission of 1917, the annual attendance figure was approximately 1075 million.

The figures for television licences are those issued by the BBC.

Television licences were not required before June 1946. When the service closed down in 1939, there were already more than 20,000 viewers, according to the BBC Handbook.

Table 2

Films registered with the Department of Trade 1930–80

Year	British films				EEC films*	Foreign films			
	Over 72 mins	33⅓–72 mins	Total over 33⅓ mins	Under 33⅓ mins	Under 33⅓ mins	Over 72 mins	33⅓–72 mins	Total over 33⅓ mins	Under 33⅓ mins
1929/30			96	180				506	885
1934/35			190	123				477	697
1939/40			108	207				399	508
1945	40	36	76	174		191	183	374	295
1950	74	49	123	238		308	153	461	524
1955	82	40	122	310		268	91	359	316
1960	79	44	123	285		254	67	321	175
1965	69	22	91	227		233	23	256	166
1970	85	11	96	108		275	14	289	61
1975	70	13	83	69	59	212	16	228	38
1980	41	16	57	66	38	178	12	180	16

The statistics are those issued by the Department of Trade.

* From 1973 onwards films were registered as being eligible for British or Community quota.

Table 3

Films submitted to the British Board of Film Censors

		'U'	'A'	'AA'	'H' until 1950 'X' from 1951	Refused	
1930	Long	490	366			12	2303
	Short	1399	20			(+ 16 outstanding)	2117
1935	Long	368	318			17	
	Short	1382	32				1754
1939	Long	269	312		11	3	
	Short	1121	38				
1945		165	301		3	5	469
1950		332	227		1	8	565
1955		271	186		35	10	500
1960		199	181		98	3	588
1965		155	144		95	25(11)	397
1970		104(9)	84(31)	77(29)	212(97)	17(3)	502
1975		74(5)	96(32)	73(12)	164(98)	4	424
1980		25	82(9)	84(4)	124(54)		319

The statistics are those issued by the British Board of Film Censors.

The figures for 1930–39 cover all films submitted to the Board. 'Long' films are those of over 33⅓ minutes' duration; 'short' films, under 33⅓ minutes' duration.

The figures for 1945–80 cover films of 45 minutes or more, including documentaries and cartoons. The figures between brackets indicate the number of films cut to conform with each category, except those in the column headed 'Refused'; here the figures between brackets indicate the number passed 'X' in subsequent years, generally with cuts.

Table 4

	Number of cinemas	Seating capacity (thousands)
1910	1600	
1915	3500	
1925	3878	
1935	4448	
1940	4671	
1945	4703	
1950	4660	4221
1955	4483	4087
1960	3034	2960
1965	1971	2013
1970	1529	1466
1975	1530	879
1980	1652	688

Growth of multi cinemas

	Single cinemas	Double cinemas	Triple cinemas	Other multi cinemas	Total
1970	1461	52		16	1529
1975	848	198	387	97	1530
1980	584	284	537	157	1562

The statistics from 1935 onwards are those issued by the Department of Trade.

Early estimates of the number of cinemas vary considerably. Figures prior to 1935 come from the *Cinematograph Exhibitors' Diary* and the *Kinematograph Year Book*, and are probably on the low side.

Table 5

Distribution

	Total of films distributed	Films distributed by major American companies	Percentage of total distributed by major American companies	Total of British films distributed	British films distributed by major American companies	Percentage of British films distributed by major American companies
1926	580	266	46	18	2	11
1929	504	263	52	52	16	31
1950	400	221	55	72	7	10
1958	360	243	67	84	35	42
1971	235	177	75	74	44	59
1980	188	82	44	36	8	22

The statistics 1926–71 are reprinted from the publication issued by the ACTT, *Nationalising the Film Industry*. Figures do not cover all films released but the number of films released by the major distributing companies. The figures for 1980 are based on the listing published in the *Screen International Film and TV Year Book*.

Pattern of exhibition

Year	Number of circuits with 10 or more cinemas	Percentage of cinemas owned by circuits with 10 or more cinemas	Percentage of cinemas controlled by the 2 major circuits	The major circuits	
1915		6			
1935	34	27.5	9.8	ABC	247
				Gaumont – British	189
				Union Cinema Co.	128
				PCT	103
1950	47	46.3	20.9	CMA	560
				ABC	414
				Union Cinema Co.	119
				Essoldo	93
1960	33	57.7	25.7	CMA	457
				ABC	324
				Essoldo	172
				Star	117
1970	19	65	31.5	Rank	256
				ABC	226
				Classic	83
				Star	68
1980	10	63.8	39.3	EMI	330
				Rank	284
				Star/Cinecenta	150
				Classic	130

The statistics have been compiled from cinema listings published in the *Kinematograph Year Books* and *Screen International Film and TV Year Book*.

ABC: Associated British Cinemas Ltd. CMA: Circuits Management Association. PCT: Provincial Cinematograph Theatres. The Gaumont-British and Odeon circuits came under the control of CMA in 1948.

Table 7

Imported capital for film production by British subsidiaries of the major American film companies

	£ millions
1965	14.9
1966	18.0
1967	22.8
1968	31.3
1969	20.9
1970	12.8
1971	18.6
1972	14.0
1973	4.8
1974	2.9
1975	4.2
1976	4.8
1977	5.3
1978	7.9
1979	6.0

The statistics are those issued by the Department of Trade.

This table covers the total receipts by the United Kingdom subsidiaries of the major American film companies in respect of film production and therefore differs from Table 8, which sets out the net receipts (ie: capital imported for film production less capital exported for film production abroad.)

Table 8

Net receipts from overseas for the performance and production of films, 1965–79

	Performances of films			Production of films			Total receipts		
	United Kingdom subsidiaries of major American companies (£ millions)	Other companies	All companies	United Kingdom subsidiaries of major American companies	Other companies	All companies	United Kingdom subsidiaries of major American companies	Other companies	All companies
1965	(10.4)	3.7	(6.7)	12.6	.3	12.9	2.2	4.0	6.2
1966	(10.2)	4.6	(5.6)	13.0	1.3	14.3	2.8	5.9	8.7
1967	(6.2)	3.5	(2.7)	17.3	9.5	26.8	11.1	13.0	24.1
1968	(8.9)	3.2	(5.7)	26.4	2.4	28.8	17.5	5.6	23.1
1969	(8.5)	4.0	(4.5)	13.1	5.2	18.3	4.6	9.2	13.8
1970	(6.6)	2.9	(3.7)	11.9	3.2	15.1	5.3	6.1	11.4
1971	(7.9)	4.8	(3.1)	15.3	2.4	17.7	7.4	7.2	14.6
1972	(11.6)	3.6	(8.0)	13.8	2.6	16.4	2.2	6.2	8.4
1973	(8.0)	3.4	(4.6)	3.8	2.7	6.5	(4.2)	6.1	1.9
1974	(9.4)	7.2	(2.2)	2.6	6.1	8.7	(6.8)	13.3	6.5
1975	(10.4)	17.4	7.0	3.3	6.1	9.4	(7.1)	23.5	16.4
1976	(11.1)	17.5	6.4	4.3	8.8	13.1	(6.8)	26.3	19.5
1977	(14.5)	24.2	9.7	4.9	15.8	20.7	(9.6)	40.0	30.4
1978	(21.3)	34.7	13.4	3.9	25.2	29.1	(17.4)	59.9	42.5
1979	(24.7)	33.2	8.5	2.0	24.1	26.1	(22.7)	57.3	34.6

The statistics are those issued by the Department of Trade.

In the 1979 enquiry, revisions were made to the figures to allow for smaller film companies not adequately covered in previous enquiries. In this table, the revised figures have been used from 1974 onwards.

Figures in brackets: negative – i.e. represent a net overseas expenditure.

Table 9

	Employment in studios				Employment in cinemas		
	Technical	Craft Grades	Other grades including clerical	Total	Full-time	Part-time	Total
1936	1000*	5000*	1000*	7000*			
1945	997	2803	876	4676			
1948	1728	4186	1704	7618			
1950	674	1656	1092	3422	51,719	33,996	85,715
1955	721	1769	992	3482	44,273	37,141	81,414
1960	593	1730	818	3141	28,168	24,933	53,101
1965	544	2216	859	3619	18,609	19,137	37,746
1970					12,005	16,084	28,089
1975					7618	11,822	19,440
1980					6420	10,054	16,474

The statistics for employment in cinemas are those issued by the Department of Trade. The figures for employment in studios are those published by the *Kinematograph Year Book* and refer only to regular employment (not freelance labour) in the production of feature films.

* Approximate figures.

Table 10

Analysis of production costs

	Story and script	Producer and director	Production unit salaries	Craft labour	Sets and materials	Acting	Film and laboratory charges	Studio facilities	Type factor	Finance and insurance	Miscellaneous
	%	%	%	%	%	%	%	%	%	%	%
1930s	4.7	11.3	8.9	6.7	2.7	18.2	9.2	18.1	5.2	9.0	6.0
	7.9	14.5	5.6	6.4	4.9	17.5	8.0	17.8	2.9	10.7	3.8
1950s	10.4	9.5	7.6	7.7	6.4	18.5	4.2	11.3	1.3	16.6	6.5
	3.2	8.1	10.4	8.0	3.5	12.7	11.5	11.3	2.5	18.0	10.8
1970s	6.7	9.5	15.6	1.6	6.0	18.0	10.6	6.1	1.6	2.2	22.1
	1.2	4.2	16.6	4.4	6.6	21.5	5.1	6.6	2.2	11.5	20.1

These figures relate to film budgets held in the library of the British Film Institute.

Costs shown under the heading 'Type factor' include the main items that vary according to the type of film that is being made – for example, music, costumes and location expenses.

Table II

Distribution of box-office receipts

	Gross box-office receipts (£ millions) (at then current prices)	*(£ millions) (at 1980 prices)	Entertainment duty	Payments to the British Film Production Fund	Net receipts	Payments for film hire	Exhibitors' share after paying film hire
1935	38.7		5.8		32.9		
1940	44.9	(485.4)	6.7		38.2		
1945	114.2	(1027.8)	40.8		73.4		
1950	105.2	(779.5)	36.8	0.4	68.0	24.1	43.8
1955	105.8	(632.7)	33.4	2.7	69.8	24.5	45.3
1960	63.6	(338.4)	2.0	3.8	57.8	19.6	38.2
1965	61.7	(278.9)		4.6	57.1	20.9	36.2
1970	59.0	(213.0)		4.2	54.8	18.4	36.4
1975	71.2	(139.6)		4.9	66.3	21.4	44.9
1980	135.7	(135.7)		5.8	129.9	42.2	87.7

The statistics are those issued by the Department of Trade. Entertainment duty was repealed from 10 April 1960. Payments to the British Film Production Fund started in September 1950.

* This column, in which the purchasing power of the pound in 1980 has been reckoned as a constant 100p, shows the comparable figures for box-office receipts from 1940 onwards; VAT is included where relevant.

Select Bibliography
The British Cinema
Susan Daws

The arrangement of this select bibliography is largely alphabetical by author within each subject field, books and pamphlets being listed before periodical articles. In the section on legislation, however, the arrangement is chronological, with items of secondary legislation grouped under the principal enabling statute; here, items no longer in force are marked with an asterisk. In the section on personalities at the end, the arrangement is first by function (director, screen-writers, and so on); then, under each heading, general books are followed by biographies and autobiographies, alphabetically by subject. In cases where a person performed more than one function, books about him will be found under that function for which he is best known. For example, Nicolas Roeg is under the heading 'Directors', and not under 'Cinematographers'.

The bibliography is classified under the following headings and sub-headings:

The industry: General; History; British Film Industry; Copyright; Economics; Statistics; Film Companies and Studios; Censorship

Government and the Cinema: Government Reports; Legislation: General Articles; Statutes and Statutory Instruments: Film; Statutes and Statutory Instruments: Broadcasting; Co-production Treaties; Annual Reports

Cinemas and their Audiences: Distribution; Cinemas: General; Cinemas: Listed Alphabetically by Location; Films in the United Kingdom; Films Abroad

Films of Fact: Documentaries; Colonial Films; Short Films; Newsreels; History and Film; Independent and Free Cinema; Propaganda; Education; Film Schools; Scientific and Industrial Films

British Films: British Character in Films; Films: General; Films: Listed Alphabetically by Title; Adventure Films; Comedy Films; Horror Films

Personalities: Pioneers; Producers; Screenwriters; Directors; Art Designers; Cinematographers; Editors; Composers; Actors: General; Actors: Listed Alphabetically

The Industry

General

Alexander, Donald, *Facts about Films* (London Bureau of Current Affairs, 1946) (Current Affairs, no. 15)

Andrews, Cyril Bruyn, *The Theatre, the Cinema and Ourselves* (London, Clarence House Press, 1947)

Balcon, Michael, *Film Production and Management* (London, British Institute of Management, 1950, Occasional Papers, no. 4)

Realism or Tinsel, paper delivered to the Workers' Film Association, 1943

Belmans, Jacques, *Jeune cinéma anglais* (Lyon, SERDOC, 1967: Premier Plan, no. 44)

Blakeston, Oswell, ed., *Working for the Films* (London, Focal Press, 1947)

Butler, Ivan, *Cinema in Britain: an Illustrated Survey* (London, Tantivy Press, 1973)

Central Office of Information: Reference Division, *The Film in Britain* (London, Central Office of Information, 1963)

Film Production Association of Great Britain, *Britain: World Film Centre 1976* (London, Film Production Association of Great Britain, 1976)

Furniss, Harry, *Our Lady Cinema* (Bristol, Arrowsmith, 1914)

Gifford, Denis, *British Cinema: an Illustrated Guide* (London, Zwemmer, 1968: International Film Guide Series)

The British Film Catalogue 1895–1970: a Guide to Entertainment Films (Newton Abbot, David and Charles, 1973)

Cinema Britanico (Rio de Janeiro, Cinemateca do Museu, 1963)

The Illustrated Who's Who in British Films (London, Batsford, 1978)

Kolodynski, Andrzej, *100 filmow angielskich* (Warsaw, Wydawnictwa Artystyczne i Filmowe, 1975)

Labour Party, *The Arts and the People: Labour's Policy towards the Arts* (London, Labour Party, 1977)

Lovell, Alan, ed., *Art of the Cinema in Ten European Countries* (Strasbourg, Council of Europe, 1967: Education in Europe, Sec. IV, no. 7)

Lovell, Alan, *Breakthrough in Britain* (London, British Film Institute Education Department, 1967: Study Unit 1)

The British Cinema: the Unknown cinema, seminar paper (London, British Film Institute Education Department, 1969)

Manvell, Roger, *New Cinema in Britain* (London, Studio Vista, 1969)

New Cinema in Europe (London, Studio Vista, 1966)

Minney, Rubeigh James, *Talking of Films* (London, Home and Van Thal, 1947)

Noble, Peter, *Spotlight on Filmland: a Book about British Films* (London, Ward and Hitchon, 1947)

Towers, Harry Alan, and Leslie Mitchell, *The March of the Movies* (London, Sampson Low Marston, 1947)

Vermilye, Jerry, *The Great British Films* (Secaucus, N.J., Citadel Press, 1978)

Warren, Low, *The Film Game* (London, Werner Laurie, 1937)

Zambelli, Enrico Carlo, *Introduzione al cinema inglese* (Naples, Edizioni Cinema Sera, 1967)

General: Periodical Articles

Dusinberre, Deke. 'On Expanding Cinema, *Studio International* 190 (November/December 1975), pp. 220–24

Fothergill, Dorothy, 'Quality of Film in Britain', *Month*, 13 (February 1980), pp. 49–51

Gray, J. C. 'The Outlook for British Films', *Political Quarterly* (October/December 1950), pp. 384–94

Harris, Sir Sidney, 'Public Taste in the Cinema', *English*, 8, no. 44 (1950), pp. 55–9

Houston, Penelope, 'The Undiscovered Country', *Sight and Sound*, 25, no. 1 (summer 1955), pp. 10–14

Hutchinson, Tom, 'By their Films shall ye know them', *Twentieth Century*, 175 (summer 1966), pp. 18–19

Kauffmann, Stanley, 'England; with a Note on Ireland', in Stanley Kauffmann, *A World on Film, Criticism and Commentary* (New York, Harper and Row, 1966), pp. 177–220

Lovell, Alan, 'Notes on British Film Culture', *Screen*, 13, no. 2 (summer 1972), pp. 5–15

Macdonald, Dwight, 'England', in *Dwight Macdonald on movies* (Englewood Cliffs, N.J., Prentice-Hall, 1969), pp. 388–411

Mayersberg, Paul, 'A National Cinema', *New Society*, 31 August 1967, pp. 296–7

Perkins, V. F., 'The British Cinema', in Ian Cameron, ed., *Movie reader* (London, November Books, 1972), pp. 7–11

'Supporting the British Cinema', *Movie*, no. 16 (Winter 1968–9) pp. 13–15

Ralph, J. D., 'Films and the Festival of Britain 1951', in Roger Manvell, ed., *The Year's Work in the Film, 1950* (London, Longman, for the British Council, 1951), pp. 60–62

Rhode, Eric, 'British Filmmakers', *Listener*, 26 September 1968, pp. 385–7

Taylor, John Russell, 'Tomorrow, the World: Some Reflections on the Unenglishness of English Films, *Sight and Sound*, 43, no. 2 (spring 1974), pp. 80–83

Wollen, Peter, Alan Lovell and Sam Rohdie, interview with Ivor Montagu (on British cinema), *Screen*, 13, no. 3 (autumn 1972), pp. 71–113; corrections and additions by Montagu, *Screen*, 13, no. 4 (winter 1972/3), pp. 154–5

'The British Cinema', *Movie*, no. 1 (June 1962), pp. 2–9

History

Armes, Roy, *A Critical History of the British Cinema* (London, Secker and Warburg, 1978. 'Cinema Two' series)

Balcon, Michael, Ernest Lindgren, Forsyth Hardy and Roger Manvell, *Twenty Years of British Film, 1925–1945* (London, Falcon, 1947)

Barnes, John, *The Beginnings of the Cinema in England* (Newton Abbot, David and Charles, 1976)

Betts, Ernest, *The Film Business: a History of British Cinema 1896–1972* (London, Allen and Unwin, 1973)
Inside Pictures, with some Reflections from the Outside (London, Cresset Press, 1960)

Brown, Pat, *The First Fifty Years: a History of the Finchley Cine Society, 1930–1980* (New Barnet, Herts., John Morin for Finchley Cine Society, 1980)

Chanan, Michael, *The Dream that kicks: the Prehistory and Early Years of Cinema in Britain* (London, Routledge and Kegan Paul, 1980)

Durgnat, Raymond, *A Mirror for England: British Movies from Austerity to Affluence* (London, Faber and Faber, 1970)

Grenfell, David, *An Outline of British Film History, 1896–1962* (unpublished typescript, 1963)

Lefevre, Raymond and Roland Lacourbe, *30 ans de cinéma Britannique* (Paris, Editions Cinéma 76, 1976)

Low, Rachel and Roger Manvell, *The History of the British Film, 1896–1906* (London, Allen and Unwin, 1948)
The History of the British Film, 1906–1914 (London, Allen and Unwin, 1949)
The History of the British Film, 1914–1918 (London, Allen and Unwin, 1950)
The History of the British Film, 1918–1929 (London, Allen and Unwin, 1971).
The History of the British Film, 1929–1939: Documentary and Educational Films of the 1930s (London, Allen and Unwin, 1979)
The History of the British Film, 1929–1939: Films of Comment and Persuasion of the 1930s (London, Allen and Unwin, 1979)

MacPherson, Don, ed., *Traditions of Independence: British Cinema in the Thirties* (London, British Film Institute, 1980)

Malassinet, Alain, *Société et cinéma: les années 1960 en Grande-Bretagne; essai d'interprétation sociologique* (Paris, Lettres Modernes/ Minard, 1979: Etudes Cinématographiques, nos 115–121)

Oakley, Charles, *Where we came in: 70 Years of the British Film Industry* (London, Allen and Unwin, 1964)

Perry, George, *The Great British Picture Show* (London, Hart-Davis Mac-Gibbon, 1974)

'Progress of British films, pt 1' (Glasgow, McKenzie Vincent and Co., ?1946)

'Progress of British films, pt 2' (Glasgow, McKenzie Vincent and Co., ?1946)
'Progress of British films, 1946–47' (Glasgow, McKenzie Vincent and Co., ?1946)
Scottish Film Council, *Fifty Years at the Pictures* (Glasgow, Scottish Film Council, 1946)
Venice, *Mostra internazionale d'arte cinematografica. Retrospettiva del film inglese del 1895 al 1948* (Venice, 18th Mostra Internazionale d'arte Cinematografica, 1957)
Venice, *Mostra internazionale d'arte cinematografica*. Retrospettiva dedicata *al film inglese di guerra (1940/1945)*, ed. British Film Institute (Venice, 21st Mostra Internazionale d'arte Cinematografica, 1960)

History: Periodical Articles

Anstey, Edgar, 'Development of Film Technique in Britain', in Roger Hanvell, ed., *Experiment in the Film* (London, Greywalls Press, 1949), pp. 234–65.
Aylott, Dave, 'Reminiscences of a showman', *Cinema Studies*, 2 January 1965), pp. 3–6
Bowler, S., 'Fiftieth Anniversary', *British Journal of Photography*, 27 February 1981, p. 228.
Crow, Duncan, 'The Advent of Leviathan (1927–1936)', *Sight and Sound*, 23, no. 4 (April–June 1954) pp. 191–3, 222
Curtis, David, 'English Avant-garde Film: an Early Chronology', *Studio International*, 190 (November/December 1975) pp. 176–82.
East, John M., 'The Birth of the Cinema Trade in Scotland), *Scotland's Magazine*, 69 (December 1973) pp. 27–9.
'Looking back – when Croydon was the Film Capital of Britain', in Maurice Speed *Film Review 1977–78* (London, W. H. Allen, 1977) pp. 102–9.
Ellis, John, 'Art, Culture and Quality – Terms for a Cinema in the Forties and Seventies', *Screen*, 19, no. 3 (autumn 1978) pp. 9–49.
Elvin, George, 'Planned Production', *Sight and Sound*, 13, no. 50 (July 1944), pp. 30–31.
French, Philip, 'The Alphaville of Admass, or how we learned to stop worrying and love the Boom', *Sight and Sound*, 35, no. 3 (summer 1966), pp. 106–11.
Gunston, David, 'Railways on the Screen', *Railway Magazine*, February 1958, pp. 86–90.
Honri, B. 'Milestones in Motion Picture Production', *British Kinematography, Sound and Television*, 51 (April 1969), p. 94.
'Circle of Technical Trends and Portents', *British Kinematography, Sound and Television*, 52 (May 1970) pp. 130–32.
'Then, now and the Future', *British Journal of Photography*, 31 January 1975, pp. 80–83.

Kimbley, D. 'How the B.K.S. began: the developments of 1928–32', *BKSTS Journal*, 63 (January 1981, p. 123.

Paul, R. W., C. M. Hepowrth and W. G. Barker, 'Before 1910: Kinematograph Experiences', *Proceedings of the British Kinematograph Society*, no. 38 (1936), pp. 2–16.

Rhode, Eric, 'The British Cinema in the Seventies', *Listener*, 14 August 1969, pp. 201–3.

Seton, Marie, 'The British Cinema, 1896–1907', *Sight and Sound*, 6, no. 21 (spring 1937), pp. 5–8.

'The British Cinema, 1907–1914', *Sight and Sound*, 6, no. 22 (summer 1937), pp. 64–7.

'The British Cinema, 1914', *Sight and Sound*, 6, no. 23 (autumn 1937), pp. 126–8.

'War', *Sight and Sound*, 6, no. 24 (winter 1937–8), pp. 182–5.

Slide, Anthony, 'Bioscope Shows at Hull Fair', *Cinema Studies*, 2 (June 1965), pp. 7–9.

Smith, Trevor, 'British Film Pioneers. Pt 1: 1896–1908', *Flickers*, no. 34 (October 1976) pp. 17–19.

'British Film Pioneers. Part 2: 1908–1914', *Flickers*, no. 35 (February 1977) pp. 16–19.

'British Film Pioneers. Part 3: 1914–1918', *Flickers*, no. 36 (January 1978), pp. 3–8.

'British Film Pioneers. Part 4: 1919–1923', *Flickers*, no. 37 (October 1978), pp. 3–11.

'British Film Pioneers. Part 5: 1919–1923', *Flickers*, no. 38 (1979), pp. 3–12.

'British Film Pioneers. Part 6: 1924–1928', *Flickers*, no. 39 (January 1980), pp. 15–18.

'British Film Pioneers. Part 7: 1924–1928 (cont.)', *Flickers*, no. 40 (March 1980), pp. 16–20.

'British Film Pioneers. Part 8: a New Melting Pot', *Flickers*, no. 41 (June 1980), pp. 8–10.

Wilcox, Herbert, 'British Films – Past and Future', *Royal Society of Arts Journal*, 112 (June 1964), pp. 514–22.

Wratten, I. D., 'Early Years of the British Kinematograph Society', *BKSTS Journal*, 63 (January 1981), pp. 14–15.

British Film Industry

Association of Cinematograph, Television and Allied Technicians, *Nationalizing the Film Industry*, report of the ACTT Nationalization Forum, August 1973 (London, Association of Cinematograph, Television and Allied Technicians, 1973)

Bond, Ralph, *Monopoly: the Future of British Films* (London, Association of

Ciné-Technicians, 1946)

Boughey, Davidson, *The Film Industry* (London, Pitman, 1921: 'Common Commodities and Industries' series).

British Film Academy, *The Film Industry in Great Britain: some Facts and Figures* (London, British Film Academy, 1950)

Chanan, Michael, *Labour Power in the British Film Industry* (London, British Film Institute, 1976)

Communist Party, *The Film Industry: a Memorandum* (London, Communist Party, 1947)

Federation of British Industries, *The Activities of the British Film Industry, presented to the Delegates to the Monetary and Economic Conference of the Federation of British Industries, London 12 July 1933* (London, Federation of British Industries, 1933)

Film Centre, *The Film Industry in Six European Countries: a Detailed Study of the Film Industry in Denmark compared with that in . . . the United Kingdom* (Paris, UNESCO, 1950)

Film Industry Employees' Council, *The Crisis of British Films* (London, Film Industry Employees' Council, ?1951)

Film Production Association of Great Britain, the EEC and the film industry: a transcript of a conference convened by the Film Production Association at the National Film Theatre, 15 December 1971 (unpublished paper)

Foot, Paul, *The Politics of Harold Wilson* (Harmondsworth, Penguin Books, 1968). Chapter 2 is concerned with Wilson's time at the Board of Trade.

Kelly, Terence, Graham Norton and George Perry, *A Competitive Cinema* (London, Institute of Economic Affairs, 1966)

Labour Party, *Proposals for Improvement in the British Film Industry*, report of the Films Sub-committee of the Trade and Industry Group of the Labour Party (London, Labour Party, 1946)

Mullally, Frederic, *Films – an Alternative to Rank: an Analysis of Power and Policy in the British Film Industry* (London, Socialist Book Centre, 1946)

Political and Economic Planning, *The British Film Industry; a Report on its History and Present Organization with Special Reference to the Economic Problems of British Feature Film Production, May 1952.* (London, Political and Economic Planning, 1952; Supplement, 1958)

Porter, Vincent, ed., *British Film Production within the EEC; Background Papers* (London, Polytechnic of Central London, 1972)

Walker, Alexander, *Hollywood, England: the British Film Industry in the Sixties* (London, Joseph, 1974)

Wood, Linda, *British Film Industry* (London, British Film Institute Library Services, 1980: Information Guides, no. 1)

British Film Industry: Periodical Articles

Adam, Nicolas, 'Copybook Profits', *New Statesman*, 11 January 1974, pp. 38–40

Balcon, Michael, 'Rationalize!', *Sight and Sound*, 9, no. 36 (winter 1940/41), pp. 62–3

Cameron, Ian, 'Saving the Cinema', *Spectator*, 7 February 1964, pp. 178–80
'The Hard Night Out: the Federation of British Film Makers Report', *Spectator*, 10 July 1964, pp. 45–6

Clayton, Bertram, 'The State and the Films', *Quarterly Review*, January 1949, pp. 104–15

Crow, Duncan, 'The Protected Industry. No. 1: The Need for Protection', *Sight and Sound*, 19, no. 8 (December 1950), pp. 317–18
'The Protected Industry. No. 2: The Quota and the Fund', *Sight and Sound*, 19, no. 9 (January 1951), pp. 357–8
'The Protected Industry. No. 3: Closing the Gap', *Sight and Sound*, 19, no. 10 (February 1951), pp. 391–2
'The Protected Industry. No. 4: Protecting the Producer', *Sight and Sound*, 19, no. 11 (March 1951), pp. 429–30
'The Protected Industry. No. 5: Summing up', *Sight and Sound*, 19, no. 12, (April 1951), pp. 460, 488

Davenport, Nicholas, 'The Film Crisis', *Spectator*, 20 December 1963, pp. 830–31
'The State Muddle in Films', *Spectator*, 28 October 1966, pp. 562–3
'The Film Crisis', *Spectator*, 18 September 1971, p. 424

Dickinson, Margaret and Simon Hartog, interview Sir Harold Wilson, *Screen*, 22, no. 3 (1981), pp. 9–22

Economist Intelligence Unit, 'In the Common Market: a Wider Screen for Britain', *Sight and Sound*, 31, no. 1 (winter 1961/62), pp. 32–34

Elvin, George H., 'British Labour Problems', *Sight and Sound*, 10, no. 40 (spring 1942), pp. 79–81

Eves, Vicki, 'The Structure of the British Film Industry', *Screen*, 11, no. 1 (January/February 1970), pp. 41–54

Fay, Gerard, 'The British Film Industry: its Crisis and its Future', *World Review*, June 1948, pp. 43–6

Foreman, Carl, 'Films and Film-making in the Seventies', *Royal Society of Arts Journal*, 121 (October 1973), pp. 699–706

Forsyth, Bill, 'British Cinema: 1981 to . . .', paper delivered at the Symposium held at the National Film Theatre, 4 November 1981, *Sight and Sound*, 50, no. 4 (autumn 1981), p. 243

Gillett, John, 'State of the Studios', *Sight and Sound*, 33, no. 2 (spring 1964), pp. 55–61

Gordon, David, 'Ten Points about the Crisis in the British Film Industry', *Sight and Sound*, 43, no. 2 (spring 1974), pp. 66–72
'British National Pictures rides again', *Sight and Sound*, 45, no. 2 (spring 1976), pp. 81–2

Hill, Derek, 'Defence through FIDO', *Sight and Sound*, 28, nos 3, 4 (summer/autumn 1959), pp. 183–4

Houston, Penelope, 'Time of Crisis', *Sight and Sound*, 27, no. 4 (spring 1958), pp. 167–75

'Whose Crisis?', *Sight and Sound*, 33, no. 1 (winter 1964), pp. 26–28,50

'England, their England', *Sight and Sound*, 35, no. 2 (spring 1966), pp. 54–6

'Interim Inaction', *Sight and Sound*, 50, no. 3 (summer 1981), p. 150

Hunnings, Neville, 'The Film Industry and the EEC', *Sight and Sound*, 41, no. 2 (spring 1972), pp. 82–5

Isaacs, Jeremy, 'British Cinema: 1981 to . . .', paper delivered at the Symposium held at the National Film Theatre, 4 November 1981, *Sight and Sound* 50, no. 4 (autumn 1981), pp. 241–2

Kitses, Jim, interview with Gavin Lambert (on the British cinema), *Screen*, 13, no. 2 (summer 1972), pp. 55–78

Open, M. 'Desperate Living', *Film Directions*, 4, no. 14 (1981), pp. 6–7

Porter, Vincent, 'TV Strategies and European Film Production', *Sight and Sound*, 43, no. 3 (summer 1974), pp. 163–5, 175

'Film Policy for the 80s: Industry or Culture?', *Sight and Sound*, 48, no. 4 (autumn 1979), pp. 221–3, 266

Puttnam, David, 'British Cinema: 1981 to . . .', paper delivered at the Symposium held at the National Film Theatre, 4 November 1981, *Sight and Sound*, 50, no. 4 (autumn 1981), pp. 238–40

Rix, Margaret S., 'The Shadowed Screen: Problems of the Film Industry', *Future*, 9, no. 2 (1954), pp. 32–5

Rotha, Paul, 'British Films', *World Review*, October 1948, pp. 47–51

Sainsbury, Peter, 'British Cinema: 1981 to . . .', paper delivered at the Symposium held at the National Film Theatre, 4 November 1981, *Sight and Sound*, 50, no. 4 (autumn 1981), pp. 242–3

Sinclair, Andrew, 'A Scenario for British Films', *New Statesman*, 31 August 1973, pp. 273–4

Smith, Brian, 'Nationalize!', *Sight and Sound*, 9, no. 36 (winter 1940/41), pp. 60–61

Terry, John, 'The Future of the British Film Industry', Kinnaird Lecture delivered at the Regent Street Polytechnic, November 1969, *Screen*, 11, no. 4/5 (1970), pp. 115–28

Thomas, F. L., 'Whither our Business?', *Sight and Sound*, 10, no. 40 (spring 1942), pp. 64–7

Wakely, Michael, 'Situation Hopeless but not Serious', *Films and Filming*, 16, no. 8 (May 1970), pp. 6–9

Watkins, Arthur, 'British Film Production', *Journal of the Royal Commonwealth Society* (July/August 1959), pp. 151–5

Wilson, David, 'Images of Britain', *Sight and Sound*, 43, no. 2 (spring 1974), pp. 84–7

Wyatt, Woodrow, 'Champagne for Hollywood', *New Statesman*, 20 March

1948, p. 231

'Dollars and Films', *New Statesman*, 8 May 1948, p. 368

'The American key to British Films', *The Economist*, 14 February 1976, pp. 76–7

'The Crisis we deserve', *Sight and Sound*, 39, no. 4 (autumn 1970), pp. 172–8

'The Film Crisis in Perspective', *Times Review of Industry and Technology*, February 1964, pp. 8–12

'Hollywood and Bust', *The Economist*, 29 November 1969, pp. 69–70

'Manic Depression in Wardour Street', *Economist*, 21 December 1963, pp. 1277–8

Copyright

Hunnings, Neville, 'Copyright', *Sight and Sound*, 36, no. 3 (summer 1967), pp. 138–40

'Copyright and the Pirates', *Sight and Sound*, 41, no. 3 (summer 1972), pp. 165,173

Porter, Vincent, 'Copyright or Copywrong?', *Sight and Sound*, 51, no. 1 (winter 1981/2), pp. 25–8

Economics

Department of Trade, *Review of Policy on Film Finance* (London, Department of Trade and Industry, 1979)

HM Customs and Excise, *Film Levy* (London, HM Customs and Excise, 1980) (Notice no. 111)

Klingender, F. D. and Stuart Legg, *Money behind the Screen: a Report prepared on behalf of the Film Council* (London, Lawrence and Wishart, 1937)

National Film Finance Corporation, *National Film Finance Consortium: a Memorandum* (London, National Film Finance Corporation, 1971)

Spraos, John, *The Decline of the Cinema: an Economist's Report* (London, Allen and Unwin, 1962)

Austen, David, 'Films and Finance,' *Films and Filming*, 16, no. 7 (April 1970), pp. 5–8

Caulkin, Simon, 'The Film Finance Farce', *New Statesman*, 10 September 1971, p. 328

Fletcher, Paul, 'Film, Finance and the Future', *Film Finance*, no. 4, September 1971, pp. 3–8

Griffith, Richard, 'Where are the dollars? Part 1', *Sight and Sound*, (December 1949), pp. 33–4; Part 2, *Sight and Sound*, (January 1950), pp. 39–40; Part 3, *Sight and Sound*, (March 1950), pp. 44–5

Houston, Penelope, 'New Man at the NFFC, *Sight and Sound*, 48, no. 2

(spring 1979), pp. 70–73

Hartshorn, J. E., 'Finance for Films. Part 1: The Changing Scene'. *Banker*, (December 1952), pp. 350–4

'Finance for Films. Part 2: Exhibitors under Pressure', *Banker*, (January 1953), pp. 29–34

Kerstin, J. M., 'No Hollywood on the Thames', *Encounter*, 57, September 1981, pp. 45–9

MacCann, Richard Dyer, 'Subsidy for the Screen: Grierson and Group 3, 1951–1955', *Sight and Sound*, 46, no. 3 (summer 1977), pp. 168–73

Penn, D., 'What Price Admission?', *Film Directions*, 4, no. 14 (1981), pp. 8–9

Perkins, V. F., 'Supporting the British Cinema', *Movie*, no. 16 [1966], pp. 13–15

Rotha, Paul, 'Britain's Dollar-dominated Films', *New Statesman*, 24 January 1966, pp. 925–6

Taylor, John Russell, 'Backing Britain', *Sight and Sound*, 38, no. 3 (summer 1969), pp. 112–5

'All about Eady', *Economist*, 24 November 1979, pp. 39–40

'The Bank of Soho Square', *Economist*, 2 August 1969, pp. 56–7

'British Lion: the Government and the Film Industry', *Sight and Sound*, Supplement, 1954

'Developing British Films', *Economist*, 8 March 1969, pp. 56–7

'Lap Dissolve', *Economist*, 19 July 1958, pp. 225–6

'Mr Rank, Manufacturer', *Economist*, 15 September 1956, p. 911

Round table on British films, 'Economic and Creative Problems in the British Cinema', *Sight and Sound*, 19, no. 3 (May 1950), pp. 114–22

Statistics

British Film Producers Association, 'The Film Industry: Statistical Digest', nos 1 and 2, June 1954 and June 1955

Browning, H. E. and Sorrell, 'Cinemas and Cinema-going in Great Britain', *Journal of the Royal Statistical Society*, series A, vol. 117, pt 2 (1954), pp. 133–70

Chisholm, Cecil, and Louis Nagy, 'Can British Films become an Industry?', *Business*, August 1948, pp. 37–43, 88–90

Rowson, S. 'A Statistical Survey of the Cinema Industry in Great Britain in 1934', *Journal of the Royal Statistical Society*, 99 (1936), pp. 67–129

'Films and the Future', *Economist*, 12 November 1949, pp. 1076–8

Film Companies and Studios

Barr, Charles, *Ealing Studios* (London, Cameron & Tayleur/David and Charles, 1977)

Barr, Charles, 'Projecting Britain and the British Character: Ealing Studios, part 1', *Screen*, 15, no. 1 (spring 1974), pp. 87–121; part 2, *Screen*, 15, no. 2 (summer 1974), pp. 129–63

Boulting, John, and Roy Boulting, 'The Years of the Lion', *Spectator*, 3 January 1964, p. 5; 10 January 1964, pp. 41–3

Brown, Geoff, 'Ealing, your Ealing', *Sight and Sound*, 46, no. 3 (summer 1977), pp. 164–7

Clynton, Lionel, 'Michael Balcon of Ealing', in *British Film Yearbook, 1947–48*, compiled by Peter Noble (London, British Yearbooks, 1947), pp. 67–74

Davenport, Nicholas, 'Lion Couchant', *Spectator*, 16 August 1968, pp. 239–40

'British Lion: curing the Mange', *Spectator*, 6 May 1972, p. 709

Davis, John, 'The Rank Organization redeploys Resources'; Kenneth Winckles, 'The Group ramifies'; G. Darnley-Smith, 'Electronics for Home and Factory'; T. A. Law, 'Precision in Glass and Metal': *Times Review of Industry*, May 1960, pp. 4–13

Dickinson, Thorold, 'The Work of Sir Michael Balcon at Ealing Studios', in Roger Manvell, ed., *The Year's Work in the Film, 1950* (London, Longman for the British Council, 1951), pp. 9–17

Ellis, John, 'Made in Ealing', *Screen*, 16, no. 1 (spring 1975), pp. 78–127

Eyles, Allen, Robert Adkinson and Nicholas Fry, *The House of Horror: the Story of Hammer Films* (London, Lorrimer, 1973)
The House of Horror: the Complete Story of Hammer Films (2nd ed. of above title; London, Lorrimer, 1981)

Fothergill, Richard, 'The Ealing Tradition', *Screen Education*, no. 10 (September/October 1961), pp. 20–21, 50

Glaser, Gregg, *The Formation and Early History of Pinewood Studios* (Ithaca, NY, The Author, 1975), An independent research paper for the Foreign Study program of the Department of Cinema Studies and Photography, School of Communications, Ithaca College, NY

Hall, Dennis John, 'Balcon's Britain. Part 1', *Films*, 1, no. 3 (February 1981), pp. 40–43; Part 2, *Films*, 1, no. 4 (March 1981), pp. 30–35

Honri, B., 'Film Studios of Elstree: their Origins and Development', *British Journal of Photography*, 19 November 1976, pp. 1014–16
'Film Studios of Elstree: their Continued Development into the Television Age', *British Journal of Photography*, 17 December 1976, p. 1107

Junge, Helmut, *Plan for Film Studios: a Plea for Reform*' (London, Focal Press, 1945)

Lightman, Herb A., 'The Wonderful World of Pinewood Studios', *American Cinematographer*, 48, no. 3 (March 1967), pp. 178–81, 197

Lightman, Herb A., 'London – Pinewood revisited . . .', *American Cinematographer*, 49, no. 11, November 1968, pp. 842–3, 896

Manvell, Roger, *Art and Animation: the Story of Halas and Batchelor Animation*

Studio, 1940–1980 (London, Tantivy Press, 1980)

Morgan, John, 'Wounded Lion', *New Statesman*, 3 January 1964, pp. 5–6

Murphy, Robert, 'Gainsborough Pictures: a Popular Commercial Studio', thesis submitted for the degree of Master of Arts to the Polytechnic of Central London, 1981

Newnham, John K. 'Progress Report on the Charm School', *Picturegoer*, 25 September 1948, pp. 6–7

Perry, George, *Movies from the Mansion: a History of Pinewood Studios* (London, Elm Tree Books/Hamish Hamilton, 1976)

Perry, George, *'Forever Ealing: a Celebration of the Great British Film Studio* (London, Pavilion/Joseph, 1981)

Pickard, Roy, 'The Ealing Story', *Films in Review*, 26, no. 2 (February 1975), pp. 101–7

Pirie, David, *Hammer: a Cinema Case Study* (London, British Film Institute, 1980)

Robinson, David, 'Acting with Brushes and Paint' (Richard Williams Animation), *Sight and Sound*, 42, no. 3 (summer 1973), pp. 151, 154

Seaton, Ray and Roy Martin, 'Gainsborough: the Story of the Celebrated British Film Studio,' *Films and Filming*, no. 332, May 1982, pp. 8–15 'Gainsborough in the Forties', *Films and Filming*, no. 333 (June 1982), pp. 13–18

Shivas, Mark, 'British Lion', *Movie*, no. 14 (autumn 1965), pp. 1–4

Summers, Sue, 'The Splendour of days gone by . . .' (Pinewood) *Screen International*, no. 56 (2 October 1976), pp. 12–13, 31; Pinewood filmography 1936–1976, pp. 21–24

'The British Film Industry: the Elstree Story', *Future*, 9, no. 1 (1954), pp. 15–24

The Elstree Story: Twenty-one Years of Film-making, described by Leslie Banks [and others] (London, Clerke and Cockeran, 1949)

'The Organization of Change: the Rank Organization', *Times Review of Industry and Technology*, December 1965, pp. 20–27

Censorship

Brody, Stephen, *Screen Violence and Film Censorship: a Review of Research* (London, HMSO, 1977: Home Office Research Study, no. 40)

Home Office, *Children and 'A' films:* [letter to] *the Clerk to the Licensing Authority under the Cinematograph Act 1909* [from the] *Under-Secretary of State, Home Office* (London, HMSO, 1934)

Home Office, *The System of Film Censorship* (London, Home Office, 1980)

Hunnings, Neville March, *Film Censors and the Law* (London, Allen and Unwin, 1967)

Knowles, Dorothy, *The Censor, the Drama and the Film, 1900–1934* (London, Allen and Unwin, 1934)

Montagu, Ivor, *The Political Censorship of Films* (London, Gollancz, 1929)
O'Higgins, Paul, *Censorship in Britain* (London, Nelson, 1972)
Phelps, Guy, *Film Censorship* (London, Gollancz, 1975)
Trevelyan, John, *What the Censor saw* (London, Joseph, 1973)
Wistrich, Enid, *'I don't mind the sex, it's the violence': Film Censorship explored* (London, Boyars, 1978)

Censorship: Periodical Articles

Ellis, John, 'Photography/Pornography/Art/Pornography', *Screen*, 21, no. 1 (spring 1980), pp. 81–108
Gillett, John, 'Cut and come again!', *Sight and Sound*, 27, no. 5 (summer 1958), pp. 258–60
Grey, Antony, 'The Williams Report: one Step forward, Two Steps back', *Contemporary Review*, 236 (May 1980), pp. 256–60
Hill, Derek, 'The Habit of Censorship: "We're paid to have dirty minds" ', *Encounter*, July 1960, pp. 52–62; (reply by John Trevelyan, September 1960, pp. 61–4)
Hinxman, Margaret, 'The British Board of Film Censors', in *Films in 1951, Festival of Britain* (London, *Sight and Sound* for the British Film Institute, 1951), pp. 57–8
Holbrook, David, 'Test Case at Totnes', *Spectator*, 14 July 1973, pp. 582–3
Hunnings, Neville March, ". . . and loss of Paradise": the Origins of Censorship in England', *Sight and Sound*, 27, no. 3 (winter 1957/8), pp. 151–4
'Censorship: on the way out?', *Sight and Sound*, 38, no. 4 (autumn 1969), pp. 201–2
McDougall, Gordon, 'To deprave and corrupt? An Examination of the Method and Aim of Film Censorship in Britain', *Motion*, no. 2 (winter 1961–2), pp. 5–8
Manvell, Roger, 'The Liberty of the Screen', *New Humanist*, 88 (May 1972), pp. 18–19
Perkins, V. F., 'Censorship', *Movie*, no. 6 (January 1963), p. 16
'Interview with John Trevelyan', *Movie*, no. 6 (January 1963), pp. 17–19
'Interview with Joseph Losey', *Movie*, no. 6 (January 1963), pp. 20–21
Phelps, Guy, 'Censorship and the Press', *Sight and Sound*, 42, no. 3 (summer 1973), pp. 138–40
'The Role and Problems of Local Government Film Censorship', *Local Government Studies*, 9 (October 1974), pp. 11–20
Pronay, Nicholas, 'The First Reality: Film Censorship in Liberal England', in K. R. M. Short, ed., *Feature Films as History* (London, Croom Helm, 1981), pp. 113–37
Richards, Jeffrey, 'The British Board of Film Censors and Content Control in the 1930s: Images of Britain', *Historical Journal of Film, Radio and*

Television, 1, no. 2 (October 1981), pp. 95–116

Robertson, Geoff, 'Film Censorship Merry-go-round', *New Statesman*, 28 June 1974, pp. 912, 914

'Film Censorship Blues', *New Statesman*, 27 June 1975, pp. 817–18

Robinson, David, 'Trevelyan's Social History: some Notes and a Chronology', *Sight and Sound*, 140, no. 2 (spring 1971), pp. 70–72

Trevelyan, John, 'Film Censorship in Great Britain', *Screen*, 11, no. 3 (summer 1970), pp. 19–30

Warnock, Mary, 'The Williams Report on Obscenity and Film Censorship', *Political Quarterly*, 51 (July/September 1980), pp. 341–4

Watkins, Arthur T. L., 'The Censorship of Films in Great Britain', in Roger Manvell, ed., *The Year's Work in the Film, 1950* (London, Longman for the British Council, 1951), pp. 50–54

Wilcox, John, 'The Small Knife: Studies in Censorship – Britain', *Sight and Sound*, 25, no. 4 (spring 1956), pp. 206–10

Wistrich, Enid, 'Censorship and the Local Authority', *Local Government Studies*, 9 (October 1974), pp. 1–9

Zellick, Graham, 'Films and the Law of Obscenity', *Criminal Law Review*, March 1971, pp. 126–50

'Report on the "X" ', *Sight and Sound*, 23, no. 3 (January–March 1954), pp. 123–4, 153

Government and the Cinema

Government Reports

Report [to the Home Office Departmental Committee on Celluloid]; chairman: Earl of Plymouth (London, HMSO, 1913) (Cd 7158)

Minutes of Evidence [to the Home Office Departmental Committee on Celluloid]; chairman: Earl of Plymouth (London, HMSO, 1913) (Cd 7159)

Report of a Committee appointed by the Board of Trade to consider the Position of British Films; chairman: Lord Moyne (London, HMSO, 1936) (Cmd 5320)

Minutes of Evidence taken before the Departmental Committee on Cinematograph Films; chairman: Lord Moyne (London, HMSO, 1936)

Board of Trade, *Proposals for Legislation on Cinematograph Films . . .* (London, HMSO, 1937) (Cmd 5529)

The Position of Slow-burning Films under the [Cinematograph Act 1909]; chairman: Viscount Stoneham (London, HMSO, 1939)

Tendencies to Monopoly in the Cinematograph Film Industry: Report of a Committee appointed by the Cinematograph Films Council; chairman: Albert Palache (London, HMSO, 1944)

Recommendations of the Cinematograph Films Council for New legislation on Cinematograph Films; chairman: Arnold Plant (London, HMSO, 1947)

Report of the Film Studio Committee; chairman: G. H. Gater (London, HMSO, 1948)

Report of the Committee on the British Film Institute; chairman: Sir Cyril Radcliffe (London, HMSO, 1948) (Cmd 7361)

Report of the Working Party on Film Production Costs; chairman: Sir George Gater (London, HMSO, 1949)

Cinematography Films, Distribution and Exhibition of Cinematograph Films: Report of the Committee of Inquiry . . . Nov. 28, 1949; chairman: Sir Arnold Plant (London, HMSO, 1949) (Cmd 7837)

Report of the Departmental Committee on the Employment of Children as Film Actors, in Theatrical Work and in the Ballet; chairman: D. L Bateson (London, HMSO, 1950) (Cmd 8005)

Distribution and Exhibition of Cinematograph Films: Recommendations to the President of the Board of Trade on the Report of the Committee of Enquiry [of the Cinematograph Films Council]; chairman: Earl of Drogheda (London, HMSO, 1950)

Report of the Committee on Celluloid Storage; chairman: J. I. Wall (London, HMSO, 1950) (Cmd 7929)

Report of the Departmental Committee on Children and the Cinema; chairman: K. C. Wheare (London, HMSO, 1950) (Cmd 7945)

Report of the Copyright Committee . . . ; chairman: H. S. Gregory (London, HMSO, 1952) (Cmd 8662)

The Cine Camera and Industrial Research: Report of a Conference held on April 17th and 18th 1958 (London, Department of Scientific and Industrial Research, 1958)

Report of the Departmental Committee on the Law of Sunday Observance; chairman, Lord Crathorne (London, HMSO, 1964) (Cmnd 2528)

Structure and Trading Practices of the Films Industry: Recommendations of the Cinematograph Films Council; chairman: Sydney C. Roberts (London, HMSO, 1964) (Cmnd 2324)

A Policy for the Arts: the First Steps (London, HMSO, 1965) (Cmnd 2601)

Monopolies Commission, *Report on the Supply of Films for Exhibition in Cinemas*; chairman: Ashton Roskill (London, HMSO, 1966) (1966–1967 HC. 206)

National Film School, *Report of the Committee to consider the Need for a National Film School*; chairman: Lord Lloyd of Hampstead (London, HMSO, 1967)

Report of a Committee of Investigation into a Difference between the Film Artists' Association and the Film Production Association of Great Britain over the Operation of the Employment Agency for Crowd Artistes known as Central Castings Ltd (London, HMSO, 1967) (Ministry of Labour, document 36–310)

Review of Films Legislation: Report of the Cinematograph Films Council (London, HMSO, 1968) (Cmnd 3584)

Future of the British Film Industry: Report of the Prime Minister's Working Party; chairman, John Terry (London, HMSO, 1976) (Cmnd 6372)

Proposals for the Setting up of a British Film Authority: Report of the Interim Action Committee on the Film Industry; chairman: Sir Harold Wilson (London, HMSO, 1978) (Cmnd 7071)

The Financing of the British Film Industry: Second Report of the Interim Action Committee on the Film Industry; chairman: Sir Harold Wilson (London, HMSO, 1979) (Cmnd 7597)

Report of the Committee on Obscenity and Film Censorship, November 1979; chairman: Bernard Williams (London, HMSO, 1979) (Cmnd 7772)

Statistics, Technological Developments and Cable Television: Third Report of the Interim Action Committee on the Film Industry; chairman: Sir Harold Wilson (London, HMSO, 1980) (Cmnd 7855)

Reform of the Law relating to Copyright Designs and Performers' Protection: a Consultative Document (London, HMSO, 1981) (Cmnd 8302)

Film and Television Co-operation: Fourth Report of the Interim Action Committee on the Film Industry; chairman: Sir Harold Wilson (London, HMSO, 1981) (Cmnd 8227)

The Distribution of Films for Exhibition in Cinemas and by Other Means: Fifth Report of the Interim Action Committee on the Film Industry (London, HMSO, 1982) (Cmnd 8530)

Legislation: General Articles

Rowson, S., *Memorandum on Cinematograph Films Bill* (as amended in Committee) with detailed notes on the clauses (unpublished typescript, September 1927)

Rowson, S., *The Future of the Films Act*, paper read at the conference of the Cinematograph Exhibitors Association, 26 June 1935 [n.p.: the Author, 1935]

Lockley, W. E. E., 'Changes in Cinema Legislation', *Municipal Journal*, 7 October 1955, p. 2691

'British Media Law: Cinema and Film, 1', *Screen Digest*, February 1979, pp. 30–34

'British Media Law: Cinema and Film, 2', *Screen Digest*, March 1979, pp. 53–4

'British Media Law: Television', *Screen Digest*, July 1979, pp. 130–34

'UK Media Law Update', *Screen Digest*, July 1981, pp. 127–33

Statutes and Statutory Instruments: Film

Cinematograph Act (1909) (9 Edw.7 c.30)
  * SR&O 1910/189: Cinematograph Regulations (1910)
  * SR&O 1913/566: Cinematograph Regulations (1913)

* SR&O 1923/983: Regulations made under the Cinematograph Act (1909), (1923)

* SR&O 1923/1147. Regulations made by the Secretary for Scotland under the Cinematograph Act (1909), (1923)

* SR&O 1930/361: Regulations made under the Cinematograph Act (1909), (1930)

* SI 1950/2133: Cinematograph Regulations (1950)

* SI 1952/727: Cinematograph Regulations (1952)

* SI 1953/710: Cinematograph Regulations (1953)

* SI 1955/1125: Cinematograph (Safety) (Scotland) Regulations (1955)

SI 1955/1129: Cinematograph (Safety) Regulations (1955)

SI 1958/1530: Cinematograph (Safety) Regulations (1958)

SI 1965/282: Cinematograph (Safety) Regulations (1965)

* SI 1969/1575: Cinematograph (Safety) (Scotland) (Amendment) Regulations (1969)

* SI 1971/471: Cinematograph (Safety) (Scotland) Amendment Regulations (1971)

SI 1976/1315: Cinematograph (Safety) (Amendment) Regulations (1976)

SI 1976/1621: Cinematograph (Safety) (Scotland) (Amendment) Regulations (1976)

* SI 1955/1131: Cinematograph (Children) Regulations (1955)

* SI 1955/1138: Cinematograph (Children) (Scotland) Regulations (1955)

SI 1955/1909: Cinematograph (Children) (no. 2) Regulations (1955)

* SI 1955/1912: Cinematograph (Children) (Scotland) (no. 2) Regulations (1955)

Act amended by 1968/170 Miscellaneous Fees (Variation) Order (1968)

Finance (New Duties) Act (1916) (6 & 7 Geo.5 c.11) s. 2(1)

SI 1955/1239: Entertainments Duty Regulations (1955)

Celluloid and Cinematograph Film Act (1922) (12 & 13 Geo.5 c.35)

* SR&O 1922/1054: Order of the Secretary for Scotland . . . prescribing certain fees to be paid to local authorities

* SR&O 1922/1076: Order . . . prescribing certain fees to be paid to local authorities

SR&O 1924/363: Order made by the Secretary for Scotland . . . with respect to the use of cinematograph or similar apparatus in cinematograph film stores

SR&O 1924/403: Order as to the use of cinematograph or similar apparatus upon any premises used for any purpose to which the Celluloid and Cinematograph Film Act (1922) applies

SR&O 1928/82: Manufacture of Cinematograph Film Regulations (1928)

SR&O 1939/571: Cinematograph Film Stripping Regulations (1939)

SI 1974/1841: Celluloid and Cinematograph Film Act (1922) (Repeals and Modifications) Regulations (1974)

Performing Animals (Regulation) Act (1925) (15 & 16 Geo.5 c.38) ss. 1, 2, 4, 5
* Cinematograph Films Act (1927) (17 & 18 Geo. 5 c. 29)
    * SR&O 1928/244: Cinematograph Films (Mandated Territories) Order (1928)
Sunday Entertainments Act (1932) (22 & 23 Geo.5 c.51) ss. 1 & 2
    * SR&O 1933/110: Cinematograph Fund Regulations (1933)
    SR&O 1932/828: Sunday Cinematograph Entertainments (Polls) Order (1932) (made also under the Borough Funds Act 1903 (3 Edw.7 c.14))
Children and Young Persons Act (1933) (23 & 24 Geo.5 c.12) ss. 12, 22, 23–6
    SR&O 1933/992: Licence and Regulation under s. 25 of the Children and Young Persons Act (1933)
    SI 1976/773: Children and Young Persons (Licensing for Employment Abroad) Order (1976)
Protection of Animals Act (1934) (24 & 25 Geo.5 c.21) s. 1
Public Health Act (1936) (26 Geo.5 & 1 Edw.8 c.49) s. 179
Cinematograph Films (Animals) Act (1937) (1 Edw.8 & 1 Geo.6 c.59)
* Cinematograph Films Act (1938) (1 & 2 Geo.6 c.17)
    * SR&O 1944/1426: Cinematograph Films (Labour Costs Amendment) Order (1944)
    * SR&O 1948/1831: Cinematograph Films (Exhibitors) Regulations (1948)
    * SI 1952/687: Cinematograph Films (Exhibitors) Regulations (1952)
    * SI 1956/1101: Cinematograph Films (Exhibitors) (Amendment) Regulations (1956)
    * SI 1957/1200: Cinematograph Films (Exhibitors) (Amendment) Regulations (1957)
    * SI 1960/1338: Cinematograph Films (Exhibitors) Regulations (1960)
    * SR&O 1938/266: Cinematograph Films (Registration) Regulations (1938)
    * SR&O 1941/1854: Cinematograph Films (Registration) Amendment Regulations (1941)
    * SR&O 1945/276: Cinematograph Films (Registration) Amendment Regulations (1945)
    * SR&O 1948/634: Cinematograph Films (Registration) Regulations (1948)
    * SI 1952/688: Cinematograph Films (Registration) Regulations (1952)
    * SI 1953/980: Cinematograph Films (Registration) Amendment Regulations (1953)
    * SI 1955/1827: Cinematograph Films (Registration) (Amendment) Regulations (1955)
    * SI 1957/1199: Cinematograph Films (Registration) (Amendment) Regulations (1957)
    * SI 1960/1669: Cinematograph Films (Registration) (Amendment)

Regulations (1960)
* SI 1960/2291: Films (Registration) Regulations (1960)
* SR&O 1928/131: Cinematograph Films (Renters) Regulations (1928)
* SR&O 1938/267: Cinematograph Films (Renters) Regulations (1938)
* SR&O 1941/423: Cinematograph Films (Renters) (Amendment) Regulations (1941)
* SR&O 1941/1856: Cinematograph Films (Renters)(no. 2)(Amendment) Regulations (1941)
* SR&O 1943/238: Cinematograph Films (Renters) (Amendment) Regulations (1943)
* SR&O 1948/633: Cinematograph Films (Renters' Licences) Regulations (1948)
* SI 1958/309: Cinematograph Films (Renters' Licences) (Amendment) Regulations (1958)
* SI 1960/559: Cinematograph Films (Renters' Licences) Regulations (1960)
* SI 1960/2219: Cinematograph Films (Renters' Licences) (no. 2) Regulations (1960)
* SI 1960/712: Cinematograph Films (Registration of Newsreels) Regulations (1960)
* SI 1960/1621: Cinematograph Films (Registration of Newsreels) (Amendment) Regulations (1960)
Wartime Emergency Regulations:
* SR&O 1943/430: Cinematograph Film (Control) Order (1943)
* SR&O 1943/718: General licence made by the Board of Trade under SR&O 1943/430
* SR&O 1946/1130: General licence made by the Board of Trade under SR&O 1943/430
National Health Service Act (1946) (9 & 10 Geo.6 c.81) s. 76, Sch. 10
London County Council (General Powers) Act (1947) (10 & 11 Geo.6 c.xlvi) s. 5(1) (proviso a)
Cinematograph Films Act (1948) (11 & 12 Geo.6 c.23)
SR&O 1948/1687: Cinematograph Films (Quotas) Order (1948)
SR&O 1949/661: Cinematograph Films (Quotas) Amendment Order (1949)
SI 1950/531: Cinematograph Films (Quotas) Amendment Order (1950)
Local Government Act (1948) (11 & 12 Geo.6 c.26) ss. 132,135
Cinematograph Film Production (Special Loans) Act (1949) (12, 13 & 14 Geo.6 c.20)
SI 1949/680 National Film Finance Corporation Regulations (1949)
British Film Institute Act (1949) (12, 13 & 14 Geo.6 c.35)
SI 1965/603: Transfer of Functions (Cultural Institutions) Order (1965)
* Cinematograph Film Production (Special Loans) Act (1950) (14 Geo.6 c.18)

* Cinematograph Film Production (Special Loans) Act (1952) (15 & 16 Geo.6 & 1 Eliz.2 c.20)

Customs and Excise Act (1952) (15 & 16 Geo.6 & 1 Eliz.2 c.44)
   SI 1958/1975: Import Duty Reliefs (no. 3) Order (1958)
   SI 1958/1979: Import Duty Reliefs (no. 7) Order (1958)
   SI 1958/2141: Films (Temporary Importation) Regulations (1958)
   SI 1962/918: Temporary Importation (Process and Films) (Amendment) Regulations (1962)

Cinematograph Act (1952) (15 & 16 Geo.6 & 1 Eliz.2 c.68)
   * SI 1955/1124: Cinematograph Act (1952) (Commencment in Scotland) Instrument (1955)
   * SI 1955/1128: Cinematograph Act (1952) (Commencement in England and Wales) Instrument (1955)

Cinematograph Film Production (Special Loans) Act (1954) (2 & 3 Eliz.2 c.15)

Revision of the Army and Air Force Acts (Transitional Provisions) Act (1955) (3 & 4 Eliz.2 c.20) s. 4, Sch. 3 para. 1

Children and Young Persons (Harmful Publications Act) (1955) (3 & 4 Eliz.2 c.28)

Copyright Act (1956) (4 & 5 Eliz.2 c.74) s. 13–15

*Cinematograph Films Act (1957) (5 & 6 Eliz.2 c.21)
   SI 1957/1055: British Film Fund Agency (Appointed Day) Order (1957)
   SI 1957/1056: British Film Fund Agency Regulations (1957)
   * SI 1957/1341: Cinematograph Films (Collection of Levy) Regulations (1957)
   * SI 1958/837: Cinematograph Films (Collection of Levy) (Amendment) Regulations (1958)
   * SI 1960/726: Cinematograph Films (Collection of Levy) Regulations (1960)
   * SI 1960/1185: Cinematograph Films (Collection of Levy) (Amendment) Regulations (1960)
   * SI 1962/2544: Cinematograph Films (Collection of Levy) (Amendment no. 2) Regulations (1962)
   * SI 1963/1375: Cinematograph Films (Collection of Levy) (Amendment no. 3) Regulations (1963)
   * SI 1965/1234: Cinematograph Films (Collection of Levy) (Amendment no. 4) Regulations (1965)
   * SI 1967/889: Cinematograph Films (Collection of Levy) (Amendment no. 5) Regulations (1967)
   * SI 1968/1077: Cinematograph Films (Collection of Levy) Regulations (1968)
   * SI 1970/1145: Cinematograph Films (Collection of Levy) (Amendment) Regulations (1970)
   * SI 1971/1206: Cinematograph Films (Collection of Levy) (Amendment

no. 2) Regulations (1971)
* SI 1973/728: Cinematograph Films (Collection of Levy) (Amendment no. 3) Regulations (1973)
* SI 1975/1885: Cinematograph Films (Collection of Levy) (Amendment no. 4) Regulations (1975)
* SI 1977/1330: Cinematograph Films (Collection of Levy) (Amendment no. 5) Regulations (1977)
* SI 1978/1092: Cinematograph Films (Collection of Levy) (Amendment no. 6) Regulations (1978)
SI 1979/1751: Cinematograph Films (Collection of Levy) (Amendment no. 7) Regulations (1979)
SI 1980/1178: Cinematograph Films (Collection of Levy) (Amendment no. 8) Regulations (1980)
* SI 1957/1342: Cinematograph Films (Distribution of Levy) Regulations (1957)
* SI 1958/270: Cinematograph Films (Distribution of Levy) (Amendment) Regulations (1958)
* SI 1959/725: Cinematograph Films (Distribution of Levy) (Amendment no. 2) Regulations (1959)
* SI 1960/727: Cinematograph Films (Distribution of Levy) Regulations (1960)
* SI 1960/1186: Cinematograph Films (Distribution of Levy) (Amendment) Regulations (1960)
* SI 1962/1529: Cinematograph Films (Distribution of Levy) (Amendment no. 2) Regulations (1962)
* SI 1963/1376: Cinematograph Films (Distribution of Levy) Regulations (1963)
* SI 1964/1168: Cinematograph Films (Distribution of Levy) (Amendment) Regulations (1964)
* SI 1967/890: Cinematograph Films (Distribution of Levy) (Amendment no. 2) Regulations (1967)
* SI 1968/1076: Cinematograph Films (Distribution of Levy) (Amendment no. 3) Regulations (1968)
SI 1970/1146: Cinematograph Films (Distribution of Levy) Regulations (1970)
SI 1979/1750: Cinematograph Films (Distribution of Levy) (Amendment) Regulations (1979)
SI 1980/1179: Cinematograph Films (Distribution of Levy) (Amendment no. 2) Regulations (1980)
Entertainments Duty Act (1958) (6 & 7 Eliz.2 c.9)
* SI 1958/1285: Entertainments Duty Regulations (1958)
Dramatic and Musical Performers' Protection Act (1958) (6 & 7 Eliz.2 c.44) ss. 2, 3
Obscene Publications Act (1959) (7 & 8 Eliz.2 c.66)

* Cinematograph Films Act (1960) (8 & 9 Eliz.2 c.14)
Finance Act (1960) (8 & 9 Eliz.2 c.44)
Films Act (1960) (8 & 9 Eliz.2 c.57)
    SI 1961/1187: Films (Tanganyika) Order (1961)
    SI 1964/695: Films Act (1960) (Malaysia) Order in Council (1964)
* SI 1961/1826: Films (Registration) (Amendment) Regulations (1961)
* SI 1966/420: Films (Registration) (Amendment) Regulations (1966)
* SI 1967/400: Films (Registration) (Amendment) Regulations (1967)
* SI 1970/988: Films (Registration)(Amendment) Regulations (1970)
    SI 1970/1858: Films (Registration) Regulations (1970)
    SI 1972/1925: Films (Registration) (Amendment) Regulations (1972)
* SI 1974/2131: Films (Registration) Amendment Regulations (1974)
* SI 1975/1657: Films (Registration) Amendment Regulations (1975)
* SI 1976/1254: Films (Registration) (Amendment) Regulations (1976)
* SI 1977/1667: Films (Registration) (Amendment) Regulations (1977)
    SI 1978/1632: Films (Registration) (Amendment) Regulations (1978)
    SI 1980/1181: Films (Registration) (Amendment) Regulations (1980)
    SI 1982/373: Films (Registration) (Amendment) Regulations (1982)
    SI 1961/1824: Films (Exhibitors) Regulations (1961)
    SI 1970/985: Films (Exhibitors) (Amendment) Regulations (1970)
* SI 1972/1926: Films (Exhibitors) (Amendment) Regulations (1972)
* SI 1974/2129: Films (Exhibitors) (Amendment) Regulations (1974)
* SI 1975/1656: Films (Exhibitors) (Amendment) Regulations (1975)
* SI 1976/1255: Films (Exhibitors) (Amendment) Regulations (1976)
* SI 1977/1668: Films (Exhibitors) (Amendment) Regulations (1977)
    SI 1980/1180: Films (Exhibitors) (Amendment) Regulations (1980)
    SI 1980/1819: Films (Exhibitors) (Amendment no. 2) Regulations (1980)
    SI 1982/372: Films (Exhibitors) (Amendment) Regulations (1982)
    SI 1977/1306: Films (Exemption from Quota) Order (1977)
    SI 1961/1825: Films (Registration of Newsreels) Regulations (1961)
    SI 1964/1281: Films (Registration of Newsreels) (Amendment) Regulations (1964)
* SI 1970/987: Films (Registration of Newsreels) (Amendment) Regulations (1970)
* SI 1974/2130: Films (Registration of Newsreels) (Amendment) Regulations (1974)
* SI 1975/1658: Films (Registration of Newsreels) (Amendment) Regulations (1975)
* SI 1976/1253: Films (Registration of Newsreels) (Amendment) Regulations (1976)
    SI 1977/1666: Films (Registration of Newsreels) (Amendment) Regulations (1977)
    SI 1961/1827: Films (Renters' Licences) Regulations (1961)
* SI 1970/986: Films (Renters' Licences) (Amendment) Regulations (1970)

* SI 1974/2132: Films (Renters' Licences) (Amendment) Regulations (1974)
* SI 1975/1659. Films (Renters' Licences) (Amendment) Regulations (1975)
* SI 1976/1252: Films (Renters' Licences) (Amendment) Regulations (1976)
* SI 1977/1669: Films (Renters' Licences) (Amendment) Regulations (1977)
  SI 1980/1188: Films (Renters' Licences) (Amendment) Regulations (1980)
  SI 1982/374: Films (Renters' Licences) (Amendment) Regulations (1982)
  SI 1965/1856: Films Co-production Agreement (France) Order (1965) [brings Cmnd. 2781 into force]
  SI 1967/1679: Films Co-production Agreement (Italy) Order (1967) [brings Cmnd. 3434 into force]
  SI 1975/623: Films Co-production Agreement (Federal Republic of Germany) Order (1975) [brings Cmnd 5972 into force]
  SI 1975/1838: Films Co-production Agreement (Government of Canada) Order (1975) [brings Cmnd 6274 into force]
Charities Act (1960) (8 & 9 Eliz.2 c.58)
Factories Act (1961) (9 & 10 Eliz.2 c.34) s. 175(2)(h) & (l)
Public Health Act (1961) (9 & 10 Eliz.2 c.64) Part III
London Government Act (1963) (1963 c. 33) s. 52
Children and Young Persons Act (1963) (1963 c. 37) ss. 37–44
  SI 1968/1728: Children (Performances) Regulations (1968)
Performers' Protection Act (1963) (1963 c. 53)
Films Act (1964) (1964 c. 52)
Obscene Publications Act (1964) (1964 c. 74)
Local Government Act (1966) (1966 c. 42) Sch. 3
  SI 1968/170: Miscellaneous Fees (Variation) Order (1968)
* SI 1978/1387: Fees for Cinematograph Licences (Variation) Order (1978)
  SI 1980/1398: Fees for Cinematograph Licences (Variation) Order (1980)
Films Act (1966) (1966 c. 48)
Local Government (Scotland) Act (1966) (1966 c. 51) s. 42(2)
Private Places of Entertainment (Licensing) Act (1967) (1967 c. 19) s. 2(3)
Criminal Justice Act (1967) (1967 c. 80) ss. 92, 106(2)(e), Sch. 3
Films Act (1970) (1970 c. 26)
* SI 1975/1884: Cinematograph Films (Limits of Levy) Order (1975)
  SI 1979/395: Cinematograph Films (Limits of Levy) Order (1979)
Courts Act (1971) (1971 c. 23) s. 56(2)
Fire Precautions Act (1971) (1971 c. 40) s. 12(12)
Sunday Cinema Act (1972) (1972 c. 19)
Performers' Protection Act (1972) (1972 c. 32)
European Communities Act (1972) (1972 c. 68) s. 8: directives which came

into force in the United Kingdom on accession to the Communities:
    Film Directive no. 1, 15 October 1963: *Journal Officiel*, 63/607/CEE
    Film Directive no. 2, 13 May 1965: *Journal Officiel*, 65/264/CEE
    Film Directive no. 3, 15 October 1968: *Journal Officiel*, 68/369/CEE
    Film Directive no. 4, 29 September 1970: *Journal Officiel*, 70/451/CEE
Local Government Act (1972) (1972 c. 70) ss. 180(2), 204, 272(1)
Employment of Children Act (1973) (1973 c. 24)
Local Government Act (1973) (1973 c. 65) s. 209,237
Local Government Act (1974) (1974 c. 7) ss. 35,42(2)
Health and Safety at Work Act (1974) (1974 c. 37)
    SI 1974/1841: Celluloid and Cinematograph Film Act (1922) (Repeals and
    Modifications) Regulations (1974)
    SI 1980/1314: Celluloid and Cinematograph Film Act (1922) (Exemptions)
    Regulations (1980)
* Cinematograph Films Act (1975) (1975 c. 73)
Local Government (Miscellaneous Provisions) Act (1976) (1976 c. 57)
ss. 19–22
Statute Law (Repeals) Act (1978) (1978 c. 45)
Films Act (1979) (1979 c. 9)
Films Act (1980) (1980 c. 41)
National Film Finance Corporation Act (1981) (1981 c. 15)
Film Levy Finance Act (1981) (1981 c. 16)
Indecent Displays (Control) Act (1981) (1981 c. 42)

Statutes and Statutory Instruments: Broadcasting

Wireless Telegraphy Act (1949) (12,13 & 14 Geo.6 c.54)
* Television Act (1954) (2 & 3 Eliz.2 c.55)
* Television Act (1963) (1963 c. 50)
* Television Act (1964) (1964 c. 21)
    SI 1964/1202: Television Act (1964) (Channel Islands) Order (1964)
    SI 1965/601: Television Act (1964) (Isle of Man) Order (1965)
    SI 1969/1370: Television Act (1964) (Channel Islands) Order (1969)
    SI 1969/1372: Television Act (1964) (Isle of Man) Order (1969)
    * SI 1971/309: Television Act (1964) (Additional Payments) Order (1971)
Marine Broadcasting (Offences) Act (1967) (1967 c. 41)
    SI 1967/1274: Marine etc, Broadcasting (Offences) (Guernsey) Order
    (1967)
    SI 1967/1275: Marine etc, Broadcasting (Offences) (Jersey) Order (1967)
    SI 1967/1976: Marine etc, Broadcasting (Offences) (Isle of Man) Order
    (1967)
Wireless Telegraphy Act (1967) (1967 c. 72)
Post Office Act (1969) (1969 c. 48) ss. 89–92
Sound Broadcasting Act (1972) (1972 c. 31)

408 / Select Bibliography

SI 1973/1087: Sound Broadcasting Act (1972) (Channel Islands) Order (1973)

SI 1973/1088: Sound Broadcasting Act (1972) (Isle of Man) Order (1973)

★ Independent Broadcasting Authority Act (1973) (1973 c. 19)

SI 1976/1778: Independent Broadcasting Authority Act (1973) (Isle of Man) Order (1976)

SI 1979/114: Independent Broadcasting Authority Act (1973) (Channel Islands) Order (1979)

★ Independent Broadcasting Authority Act (1974) (1974 c. 16)

★ Independent Broadcasting Authority Act (no. 2) (1974) (1974 c. 42)

★ Independent Broadcasting Authority Act (1978) (1978 c. 43)

SI 1979/461: Independent Broadcasting Authority Act (1978) (Isle of Man) Order (1979)

Independent Broadcasting Authority Act (1979) (1979 c. 35)

SI 1980/189: Independent Broadcasting Act (1979) (Channel Islands) Order (1980)

★ Broadcasting Act (1980) (1980 c. 64)

SI 1980/1907: Broadcasting Act (1980) (Commencement no. 1) Order (1980)

SI 1981/759: Broadcasting Act (1980) (Commencement no. 2) Order (1981)

Broadcasting Act (1981) (1981 c. 68)

Co-production Treaties

Film Production Association of Great Britain and Federation of Film Unions, *Co-production: (guide to the Anglo-French and Anglo-Italian Co-production Treaties* (London, Film Production Association and Federation of Film Unions, 1971)

France, no. 1 (1965): *Film Co-production Agreement between the Government of the United Kingdom . . . and the Government of the French Republic. 21 Sept. 1965* (London, HMSO, 1965) (Cmnd 2781)

Extended 3 May 1967. Treaty Series (1967), no. 63. (Cmnd 3349).

Italy, no. 1 (1967): *Films Co-production Agreement between the Government of the United Kingdom . . . and the Government of the Italian Republic. Sorrento, 30 Sept. 1967* (London, HMSO, 1967) (Cmnd 3434)

Federal Republic of Germany, no. 2 (1975): *Films Co-production Agreement between the Government of the United Kingdom . . . and the Government of the Federal Republic of Germany. 30 Jan. 1975* (London, HMSO, 1975) (Cmnd 5972); also Treaty Series, no. 103 (1975)

Canada no. 1 (1975): *Films Co-production Agreement between the Government of the United Kingdom . . . and the Government of Canada. London, 12 Sept. 1975* (London, HMSO, 1975) (Cmnd 6274); also Treaty Series, no. 8 (1976) (Cmnd 6380)

Annual Reports

British Film Fund Agency *Annual Report, 1958–* (London, HMSO, 1959–)
Cinematograph Exhibitors' Association of Great Britain and Ireland, *Annual Report, 1920–* (London, Cinematograph Exhibitors' Association, 1920–)
Cinematograph Films Council, *Annual Report, 1939–* (London, HMSO, 1939–)
Exchequer and Audit Department, *Account prepared pursuant to Section 8(2) of the Cinematograph Film Production (Special Loans) Act 1949 . . . Annual* (London, HMSO)
Exchequer and Audit Department, *Cinematograph Fund. Account of the Cinematograph Fund established pursuant to Section 2 of the Sunday Entertainments Act, 1932 . . . Annual* (London, HMSO)
Film Production Association of Great Britain, *Annual Report, 1967/8–* (London, Film Production Association, 1968–)
National Film Finance Corporation. *Annual report . . . , 1950–*. (London: HMSO, 1950–)

Cinemas and their Audiences

Distribution

Box, Sidney, *Film Publicity: a Handbook on the Production and Distribution of Propaganda Films* (London, Lovat Dickson, 1937)
Edson, Barry, 'Commercial Film Distribution and Exhibition in the UK' *Screen*, 21, no. 3 (1980), pp. 36–44
'Percolating pictures' *Film Directions*, 4, no. 14 (1981), pp. 13–16
Hart, Romaine, and Peter Dally, 'Independent Audiences: Screen Cinemas, paper delivered at the symposium held at the National Film Theatre, 4 November 1981, *Sight and Sound*, 50, no. 4 (autumn 1981), pp. 254–5
Hart-Williams, Nick, *et al.*, 'Other and Essential: a Survey of Independent Distributors/Exhibitors, *Sight and Sound*, 45, no. 4 (autumn 1976), pp. 207–11
Montagu, Ivor, 'Old Man's Mumble: Reflections on a Semi-centenary', *Sight and Sound*, 44, no. 4 (autumn 1975), pp. 220–24,247
Wall, Joseph, 'The Public in Relation to Cinema in Ireland today', *Studies*, 67 (winter 1978), pp. 343–6
Whitaker, Sheila, 'Independent Audiences: Tyneside Cinema', paper delivered at the symposium held at the National Film Theatre, 4 November 1981, *Sight and Sound*, 50, no. 4 (autumn 1981), p. 255
'Cinemas and Circuits', *Economist*, 18 September 1954, pp. 915–17
'When screens overlap (Rank/ABC/TV)', *Economist*, 17 September 1955, pp. 963–4

Cinemas: General

Atwell, David, *Cathedrals of the Movies: a History of British Cinemas and their Audiences* (London, Architectural Press, 1980)
Benfield, Robert, *Bijou Kinema: a History of Early Cinema in Yorkshire* (Sheffield, Sheffield City Polytechnic, 1976)
Bennett, Richard, *A Picture of the Twenties* (London, Studio Vista, 1961)
Bern, Leslie, *Cinemas in Portsmouth* (Portsmouth, Portsmouth Reference and Information Centre, 1975)
Bird, John H. *Cinema Parade: 50 Years of Film Shows* (Birmingham, Cornish, 1947)
Braithwaite, P., 'The cinema industry 1950–1970 and its customers', thesis submitted for a CNAA degree in Business Studies, 1970
Ceram, C. W., *The Archaeology of the Cinema* (London, Thames and Hudson, 1965)
Chadwick, Stanley, *The Mighty Screen: the Rise of the Cinema in Huddersfield.* (Huddersfield, Venturers Press, 1953)
Downie, Craig Ross, '*Coming soon, an Account of Dundee's Cinema Era*', thesis submitted to the Department of Architecture, University of Dundee, 1979
Elgood, David, *City Cinemas (1903–1978): a Brief History of Cinema in Norwich* (Norwich, Norfolk and Norwich Film Theatre, 1978)
Field, Audrey, *The Picture Palace: a Social History of the Cinema* (London, Gentry Books, 1974)
George, Eric A., *The Cinema in Bournemouth, Poole and Christchurch* (Bournemouth, Bournemouth Local Studies Publications, 2nd rev. ed. [?1980])
Reminiscences of the Cinema in Bournemouth' (Bournemouth, Bournemouth Local Studies Publications, 1978, (publications, no. 639)
Key Note Business Information, *Cinemas and Theatres* (London, Key Note Publications, 1979; 2nd ed., 1982)
Knopp, Leslie, *The Cinematograph Regulations 1955* (London, Cinema Press, 1955)
McAlley Associates Ltd *The Cinema and its Customers (a Pilot Study)*, prepared for the Barclay Committee (London, McAlley Associates, 1968)
Morgan, Guy, *Red Roses Every Night: an Account of London Cinemas under Fire* (London, Quality Press, 1948)
Peart, Stephen, *The Picture House in East Anglia* (Lavenham, Terence Dalton, 1980)
Peck, G. C., *Bedfordshire Cinemas* (Bedford, Bedfordshire County Council, 1981)
Quinn, James, *Outside London: a Report to the Governors of the British Film Institute* (London, British Film Institute, 1965)
Richardson, Alan A., *The Cinema Theatres of Salisbury* (Salisbury, the author, 1981)

Ritchie, N. N., *The Design of Cinemas in Britain up to 1940* (Manchester, Manchester University School of Architecture, 1965)

Sharp, Dennis, *The Picture Palace, and Other buildings for the Movies.* (London, Hugh Evelyn, 1969)

Tonkin, W. G. S., *Showtime in Walthamstow* (London, Walthamstow Antiquarian Society, 1967)

Business Monitor: M2 – Cinemas (London, HMSO, Annual)

Cinemas: General Periodical Articles

Adam, Nicolas, 'The Last Picture Palaces', *Illustrated London News*, April 1974, pp. 41–3

Alloway, Lawrence, 'Architecture and the Modern Cinema', *Listener*, 22 June 1961, pp. 1085–6

Atkinson, R., 'The Design of the Picture Theatre', *Royal Institute of British Architects Journal*, June 1921, pp. 441–5

Atwell, D., 'Rise and Fall of the London Picture Palace', *Journal of the Royal Institute of British Architects*, 80 (January 1973), pp. 8–10

Benton, C., 'Palaces of Entertainment', *Architectural Design*, 49, no. 10/11 (1979) Supplement, pp. 52–5

Bidwell, Denis 'Fifty Years of Cinema in Ampthill', *Bedfordshire Magazine*, 16 (winter 1978), pp. 294–6

Cradduck, K. S. 'Planning for the Film Industry', *Architects Journal*, 6 May 1948, p. 412

Crew, Kathleen, 'When the Cinema came to Stourbridge', *Blackcountryman*, 12 (summer 1979), pp. 15–16

Durgnat, Raymond, 'Movie Eye', *Architectural Review*, 137 (March 1965), pp. 186–93

Everson, William K., 'Memoirs of a Film-spent Youth', *Focus on Film*, no. 10 (summer 1972), pp. 51–6

Eyles, Allen, 'The Cinemas of Henry Elder', *Picture House*, no. 1 (spring 1982), pp. 8–12

'The Cinemas of Kentish Town', *Focus on Film*, no. 4 (September/October 1970), pp. 58–9; additional photographs, no. 5 (winter (November/December) 1970), p. 58

'The Cinemas of Norwood', *Focus on Film*, no. 6 (spring 1971), pp. 55–8

' "A Romance of Finance": Oscar and the Odeons', *Focus on Film*, no. 22 (autumn 1975), pp. 38–50; chronology, pp. 51–7

'Saving the Supers', *Focus on Film*, no. 8(1971), pp. 15–16

'Union Cinemas', *Focus on Film*, no. 37 (March 1981), pp. 33–42

'Vanished Cinemas', *Focus on Film*, no. 36 (October, 1980), pp. 48–51

Happe, B. 'Wide-screen comes to Britain', *BKSTS Journal*, 63 (January 1981), pp. 76–9

Montagu, Ivor, 'Birmingham Sparrow: In Memoriam Iris Barry, 1896–1969',

Sight and Sound, 39, no. 2, (spring 1970), pp. 106–8

Price, Cecil, 'Early Cinemas in Wales', *Dock Leaves*, 8, no. 21, (1957), pp. 45–9

Pulman, R. E. 'Recent Developments in Cinema Construction and Equipment in England', *British Kinematography, Sound and Television*, 49 (April 1967), pp. 88–96

Richardson, Alan A. 'The Way it was: Picture-going in Salisbury', *Focus on Film*, no. 26 (1977), pp. 41–3,47

Robinson, David 'Building a Cinema', *Sight and Sound* 26, no. 3 (winter 1956/7), pp. 137–9,166

Smith, Trevor, 'Luxuriant Splendour: the Early Picture Palaces, Part 1', *Flickers*, no. 42 (October 1980), pp. 12–16

'Luxuriant Splendour: the Early Picture Palaces, Part 2', *Flickers*, no. 43 (January 1981), pp. 14–18

'Luxuriant Splendour: the Early Picture Palaces, Part 3', *Flickers*, no. 44 (June 1981), pp. 13–17

Standley, Philip, 'Cinemas in Bedford, 1898–1978', *Bedfordshire Magazine*, 17 (winter 1979), pp. 122–7

Thomson, David 'I remember when it was a Cinema', *Sight and Sound*, 46, no. 3 (summer 1977), pp. 134–8

Threadgall, D. R., 'Preserved for Posterity' (Electric Palace, Harwich), *BKSTS Journal* 58 (April 1976), pp. 107–9

Wylson, Anthony and Leslie Knopp, 'Cinema Design', *Architects Journal*, 1 March 1967, pp. 563–79

'Cinemas: Construction and Legislation', *Architects Journal*, 17 May 1967, information sheet 1472

'Cinema Spaces', *Architects Journal*, 9 September 1964, information sheet 1274

'Design Guide: Cinema Buildings', *Architects Journal*, 1 March 1967, pp. 567–79

'Film Projection and Cinema Design', *Architects Journal*, 9 September 1964, supplement

'Modern Cinemas', *Architects Journal*, 7 November 1935, whole issue

Cinemas: Listed Alphabetically by Location

Thomson, Michael, 'The Capitol, Aberdeen', *Focus on Film*, no. 32 (April 1979), pp. 50–51

Ferris, B., 'Building of the Globe Kinema (Acton)' (1918–1920), *Building Technology and Management*, 19 (April 1981), pp. 3–6

'Barnsley: Gaumont Cinema; T. P. Bennett and Son, Architects', *Builder*, 21 December 1956, pp. 1053–6

Squires, John, 'Granada Bedford: the Early Days', *Picture House*, no. 1 (spring 1982), pp. 3–5

Fernee, John, 'Beaufort, Birmingham', *Focus on Film*, no. 32 (April 1979), pp. 48–9

'Birmingham: Cinephone Cinema; H. Werner Rosenthal, Architect', *Architectural Review*, November 1956, pp. 327–8

Eyles, Allen, 'Futurist Birmingham; Granada, Clapham Junction', *Focus on Film*, no. 35 (April 1980), pp. 47–50

Gray, Richard, 'The Odeon, Birmingham', *Picture House*, no. 1 (spring 1982), pp. 5–8

Dolling, Ray, 'The Eltham Cinema-theatre', *Picture House*, no. 1 (spring 1982), p. 15

'Hull: Cecil Cinema; Gelder and Kitchen, Architects', *Builder*, 3 August 1956, pp. 193–7

'Warehouses Conversion: Hull – Theatre Cinema and Workshops' *Architectural Review*, 167 (January 1980), p. 18

Atwell, David, 'ABC (Forum), Liverpool', *Focus on Film*, no. 34 (December 1978), pp. 48–50

'The Brixton Astoria', *Focus on Film*, no. 20 (spring 1975), pp. 58–9

'London: Columbia Theatre, First Post-war Cinema in the West End; Sir John Burnet, Tait and Partners, Architects', *Architectural Review*, 19 February 1959, pp. 294–6

'Cinema at Curzon Street, London, W1; Sir John Burnet, Tait and Partners, Architects', *Architects Journal*, 27 July 1966, pp. 231–8

'London: Cinema at Dean House, Dean Street W1 for RKO Pictures: Elsom and Pearlman, Architects', *Architects Journal*, 29 June 1950, pp. 792–5

'Cinema at Elephant & Castle, London SE1: Erno Goldfinger, Architect', *Architects Journal*, 19 April 1967, pp. 949–59

Carter, John, 'Odeon Cinema (Elephant and Castle): Building Revisited', *Architects Journal*, 17 September 1969, p. 709

'Odeon Building, Haymarket', *Architect and Surveyor*, 7 (July/August 1962), pp. 67–71

Eyles, Allen, 'Carlton Theatre, Haymarket', *Focus on Film*, no. 28 (1977), pp. 48–9

'Empire, Leicester Square', *Focus on Film*, no. 31 (November 1978), pp. 48–50

'Odeon, Lewisham', *Focus on Film*, no. 29 (1978), pp. 49–50

Crawley, G. 'New Odeon Marble Arch, London W1', *British Journal of Photography*, 17 February 1967, p. 116

Wylson, Anthony, 'Cinemas: some Case Studies – 1. Odeon, Marble Arch; 2. Scala Superama, Birmingham; 3. Odeon, Nottingham; 4. Windmill Cinema, London; 5. Dilly Cine-Club, London; 6. Compton Cinema Club, Birmingham; 7. 40 Birmingham Square, London W1', *Architects Journal*, 19 June 1968, pp. 1405–24

'Cinema, Mayfair, London: Interior Design', *Architectural Review*, vol. 140 (August 1966), pp. 115–18

'Studio and Cinema, Mayfair, London: Interior Design', *Architectural Review*, 140 (November 1966), pp. 351–3

'National Film Theatre, Lambeth; Hubert Bennett, Architect to the London County Council', *Architectural Review*, July 1958, pp. 40–41

'National Film Theatre, South Bank', *Builder*, 20 July 1956, pp. 92–3

'National Film Theatre, South Bank', *Builder*, 25 October 1957, pp. 710–11

Brown, R., 'England's First Cinema' (Olympia), *British Journal of Photography*, 24 June 1977, p. 520

'Interior Design: Cinema, Oxford Street, London', *Architectural Review*, 138 (September 1965), pp. 197–200

'Cinemas in Lower Regent Street', *Architects Journal*, 17 July 1968, pp. 95–102

'Two Private Theatre Conversions: Preview Theatre, Audley Square, and Dubbing Theatre, Soho Square; J. D. Morgan and D. C. Branch, Architects', *Builder*, 27 September 1957, pp. 538–41

'Shell-Mex, London: Conversion of Offices into a Private Cinema; Norman R. Branson, Architect', *Art and Industry*, May 1954, pp. 168–71

'Shepherds Bush: The Gaumont, formerly Shepherds Bush Pavilion, Reconstruction', Frank T. Verity, Architect, S. Beverley, Architect for Reconstruction, *Builder*, 16 September 1955, pp. 469–71

'New Filming and Production Technique: Todd-AO at London's Dominion theatre, Tottenham Court Road, *Engineering*, 2 May 1958, pp. 548–9

'Equipping for Todd-AO: Installations at the Dominion and Manchester Gaumont Theatres', *British Journal of Photography*, 25 April 1958, pp. 218–19

Dewes, R. H. 'My Nottingham Venture: recalling a Cinema Development of 1921', *Focus on Film*, no. 32 (April 1979), pp. 43–7

'Rye, Sussex: the Regent Cinema; David E. Nye, Architect', *Builder*, 9 April 1948, pp. 417–20

'St Helier, Jersey: Odeon Cinema; T. P. Bennett and Son, Architects', *Architects Journal*, 16 October 1952, pp. 466–8

'Plymouth: The Drake', *Builder*, 7 November 1958, pp. 778–80

'Shrivenham, Berks: Cinema for the Army Kinema Corporation; Thurlow, Lucas and Janes, Architects', *Builder*, 15 March 1957, pp. 493–6

Eyles, Allen, 'Odeon Southport; Playhouse Edinburgh', *Focus on Film*, no. 33 (August 1979), pp. 40–43

Films in the United Kingdom

Box, Kathleen, *The Cinema and the Public: an Inquiry into Cinema-going Habits and Expenditure made in 1946* (London, Central Office of Information, 1947; Social Survey Report, new series, no. 106)

Mayer, J. P., *British Cinemas and their Audiences; Sociological Studies* (London, Dobson, 1948)

Sociology of Film, Studies and Documents (London, Faber and Faber, 1946)

National Council of Public Morals, Cinema Commission of Inquiry. *The Cinema, its Present Position and Future Possibilities; Report and Evidence taken by the Cinema Commission of Inquiry instituted by the National Council of Public Morals* (London, Williams and Norgate, 1917)

Ward, J. C., *Children and the Cinema: an Inquiry made by the Social Survey in October 1948 for a Departmental Committee* . . . (London, Central Office of Information, 1949; Social Survey Report, New Series, no. 131)

'*Children out of School: an Inquiry into the Leisure Interests and Activities of Children out of School Hours, carried out for the Central Advisory Council for Education (England) in November/December 1947* (London, Central Office of Information, 1948; Social Survey Report, New Series, no. 110)

Moss, Louis and Kathleen Box, *The Cinema Audience: an Inquiry made by the Wartime Social Survey for the Ministry of Information* (London, Ministry of Information, 1943; Social Survey Report, New Series, 37b)

England, Leonard, 'What the Cinema means to the British Public', in Roger Manvell, ed., *The Year's Work in the Film, 1949* (London, Longman for the British Council, 1950), pp. 62–8

Gray, Barbara, 'The Social Effects of the Film' (on children), *Sociological Review*, 42, no. 7 (1950), pp. 135–44

Keir, Gertrude, 'Children and the Cinema', *British Journal of Delinquency*, 1, no. 3 (1951), pp. 225–9

Low, Rachel, 'The Implications behind the Social Survey', in Roger Manvell, ed., *The Penguin Film Review, no. 7* (Harmondsworth, Penguin, 1948), pp. 107–12

Powell, Dilys, 'The Development of the Film in Educational and Social Life', *Journal of the Royal Society of Arts*, 14 January 1949, pp. 120–29

Vargas, A. L. 'British Films and their Audience', in Roger Manvell, ed., *The Penguin Film Review, no. 8* (Harmondsworth, Penguin, 1949), pp. 71–6

Wall, W. D., and W. A. Simson, 'The Effects of Cinema Attendance on the Behaviour of Adolescents as seen by their Contemporaries, *British Journal of Educational Psychology*, February 1949, pp. 53–61

'The Film Choices of Adolescents', *British Journal of Educational Psychology*, June 1949, pp. 121–36

'The Emotional Responses of Adolescent Groups to Certain Films', *British Journal of Educational Psychology*, November 1950, pp. 153–63

'The Responses of Adolescent Groups to Certain Films', *British Journal of Educational Psychology*, June 1951, pp. 81–8

Wilkinson, F., 'The Cinema as a Social Force', *Visual Education*, October 1958, pp. 4–6

'Social Survey Report on the Cinema and the Public', *Board of Trade Journal*, 20 September 1947, pp. 1628–9

Films Abroad

Ministry of Information, *British Films for Liberated Europe* (London, Ministry of Information, 1944)

Auriol, Jean George, 'The British Film Abroad: a Study of Critical Reactions', in Roger Manvell, ed., *The Year's Work in the Film, 1949*, (London, Longman for the British Council, 1950), pp. 46–54

Koval, Francis, 'British Films in Europe', *Sight and Sound*, 20, no. 1 (May 1951), pp. 10–11

Middleton, Jane, 'The British Council's Work in Films', in Roger Manvell, ed., *The Year's Work in the Film, 1950*, (London, Longman, for the British Council, 1951), pp. 71–3

Queval, Jean, 'France looks at British Films', *Sight and Sound*, 19, no. 5 (July 1950), pp. 198–200

Roud, Richard, 'Britain in America', *Sight and Sound*, 26, no. 3 (winter 1956/7), pp. 119–23

Wollenberg, H. H., 'British Films Overseas', *Sight and Sound*, 15, no. 60 (winter 1946/7), p. 146

'Celluloid Ambassadors', *Sight and Sound*, 17, no. 65 (spring 1948), p. 39

Films of Fact

Documentaries

Arts Enquiry, *The Factual Film: a Survey sponsored by the Dartington Hall Trustees, Published on behalf of the Arts Enquiry* by *Political and Economic Planning* (London, Oxford University Press, 1947)

Barrot, Olivier, et al., *L'Angleterre et son cinéma: le courant documentaire 1927/1965* (Paris, Filmeditions, 1977); *Cinema D'Aujourd'hui*, no. 11 (February/March 1977), whole issue

Gimenez, Manuel Horacio, *Escuela documental Inglesa* (Santa Fe, Editorial Documento del Instituto de Cinematografia de la Universidad Nacional del Litoral, 1961)

Lovell, Alan and Jim Hillier, *Studies in Documentary* (London, Secker and Warburg, 1972; 'Cinema One' no. 21.)

Orbanz, Eva, ed., *Journey to a Legend and Back: the British Realistic Film* (Berlin, Volker Spiess, 1977)

Reemtsen, Rolf, *Die englische Dokumentarfilmschule in den dreissiger Jahren: zur Begriffsbestimmung des Dokumentarismus im Film*, Inaugural-Dissertation zur Erlangung des Doktorgrades der Philosophischen Fakultät der Universität zu Köln, 1976

Ripley, A. Crooks, *Vaudeville Pattern* (London, Brownlee, 1942)

Rotha, Paul, *Documentary Diary: an Informal History of the British Documentary Film, 1928–1939* (London, Secker and Warburg, 1973)

Sussex, Elizabeth, *The Rise and Fall of British Documentary: the Story of the Film Movement founded by John Grierson* (London, University of California Press, 1975)

Wyver, John, ed., *Nothing but the Truth: Cinéma vérité and the Films of the Roger Graef Team* (London, British Film Institute, 1982)

Documentaries: Periodical Articles

Angus, Alfred, 'A Mutoscopic Romance: the Fight to photograph Captain Dreyfus in the Prison Yard at Rennes', *Penny Pictorial Magazine*, 23 September 1899, pp. 101–4

Anstey, Edgar, 'The Year's Work in the Documentary', in Roger Manvell, ed., *The Year's Work in the Film, 1949* (London, Longman for the British Council, 1950), pp. 30–36

'Geography and the Documentary Film: Britain up to 1945', *Geographical Magazine*, March 1957, pp. 541–50

Berger, John, 'Look at Britain!', *Sight and Sound*, 27, no. 1 (summer 1957), pp. 12–14

Ellis, J., 'Victory of the Voice?', *Screen*, 22, no. 2 (1981), pp. 69–72

Furse, Sir William, 'The Imperial Institute and the Films of the Empire Marketing Board', *Sight and Sound*, 2, no. 7 (autumn 1933), pp. 78–9

Graef, Roger and David Wilson, 'Decisions, Decisions: a Discussion between Roger Graef, Dai Vaughan, Terence Twigg, Iain Bruce and Ian Woolf about Approaches to TV Documentary', *Sight and Sound*, 45, no. 1 (winter 1975/6), pp. 2–7

Grierson, John, 'Empire Marketing Board', in Forsyth Hardy, ed., *Grierson on Documentary* (London, Collins, 1946), pp. 97–101

'Public Relations', *Sight and Sound*, 19, no. 5 (July 1950), pp. 201–4

Hardy, Forsyth, 'John Grierson and the Documentary Idea', in *Films in 1951, Festival of Britain* (London, *Sight and Sound* for the British Film Institute, 1951), pp. 55–6

Harrison, Norman K., 'The Production of BBC Documentary Films in the Far East', *British Journal of Photography*, 16 December 1955, pp. 627–9

Holmes, Winifred, 'Bill Smith and Mrs Brown like the Latest Documentaries', *Sight and Sound*, 9, no. 33 (spring 1940), pp. 10–11

Kuhn, A., '*Desert Victory* and the People's War', *Screen*, 22, no. 2 (1981), pp. 45–68

Mackie, Philip, 'One for the Road', *Sight and Sound*, January 1950, pp. 43–4

Manvell, Roger, 'Documentary Film Progress', *Britain Today*, August 1949, pp. 37–40

Price, Peter, 'The Sulky Fire, part 3: 'The Light that failed', *Sight and Sound*, 22, no. 3 (January/March 1953), p. 139

Road, Sinclair, 'The Year's Work in the Documentary Film', in Roger Manvell, ed., *The Year's Work in the Film, 1950* (London, Longman for the

British Council, 1951); pp. 25–30

Robinson, David, 'Looking for Documentary – 1: The Background to Production', *Sight and Sound*, 27, no. 1 (summer 1957), pp. 6–11
'Looking for Documentary – 2: The Ones that got Away', *Sight and Sound*, 27, no. 2 (autumn 1957), pp. 70–75

Smith, Janet Adam, 'Filming Everest', *Sight and Sound*, 23, no. 3 (January/March 1954), pp. 138–9

Strasser, Alex and Basil Wright, 'Problems of Filmmaking', *Engineering*, 12 April 1957, pp. 450–52

Sussex, Elizabeth, 'The Golden Years of Grierson', *Sight and Sound*, 41, no. 3 (summer 1972), pp. 149–53

Tallents, Sir Stephen, 'The Birth of British Documentary', *Journal of the University Film Association*, 20, no. 1 (1968), pp. 15–21; 20, no. 2 (1968), pp. 27–33; 20, no. 3 (1968), pp. 61–6

Ward, Kenneth, 'British Documentaries of the 1930s', *History*, 62 (October 1977), pp. 426–31

Winston, Brian, 'Documentary: I think we are in trouble', *Sight and Sound*, 48, no. 1 (winter 1978/9), pp. 2–7

Wright, Basil, 'The British Documentary: Today and Tomorrow' in F. Maurice Speed, ed., *Film Review 1947*, (London, Macdonald, 1947), pp. 114–5
'Realist Review', *Sight and Sound*, 10, no. 38 (summer 1941), pp. 20–21
'Geography and the Documentary Film: Britain, since 1945', *Geographical Magazine*, April 1957, pp. 583–95

Wright, Basil and Paul Rotha, 'The Progress of the Factual Film: Grierson the Pioneer; the Future Outlook', in A. G. Weidenfeld, ed., *The Public's Progress* (London, Contact Publications, 1947), pp. 64–73

Wright, John, 'Sussex on the Screen', *Sussex County Magazine*, August 1949, pp. 260–62

Colonial Films

British Film Institute, *The Film in Colonial Development: a Report of a Conference, held in London, January 16, 1948* (London, British Film Institute, 1948)

Mann, John, ed., *The Empire on Film* (London, BBC/Time Life Books, 1973), BBC/Time Life Books, no. 80: *The British Empire*

Milton, Meyrick, *Concerning Legislation to encourage Empire Films* (London, Austin Leigh, 1927)

Champion, A. M., 'With a Mobile Cinema Unit in Kenya', *Overseas Education*, October 1948, pp. 788–92

Glencross, Barbara, 'The Film and Native Cultures', *East and West Review*, October 1948, pp. 125–7

Grierson, John, 'National Film Services in the Dominions', *United Empire*,

November/December 1948, pp. 277–81

'Come, come, is it really R.I.P.?' (On the dissolution of the Crown Film Unit), *Sight and Sound*, 21, no. 4 (April–June 1952), p. 143

Holmes, Winifred, 'British Films and the Empire', *Sight and Sound*, 5, no. 19 (autumn 1936), pp. 72–4

Kearney, Neville, 'The Work of the Film Division of the British Council', *Photographic Journal*, July 1944, pp. 231–3

Keller, Hans, 'A Film Analysis of the Orchestra: a Considered Review of the Crown Film Unit Production "Instruments of the Orchestra" ', *Sight and Sound*, 16, no. 61 (spring 1947), pp. 30–1

Manvell, Roger, and William Sellers, 'The Growth of Film Units in British Overseas Territories', *Geographical Magazine*, January 1958, pp. 365–74

Neville, Alan J., 'Tanganyika's Film-making Experiment', *New Commonwealth*, 21 July 1952, pp. 69–71

Pearson, George, 'The Film in Colonial Development', *Photographic Journal*, Sec. A. August 1948, pp. 172–5

'Visual Education by Film in the Colonies', *United Empire*, July/August 1951, pp. 206–10

Sellers, William, 'Making Films with the Africans', in Roger Manvell, ed., *The Year's Work in the Film, 1950* (London, Longman for the British Council, 1951), pp. 37–43

'Making Films in and for the Colonies', *Journal of the Royal Society of Arts*, 16 October 1953, pp. 829–37

'Mobile Cinema Shows in Africa', *Colonial Review*, March 1955, pp. 13–14

Smith, K. Lockhart, 'Film Uses in Commonwealth Development', *New Commonwealth*, 31 March 1958, pp. 323–6

Smyth, Rosaleen 'The Development of British Colonial Film Policy, 1927–1939 with Special Reference to East and Central Africa', *Journal of African History*, 20 (1979), pp. 437–50

Short Films

Knight, Derrick, and Vincent Porter, *A Long Look at Short Films: an ACTT Report on the Short Entertainment and Factual Film* (London, Pergamon, 1967)

Rank Organization, *No Case for Compulsion* (London, Rank, 1967)

Reid, Adrian, ' "Let's wait till the big picture starts" ', *Sight and Sound*, 19, no. 3 (May 1950) pp. 139–40

'The Supporting Film', *Sight and Sound*, 19, no. 4 (June 1950), pp. 178–80

Robinson, David, and Ian Wright, 'Shorts and Cinemas', *Sight and Sound*, 36, no. 2 (spring 1967), pp. 63–7, 105

Woolfe, Bruce, 'I remember', *Sight and Sound*, 10, no. 37 (spring 1941), pp. 8–9

Newsreels

Hogenkamp, Bert, *Workers Newsreels in the 1920s and 1930s*. (London, Communist Party History Group, 1980; 'Our History' pamphlet, no. 68)

Mitchell, Leslie, *Leslie Mitchell Reporting* (London, Hutchinson, 1981)

Aldgate, Tony, 'British Newsreels and the Spanish Civil War', *History*, 58 (February 1973), pp. 60–63
'Newsreel Scripts: a Case-study', *History*, 61 (October 1976), pp. 390–2
'1930s Newsreels: Censorship and Controversy', *Sight and Sound*, 46, no. 3 (summer 1977), pp. 154–7

Harris, Leslie. 'Presenting the World to the World . . .', *Flickers*, no. 45 (September 1981), pp. 5–10

Hogenkamp, Bert, 'Film and the Workers' Movement in Britain 1929–1939', *Sight and Sound* 45, no. 2 (spring 1976), pp. 68–76

Lewis, Jonathan, 'Before Hindsight', *Sight and Sound*, 46, no. 2 (spring 1977), pp. 68–73

Manvell, Roger, 'Films and the British Working Class', *Humanist*, 83 (March 1968), pp. 73–6

Pronay, Nicholas, 'British Newsreels in the 1930s: 1 – Audience and Producers', *History*, 56, October 1971, pp. 411–18
'British Newsreels in the 1930s: 2 – Their Policies and Impact', *History*, 57 (February 1972), pp. 63–72

Thomas, Howard, 'A Preview of Tomorrow's Newsreels', *Photographic Journal*, Sec. A, December 1953, pp. 306–12

Wegg-Prosser, Victoria, 'The Archive of the Film and Photo League', *Sight and Sound*, 46, no. 4 (autumn 1977), pp. 245–7

History and Film

Smith, Paul, ed., *The Historian and Film* (Cambridge, Cambridge University Press, 1976)

Aldgate, Tony, 'Ideological Consensus in British Feature Films, 1935–1947', in K. R. M. Short, ed., *Feature Films as History* (London, Croom Helm, 1981), pp. 94–112

Chandler, D. G., 'War and the Past: the Historian and the Media', *History Today*, 31 (August 1981), p. 54

Coultass, Clive, 'Film as an Historical Source: its Use and Abuse', *Archives*, 13 (spring 1977), pp. 12–19

Curran, Jim, Paul Nunn, Tony Riley, 'First Ascent reconstructed', *Illustrated London News*, 268 (October 1980), pp. 67–9

Duckworth, John, 'History on the Screen', *Teaching History*, no. 29 (February 1981), pp. 32–5

Houston, Penelope, 'Witnesses of War', *Sight and Sound*, 43, no. 2 (spring 1974), pp. 110–2

Strebel, Elizabeth Grottle, 'Primitive Propaganda: the Boer War Films', *Sight and Sound*, 46, no. 1 (winter 1976/7), pp. 45–7

Independent and Free Cinema

Darian, Adina, *Free cinema: furisii filmului britanic* (Bucharest, Editura Meridane, 1970)

Ellis, John, ed., *1951–76: British Film Institute Productions; a Catalogue of Films made under the Auspices of the Experimental Film Fund 1951–1966 and the Production Board 1966–1976* (London, British Film Institute, 1977)

Fink, Guido, *Il cinema inglese indipendente* (Monza, Circolo Monzese del Cinema, 1964); 'Cinestudio', no. 13)

Issari, M. Ali, and Doris A. Paul, 'The Free Cinema', in *What is Cinéma Vérité?* (Metuchen, N. J., Scarecrow Press, 1979); pp. 52–7

Lovell, Alan, ed., *British Film Institute Production Board* (London, British Film Institute, 1976)

Stoneman, Rod, and Hilary Thompson ed., *The New Social Function of Cinema: Catalogue of British Film Institute Productions 1979/80* (London, British Film Institute, 1981)

Anderson, Lindsay, 'Il Free Cinema vent'anni dopo', in *Free Cinema* (booklet produced for Laboratorio 80 di Bergamo . . . 1982), pp. 15–16

Andrews, Nigel, 'Production Board Films', *Sight and Sound*, 48, no. 1 (winter 1978/9), pp. 53–5

Arts Council of Great Britain, *Perspectives on British Avant-garde Film* (programme notes for a season of films held at the Hayward Gallery, 2 March–24 April 1977.) (London, Arts Council, 1977)

Brownlow, Kevin, et al., 'Alternative Routes: Mason, Graef, Frears, Brownlow', *Sight and Sound*, 41, no. 4 (autumn 1972), pp. 186–91

Caughie, John, *'Because I am King* and Independent Cinema', *Screen*, 21, no. 4 (1980/81), pp. 8–16

Dawson, Jan, and Claire Johnston, 'More British Sounds', *Sight and Sound*, 39, no. 3 (summer 1970), pp. 144–7

Ellis, John, 'Production Board Policies', *Screen*, 17, no. 4 (winter 1976/7), pp. 9–23

Gillett, John, 'Happening here', *Sight and sound*, 34, no. 3 (summer 1965), pp. 138–41

Houston, Penelope, 'Captive or Free', *Sight and Sound*, 27, no. 3 (winter 1957/8), pp. 116–20

Hurst, Brian Desmond, 'The lady vanishes', *Sight and Sound*, 19, no. 6 (August 1950), pp. 253–5

Johnston, Claire, and Jan Dawson, 'Declarations of Independence', *Sight and Sound*, 39, no. 1 (winter, 1969/70), pp. 28–32

Lambert, Gavin, 'Free Cinema', *Sight and Sound*, 25, no. 4 (spring 1956), pp. 173–7

Lassally, Walter, 'The Dead Hand', *Sight and Sound*, 29, no. 3 (summer 1960), pp. 113–15

Lovell, Alan, 'Free Cinema: temi e contesto', in *Free Cinema* (booklet produced for Laboratorio 80 di Bergamo . . . 1982), pp. 9–14

Perkins, V. F., 'Forced to be Free: or doing Business in a Great Art', *Movie*, no. 15 (1966), pp. 17–19

Robinson, David, 'Around Angel Lane', *Sight and Sound*, 39, no. 3 (summer 1970), pp. 132–3

Scott, James, 'Independent Cinema', *Stills*, 1, no. 4 (winter 1982), pp. 40–42

Sutherland, Allan T., 'The Setting up of *Nighthawks*', *Sight and Sound*, 48, no. 1 (winter 1978/9), pp. 50–52

Walsh, Ann, 'Independent Frame: an Innovation in Film Production', *British Journal of Photography*, 27 May 1949, pp. 243–4

'The Cost of Independence: an Enquiry', *Sight and Sound*, 30, no. 3 (summer 1961), pp. 107–13

'The Eleventh Hour', *Scope*, January 1949, pp. 70–79

Propaganda

Thorpe, Frances, and Nicholas Pronay, *British Official Films in the Second World War: a Descriptive Catalogue* (Oxford, Clio Press, 1980)

Forman, Lady Helen, 'Film Propaganda and the War', paper delivered at a conference held at the Imperial War Museum, 1973 (unpublished)

Furhammar, Leif and Folke Isaksson, 'Britain: Democracy at War', in *Politics and Film*, trans. Kersti French (London, Studio Vista, 1971), pp. 78–86

Hollins, T. J., 'The Conservative Party and Film Propaganda between the Wars', *English Historical Review*, 96 (April 1981), pp. 359–69

Porter, Vincent, and Chaim Litewski, 'The Way ahead: Case History of a Propaganda Film', *Sight and Sound*, 50, no. 1 (spring 1981), pp. 84–5

Education

Birkenhead Vigilance Committee, *The Cinema and the Child: a Report of Investigations (June–October 1931)* (Birkenhead, the Committee, 1931)

Field, Mary, *Good Company: the Story of the Children's Entertainment Film Movement in Great Britain, 1943–1950* (London, Longmans, 1952)

Beales, H. L., and R. S. Lambert, 'Living History', *Sight and Sound*, 5, no. 18 (summer 1936), pp. 18–20

Beattie, Nicholas, 'Film in the A-level Modern Language Course: a Proposal', *Screen*, 12, no. 3 (autumn 1971), pp. 121–7

Cons, G. J., 'The Geographical Film in Education', *Geographical Magazine*, January 1959), pp. 456–66

Cook, Jim, 'Teaching Industry', *Screen Education*, no. 16 (autumn 1975), pp. 4–18

Coubro, Gerry, 'Art History and Film Studies in Art Colleges', *Screen*, 12, no. 3 (autumn 1971), pp. 115–18

Duckworth, John, 'Film and the History Teacher', *Teaching History*, no. 19 (October 1977), pp. 8–9

Elliott, B. J., 'Genesis of the History Teaching Film', *Teaching History*, no. 19 (October 1977), pp. 3–6

Exton, Richard, and Heather Hillier, ' "Film as Industry" in the ILEA Sixth Form Film Study Course', *Screen Education*, no. 16 (autumn 1975), pp. 36–9

Field, Mary, 'Children's Taste in Films', *National Froebel Foundation Bulletin*, 98 (February 1956), pp. 2–10

'Nature Films in geography', *Geographical Magazine*, June 1958, pp. 72–81

Gilman, Ian, and Michael Walker, ' "Film as Industry" in the GCE Mode III O-level in Film Studies', *Screen Education*, no. 16 (autumn 1975), pp. 31–5

Grenvill, J. A. S., 'The Use of Film in Schools', *History*, 58 (October 1973), pp. 397–9

Gwynne, Terence and Ian Willis, 'The Role of Feature Films in the Teaching of History', *Teaching History*, 3 (May 1974), pp. 204–8

Hillier, Jim, 'Tyneside: the North East Educational Film Project', *Screen*, 12, no. 3 (autumn 1971), pp. 51–5

Holland, Joanna, 'Upsurge in Interest in the use of Films', *Times Higher Educational Supplement*, 12 January 1973, p. 8

Hunter, William, 'Crisis in Production: the Present Position and a Possible Solution', *Sight and Sound*, 9, no. 34 (summer 1940), pp. 25–7, 36

Knight, Roy, 'Film in English Teaching', *Screen*, 11, no. 6 (November/December 1970), pp. 67–74

MacArthur, Colin, 'The Cinema and the Teacher: Teaching with Film and Film Teaching', *Visual Education*, March 1969, p. 23

Pegge, C. Denis, 'Cinematography and the University', *Nature*, no. 164 (1949), pp. 413–15

Roberts, Martin, and Robert Wolfson, 'Teaching with Film', *History*, 62 (June 1977), pp. 249–51

Toms, V. G., 'The Film Archives of the Imperial War Museum and the Teaching of Twentieth Century History in a College of Education', *Education for Teaching*, 77 (autumn 1968), pp. 65–9

Turnbull, L., 'The Use of Film in the Teaching of History', *Screen Education Notes*, no. 6, (spring 1973), pp. 9–20

'Films in Education' (4 articles by Colin Young et al.), *Times Educational Supplement*, 8 January 1971, pp. 35–8

'Films in Education' (9 articles by C. L. Hewitt et al.), *Times Educational Supplement*, 21 January 1972), pp. 41–8

'Films in Education', (15 articles by Anna Sproule et al.), *Times Educational*

Supplement, 2 February 1973, pp. 51–62

'Film in Education' (11 articles by Adrian Hope et al.), *Times Educational Supplement*, 18 January 1974, pp. 51–8

'Film in Education' (11 articles by Vincent Porter et al.), *Times Educational Supplement*, 17 January 1975, pp. 51–8

'Focus on Film' (10 articles by Paul Medlicott et al.), *Times Educational Supplement*, 9 January 1970, pp. 33–40

'Powerful Role of the Film' (6 articles), *Times Educational Supplement*, 10 January 1969, pp. 75–86

Film Schools

Crofts, Stephen, 'Film Education in England and Wales', *Screen*, 11, no. 6 (November/December 1970), 3–22

Kulik, Karol, ed., 'After School', contributions by Jana Bokova, Chris King, Steve Morrison, Mike Radford, Diane Tammes, *Sight and Sound*, 46, no. 4 (autumn 1977), pp. 200–4

Lovell, Alan, 'The British Film Institute and Film Education', *Screen*, 12, no. 3 (autumn 1971), pp. 13–26

Robinson, David, 'Film Schools: Active and Passive', *Sight and Sound*, 44, no. 3 (summer 1975), pp. 166–9

Stone, Margaret, 'Let's keep this film school: its the only one we have' (London School of Film Technique), *Motion*, no. 2 (winter 1961/2), pp. 36, 39

Young, Colin, 'National Film School', *Sight and Sound*, 41, no. 1 (winter 1971/2), pp. 5–8

Scientific and Industrial Films

The Film in Scientific Research: Report of a Working Party, chairman: W. L. Francis (London, Department of Scientific and Industrial Research, 1963)

Anstey, Edgar, 'Films in Alliance with Industry', *Journal of the Royal Society of Arts*, March 1959, pp. 242–54

Coe, Brian W., 'Eighty-two years of Scientific Cinematography', *Discovery*, August 1956, pp. 332–8

Cox, Frank H. W., 'Films for Industry', *British Journal of Photography*, 24 August 1956, pp. 414–7; 21 September 1956, pp. 466–8; 12 October 1956, pp. 510–11; 2 November 1956, pp. 558–61; 30 November 1956, pp. 616–19

Legg, Stuart, 'Shell Film Unit: Twenty-one Years', *Sight and Sound*, 23, no. 4 (April–June 1954), pp. 209–11

Maddison, John, 'All Wardour Street to a Liver Fluke', in *Films in 1951, Festival of Britain* (London, *Sight and Sound* for the British Film Institute, 1951), pp. 67–8

'The Year's Work in the Specialized Film', in Roger Manvell, ed., *The Year's Work in the Film, 1950* (London, Longman, for the British Council, 1951), pp. 31–6
'The Year's Work in the Specialized Film, seen in its Historical Perspective', in Roger Manvell, ed., *The Year's Work in the Film, 1949*, (London, Longman, for the British Council, 1950), pp. 37–45
Michaelis, A. R., 'Scientific Cinematography in Great Britain', *Nature*, no. 178 (1956), pp. 728–9
Paterson, R. N., 'Films: their Use in Architecture and Building', *Architects Journal*, 20 March 1947, pp. 229–31

British Films

British Character in Films

Anstey, Edgar, 'The Regional Life of Britain as seen through British Films', in Roger Manvell, ed., *The Year's Work in the Film, 1950*, (London, Longman for the British Council, 1951), pp. 44–9
Bannister, Edith, 'Britain on the Screen', *Special Libraries*, November 1943. pp. 452–4
Eves, Vicki, 'Britain's Social Cinema', *Screen*, 10, no. 6 (November/December 1969), pp. 51–66
French, Philip, 'Marriage in the British Cinema', *Twentieth Century*, 172, (spring 1964), pp. 107–16
Jarvie, I. C., 'Fanning the Flames: anti-American Reaction to "Operation Burma"' (*Objective Burma*), *Historical Journal of Film, Radio and Television*, 1, no. 2 (October 1981), pp. 117–37
Lambert, R. S.,'The Screen Englishman', *Sight and Sound*, 13, no. 51 (October 1944), p. 60
Manvell, Roger, 'Britain's Self-portraiture in Feature Films', *Geographical Magazine*, August 1953, pp. 222–34
McArthur, Colin, *Scotch Reels: Scotland in Cinema and Television* (London, British Film Institute, 1982)
Pontecorvo, Lisa, 'Film as a Record of British Industry and Social Life', *Business Archives*, no. 30 (June 1969), pp. 25–6
Richards, Jeffrey, 'Ronald Colman and the Cinema of Empire', *Focus on Film*, no. 4 (September/October 1970), pp. 42–55
'The Cinema of Empire', in *Visions of Yesterday* (London, Routledge, 1973), pp. 2–220
Tallents, Sir Stephen, *The Projection of England* (London, Faber and Faber, 1932)

Films: General

Forman, Denis, *Films 1945–1950* (London, Longmans for the British Council, 1952)

Huntley, John, *British Technicolour Films* (London, Skelton Robinson, 1949)
Railways in the Cinema (London, Ian Allen, 1969)

Powell, Dilys, *Films since 1939* (London, Longmans for the British Council, 1947)

Anderson, Lindsay, 'British Films: the Descending Spiral', *Sequence*, no. 7 (spring 1949), pp. 6–11

Bradbury, Nicola, 'Filming James', *Essays in Criticism*, 29 (October 1979), pp. 293–301

Dixon, Campbell, 'The Year's Work in the Feature Film: a Personal Impression', in Roger Manvell, ed., *The Year's Work in the Film, 1949* (London, Longman for the British Council, 1950), pp. 23–9

Durgnat, Raymond, 'The Great British Phantasmagoria', *Film Comment*, 13, no. 3 (May–June 1977), pp. 48–53

Kael, Pauline, 'Commitment and the Strait-jacket', *Film Quarterly*, 15, no. 1 (fall 1961), pp. 4–13

Monahan, James, 'The Year's Work in the Feature Film', in Roger Manvell, ed., *The Year's Work in the Film, 1950* (London, Longmans for the British Council, 1951), pp. 18–24

Perkins, V.F., 'The British Cinema', *Movie*, no. 1, (1962), pp. 2–9

Pirie, David, 'New Blood', *Sight and Sound*, 40, no. 2 (spring 1971), pp. 73–5

Ray, Cyril, 'These British Movies', *Harper's*, June 1947, pp. 516–23

Riley, Phillip, 'Second Thoughts on British Films', *London Magazine* (NS), 1 (July 1961), pp. 91–6

Robinson, David, 'Case Histories of the Next Renascence', *Sight and Sound*, 38, no. 1 (winter 1968/9), pp. 36–40

Rotha, Paul, 'Films from Home and Abroad', *National and English Review*, September 1952, pp. 160–3

Films: Listed Alphabetically by Title

Jones, Gareth, 'Akenfield', *Sight and Sound*, 42, no. 4 (autumn 1973), pp. 192–3

Pardoe, Bill, 'Early Local Film Relics: "Bladys of the Stewpony" ', *Blackcountryman*, 8 (spring 1975), pp. 7–8

Mass Observation, 'Film and Public: "Chance of a Lifetime" ', *Sight and Sound* 19, no. 9 (January 1951), pp. 349–50

Miles, Bernard, 'Chance of a Lifetime', *World Review*, February 1950, pp. 38–44

Barr, Charles, ' "Straw Dogs", "A Clockwork Orange" and the Critics', *Screen*, 13, no. 2 (summer 1972), pp. 17–31

Eyles, Allen, 'Ken Hughes and "Cromwell" ', *Focus on Film*, no. 4 (September/October 1970), pp. 18–23

Powell, Michael, '20,000 feet on Foula' (*Edge of the World*), (London, Faber and Faber, 1938)

Mathers, Pete, 'Brecht in Britain – from Theatre to Television' (*The Gangster Show*), *Screen*, 16, no. 4 (winter 1975/6), pp. 81–100

Burch, Noel, ' "Hogarth", "England Home and Beauty" – Two Recent British Films and the Documentary Ideology', *Screen*, 19, no. 2 (summer 1978), pp. 119–28

Lovell, Alan, 'Brecht in Britain – Lindsay Anderson' (*If* and *O Lucky Man*), *Screen*, 16, no. 4 (Winter 1975/6), pp. 62–80

Robinson, David, 'Anderson shooting "If" ', *Sight and Sound*, 37, no. 3 (summer 1968), pp. 130–1

Levin, Bernard, ' "I'm all right Jack" ' *Spectator*, 6 April 1962, pp. 435–7

Collier, John W., *A Film in the Making: 'It Always Rains on Sunday'* (London, World Film Publications, 1947)

Brownlow, Kevin, *How it Happened Here* (London, Secker and Warburg in association with the British Film Institute, 1968)

Taylor, John Russell, 'The "Kes" Dossier', *Sight and Sound*, 39, no. 3 (summer 1970), pp. 130–31

Barr, Charles, ' "King and Country" ', *Movie*, no. 12 (spring 1965), pp. 25–7

Buscombe, Edward, *Making 'Legend of the Werewolf'* (London, British Film Institute, 1976)

Harcourt, Peter, 'I'd rather be like I am: Some Comments on "The Loneliness of the Long Distance Runner" ', *Sight and Sound*, 32, no. 1 (winter 1962/3), pp. 16–9

Robinson, David, ' "Look Back In Anger" ', *Sight and Sound*, 28, nos. 3, 4 (summer/autumn 1959), pp. 122–3, 179

Johnston, Claire, and Paul Willemen, 'Brecht in Britain – The Independent Political Film' (*The Nightcleaners*), *Screen*, 16, no. 4 (winter 1975/6), pp. 101–18

Wilson, David, ' "O Lucky Man" ', *Sight and Sound*, 42, no. 3 (summer 1973), pp. 126–9

Stone, Andrew, 'A Method of making Films' (*The Password is Courage*), *Movie*, no. 4 (November 1962), pp. 28–9

Houston, Penelope, ' "Room at the top" '?, *Sight and Sound*, 28, no. 2 (spring 1959), pp. 56–9

James, David, '*Scott of the Antarctic': the Film and its Production* (London, Convoy, 1948)

Frend, Charles, ' "Scott of the Antarctic": the Making of the Film', *Photographic Journal*, Sec. A, August 1949, pp. 192–4

Anderson, Lindsay, ed., *Making a Film: the Story of 'Secret People'* (London, Allen and Unwin, 1952)

Belmans, Jacques, 'Demystifications anglaises' (*A Taste of Honey*), *La Nouvelle Etape*, September/October 1962), pp. 43–7

Vas, Robert, 'Arrival and Departure' (*This Sporting Life*), *Sight and Sound*, 32, no. 2 (spring 1963), pp. 56–9

Honri, B., 'Filming "The Titfield Thunderbolt" ', *Railway Magazine*, March 1953, pp. 163–7, 193

Hoggart, Richard, ' "We are the Lambeth Boys" ', *Sight and Sound*, 28, nos. 3, 4 (summer/autumn 1959), pp. 164–5

Houston, Penelope, ' "Winstanley" ', *Sight and Sound*, 44, no. 4 (autumn 1975), pp. 232–3

Strick, Philip, ' "Zardoz" and John Boorman', *Sight and Sound* 43, no. 2 (spring 1974), pp. 73–4

Adventure Films

Brosnan, John, *James Bond in the Cinema* (London, Tantivy Press, 1972)

Rubin, Steven Jay, *The James Bond Films: a behind the Scenes History* (London, Talisman Books, 1981)

Bennett, Tony, 'Text and Social Process: the Case of James Bond', *Screen Education*, no. 41, (winter/spring 1982), pp. 3–14

Houston, Penelope, '007', *Sight and Sound*, 34, no. 1 (winter 1964), pp. 14–16

Comedy Films

Eastaugh, Kenneth, *The Carry-on Book*, (Newton Abbot, David and Charles, 1978)

Thompson, John O., *Monty Python: Complete and Utter Theory of the Grotesque* (London, British Film Institute, 1982)

Cameron-Wilson, James, 'What a Carry-on!', in F. Maurice Speed, ed., *Film Review 1979–80* (London, W. H. Allen, 1979), pp. 121–6

Flanagan, Bud, 'Knowing your Audience', *Twentieth Century*, 170 (July 1961), pp. 35–9

Raynor, Henry, 'Nothing to laugh at', *Sight and Sound*, 19, no. 2 (April 1950), pp. 68–73

Richardson, Gina, 'Carry on carries on', *Time and Tide*, 17–23 December 1964, p. 29

Rogers, Peter, 'Carrying on in the Cinema', *Twentieth Century*, 170 (July 1961), pp. 66–72

Horror Films

Pirie, David, *A Heritage of Horror: the English Gothic Cinema 1946–1972* (London, Gordon Fraser, 1973)

Personalities

Pioneers

Mellor, G. J., *Picture Pioneers: the Story of the Northern Cinema 1896–1971* (Newcastle-upon-Tyne, Frank Graham, 1971)

Sutherland, Allan T., 'The Yorkshire Pioneers', *Sight and Sound*, 46, no. 1 (winter 1976/7), pp. 48–51

Honri, B., 'Will G. Barker . . . his Studios and Techniques. Part 1', *British Journal of Photography*, 16 February 1973, p. 150; Part 2: *British Journal of Photography*, 23 February 1973, pp. 176–8

Allister, Ray, *Friese-Greene: Close-up of an Inventor* (London, Marsland, 1948)

Coe, B., 'William Friese-Greene and the Origins of Cinematography. Part 1', *Photographic Journal*, vol. 102, March 1962, pp. 92–104; Part 2, *Photographic Journal*, vol. 102, April 1962, pp. 121–7. (Reprinted in *Screen*, 10, no. 2 (March/April 1969), pp. 25–41; 10, no. 3 (May/June 1969), pp.72–83; 10, no. 4/5 (July/October 1969), pp. 129–147

Honri, B., 'William Friese-Greene – an Appreciation', *British Journal of Photography*, 25 June 1971, pp. 576–7

Segaller, Denis, 'The Inventions of Friese-Greene', *Discovery*, November 1951, pp. 343–6

Haas, Robert Bartlett, *Muybridge: Man in Motion* (Berkeley, University of California Press, 1976)

Hendricks, Gordon, *Eadweard Muybridge: the Father of the Motion Picture* (London, Secker and Warburg, 1975)

Producers

Price, Peter, 'The Impresario Urge', *Sight and Sound*, 19, no. 7 (November 1950), pp. 290–3

Balcon, Michael, *Michael Balcon presents: a Lifetime of Films* (London, Hutchinson, 1969)

Danischewsky, Monja, ed., *Michael Balcon's 25 Years in Films* (London, World Film Publications, 1947)

Brown, Geoff, ed., *Der Produzent: Michael Balcon und der englische Film* (Berlin, Volker Speiss, 1981); compiled by Stiftung Deutsche Kinemathek, for the Retrospektive Internationale Filmfestspiele, Berlin, 1981

Danischewsky, Monja, *White Russian, Red Face* (London, Gollancz, 1966)

Balcon, Michael, 'Thiry Years of Film Production' *British Journal of Photography*, 8 July 1949, pp. 312–3

Koval, Francis, 'Sir Michael Balcon and Ealing', in *Films in 1951, Festival of Britain* (London, *Sight and Sound* for the British Film Institute, 1951), pp. 8–9, 58

Box, Muriel, *Odd Woman out: an Autobiography* (London, Frewin, 1974)

Davies, Hunter, *The Grades: the First Family of British Entertainment* (London, Weidenfeld and Nicolson, 1981)

Freeman, Rita Grade, *My Fabulous Brothers: the Story of the Grade Family* (London, W. H. Allen, 1982)

Korda, Michael, *Charmed Lives: a Family Romance* (New York, Random House, 1979)

Kulik, Karol, *Alexander Korda: the Man who could work Miracles* (London, W. H. Allen, 1975)

Tabori, Paul, *Alexander Korda* (London, Oldbourne, 1959)

Dixon, Cambell, 'Sir Alexander Korda', in *Films in 1951, Festival of Britain* (London, *Sight and Sound* for the British Film Institute, 1951), pp. 6–7

Richardson, Ralph, 'Sir Alexander Korda', *Sight and Sound*, 25, no. 4 (spring 1956), pp. 214–5

Brown, Geoff, *Launder and Gilliat* (London, British Film Institute, 1977)

Montagu, Ivor, *The Youngest Son: Autobiographical Sketches* (London, Lawrence and Wishart, 1970)

Pearson, George, *Flashback: the Autobiography of a British Filmmaker* (London, Allen and Unwin, 1957)

Limbacher, James L., 'The Influence of J. Arthur Rank on the History of the British Film'. Submitted in partial requirement for the Seminar in the British Film, Summer 1971, Temple University, Philadelphia, Pennsylvania

Wood, Alan, *Mr Rank: a Study of J. Arthur Rank and British Films* (London, Hodder and Stoughton, 1952)

McNeil, Ann, 'J. Arthur Rank', in *Films in 1951, Festival of Britain* (London, *Sight and Sound* for the British Film Institute, 1951), pp. 5, 15

Wilcox, Herbert, *Twenty-five Thousand Sunsets* (London, Bodley Head, 1967)

Screenwriters

Sadoul, Georges, *British Creators of Film Technique; British Scenario Writers, the Creators of the language of D. W. Griffith, G. A. Smith, Alfred Collins, and Some Others* (London, British Film Institute, 1948)

Hill, Derek, 'A Writers' Wave?', *Sight and Sound*, 29, no. 2 (spring 1960), pp. 56–60

Bell, Mary Haley, *What shall we do tomorrow?: an Autobiography* (London, Cassell, 1968)

Clarke, T. E. B., *This is where I came in* (London, Joseph, 1974)

Morley, John, 'The Screenwriter: T. E. B. Clarke', in *Films in 1951, Festival of Britain* (London, *Sight and Sound* for the British Film Institute, 1951). p. 14

Kneale, Nigel, 'Not quite so Intimate', *Sight and Sound*, 28, no. 2 (spring 1959), pp. 86–8

Mortimer, John, *Clinging to the Wreckage: a Part of Life* (London, Weidenfeld and Nicolson, 1982)

Darlow, Michael, and Gillian Hodson, *Terence Rattigan: the Man and his Work* (London, Quartet Books, 1979)

Shaughnessy, Alfred, *Both Ends of the Candle* (London, Owen, 1978)

Sherriff, Robert Cedric, *No Leading Lady: an Autobiography* (London, Gollancz, 1969)

Speight, Johnny. *It stands to Reason: a Kind of Autobiography* (London, Joseph, 1973)

Travers, Ben, *Vale of Laughter: an Autobiography* (London, Bles, 1957) *A-sitting on a Gate: Autobiography* (London, W. H. Allen, 1978)

Directors

Levin, G. Roy, *Documentary Explorations: 15 Interviews with Film Makers* (New York, Doubleday, 1971), pp. 29–110; interviews with Basil Wright, Lindsay Anderson, Richard Cawston, Tony Garnett and Ken Loach

Phillips, Gene, D., *The Movie Makers: Artists in an Industry* (Chicago, Nelson-Hall, 1973), pp. 135–231; on Carol Reed, David Lean, Joseph Losey, Bryan Forbes, John Schlesinger and Ken Russell

Sussex, Elizabeth, *Lindsay Anderson* (London, Studio Vista, 1969)

British Feature Directors: an Index to their Work', *Sight and Sound*, 27, no. 6 (autumn 1958), pp. 289–304

Anderson, Lindsay, 'Notes from Sherwood', *Sight and Sound*, 26, no. 3 (winter 1956/7), pp. 159–60

Gregor, Ulrich, 'Lindsay Anderson', in Ulrich Gregor, *Wie sie Filmen: fünfzehn Gespräche mit Regisseuren der Gegenwart* (Gütersloh, Sigbert Mohn Verlag, 1966), pp. 228–42

Taylor, John Russell, 'Lindsay Anderson', in J. R. Taylor, *Directors and Directions: Cinema for the Seventies* (London, Eyre Methuen, 1975), pp. 69–99

Belmans, Jacques, *Anthony Asquith 1902–1968* (Paris, Anthologie du Cinéma, 1972; 'Anthologie du Cinéma', no. 67

Minney, Rubeigh James, *Puffin Asquith: a Biography of the Hon. Anthony Asquith* . . . (London, Frewin, 1973)

De La Roche, Catherine, 'The Director's Approach to Film-making: John and Roy Boulting', unpublished script of BBC interview, 1947

Trewin, John Courtenay, *Peter Brook: a Biography* (London, Macdonald, 1971)

Churchill, Clarissa, 'Peter Brook: a Profile of a Producer', in A. G. Weidenfeld, ed., *Uncommon Pleasures* (London, Contact Publications, 1949), pp. 25–9

Houston, Penelope and Tom Milne, 'Interview with Peter Brook', *Sight and Sound*, 32, no. 3 (summer 1963), pp. 108–13

Taylor, John Russell, 'Peter Brook, or the Limitations of Intelligence', *Sight and Sound*, 36, no. 2 (spring 1967), pp. 80–4

Brunel, Adrian, *Film Production* (London, Newnes, 1936)
    Nice Work: the Story of 30 Years in British Film Production (London, Forbes Robertson, 1949)

Carstairs, John Paddy, *Hadn't we the Gaiety?* (London, Hurst and Blackett, 1940)
    Honest Injun: a Light-hearted Autobiography (London, Hurst and Blackett, 1942)

Klaue, Wolfgang, *Alberto Cavalcanti* (Berlin, Staatlichen Filmarchiv der DDR und Club der Filmschaffenden der DDR, 1962)

Hillier, Jim, Alan Lovell, and Sam Rohdie, 'Interview with Alberto Cavalcanti', *Screen*, 13, no. 2 (summer 1972), pp. 36–53

Sussex, Elizabeth, 'Cavalcanti in England', *Sight and Sound*, 44, no. 4 (autumn 1975), pp. 205–11

Cowie, Peter, 'Clayton's Progress', *Motion*, no. 3 (spring 1962), pp. 34–6

Dean, Basil, *Seven Ages: an Autobiography 1888–1927* (London, Hutchinson, 1970)
    Mind's Eye: an Autobiography, 1927–1972 (London, Hutchinson, 1970)

Cameron, Ian, and Mark Shivas, 'What's new Pussycat?' (interview with Clive Donner), *Movie*, no. 14 (autumn 1965), pp. 12–16

Perkins, V. F., 'Clive Donner and *Some People*', *Movie*, no. 3 (October 1962), pp. 22–5

Forbes, Bryan, *Notes for a Life* (London, Collins, 1974)

Brown, Geoff, ed., *Walter Forde* (London, British Film Institute, 1977)

Madden, Paul, and David Wilson, 'Getting in Close: an Interview with Jack Gold', *Sight and Sound*, 43, no. 3 (summer 1974), pp. 134–7

Spiers, David, 'Interview with Jack Gold', *Screen*, 10, no. 4/5 (July/October 1969), pp. 115–28

Lockhart, Freda Bruce, 'Interview with Hamer', *Sight and Sound*, 21, no. 2 (October/December 1951), pp. 74–5

Combs, Richard, and Tom Milne, 'The Romantic Englishman: Anthony Harvey interviewed', *Sight and Sound*, 48, no. 4 (autumn 1979), pp. 210–4

Hepworth, Cecil, *Came the Dawn: Memories of a Film Pioneer* (London, Phoenix House, 1951)
    'Those were the Days', in R. Manvell, ed., *The Penguin Film Review*, no. 6 (Harmondsworth, Penguin, 1948), pp. 33–9

Weybridge Museum, *If it moves – film it: a History of Film-making in Walton-on-Thames, 1900–1939, commemorating the Work of Cecil Hepworth and Clifford Spain* (Weybridge, Weybridge Museum, 1973)

Honri, B., 'Cecil M. Hepworth – his Studios and Techniques', *British Journal of Photography*, 15 January 1971, p. 48

Smith, John M., 'Conservative Individualism: a Selection of English Hitchcock', *Screen*, 13, no. 3 (autumn 1972), pp. 51–70

Gough-Yates, Kevin, 'Seth Holt', *Screen*, 10, no. 6 (November/December

1969), pp. 4–23

Eyles, Allen, 'A Passion for Cinema: Ken Hughes', *Focus on Film*, no. 6 (spring 1971), pp. 42–51

Hardy, Forsyth, *John Grierson: a Documentary Biography* (London, Faber and Faber, 1979)

Powell, Dilys, et al. *Humphrey Jennings, 1907–1950: a Tribute* (London? Humphrey Jennings Memorial Fund Committee, 1950)

Anderson, Lindsay, 'Only connect: some Aspects of the Work of Humphrey Jennings', *Sight and Sound*, 23, no. 4 (April/June 1954), pp. 181–3, 186

Lambert, Gavin, 'Jennings' Britain', *Sight and Sound*, 20, no. 1 (May 1951), pp. 24–6

Millar, Daniel, 'Fires were started' (Humphrey Jennings), *Sight and Sound*, 38, no. 2 (spring 1969), pp. 100–4

Wright, Basil, 'Humphrey Jennings', *Sight and Sound*, 19, no. 8 (December 1950), p. 311

Buache, Freddy, *Cinéma anglais: autour de Kubrick et Losey* (Lausanne, Editions L'Age d'Homme, 1978)

Price, James, 'Stanley Kubrick's Divided World', *London Magazine*, 4, (May 1964), pp. 67–70

Strick, Philip, and Penelope Houston, 'Interview with Stanley Kubrick', *Sight and Sound*, 41, no. 2 (spring 1972), pp. 62–6

De La Roche, Catherine, 'A Director's Approach to Filmmaking: David Lean', unpublished script of BBC interview, 1947

Higham, Charles, 'David Lean', *London Magazine*, 4 (January 1965), pp. 74–82

Lee, Norman, *Log of a Film Director* (London, Quality Press, 1949)

French, Philip, 'Richard Lester', *Movie*, no. 14 (autumn 1965), pp. 5–11

McBride, Joseph, 'Running, jumping and standing still: an Interview with Richard Lester', *Sight and Sound*, 42, no. 2 (spring 1973), pp. 75–9

Milne, Tom, ed., *Losey on Losey* (London, Secker and Warburg, 1967; 'Cinema One', no. 2)

Jacob, Gilles, 'Joseph Losey, or the Camera calls', *Sight and Sound*, 35, no. 2 (spring 1966), pp. 62–7

Mackendrick, Alexander, 'A Film Director and his Public', *Listener*, 23 September 1954, pp. 482–3, 489

Brown, Geoff, 'Richard Massingham: the Five-inch Film-maker', *Sight and Sound*, 45, no. 3 (summer 1976), pp. 156–9

Zito, Bobbi Leigh, 'Alan Parker: Interview', *Focus on Film*, no. 35 (April 1980), pp. 4–8

Christie, Ian, ed., *Powell, Pressburger and others* (London, British Film Institute, 1978)

Badder, David, 'Powell and Pressburger: the War Years', *Sight and Sound*, 48, no. 1 (winter 1978/9), pp. 8–12

Green, O. O., 'Michael Powell', *Movie*, no. 14 (autumn 1965), pp. 17–20

Thomson, D., 'The Films of Michael Powell: a Romantic Sensibility', *American Film*, 6, no. 2 (November 1980), pp. 47–8, 50–2

Williams, T., 'Michael Powell', *Films and Filming*, no. 326 (November 1981), pp. 10–16

De La Roche, Catherine, 'The Director's Approach to Film Making: Carol Reed', unpublished script of BBC interview, 1948

Voight, Michael, 'Pictures of Innocence: Sir Carol Reed', *Focus on Film*, no. 17 (spring 1974), pp. 17–38

Wright, Basil, 'A Study of Carol Reed', in Roger Manvell, ed., *The Year's Work in the Film, 1949* (London, Longman for the British Council, 1950), pp. 11–22

'Carol Reed', in *Films in 1951, Festival of Britain* (London, *Sight and Sound* for the British Film Institute, 1951), pp. 10–13

Wood, Robin, 'In Memoriam Michael Reeves', *Movie*, no. 17 (1966), pp. 2–6

Lellis, George, 'Recent Richardson – cashing the Blank Cheque', *Sight and Sound*, 38, no. 3 (summer 1969), pp. 130–3

Stokes, Sewell, 'Filming a Borstal' (Tony Richardson), *Listener*, 1 November 1962, pp. 715–6

Kolker, Robert Phillip 'The Open Texts of Nicolas Roeg', *Sight and Sound*, 46, no. 2 (spring 1977), pp. 82–4, 113

Milne, Tom, and Penelope Houston, '*Don't look now*: Nicolas Roeg interviewed', *Sight and Sound*, 43, no. 1 (winter 1973/4), pp. 2–8

Baxter, John, *An Appalling Talent* (Ken Russell) (London, Joseph, 1974)

Phillips, Gene, 'On *Yanks* and other Films: John Schlesinger', *Focus on Film*, no. 31 (November 1978), pp. 4–7

Spiers, David, 'John Schlesinger', *Screen*, 11, no. 3 (summer 1970), pp. 3–18

Tennyson, Charles, *Penrose Tennyson* (London, privately published by A. S. Atkinson, 1943)

Watt, Harry, *Don't look at the Camera* (London, Elek, 1974)

Art Designers

Carrick, Edward, compiled by *Art and Design in the British Film: a Pictorial Directory of British Art Directors and their Work* (London, Dobson, 1948)

Myerscough-Walker, R., *Stage and Film Décor* (London, Pitman, 1940)

Carrick, Edward, 'The Influence of the Graphic Artist on Films', *Journal of the Royal Society of Arts*, 24 March 1950, pp. 368–84

'The Artist and the Film', *Studio*, December 1951, pp. 161–7

Hardy, H. Forsyth, 'Designers and British Film Advance', *Architectural Design*, March 1948, pp. 58–9

Howard, Tom, 'The Role of the Special Effects Department', *Photographic Journal*, August 1944, pp. 262–5

Hudson, Roger, 'Three Designers' (conversations with Ken Adam, Edward

Marshall and Richard Macdonald). *Sight and Sound*, 34, no. 1 (winter 1964/5), pp. 26–31

Martin, Geoffrey, 'The Designer and the Cartoon Film', *Art and Industry*, September 1953, pp. 94–9

Newton, Eric, 'Film Décor', in Roger Manvell, ed., *The Year's Work in the Film, 1949* (London, Longman for the British Council, 1950), pp. 55–61

Pierce, Betty, 'The Work of the Film Architect: 1. The Art Director', *Official Architect*, September 1950, pp. 515–7; '2. The Drawing Office', *Official Architect*, October 1950, pp. 573–5; '3. Construction and materials', *Official Architect*, November 1950, pp. 631–5; '4. Decoration, Furnishing and Trick Effects', *Official Architect*, December 1950, pp. 694–7

Spencer, Charles, *Cecil Beaton: Stage and Film Design* (London, Academy Editions, 1975)

Beaton, Cecil, *The Happy Years: Diaries 1944–48* (London, Weidenfeld and Nicolson, 1972)

The Restless Years: Diaries 1955–63 (London, Weidenfeld and Nicolson, 1976)

The Parting Years: Diaries 1963–1974 (London, Weidenfeld and Nicolson, 1978)

Self Portrait with Friends: the Selected Diaries of Cecil Beaton, 1926–1974 (London, Weidenfeld and Nicolson, 1979)

Nathan, Archie, *Costumes by Nathan* (London, Newnes, 1960)

Cinematographers

Hudson, Roger, 'The Secret Profession: Interviews with Lighting Cameramen Douglas Slocombe and Walter Lassally', *Sight and Sound*, 34, no. 3 (summer 1965), pp. 112–7

Edwards, Mark, 'The Cameraman: Jack Cardiff', in *Films in 1951, Festival of Britain* (London, *Sight and Sound* for the British Film Institute, 1951), p. 15

Duncan, Charles, *A Photographic Pilgrim's progress: being the Adventures of an Itinerant Photographer among Cameras, Cabbages and Kings* (London, Focal Press, 1954)

Grant, Ian, *Cameramen at war* (Cambridge, Patrick Stephens, 1980)

Grant, Ian, 'A Cameraman at war', *Army Quarterly*, October 1951, pp. 70–6

Hopkinson, Peter, *Split Focus: an Involvement in Two Decades* (London, Hart-Davis, 1969)

Hudson, Will E., *Icy Hell: Experiences of a Newsreel Cameraman in the Aleutian Islands, Eastern Siberia and the Arctic Fringe of Alaska* (London, Constable, 1937)

Malins, Geoffrey H., ed. Low Warren, *How I filmed the War: a Record of the Extraordinary Experiences of the Man who filmed the Great Somme Battles* (London, Jenkins, 1920)

Wood, Franklyn, *The Naked Truth about Harrison Marks* (Hemel Hempstead, Colonna Press, 1967)

Eyles, Allen, 'Behind the Cameras: Oswald Morris', *Focus on Film*, no. 8 (1971), pp. 28–37

Noble, Ronald, *Shoot first!: Assignments of a Newsreel Cameraman* (London, Harrap, 1955)

Arnold, H. J. P., *Photographer of the World: the Biography of Herbert Ponting* (London, Hutchinson, 1969)

Niogret, H., 'Entretien avec Douglas Slocombe', *Positif*, no. 246 (September 1981), pp. 2–10

Stobart, Tom, *Adventurer's Eye: the Autobiography of Everest Film-man Tom Stobart* (London, Odhams, 1958)

Editors

Hudson, Roger, 'Putting the Magic in it: Two Editors, James Clark and Anthony Harvey, discuss their Work', *Sight and Sound*, 35, no. 2 (spring 1966), pp. 78–83

Gladwell, David, 'Editing Anderson's *If . . .*', *Screen*, 10, no. 1 (January/February 1969), pp. 24–33

Reisz, Karel, 'The Editor: Jack Harris', in *Films in 1951, Festival of Britain* (London, *Sight and Sound* for the British Film Institute, 1951), p. 16

Composers

Huntley, John, *British Film Music* (London, Skelton Robinson, 1947)
  'British Film Music', in R. Manvell, ed., *The Penguin Film Review*, no. 6 (Harmondsworth, Penguin, 1948), pp. 91–6
  'Film Music Recordings of 1949', in Roger Manvell, ed., *The Year's Work in the Film, 1949* (London, Longman for the British Council, 1950), pp. 87–90
  'The music of *Hamlet* and *Oliver Twist*', in R. Manvell, ed., *The Penguin Film Review*, no. 8 (Harmondsworth, Penguin, 1949), pp. 110–6

Walsh, Ann, 'Music in the Film: its Possibilities and Uses', *British Journal of Photography*, 18 February 1949, pp. 73–4; 11 March 1949, pp. 110–1

Palmer, Christopher, 'British Composers for the Film: John Addison and Ron Goodwin', *Performing Right*, no. 6 (November 1971), pp. 20–5

Thomas, Tony, 'John Addison', in Tony Thomas, ed., *Film Score: the View from the Podium* (South Brunswick and New York, A. S. Barnes; London, Yoseloff, 1979), pp. 197–208

Lindgren, Ernest, 'The Composer: William Alwyn', in *Films in 1951, Festival of Britain* (London, *Sight and Sound* for the British Film Institute, 1951), pp. 19–20

Wright, Basil, 'Britten and Documentary', *Musical Times*, November 1963, pp. 779–80

Collier, Graham, *Cleo and John: a Biography of the Dankworths* (London, Quartet Books, 1976)

Hall, Henry, *Here's to the Next Time: Autobiography* (London, Odhams, 1955)

Levy, Louis, *Music for the Movies* (London, Sampson Low, Marston, 1948)

Kemp, Jeffrey, 'Write what the Film needs: an Interview with Elizabeth Lutyens', *Sight and Sound*, 43, no. 4 (autumn 1974), pp. 203–5, 248

Simon, Larry, 'Music and Film: an Interview with Michael Nyman', *Millenium Film Journal*, nos 10/11 (fall/winter 1981/2), pp. 223–34

Actors: General

Gielgud, Sir John, *Distinguished Company* (London, Heinemann, 1972)

Noble, Peter, ed., *British Screen Stars* (London, British Yearbooks, 1946)

Brown, Ivor, 'British Acting – the New Names', *Britain Today*, March 1950, pp. 31–4.

Tenent, Rose, 'The Life of a Film-extra', *Chambers's Journal*, Nov. 1952, pp. 653–4.

Actors: Listed Alphabetically

Ackland, Rodney and Elspeth Grant, *The Celluloid Mistress, or the Custard Pie of Dr Caligari* (London, Wingate, 1954)

Ackland, Rodney, 'Greed: a Personal Note', in Peter Noble, *Hollywood Scapegoat, the Biography of Erich von Stroheim* (London, Fortune Press, 1950)

Aherne, Brian, *A Proper Job* (Boston, Houghton Mifflin, 1969)

Cottrell, John, *Julie Andrews* (London, Mayflower Books, 1969)

Windeler, Robert, *Julie Andrews: a Biography* (New York, Putnam, 1970)

Arliss, George. *Up the Years from Bloomsbury* (Boston, Little Brown, 1927; published in Great Britain under the title *On the stage*, Murray, 1928)
George Arliss, by Himself (London, Murray, 1940)
My Ten Years in the Studios (Boston, Little, Brown, 1940)

Keown, Eric, *Peggy Ashcroft: an Illustrated Study of her Work, with a List of her Appearances on Stage and Screen* (London, Rockliff, 1955)

Askey, Arthur, *Before your Very Eyes* (London, Woburn Press, 1975)

Storey, Anthony, *Stanley Baker: Portrait of an Actor* (London, W. H. Allen, 1977)

Baxter, Stanley, and Ken Hoare, *Stanley Baxter on Screen* (London, Joseph in association with M. and J. Hobbs, 1980)

Bloom, Claire, *Limelight and after: the Education of an Actress* (London, Weidenfeld and Nicolson, 1982)

Bogarde, Dirk, *Snakes and Ladders* (London, Chatto and Windus, 1978)

Bodeen, DeWitt, 'Dirk Bogarde', *Films in Review*, 31, no. 9 (November 1980), pp. 513–28

Claire, Vivian, *David Bowie* (London, Flash Books, 1977)

Brambell, Wilfrid, *All above Board: an Autobiography* (London, W. H. Allen, 1976)

Marshall, Michael, *Top Hat and Tails: the Story of Jack Buchanan* (London, Elm Tree Books, 1978)

Bull, Peter, *I know the Face but . . .* (London, Davies, 1959)
   I say, look here!: the rather Random Reminiscences of a round Actor in the Square (London, Peter Davies, 1965)

Cottrell, John, and Fergus Cashin, *Richard Burton: a Biography* (London, Barker, 1971)

David, Lester, and Jhan Robbins, *Richard and Elizabeth* (New York, Funk and Wagnalls, 1977)

Ferris, Paul, *Richard Burton* (London, Weidenfeld and Nicolson, 1981)

Waterbury, Ruth, *Richard Burton* (London, Mayflower Books, 1965)

Bygraves, Max, *I wanna tell you a Story* (London, W. H. Allen, 1976)

Hall, William, *Raising Caine: the Authorized Biography* (London, Sidgwick and Jackson, 1981)

Carmichael, Ian, *Will the Real Ian Carmichael . . .* (London, Macmillan, 1979)

Churchill, Sarah, *Keep on dancing: an Autobiography* (London, Weidenfeld and Nicolson, 1981)

Collier, Constance, *Harlequinade* (London, John Lane, 1929)

Collins, Joan, *Past Imperfect: an Autobiography* (London, W. H. Allen, 1978)

Colman, Juliet Benita, *Ronald Colman: a very Private Person* (London, W. H. Allen, 1975)

Wild, Roland, *Ronald Colman* (London, Rich and Cowan, 1933)

Gant, Richard, *Sean Connery: Gilt-edged Bond* (London, Mayflower Books, 1967)

Morley Sheridan, *Gladys Cooper: a Biography* (London, Heinemann, 1979)

Stokes, Sewell, *Without Veils: the Intimate Biography of Gladys Cooper* (London, Davies, 1953)

Courtneidge, Cicely, *Cicely* (London, Hutchinson, 1953)

Hulbert, Jack, *The Little Woman's always Right* (Cicely Courtneidge) (London, W. H. Allen, 1975)

Coward, Sir Noel, *Present Indicative* (London, Heinemann, 1937)
   Future Indefinite (London, Heinemann, 1954)

Lesley, Cole, *The Life of Noel Coward* (London, Cape, 1976)

Lesley, Cole, Graham Payn and Sheridan Morley, *Noel Coward and his Friends* (London, Weidenfeld and Nicolson, 1979)

Morley, Sheridan, *A Talent to amuse: a Biography of Noel Coward* (London, Heinemann, 1969)

Culver, Roland, *Not quite a Gentleman* (London, Kimber, 1979)

De Casalis, Jeanne, *Things I don't remember: Short Stories and Impressions* (London, Heinemann, 1953)

Denison, Michael, *Overture and Beginners* (London, Gollancz, 1973)

Trewin, J. C., *Robert Donat: a Biography* (London, Heinemann, 1968)

Richards, Jeffrey, 'A Star without Armour: Robert Donat', *Focus on Film*, no. 8 (1971), pp. 17–27

Dors, Diana, *Swingin' Dors* (London, World Distributors, 1960)
For Adults Only (London, W. H. Allen, 1978)
Behind Closed Dors (London, W. H. Allen, 1979)
Dors by Diana (London, Macdonald Futura, 1981)

Emery, Dick, *In Character: a Kind of Living Scrapbook* (London, Futura, 1974)

Batters, Jean, *Edith Evans: a Personal Memoir* (London, Hart-Davis Mac-Gibbon, 1977)

Forbes, Bryan, *Ned's Girl: the Authorized Biography of Dame Edith Evans* (London, Elm Tree Books, 1977)

Trewin, J. C., *Edith Evans: an Illustrated Study of Dame Edith's Work, with a List of her Appearances on Stage and Screen* (London, Rockliff, 1954)

Farrar, David, *No Royal Road* (Eastbourne, Mortimer Publications, 1948)

Fisher, John, *What a Performance: a Life of Sid Field* (London, Seeley Service, 1975)

Aza, Bert, *Our Gracie* (London, Pitkins, 1951)

Burgess, Muriel, with Tommy Keen, *Gracie Fields* (London, W. H. Allen, 1980)

Fields, Gracie, *Sing as we go* (London, Muller, 1960)

Richards, Jeffrey, 'Gracie Fields: the Lancashire Britannia', *Focus on Film*, no. 33 (August 1979), pp. 27–35; *Focus on Film*, no. 34 (December 1979), pp. 23–38

Dundy, Elaine, *Finch, Bloody Finch* (London, Joseph, 1980)

Faulkner, Trader, *Peter Finch: a Biography* (London, Angus & Robertson, 1979)

Finch, Yolande, *Finchy: my Life with Peter Finch* (London, Arrow Books, 1980)

Flanagan, Bud, *My Crazy Life: the Autobiography of Bud Flanagan* (London, Muller, 1961)

Fletcher, Cyril, *Nice One, Cyril: being the Odd Odyssey and the Anecdotage of a Comedian* (London, Barrie and Jenkins, 1978)

Fisher, John, *George Formby* (London, Woburn-Futura, 1975)

Randall, Allan, and Ray Seaton, *George Formby: a Biography* (London, W. H. Allen, 1974)

French, Harold, *I swore I never would* (London, Secker and Warburg, 1970)

Gielgud, John, *Early Stages* (London, Macmillan, 1939; new ed., London, Falcon Press, 1953)
An actor and his Time (London, Sidgwick and Jackson, 1979)

Hayman, Ronald, *John Gielgud* (London, Heinemann, 1971)

Gingold, Hermione, *The World is Square* (London, Home and Van Thal,

1945)

Green, Martyn, *Here's a How-de-do: travelling with Gilbert and Sullivan* (London, Reinhardt, 1952)

Grenfell, Joyce, *Joyce Grenfell requests the Pleasure* (London, Macmillan, 1976)

　In Pleasant Places (London, Macmillan, 1979)

　Joyce, by herself and her Friends (London, Macmillan, 1980)

Tynan, Kenneth, *Alec Guinness* (London, Rockliff, 1953)

Phillips, Gene, 'Sir Alec Guinness: Talent has many Faces', *Focus on Film*, no. 11 (autumn 1972), pp. 16–26

Hampshire, Susan, *Susan's Story: an Autobiographical Account of my Struggle with Words* (London, Sidgwick and Jackson, 1981)

Hancock, Freddie and David Nathan, *Hancock* (London, Kimber, 1969)

Oakes, Phillip, *Tony Hancock* (London, Woburn-Futura, 1975)

Grundy, Bill, *That Man: a Memory of Tommy Handley* (London, Elm Tree Books, 1976)

Hardwicke, Sir Cedric, A Victorian in Orbit: the Irreverent Memoirs of Sir Cedric Hardwicke (London, Methuen, 1961)

Hare, Robertson, *Yours Indubitably* (London, Hale, 1956)

Harrison, Rex, *Rex: an Autobiography* (London, Macmillan, 1974)

Hickey, Des, and Gus Smith, *The Prince: being the Public and Private Life of Larushka Mischa Skikne . . . otherwise known as Laurence Harvey* (London, Frewin, 1975)

Hawkins, Jack, *Anything for a Quiet Life* (London, Elm Tree Books and Hamish Hamilton, 1973)

Seaton, Ray, and Roy Martin, *Good Morning Boys: Will Hay, Master of Comedy* (London, Barrie and Jenkins, 1978)

Eyles, Allen, 'Will Hay & Co'., *Focus on Film*, no. 34 (December 1979), pp. 4–18

Henderson-Bland, R., *Actor-soldier-poet* (London, Heath Cranton, 1939)

Henrey, Robert, *A Film Star in Belgrave Square* (London, Davies, 1948)

Henson, Leslie, *My Laugh-Story: the Story of my Life up to Date* (London, Hodder and Stoughton, 1926)

　Yours faithfully: an Autobiography (London, Long, 1948)

Hicks, Seymour, *Between Ourselves* (London, Cassell, 1930)

　Night Lights: Two Men talk of Life and Love and Ladies (London, Cassell, 1938)

　Me and my Missus: Fifty Years on the Stage . . . (London, Cassell, 1939)

Hillman, June, *The Glass Ladder* (London, Heinemann, 1960)

Hird, Thora, *Scene and Hird* (London, W. H. Allen, 1976)

Holloway, Stanley, and Dick Richards, *Wiv a little Bit o' Luck: the Life Story of Stanley Holloway* (London, Frewin, 1967)

Colvin, Ian, *Flight 777* (Leslie Howard) (London, Evans, 1957)

Howard, Leslie, ed., Ronald Howard, *Trivial Fond Records* (London,

Kimber, 1982)

Howard, Leslie Ruth, *A quite Remarkable Father* (London, Longman, 1960)

Howard, Ronald, *In Search of my father: a Portrait of Leslie Howard* (London, Kimber, 1981)

Richards, Jeffrey, 'The Thinking Man as Hero: Leslie Howard', *Focus on Film*, no. 25 (summer/autumn 1976), pp. 37–50

Howerd, Frankie, *On the way I lost it: an Autobiography* (London, W. H. Allen, 1976)

Scaduto, Anthony, *Mick Jagger* (London, W. H. Allen, 1974)

Kendall, Henry, *I remember Romano's* (London, Macdonald, 1960)

Braun, Eric, *Deborah Kerr* (London, W. H. Allen, 1977)

Lane, Lupino, *How to become a Comedian* (London, Muller, 1945)

White, James Dillon, *Born to star: the Lupino Lane Story* (London, Heinemann, 1957)

Lang, Matheson, *Mr Wu looks back: Thoughts and Memories* (London, Stanley Paul, 1941)

Lauder, Harry, *Roamin' in the Gloamin'* (London, Hutchinson, 1928)

Higham, Charles, *Charles Laughton: an Intimate Biography* (London, W. H. Allen, 1976)

Lanchester, Elsa, *Charles Laughton and I* (London, Faber and Faber, 1938)

Laughton, Tom, *Pavilions by the Sea: the Memoirs of a Hotel-keeper* (London, Chatto and Windus, 1977); contains reminiscences of Charles Laughton, the author's brother

Singer, Kurt, *The Charles Laughton Story* (London, Robert Hale, 1954)

Aldrich, Richard Stoddard, *Gertrude Lawrence as Mrs A.: an Intimate Biography of the Great Star by her Husband* (London, Odhams, 1955)

Lawrence, Gertrude, *A Star danced* (London, W. H. Allen, 1945)

Morley, Sheridan, *Gertrude Lawrence* (London, Weidenfeld and Nicolson, 1981)

Laye, Evelyn, *Boo, to my Friends* (London, Hurst and Blackett, 1958)

Lee, Christopher, *Tall, Dark and Gruesome: an Autobiography* (London, W. H. Allen, 1977)

Dent, Alan, *Vivien Leigh: a Bouquet* (London, Hamilton, 1969)

Edwards, Anne, *Vivien Leigh: a Biography* (London, W. H. Allen, 1977)

Robyns, Gwen, *Light of a Star* (Vivien Leigh) (London, Frewin, 1968)

Kidd, Paul, *Mark Lester: the Boy, his Life and his Films* (Ilfracombe, Arthur H. Stockwell, 1975)

Lillie, Beatrice, *Every Other Inch a Lady* (New York, Dell, 1972)

Lockwood, Margaret, *Lucky Star: Autobiography* (London, Odhams, 1955)

Loder, John, *Hollywood Hussar* (London, Baker, 1977)

Love, Bessie, *From Hollywood with love* (London, Elm Tree Books, 1977)

Lupino, Stanley, *From the Stocks to the Stars: an Unconventional Autobiography* . . . (London, Hutchinson, 1934)

McCowan, Alec, *Double Bill* (London, Elm Tree Books, 1980)

MacLiammoir, Micheal, *Each Actor on his Ass* (London, Routledge, 1961)

Maltby, H. F., *Ring up the Curtain: being the Stage and Film Memoirs of H. F. Maltby* (London, Hutchinson, 1950)

Maschwitz, Eric, *No Chip on my Shoulder* (London, Jenkins, 1957)

Mason, James, *Before I forget: Autobiography and Drawings* (London, Hamilton, 1981)

Monaghan, J. P., *The Authorized Biography of James Mason* (London, World Film Publications, 1947)

Nogueira, Rui, 'James Mason talks about his Career in the Cinema', *Focus on Film*, no. 2 (March/April 1970), pp. 18–43

Massey, Raymond, *When I was Young* (Boston, Little Brown, 1976)
  A Hundred Different Lives: an Autobiography (London, Robson, 1979)

Matthews, A. E., *Matty: an Autobiography* (London, Hutchinson, 1952)

Matthews, Jessie, *Over my Shoulder: an Autobiography by Jessie Matthews as told to Muriel Burgess* (London, W. H. Allen, 1974)

Thornton, Michael, *Jessie Matthews: a Biography* (London, Hart-Davis MacGibbon, 1974)

Braun, Eric, Jessie Matthews in Perspective *Films*, 1, no. 10 (September 1981), pp. 20–24

Maynard, Bill, *The Yo-yo Man: an Autobiography* (London, Golden Eagle, 1975)

East, John M., *Max Miller, the Cheekie Chappie* (London, W. H. Allen, 1977)

Mills, John, *Up in the Clouds, Gentlemen Please* (London, Weidenfeld and Nicolson, 1980)

Milton, Billy, *Milton's Paradise Mislaid: an Autobiography* (London, Jupiter Books, 1976)

Mitchell, Yvonne, *Actress* (London, Routledge, 1957)

More, Kenneth, *Happy go Lucky: my Life* (London, Hale, 1959)
  Kindly Leave the Stage (London, Joseph, 1965)
  More or Less (London, Hodder and Stoughton, 1978)

Holman, Dennis, *Eric and Ernie: the Autobiography of Morecambe and Wise* (London, W. H. Allen, 1973)

Morecambe, Eric, and Ernie Wise, *There's no Answer to that!* (London, Barker, 1981)

Morley, Margaret, *Larger than Life: the Biography of Robert Morley* (London, Robson, 1979)

Morley, Robert, and Sewell Stokes. *Robert Morley, Responsible Gentleman* (London, Heinemann, 1966)

Nares, Owen, *Myself and Some Others: Pure Egotism* (London, Duckworth, 1925)

Neagle, Anna, 'Portraying Edith Cavell and other Nurses', *Nursing Mirror*, 10 October 1958, supplement, pp. i–ii
  There's always Tomorrow: an Autobiography (London, W. H. Allen, 1974)

Nesbitt, Cathleen, *A Little Love and Good Company* (London, Faber and

Faber, 1975)

Niven, David, *The Moon's a Balloon: Reminiscences* (London, Hamilton, 1971)

Bring on the Empty Horses (London, Hamilton, 1975)

Oliver, Vic, *Mr Showbusiness: the Autobiography of Vic Oliver* (London, Harrap, 1954)

Barker, Felix, *The Oliviers: a Biography* (London, Hamilton, 1953)

Cottrell, John, *Laurence Olivier* (London, Weidenfeld and Nicolson, 1975)

Fairweather, Virginia, *Cry God for Larry: an Intimate Memoir of Sir Laurence Olivier* (London, Calder and Boyars, 1969)

Kiernan, Thomas, *Olivier: the Life of Laurence Olivier* (London, Sidgwick and Jackson, 1981)

Olivier, Lawrence, *Confessions of an Actor* (London, Weidenfeld and Nicolson, 1982)

Palmer, Lilli, *Dicke Lilli – gutes Kind* (Zurich, Droemer Knaur, 1974; Eng. ed. *Change Lobsters and Dance* (London, W. H. Allen, 1976)

Pertwee, Roland, *Master of None* (London, Davies, 1940)

Pickles, Wilfred, *Between You and Me: the Autobiography of Wilfred Pickles* (London, Laurie, 1949)

Wilfred Pickles invites you to have Another Go (Newton Abbot, David and Charles, 1978)

Powell, Sandy, *Can you hear me, mother?: Sandy Powell's Lifetime of Music-hall: Sandy Powell's story told to Harry Stanley* (London, Jupiter Books, 1976)

Rathbone, Basil, *In and out of Character* (New York, Doubleday, 1962)

Ray, Ted, *Raising the Laughs* (London, Laurie, 1952)

Findlater, Richard, *Michael Redgrave, Actor* (London, Heinemann, 1956)

Redgrave, Michael, *Mask or Face: Reflections in an Actor's Mirror* (London, Heinemann, 1958), 'I am not a Camera', pp. 120–48

Reed, Oliver, *Reed all about me: the Autobiography of Oliver Reed* (London, W. H. Allen, 1979)

Reeve, Ada, *Take it for a Fact: a Record of my 75 years on the Stage* (London, Heinemann, 1954)

Rix, Brian, *My Farce from my Elbow: an Autobiography* (London, Secker and Warburg, 1975)

Cotes, Peter, *George Robey: the Darling of the Halls* (London, Cassell, 1972)

Robey, George, *Looking back on Life* (London, Constable, 1933)

Dunbar, Janet, *Flora Robson* (London, Harrap, 1960)

Keown, Eric, *Margaret Rutherford* (London, Rockliff, 1956)

Rutherford, Margaret, *Margaret Rutherford: an Autobiography* (London, W. H. Allen, 1972)

Aherne, Brian, George Sanders and Benita Hume, *A Dreadful Man: (a Personal Intimate Book about George Sanders)* (New York, Simon and Schuster, 1979)

Sanders, George, *Memoirs of a Professional Cad* (New York, Putnam, 1960)

Scott, Janette, *Act One* (London, Nelson, 1953)

Evans, Peter, *Peter Sellers: the Mask behind the Mask* (Englewood Cliffs, N. J. Prentice-Hall, 1968)

Sylvester, Derek, *Peter Sellers* (London, Proteus, 1981)

Walker, Alexander, *Peter Sellers: the Authorized Biography* (London, Weidenfeld and Nicolson, 1981)

Sinden, Donald, *A Touch of the Memoirs* (London, Hodder and Stoughton, 1982)

Kennedy, John, *Tommy Steele – the Facts about a Teenage Idol and an 'Inside' Picture of Showbusiness* (London, Souvenir Press, 1958)

Stuart, John, *Caught in the Act* (London, The Silent Picture, 1971)

Tauber, Diana Napier, *Richard Tauber* (Glasgow, Art and Educational Publishers, 1949)

My Heart and I (biography of Richard Tauber) (London, Evans, 1959)

Terry-Thomas, *Filling the Gap* (London, Parrish, 1959)

Thesiger, Ernest, *Practically True* (London, Heinemann, 1927)

Casson, John, *Lewis and Sybil: a Memoir* (London, Collins, 1972)

Morley, Sheridan, *Sybil Thorndike: a Life in the Theatre* (London, Weidenfeld and Nicolson, 1977)

Sprigge, Elizabeth, *Sybil Thorndike Casson* (London, Gollancz, 1971)

Thorndike, Russell, *Sybil Thorndike* (London, Thornton Butterworth, 1929)

Trewin, J. C., *Sybil Thorndike: an Illustrated Study of Dame Sybil's Work, with a List of her appearances on Stage and Screen* (London, Rockliff, 1955; 'Theatre World Monograph', no. 4)

Todd, Ann, *The Eighth Veil* (London, William Kimber, 1980)

Train, Jack, *Up and down the Line* (London, Odhams, 1956)

Twiggy, *Twiggy: an Autobiography* (London, Hart-Davis MacGibbon, 1975)

Ustinov, Peter, *Dear Me* (London, Heinemann, 1977)

Vanbrugh, Irene, *To tell my Story* (London, Hutchinson, 1948)

Warner, Jack, *Jack of all Trades: an Autobiography* (London, W. H. Allen, 1975)

Wilding, Michael, *Apple Sauce: the Story of my Life, as told to Pamela Wilding* (London, George Allen and Unwin, 1982)

Findlater, Richard *Emlyn Williams* (London, Rockliff, 1956)

Williams, Emlyn, *George: an Early Autobiography, 1905–1927* (London, Hamilton, 1961)

Emlyn: an Early Autobiography, 1927–1935 (London, Bodley Head, 1973)

McCallum, John, *Life with Googie* (Googie Withers) (London, Heinemann, 1979)

Harwood, Ronald, *Sir Donald Wolfit CBE: his Life and Work in the Unfashionable Theatre* (London, Secker and Warburg, 1971)

Wolfit, Donald, *First Interval: the Autobiography of Donald Wolfit* (London, Odhams 1954)

Elley, Derek, 'Experiences: an Interview with Susannah York', *Focus on Film*, no. 9 (spring 1972), pp. 25–30
Elley, Derek, 'Wistfulness and Dry Hankies: Susannah York', *Focus on Film*, no. 10 (summer 1972), pp. 42–50